From Pain to Violence:

The Traumatic Roots of Destructiveness

From Pain to Violence:

The Traumatic Roots of Destructiveness

Felicity de Zulueta

Whurr Publishers
London

© 1993 Whurr Publishers Ltd
First published 1993 by
Whurr Publishers Ltd
19b Compton Terrace, London N1 2UN, England

Reprinted 1994, 1996, 1998, 2000, 2001 and 2003

British Library Cataloguing in Publication Data
A catalogue record for this book is available from the
British Library.

ISBN: 1-870332-79-2

Photoset by Stephen Cary
Printed and bound in the UK by Athenæum Press Ltd,
Gateshead, Tyne & Wear

Contents

Introduction

Violence is all around us. No one can feel safe from its effects. We can experience it in the intimacy of our home life, we can expect it in the street; we are bombarded with daily news of terrorism, war, murder, rape, torture and ecological disasters. We are the 'children' of those who survived two devastating world wars. We have witnessed some of the early effects of a weapon so destructive it defies the imagination. We live in its 'nuclear' shadow, scarcely able even to acknowledge its existence.

And now, with the end of the 'cold war', we are confronted by the fact that neo-Nazism, racism, nationalism and all the violence these beliefs bring with them are coming back to haunt us in Europe. The future is one of uncertainty and fear. Whether we live in the concrete jungle of New York or in the threatened rain forests of Borneo, every one of us knows that we are capable of destroying ourselves. The dim awareness of what could be is always with us, colouring the lives of many with a sense of deep despair about our very humanity. No wonder violence preoccupies us so much, for we are, as a species, quite alone in our capacity to murder in cold blood, to torture one another and to threaten our species' very existence.

Man's need to understand himself, to make sense of his cruelty has never been greater. There is already a vast literature on aggression in our species with some 20000–30000 references on the subject. So, one may well ask, why write yet another book on violence?

The fact is that there are so many different views concerning the origins of human violence, that it is clear we still do not understand why 'we are the cruellest and most ruthless species that has ever walked the earth' (Storr, 1968, p. 9).

What is interesting about most of the work on the subject of human aggression and cruelty is that it is based on the premise that we are essentially individuals driven by our inherited instincts. The 'other' acts essentially as a provider or as an outlet for these drives. For example, a well-known ethologist like Konrad Lorenz describes very clearly the intraspecific fighting behaviour seen in fish, geese and other animals. . He then goes on to extrapolate his findings with regard to mankind: 'Intraspecific aggression bred into man a measure of aggression drive for which in the social order of today he finds no adequate outlet' (1968, p. 209).

The basic assumption here is that we operate as individuals with innate drives which need to be discharged. To deprive man of such an outlet is what leads to more aggression, to wars and other forms of violence. The implications are that outlets for our aggression must be found and that those who are working for peace are, according to Lorenz, 'at a decided disadvantage' (Lorenz, 1968, p.246).

Such a conclusion may appear scientifically sound and quite acceptable because it fits in with Western cultural premises about the central importance of the individual in relation to society. However, it is this very premise that is being challenged today within both the field of biology and that of psychology. Paradoxically, it is because of our attempts to help the victims of war, of the concentration camps and of natural disasters that we are beginning to realise how emotionally vulnerable our species really is. What researchers have come to realise is just how much human beings matter to each other. Trauma has in fact been defined as 'the sudden cessation of human interaction' (Lindemann, 1944).

This need of one person for another comes as no surprise to those who have been studying attachment behaviour. Workers in the field have been able to show us that man is not intrinsically destructive; he need not be driven to kill and to torment. Study after study points to the same inescapable fact: the human being is inherently a socially co-operative animal. This has allowed Bowlby to conclude that 'human infants ... are preprogrammed to develop in a socially co-operative way; whether they do so or not turns in high degree on how they are treated'(1988, p.9).

Such a conclusion, with its accompanying research, is crucial to those who are concerned with violence as a human phenomenon which can be and needs to be understood if it is to be prevented. What these findings show is that human destructiveness, like psychological trauma, cannot be understood without recognising the intrinsic importance of human relationships in our development and in our sense of well-being. It could be that it is because we have denied this for so long that an understanding of human violence has been so elusive.

When we begin to think about human violence, we discover that we are not dealing with an instinct, a drive or a predisposition, as some would have us believe. Violence has in fact no clearly defined meaning. The *Oxford English Dictionary* interprets the term 'violence' in several different ways, one of which is 'the treatment or usage tending to cause bodily injury or forcibly interfering with personal freedom'. Implicit in this particular definition is the assumption that we are entitled to a certain degree of freedom, an abstract concept that is intrinsic to our human condition. As Stoller states: 'the brain substrates of what we call "choice" or "freedom" simply do not exist in any creature as in man' (1975).

This makes it difficult to study human violence as a biological phenomenon. A brief scan of the scientific literature on violence shows that what would be defined as violence, according to the *Oxford English Dictionary*, is in fact referred to as 'aggression'; this usually implies that it is an 'innate' behavioural manifestation of our genetic make-up. Some authors do go to the trouble of differentiating 'simple' or 'normal' aggression from violence, which they refer to as a 'transformed aggression' (Durbin and Bowlby, 1939) or 'malignant' aggression (Fromm, 1974, p.24). However, when reading their work, it is often far from clear when aggression ceases to be seen as 'normal', to become 'transformed' or 'malignant'.

In fact, the confusion cannot be avoided, because aggression is a form of social behaviour studied by ethologists, biologists and psychologists, whereas violence is more about the interpretation that is given to a form of social behaviour, an interpretation that is essentially determined by the social context in which we live. At times both terms are interchangeable but at other times they are not: an interaction deemed abusive or violent in one culture may be considered quite 'normal' in another. It is only since we have begun to study the effects of psychological trauma that we have been able to tease out the various components of our violent responses: the results have been quite surprising, for they have confirmed what psychoanalysts have always known, that the very essence of our humanness is that we invest all our experiences with meaning and that the way we interpret our experiences has a direct effect on how we respond to trauma.

So, whilst we are psychobiological entities with all that this means in terms of physical needs, behaviour patterns, genetics and biochemistry, what we do and do not do is also intrinsically linked to how we perceive ourselves and the world about us.

For instance, a man kills another man. This could be seen as an act of violence, a 'bestial act of brutality', but it could also be seen as an 'act of self-defence', a 'legitimate act of aggression for the defence of our nation', an 'act of justice for the preservation of law and order', a 'necessary step in the fight for freedom' or the 'inevitable manifestation of our instinctual drives'.

In defining an act of violence, we are giving a meaning to a form of interpersonal behaviour. Such an appraisal could be seen to be entirely subjective but it is not: how we perceive the world is intimately linked to our sense of 'self', to our beliefs and attitudes, emotions and behaviours, all of which are very much part of the social matrix to which we belong. Through our upbringing, our language and our daily social activities, we learn and absorb the culture in which we live. Through language, we in turn give a socially defined meaning to our life; we acquire a linguistic identity, a verbal sense of self which organises and defines our experiences. Thus over the last few years the abused child has been allowed to put a name to his or her experience. Through the 'help line' of Esther Rantzen, such children struggle to put the unmentionable into words and in the process their pain is validated and their trauma is given a meaning. But what if others cannot perceive your trauma? What if people cannot understand your desperate behaviour as the manifestation of being abused or tormented? What then?

Violence has to be recognised as such not only by its victims but also by those who witness it, particularly as the perpetrators of violence often fail to do just this. For such a validation of the trauma to take place, particular values need to be shared, such as the belief in our entitlement to both a certain degree of freedom and a socially sanctioned need for self-respect.

Violence is thus essentially human and it is about the meaning we give to a destructive form of behaviour which is usually taking place between people. It can also be an attack on oneself. But, whatever form it takes, the fact that humans commit acts of violence suggests that in the act itself there is a thinking 'subject' doing something to another, who, from the observer's point of view, would be defined as 'human', be it an infant as in the case of child abuse, a woman in the case of rape, or a man in the grips of torture. We will usually identify the victims as having the same capacity to think and feel as we do; we perceive them then as human.

However, how do the 'violent' members of our society see their victims? For instance, what did the men in the New York gang who attacked and raped a woman until she was unconscious say about her? They said: 'she was nothing' (Levin, 1989). Do we believe them? Was she 'nothing' to them as they attacked her with bricks, a metal pipe and a knife and then gang-raped her? To attempt to answer this question, we have to try and understand what is going on in the minds of those who torture and kill. What does such a person think he is doing? To whom does he think he is doing it? What is the victim in the eyes of the tormentor at that particular moment in time?

The study of human violence hinges, therefore, on understanding how humans develop in terms of how they perceive themselves and the 'other' and what they feel about themselves and the 'other': feelings and cognition are both involved in human destructive behaviour.

This particular work arises from a belief that those who are involved in trying to understand human behaviour have a role to play, however small it may be, in alerting others to psychological processes which exacerbate or reduce our need to be destructive. We owe it to the countless victims of Nazism, to those who died or suffered in the devastating violence of the last two World Wars and many civil wars: we owe it particularly to those who even now are suffering from man-made cruelty.

As a psychotherapist, a psychiatrist and a biologist, I have attempted to present a variety of different studies which give us a great deal of information about human violence, but we are still left with a considerable body of tentative ideas. It is my hope that these will be considered, argued against and tested. In an attempt to help the reader make sense of what is to follow, I can divulge that this book rests its particular case on seeing 'violence' as a by-product of psychological trauma and its effects on infants, children and adults. Particular attention will be given to how trauma can be processed into rage and how memories, which are 'split off' within our minds can re-emerge, even if only partly, when triggered off by the appropriate environmental stimuli.

Following in Freud's footsteps, researchers and therapists have been working with the psychological effects of trauma in all their manifestations. Their conclusions are reviewed and discussed in the following chapters because they show a link between psychological trauma and a propensity to develop destructive interpersonal relationships.

In addition to the work done with trauma victims and violent offenders, other researchers have studied the behaviour of so-called 'normal' people to see what capacity they have to be violent. Their results are revealing and confirm that most of us can become violent in the appropriate circumstances.

Although all the above mentioned research is essential in understanding violence, a parallel development in the field of psychoanalytic theory was necessary to integrate these different findings. The theoretical underpinning of the research on trauma is mainly provided by the 'object relations theory', Bowlby's 'attachment theory' and Kohut's 'self psychology', all of which stress the importance of interpersonal and, particularly, early relationships in determining the way we perceive ourselves and behave towards each other. Thus, the invalidation of our sense of self or of our sexual identity is seen to be at the root of some of our most violent behaviour. Also of great interest to the student of violence is the understanding of human defence mechanisms that allow us to deny what is painful and to 'split off' such memories and feelings. In this way we can all become potential 'Jekyll and Hyde' characters, like the respectable day-time bank manager who becomes the frightening sexual night visitor of his son's childhood.

This book is essentially divided into three parts.

Attachment gone wrong

The first part focuses on the various theoretical approaches to violence and their different historical, philosophical and psychological origins. A case of child abuse and murder is described, to introduce the reader to the more obvious links between childhood trauma and child abuse (Chapter 1). This is followed by a brief historical account of how the belief in 'original sin' came into being and what social and psychological functions it provided for Western man (Chapter 2). The third chapter provides a brief over-view of the literature on violence and aggression, stressing the polarisation of views that continues to exist in this particular field because of its links with a theory of human nature (Chapter 3). The evidence is then given concerning our physical and psychological need for the 'other' throughout our development, with particular reference to studies on attachment behaviour (Chapter 4). The effects of loss and deprivation are seen to be very important in the development of violent behaviour. These findings indicate that violence could be understood as the result of a failure in caregiving (Chapter 5). Particular emphasis is then given to the development of the self through the 'internalisation' of our different types of attachment relationships (Chapter 6). This leads on to a psychoanalytic understanding of the self in relation to 'object-relations theory' and Kohut's 'self-psychology', two psychoanalytic models which appear to be the most useful in our understanding of human attachment and destructiveness (Chapter 7). Deprivation, loss and abuse can so deplete the self that defending itself becomes of paramount importance, whatever the cost to the 'other'. This desperate need to bolster the self by whatever means contributes considerably to our understanding of the importance of the self in the origins of violence (Chapter 8).

The psychology of trauma

The second part of the book focuses more on the psychological effects of trauma on both sexes and at different ages. The unspeakable trauma of child sexual abuse is the subject of our first chapter. The psychotherapeutic treatment of a victim of child sexual abuse illustrates most clearly how the disruption and abuse of the primary attachment relationships can have devastating effects on the self and engender considerable violence, a violence which is usually turned against the self (Chapter 9). This specific account is followed by a more general study of the physiological and psychological effects of psychological trauma or 'post-traumatic stress disorder' (PTSD). Both the meaning given to the trauma, and the quality of the interpersonal relations developed by

its victims, appear to be of great importance in determining the extent
of the psychobiological damage, be it cognitive or physiological: the
greater the traumatisation, the higher the risk of later violence
(Chapter 10). The last chapter in this section looks more closely at psychobiological effects of trauma on children: links are shown to exist
between psychological trauma, child abuse and human destructiveness.
Violence can now be seen both as the extreme expression of human
rage, due to overwhelming narcissistic injuries to the self, and as the
expression of a disrupted attachment system. The compulsion to
repeat the trauma is seen to be of crucial importance in understanding
the traumatic origins of violence; the possibility that victims become
addicted to their trauma is looked at (Chapter 11).

The prevalence of psychological trauma and abuse

The third and final part of this book attempts to link the traumatic origins of violence with Western cultural requirements. Historical and
anthropological studies suggest that human beings can develop different social structures and behaviours, some of which were and still are
considerably less violent than the patriarchal and Western cultures that
now dominate the world. Primate and human studies show that the
most effective transmission of cultural values occurs through manipulation of the infant–caregiver attachment system. This is most clearly
highlighted by studies that show the traumatising effects of corporal
punishment and the implications of such a generalised form of socialisation in terms of social violence (Chapter 12).

It is the dehumanisation of the other that is at the root of all human
violence, a dehumanisation that unfortunately appears almost intrinsic
to the development of the male–female sexual role differentiation seen
in patriarchal cultures. Man's love affair with violence is examined in
terms of his vulnerable sexual identity and his resultant need to perceive women as 'objects' with all the violent consequences this entails.
Woman's masochistic collusion with this split is also addressed, as are
its implications for childrearing. In the act of making mother 'less than
human', men become men at the expense of the 'other': exploitation,
abuse, racism and violence are the result of such a cultural system
(Chapter 13). This is vividly illustrated by experiments which show how
the ordinary man and woman can torture and kill when given orders by
men in authority. The fact that the medical profession is seen to be particularly vulnerable to becoming the instrument of state torture and
genocide is of particular interest, because it illustrates the reciprocal
relationship that exists between caring and abuse, the latter being the
manifestation of attachment and love gone wrong (Chapter 14).

The final chapter focuses on a brief review of research on the 'altruistic' personality as compared to its counterpart, the authoritarian or ethnocentric personality. Links are made between these two types of personality which confirm once again the importance of certain rearing patterns and, in particular, of physical abuse in the development of violence, at the level both of the individual and of the group. The book ends by arguing the case for a marked change in our attitude to child-rearing patterns if any reduction in social violence is to be achieved (Chapter 15).

Felicity de Zulueta
July 1993

Acknowledgements

Though born of European parents, much of my childhood was spent among people of quite different cultures: with the Colombians in the wilds of the Llanos, the Malays and Dayaks of the forests of Sarawak, the African tribes of Uganda's highlands and the mixed peoples of Lebanon and Syria. Many became my friends, friends that I have now lost, but whose kindness and understanding gave me a chance to be part of their lives. I hope I have been able to convey something of what I learnt and loved with them.

As we moved from country to country, I also encountered much pain and violence and I remained puzzled: how could so much kindness turn to such hate and bloodshed? This question remained unanswered until I began training as a psychotherapist.

It was John Bowlby's work and his personal encouragement which first gave me the courage to try and answer my question. I regret that he is no longer with us to comment on my conclusions. To Dr Harold Maxwell, in particular, I owe the decision to publish this work. Supported and helped by my colleagues, Dr Jessica Kirker, Professor Hirsch, Professor Greenhalgh and others working at Charing Cross Hospital and at the Cassel Hospital, I was able to take time out to carry my project through.

My teachers, supervisors and peers in the Institute of Group Analysis assisted me through encouragement and help in clarifying my ideas. Dr Malcolm Pines, Dr Earl Hopper and Dr Dennis Brown were particularly supportive, and Dr Brian Boswood and Dr David Kay helped me reach a better understanding of the darker side of myself.

It is, however, to my patients that I owe most of my findings and conclusions and it is with them in mind that much of this was written. I hope I have done them justice.

I am also thankful to my close friends for all the personal support they have given me. But it is to Sedat that I feel particularly grateful for his help and encouragement and, perhaps most valuable of all, his criticisms and advice.

Part I
Attachment Gone Wrong

Chapter 1
A Case of Violence

' *Le coeur a ses raisons que la raison ne connait point.*'
[The heart has its reasons which reason knows nothing of.]

Pensées de Pascal

As a psychotherapist, I usually meet the victims of abuse rather than its perpetrators. When violence does erupt in our psychiatric hospitals, it is usually seen as a manifestation of a patient's 'illness', of his 'irrationality'. My first professional encounter with a child murderer whose sanity had never been questioned was therefore an important one. It left me with many questions unanswered.

In my work, I rely on feeling open and sympathetic to the people who come and see me to discuss their difficulties. On this occasion, the nurse who referred this man to me told me that he had been in jail for killing his small daughter. He now felt very depressed and wanted to see whether he could benefit from psychotherapy.

Before I went to collect my patient from the waiting room, I became aware of feeling uneasy about our meeting. I realised that he would probably appear quite ordinary, someone I would not be able to label as 'deviant'. My apparent need to see him as 'different' struck me as being out of keeping with my usual attitude to those I interview.

I knew that the man who beats up his children, or the father who forces his child to have sex with him, could be a colleague at work or my next-door neighbour. In another attempt to distance myself, I found myself focusing on the fact that the murderer was a man, not a woman like myself. But then where are the mothers when their children are being tormented and hurt? What part did this murderer's wife play in her daughter's death? Did she try to protect her? I knew that this was unlikely. The wives of men who torture their children are often their assistants, their partners in crime.

So, this anxiety I felt as I rose to collect my patient, what was it about? I realised that if my meeting was to have any meaning for me or for him, I would have to get quite close to this man, to develop some understanding of his conflicts and his feelings. I realised that to do my work, I might be reminded of my own violence, of all those feelings we do not believe we own until one day they betray themselves in a desperate wish to overcome the 'other' whom we see as the source of our pain, of our impotence or of our humiliation.

What mother or father has not felt close to losing control? Babies who cannot sleep, infants who fill our world with cries of inconsolable pain, children who want so much when we feel we have so little, all these unsuspecting little people can become tormenting characters in the living nightmares of their parents' own making. But for most of us, these powerful feelings can be recognised for what they are. We can acknowledge our rage and, fortunately, our love comes to the rescue much as our mother or father did when we were small and terrified. But, for some parents, no such memory of love and security can ever come to the rescue. These men and women were once children for whom comfort was rare, children brought up to believe that they were bad because no one seemed to care. The fear of beatings, torture and abandonment was what they knew of family life. Their bruises, burns and cuts healed with time. But what about their terror, their impotent rage, their memories of being betrayed by those who meant so much? What about that desperate need to be loved which has been so rarely met that, when it is, it turns to pain, the pain of realising what could have been? Where have all these feelings gone? Have these men and women been able to forget those traumas and leave their pain behind them?

To the casual observer that would appear to be the case, as these childhood victims set about making a living and bringing up a family. When they become parents, they often want to give their children all the love and support they failed to get. They want to be really good parents. But, for some, these childhood terrors and torments have not been allowed to disappear. Though apparently forgotten, the experiences of their parents' cruelty or indifference have been 'internalised' in the form of mental representations which will persist in their minds, albeit in an unconscious state.

It is often in the midst of their own children's screams and tears that those traumatic experiences are reactivated, even if they continue to remain unconscious. The parents recognise their childhood selves in their children's anguish, in their desperate need to be comforted and held. But, mingled with the memories of those needs, there is that other awful memory of being rejected and of feeling bad, unwanted. These painful feelings were once so unbearable that they were forgotten. Now that they are being reactivated, how can they be dealt with?

A young single mother holds her screaming child in her arms; sensing her own distress, she realises that there is still no one to hold her, to make her feel better. Her baby has unwittingly become the source of her old pain, once again revived. She needs to stop the pain. The pain is her child screaming but she can no longer feel it to be her child: this mother is back in the nightmare of her own childhood. The baby has become her tormentor, the one who hurts, whose screaming needs make the young woman feel she is bad and useless. She can no longer see her baby, for it has become the 'monster' she once was that had to be controlled, to be beaten into shape. She becomes her own mother, her own terrifying parent with whom she has identified, as so many victims do. In her raging pain this woman smashes the baby's head until the crying stops. In the silence that follows, a mother may discover herself to be a murderer.... The child she wanted to love seems dead. At this point her mind comes to the rescue. She 'forgets'. She 'splits off' the memory of her past and the memory of what she has just done to her little girl, a child she probably wants to love and protect.

It may be that this time, and possibly the next, her child survives her destructive assaults. The nightmare is forgotten again and again but, one day, it may all come true as it did for my patient.

It is doubtful that I thought all this through before meeting Mr Brown, but I was dimly aware of other patients who had been beaten and tormented during their childhood. One was a mother who had had to 'forget' what she had done and what had been done to her. All she knew was that she loved her daughter and she wanted to be a really good mother. Her girl's bruises seemed to her like some monstrous intrusion into her life for which all sorts of explanations had to be found. It was a long time before she felt safe enough to remember both what she had done to her child and what had been done to her.

Mr Brown presented himself as a pale, white-haired man in his fifties who looked much older than his age. He seemed anxious and very keen to help me with my interview, even though he admitted he might find it difficult.

The subject of his daughter emerged early on in our meeting. She was about two and a half years old when she died several years ago. He sketched out for me the life of this little girl prior to the 'incident' which led to her death. Originally, she had been looked after by her grandparents abroad while he and his wife set up home in England. They then sent for their daughter and it was not long before she was being attacked by both Mr Brown, and his wife, who, he said, hated this child from the moment she was born.

As a baby and toddler, his daughter was regularly starved and beaten. He described to me pitiful scenes of this pale little girl wandering about barefoot outside in the freezing cold: she was so cold that her feet stuck to the ice. In his attempt to warm them up, her father said he burnt them with lighted cigarettes and hot coals. She ended up being taken to the casualty department, her feet covered in blisters.

On the day of the fatal 'incident', this 'little waif', as he described her, had been locked up in her room without having been cleaned or fed. On his return from work, his wife told him to go upstairs and clean 'the thing'. Mr Brown found his daughter in a mess of faeces and urine and proceeded to clean her up. He then brought her downstairs into the sitting room and began to bully her into talking to him. The little girl would not talk. She stood in silence, looking pale and visibly distressed. He desperately wanted her to speak, to make him feel better about her. He recalls going up to her and shaking her. Nothing else.... That night he put her to bed and he must have been worried about her, for he told his wife to keep an eye on her. The next morning, their daughter was found dead. Mr Brown was later tried and committed to jail for manslaughter.

As he recounted all these events, he spoke in a quiet manner with little emotion; I could not help wondering where all his feelings had gone. He seemed to have 'split' himself off from the violence which drove him to kill his child. He had no recollection of beating his daughter but he knew she had died from injuries to her chest. Though he was judged to be the killer it was clear that he wanted his wife to take the blame for what had happened, listing all the terrible things she had also done to their daughter.

Sensing that we could get no closer to what really took place between this child and her parents, I asked Mr Brown to tell me about his own childhood. He began by talking about his mother and his face lit up as he described her to me. She was a devoted mother who unfortunately fell ill with tuberculosis when he was a small child. She often had to go to hospital for treatment. He missed her so much that he would walk several miles in order to see her. It was during the war and food was scarce. Mr Brown recalls how his mother would give him and his brothers and sisters the bread, butter and jam she had in hospital so that they had something to eat. 'She was like an angel', he said. She died when he was only eight and he remembers feeling distraught at her funeral.

From then on, Mr Brown was left to the mercies of his father, a man whose violence he clearly feared though he seemed keen not to be too critical of him. This may have been because Mr Brown did not want to get close to his own feelings about this man. What he told me next seemed to confirm this possibility. He described his mother coming home one day from one of her many stays in hospital. She celebrated this by cooking for her family their treat of treats, a dish of fried potatoes. During that same visit he found his father beating her up. Though he was only a lad of seven, Mr Brown grabbed an axe and threatened his father with it.

Later on in his childhood, his father injured his arm and he asked his son to take over his cobbler's business. Mr Brown proved to be quite good at it. However, one day, he recalls that he was finishing off a lady's boot, when his knife slipped and pierced the leather. His father saw this and in a fury he picked up a huge knobbly stick and began beating his son on the back of his head. The boy tore down the village street, blood pouring from his scalp wound with his father at his heels. A kindly neighbour came to his rescue. With visible satisfaction he remembered the woman verbally attacking his father. For once in his life someone had stood up for him.

Though he scarcely mentioned them, Mr Brown had seven brothers and sisters, two of whom died in infancy. He told me of how, one day, he and his brother were coming back from the woods with fire-wood when his brother fell into a nearby river. Though Mr Brown could not swim, he had leapt into the water to rescue his brother. As I expressed some admiration for this gesture, he hastened to put me right by telling me he had only done it out of fear of what his father would do to him if he came home without his brother.

At this point, I attempted to explore whether Mr Brown could begin to acknowledge how much he had missed as a result of his mother's illness. I recalled how earlier on in the interview he had clearly had to cling to a very idealised memory of her, painting her as an 'angel'. So, although I agreed that his mother could not be blamed for her illness, I suggested that there had been a little boy who may have felt that he had had so little of her, he had suffered considerably as a result.

He could acknowledge such feelings and this led him to link his experience of his 'little waif of a daughter' with the picture he had of his pale sick mother in hospital. It seemed likely that his unconscious rage against his mother, who failed to care for him, was finally discharged on his daughter. Like his mother, she had appeared helpless and neglected, evoking in him his own desperate needs and his old pain. He had not been able to find in himself the love she needed from him. Instead, he had coped with his own pain by identifying with his father and his destructive rage, a rage which at least had the positive affect of giving him the power to inflict the pain he had once had to suffer.

It is likely that in the final assault on his daughter, Mr Brown did not 'see' his child before him. What he probably saw and felt were his old feelings and memories being brought back to life, those unbearable moments of pain and deprivation which had been 'split off' in his mind, locked away from his daily memory and experience, just as they now were in our interview. Splitting is a dissociative process that allows us to cope with the overwhelming anxiety of feeling utterly helpless in the face of abandonment and abuse. The passive man in the chair before me, who looked at me with his rather washed-out blue eyes, could not remember what took place in his mind the night he killed his daughter.

Clearly no one will ever really know what happened between this man, his child and his wife. Their daughter seems to have been an object of abuse for both of them during most of her short life. We do not know either what part she played in her mother's inner world, though we know that Mrs Brown probably referred to her as 'the thing'. In some strange way, she was to become the 'little waif' who reminded Mr Brown of his long-lost mother whose helplessness and sickness were to be her undoing: this same helplessness was to be his child's undoing.

It seems likely that as he shook and bullied his daughter, Mr Brown wanted something from her which as a child of two she could not give him; it was probably the same thing he wished his mother could have given him, the feeling that he was a good and valuable person. But both his mother and daughter died, leaving him with the terrible guilt of having betrayed his 'angel mother' and of having murdered his own child.

A few weeks after I met him, Mr Brown was dying in hospital with a hitherto undiagnosed cancer. The illness may have come as a relief to him because it became clear, in subsequent discussions, that his main reason for seeing me was to be rescued from the terrible, violent feelings he now feared would soon overwhelm him.

However, on the day we met, I was left with many sad thoughts and many questions unanswered. If his story is a typical one of parents who seriously hurt and murder their children, it is also very much the description of what countless victims of abuse go through during their tormented childhoods: Mr Brown was first a victim of his parents' failings before he became a victimiser.

We now know that abuse is believed to be 20 times more likely if one of the parents was abused as a child. However, it is also very important to note that not all abused children repeat this pattern with their own children; about a third of mothers who were abused as girls apparently take good care of their children (Egeland, Jacobvitz and Papatola, 1987, p.270). Clearly, understanding how these childhood victims become victimisers and how others avoid repeating the pattern of abuse is crucial if we are to begin to understand the origins of violence in the family and possibly in society at large.

The story of Mr Brown is an important one. He was an ordinary man who ended up murdering his daughter in a final act of violence which was probably not premeditated and of which he had no recollection. Although many may disagree with my hypothetical reconstruction of the murderer's state of mind, I would like to make the following suggestion: what if the parents who hurt, torture and kill their children are not as they appear to us? What if these people cannot always perceive the 'other', in this case their offspring, as a child to whom they are the parent? What if, under certain conditions, people bring to their present relationships the hidden or unconscious memories of their past abuse, so moulding the present into the image of their past? This phenomenon of 'projection' is a common defence mechanism used by victims of trauma. It implies that feelings usually associated with painful experiences we cannot acknowledge are 'repressed' in our unconscious as memories that can later be re-experienced when projected onto others. This tendency unconsciously to re-enact past traumas is also characteristic of the post-traumatic stress disorder which will be described in detail later on in the book.

Whilst we hope to gain some understanding of human violence by exploring the research evidence at hand, we also need to recognise how disturbing it can be to witness so-called 'normal' people like Mr Brown torturing their children, or to realise that doctors participate actively in state torture and murder. Robert Lifton wrote of the Nazi doctors he met: 'Psychologically speaking, nothing is darker or more menacing, or harder to accept than the participation of physicians in mass murder' (Lifton, 1986, p.3).

In attempting to understand violence, we may need to try to see the victim through the eyes of his or her tormentor. How does the abuser see his victim? Does the answer lie in understanding what lies behind the 'look' a 'white' man gives when he addresses another as 'nigger'? Is it in the eyes of a rapist as he overcomes his victim? Is it a look of hatred or lust, or, perhaps worse, of indifference? Faced with such a 'look', the recipient becomes aware of no longer being seen for what he is or should be. He feels he is an 'object' to be used or abused. It is in that 'look' that violence first becomes manifest, for it belongs to those of us who have learnt to see the 'other' as an object, as less than human. Violence follows easily.

In a passage of his book on his experience in Auschwitz, Primo Levi describes the 'look' that takes place between him, the Jew, and his German boss:

> ... that look was not one between two men; and if I had known how completely to explain the nature of that look, which came as if across the glass window of an aquarium between two beings who live in different worlds, I would also have explained the essence of the great insanity of the third Germany.
>
> One felt in that moment, in an immediate manner, what we all thought and said of the Germans. The brain which governed those blue eyes and those manicured hands said: 'This something in front of me belongs to a species which it is obviously opportune to suppress. In this particular case, one has to first make sure that it does not contain some utilizable element. And in my head, like seeds in an empty pumpkin: 'Blue eyes and fair hair are essentially wicked. No communication possible ...'
>
> *(Levi, 1960, pp.111–112)*

In looking at violence, we are concerned with behaviour that not only causes damage to people but which also outrages or violates them as human beings. Implicit in the concept of violence is an assumption that human beings are entitled to a certain degree of respect. It is for this reason that the cornerstone of all human persecution and extermination is the establishment of a belief system which dictates that the 'other' is essentially less than human and hence dispensable or dangerous. For such belief systems to take root, however, there must exist in the human mind the capacity or the vulnerability to make of the 'other' the object of our needs or of our fears. How can such perceptual processes develop? And if they do arise, what could their consequences be for the individual, the family and society? This will be very much the subject of this book.

Chapter 2
The Myth of Original Sin and the Death Instinct

'Behold, I was shaped in wickedness: and in sin hath my mother conceived me.'   *The Book of Common Prayer.*

When thinking of human violence, one is inevitably drawn into the longstanding debate on 'human nature': is our species intrinsically destructive, as some would have us believe, or is human violence the result of environmental pressures? These fundamental questions have usually been addressed by philosophers and may not have been seen as relevant to the scientists involved in the study of human aggression. For this reason, there are few direct references to the concept of human nature among the thousands of papers and books on the subject of human destructiveness. It is, however, questionable whether any writer's attitude to human violence could remain unaffected by his or her own views on human nature.

Although many might tend to disclaim that any such bias exists in the scientific literature on aggression, a brief foray into the history of religious ideas relating to the nature of mankind shows how deeply held are the assumptions underlying our current thinking on human nature and its behavioural manifestations. Although the idea that scientists are expressing culturally held attitudes may seem a bit far-fetched, studies in cultural anthropology and research carried out on bilingual people also confirm how attitudes and values are transmitted down the generations by virtue of the particular language people use to communicate (Zulueta, 1990). These studies vindicate the definition of culture given by the anthropologist Clifford Geertz, who sees it as

An historically transmitted pattern of meaning embodied in symbols; a system of inherited conceptions expressed in symbolic form, by means of which men communicate, perpetuate, and develop their knowledge about and attitudes towards life.

(Quoted in Pagels, 1988, p. xix)

Elaine Pagels, in her book *Adam, Eve and the Serpent*, notes how traditional Christian attitudes relating to 'human nature' are brought to all fields of study including psychology. She adds:

> We might well be astonished at attitudes that we take for granted. Augustine, one of the greatest teachers of western Christianity, derived many of these attitudes from the story of Adam and Eve: that sexual desire is sinful; that infants are infected from the moment of conception with the disease of original sin; and that Adam's sin corrupted the whole of nature itself. Even those who think of the Genesis only as literature, and those who are not Christian, live in a culture indelibly shaped by such interpretations as these.
>
> *(1988, p.xix)*

This view of mankind as inherently sinful dates to the end of the fourth century and beginning of the fifth century. At this time Christianity stopped being the religion of the persecuted, fighting for moral justice, to become the religion of emperors ruling over vast populations. Up to this point the early Christians had seen in the Gospels a message of freedom: freedom from tyrannical governments, freedom from prevailing social and sexual customs, freedom from sexual desire and freedom of the will; that is, moral freedom. However, with the establishment of the Christian Emperor Constantine, the long-standing history of Christian persecution ended. The teachings of the clergy changed alongside their Church; the belief system of the oppressed evolved into the religion of a respectable institution. As a result, the story of creation in *Genesis* acquired a new meaning with the interpretations of Augustine, a meaning that is still very much part of our culture.

It will be recalled that according to *Genesis*, God said to the first woman:

> I will increase your labour and your groaning, and in labour you shall bear children. You shall be eager for your husband, and he shall be your master.

And to the man he said:

> Because you have listened to your wife and have eaten from the tree which I forbade you, accursed shall be the ground on your account. With labour you shall win your food from it all the days of your life.

> It will grow thorns and thistles for you, none but wild plants for you to eat. You shall gain your bread by the sweat of your brow until you return to the ground; for from it you were taken. Dust you are, to dust you shall return.
>
> *(New English Bible, Genesis 3, vv. 16–19)*.

For Augustine, this meant that it was because of Adam's sin that the human race has had to suffer the frustrations of sexual desire and the anguish of mortality. In addition, mankind lost the freedom to choose.

Summing up his views, Pagels tells us how humanity, once harmonious, perfect and free, is now, through Adam's choice, ravaged by mortality and desire, while all suffering, from crop failure, miscarriage, illness and insanity, is evidence of the moral deterioration that Eve and Adam introduced (1988, p.134). Even the blight of male domination over women is to be blamed on Adam and Eve. And, through the transmission of sexual desire in conception, all of us are tainted by original sin.

Thus, since the time of Augustine, every Catholic is expected to believe that we are born in original sin and that, should we die before we have been baptised, our infant souls are doomed to a life of eternal deprivation in Limbo.

The idea that humanity is inherently wicked may well seem to most an antiquated myth and yet, even if not consciously acknowledged, our culture is steeped in man-made guilt. In Britain, this dislike of pleasure was perhaps most clearly expressed by the Puritans of the seventeenth century, who believed, like Augustine, that man was essentially sinful and who held as proof of his inherent evilness his unlimited capacity for enjoyment!

Returning to the times of Augustine, it is important to note that his views were not acceptable to all Christians. Some objected to them on the basis that they betrayed the foundations of Christian belief: the goodness of God's creation and the freedom of the human will. His most notable critic was a certain Julian of Eclanum who systematically attacked Augustine's views, essentially because Augustine refused to differentiate between what is a matter of will and what is a matter of nature. For Julian, the fact that we die and suffer is a result of the fact that we belong to nature and are mortal beings. 'If you say it is a matter of will it does not belong to nature; if it is a matter of nature it has nothing to do with guilt' (Pagels, 1988, p.144). Not so for Augustine, who virulently exposed the plight of sick and deformed children as proof of the fact that sin is transmitted from parents to children. 'If there were no sin, then infants bound by no evil, would suffer nothing harmful in body or soul under the great power of the just God' (Pagels, 1988, p.135).

In a sense the Christian belief in the goodness and justice of God makes it almost inevitable that mankind is left carrying the blame for its suffering and destruction. The Jewish God was more a god of power than goodness. If tragedy befell the Jews it was usually because they had disobeyed their God; their suffering was the result of his anger. But with Christianity, God is goodness and love; so how could man make sense of illness, pain and evil? Someone had to be made responsible for what went wrong.

Perhaps, to the early Christians, Jesus had through his death cleared mankind of the sin he would otherwise carry. However, this left man with the responsibility of choosing how to deal with natural conditions, either by making these occasions for spiritual growth or by raging against nature and its creator, thereby adding to one's suffering. In a sense, this is how Augustine reacted to pain and death.

Augustine wrote poignantly of his losses in his *Confessions*. When his best friend died from a fatal illness, he described his pain.

> What folly, to grumble at the lot man has to bear! I lived in a fever, convulsed with tears and sighs that allowed me neither rest nor peace of mind. My soul was a burden, bruised and bleeding. It was tired of the man who carried it but I found no place to set it down to rest. Neither the charm of the countryside nor the sweet scents of a garden could soothe it. It found no peace in song or laughter .... Everything that was not what my friend had been was dull and distasteful ... and life becomes a living death because a friend is lost.
>
> *(1961, pp. 78–79)*

Later, when he lost his mistress, he wrote: 'At first the pain was sharp and searing, but then the wound began to fester, and though the pain was duller there was all the less hope of a cure' (1961, p.131). Finally, when his beloved mother dies, he writes as a converted Christian for whom death is not to be grieved: 'I blamed myself for my tender feelings. I fought against the wave of sorrow .... It was misery to feel myself so weak a victim of these human emotions ...'. He begged God to heal his sorrow but his prayer was not granted, so Augustine ascribes his enduring pain to God's wish to impress upon his memory how firmly the mind is gripped by 'the bonds of habit ...' (1961, p. 201).

Augustine found it hard to accept either loss or death but he could not blame God in all his goodness for the sufferings he and others endured. The answer was to blame mankind, but he cleverly cleared the individual of personal responsibility by making Adam take the blame for our sinfulness.

Thus, the idea that the natural human condition includes not only mortality but disease and deformity was rejected by Augustine and his followers, so much so that he succeeded in persuading bishops and emperors to ascribe to the theory of original sin and brand as heretics those who held to the earlier traditions of Christian freedom. Clearly, those in power favoured a belief system that emphasised man's inability to govern himself because of his inherent depravity; such a doctrine could be seen as an instrument of social control.

Erich Fromm, in his book *The Crisis of Psychoanalysis*, was very much aware of the powerful social and political implications of Augustine's theories, particularly in relation to sexuality:

> In so far as sexual pleasure as such is declared to be something sinful, while sexual desires remain perpetually operative in every human being, moral prohibitions always become a source of production for guilt feelings, which are often unconscious or transferred to different matters.

> These guilt feelings are of great social importance. They account for the fact that suffering is experienced as just punishment for one's own guilt, rather than blamed on the defects of the social organization. They eventually cause emotional intimidation, limiting people's intellectual – and especially their critical – capacities, while developing an emotional attachment to the representatives of social morality.
>
> *(1970, p.137)*

The implications are that, if men are made to feel inherently guilty, they are easier to control; this has obvious political advantages for those who want to govern us and such an outcome may go some way to explaining why Augustine's beliefs are still with us today.

However, as Elaine Pagels points out, his doctrine may not have survived 15 centuries for this reason alone. Her alternative explanation is a fascinating one and very much in keeping with current psychological thinking. As she says, it is natural for man when faced with disaster or pain to blame himself for his misfortunes, to seek an answer to the inevitable question of 'why me?'. This search for a meaning in the face of trauma is as evident in individuals as it is in established religions.

Four thousand years ago, the Sumerian people sang the praises of their goddess Inanna, queen of heaven and earth:

> When all the lands and people of Sumer assemble,
> Those sleeping on the roofs and those sleeping by the walls,
> When they sing your praises, and bring their concerns to you,
> You study their words.
> You render a cruel judgment against the evildoer:
> You destroy the wicked.
> You look with kindly eyes on the straightforward:
> You give that one your blessing.
>
> *(Wolkenstein and Kramer, 1984)*

Thus in those times, as nowadays, the 'bad' one got the punishment he deserved and some sort of meaning was provided to explain away the afflictions of the community.

The Greeks attributed their fate to the whims and passions of their many gods and goddesses. The ruins of their delicate temples strewn over the shores of the Mediterranean testify to a permanent discourse which took place between them and their all-powerful deities. In times of disaster, these people would offer their gods and goddesses sacrifices and prayers; in exchange, their Olympian masters might insist that one of their community should be sacrificed for order to be restored. Thus, after Oedipus became king, his once-prosperous city succumbed to the plague. This awful sickness ravaged the town and countryside, killing off both its people and their animals. Death was everywhere. A cause for this disaster had to be found. The blame was cast on Oedipus, their one-time hero, who discovers himself to be both the unknowing murderer of his father and the spouse of his own mother. The gods' orders were clear: the murderer of their old king Laios had to go if the city of Thebes was to survive and order be restored. Oedipus left, a blind and tragic man. But, through his tragedy, the Greek people found a meaning for their affliction and, through their actions, they regained some sense of control over their lives.

This need to make sense and order of our lives takes on many forms. In the rain forests of Borneo, the Dayak headhunters gave my father a beautifully carved hornbill to remember them by. It had once stood on top of a long pole during the ceremony of 'gawai kenyalang', the representative of the god of war and fertility, a link with its wild black and white counterparts in the forest. On its tail, colourfully decorated with the carved figures of a white hunter and a Dayak family, were painted words of warning against anyone who should lie in the presence of the 'kenyalang'. The bird itself was to be fed with cigarettes and nuts, a task dutifully undertaken by its owner ever since. Through these words of warning and the feeding rituals, a connection is maintained with the world beyond, to which man can attribute his mishaps and afflictions in much the same way as we still do through our superstitions.

These examples are illustrations of our need to be able both to give a reason for our sufferings and to feel in some way in control of our lives, particularly when we are most threatened. It is this need which underlies man's apparent tendency to feel guilty rather than helpless. It may also be because of this same need that the doctrine of original sin has survived as the basis of Christian religion for the last 1600 years.

The idea that our cultural heritage is to some extent determined by our psychological need to make sense of our predicament is not new. However, what perhaps is less evident, is why we choose to feel guilty in the face of disaster. It is well known to people working therapeutically with victims of trauma or incest, as well as with people who have suffered from severe emotional deprivation in childhood, that all these individuals tend to hold on to the belief that they are in some way to blame for what happened to them. This need to feel personally responsible is perplexing, particularly as the victim clings to this belief with tremendous conviction. A Scottish psychoanalyst, Ronald Fairbairn, aptly named this defensive need to feel guilty in the face of trauma, the 'moral defence'. By blaming himself for what has happened, the victim thus acquires some sense of control over his life rather than feeling totally helpless (1952, pp.65–67).

It is important to note that, according to the famous Swiss psychologist, Jean Piaget, children from about one and a half to eight years old manifest a similar form of thinking which he described as 'magical thinking'. At this stage in a child's cognitive development, not having yet differentiated clearly between her thoughts and the external world, he attributes to thoughts the power of actions (1929, pp.157–159). During this period, the death of a member of the family following a row or jealous feelings can easily be attributed by the child to her own destructive thoughts.

For example, Sigmund Freud was to lose his younger 8-month-old brother when he was himself 19 months old. The effects of this death may well have influenced the way Freud's theories developed to an extent that has only recently been acknowledged and which we shall explore later (Hamilton, 1976).

Freud wrote about the loss of his brother with insight: 'I welcomed my one-year-younger brother (who died within a few months), with ill wishes and real infantile jealousy, and ... his death left the germ of guilt in me' (Freud, 1950). 'Magical thinking', as described by Piaget, also occurs in normal adults betraying a momentary confusion between the self and the external world, particularly when very anxious. Who has not caught himself driving away a bad thought in case it should lead to the real thing?

Similar forms of thinking are of course very much present in people suffering from psychotic experiences; these, by definition, describe a mental state where the distinction between the self and external reality has broken down to a greater or lesser extent. In my psychotherapeutic work with very disturbed people, this form of thinking is often manifest.

One of my patients, who suffered from a severe manic–depressive disorder, believed he could control my thoughts by the power of his eyes. I often suffered the discomfort of his fixed blue gaze as we struggled to communicate. When it was suggested to this same young man that he could perhaps vent some of his anger towards me by symbolically using the darts' board, he looked horrified and said 'I could kill her that way'.

To this patient, there was no doubt that thoughts could kill just as they could magically put things right. Thus, when he was hypomanic or 'high', he felt endowed with such powers over life and death, that he would see himself as a deity who represented both life and death. 'I feel a failure underneath and I sometimes create a myth which takes me over', he said. Power was thus restored to him but at the price of guilt for, by being all powerful, he became all responsible. It is perhaps worth noting that when he was a little boy, his father became ill with a cancer and, throughout his childhood, this illness was kept a secret from him for reasons he never understood. The father died on the patient's fourteenth birthday. When he had a breakdown, he returned again and again to this event for which he felt in some way responsible. The need to feel guilty rather than an impotent victim of destiny betrays how deeply we need to protect ourselves from feeling totally helpless, a state tantamount to psychological annihilation.

If we return to Augustine's doctrine of original sin, we can see that for many, his view that we are inherently guilty is both simple and compelling. It accords with responses which for many people arise, as if instinctively, in the face of suffering. Augustine's answer simultaneously acknowledges and denies human helplessness and this may be the reason why it is so powerful. He personally absolves the sufferer of guilt by blaming Adam and Eve. He also assures the sufferer that pain and death are unnatural, responding to our need to be free of pain. And finally, he attributes the cause and the meaning of suffering to the sphere of moral choice, not to natural events. In this way suffering becomes a moral issue over which mankind has some illusion of control, even if it be through his or his ancestor's wickedness. As Gillian Evans writes in *Augustine on Evil*:

> A man-centred view of the problem of evil makes evil of far less account than a God-centred view. It is an optimistic explanation. Augustine's confidence grew as he saw more clearly the implications of the idea that evil springs from the will alone. He ceased to feel the deep anxiety which had troubled him when he believed that evil was something which threatened or limited God.
>
> *(1982, p.xi)*.

The use of the 'moral defence' appears to have reduced significantly Augustine's personal anxiety in the face of death.

It is of interest to learn what Julian of Eclanum made of Augustine's views in terms of his personality. According to Elaine Pagels, Julian believed that the experience of having sinned as, for example, did Adam and later Cain, leads man to perceive nature in terms of his own sinfulness. To Julian, the man who has sinned sees the world from the viewpoint of a person who is spiritually dying, '...who having failed to cultivate his own possibilities ...' would project onto life his own 'vitiated view' of nature and see bodily death as a kind of punishment. Julian saw Augustine's theories in this light. To this attack, Augustine angrily replied, 'How *else* could anyone envision "our last enemy"?' (Pagels, 1988, p.138).

I refer to Augustine's religious doctrines for several reasons: not only do they illustrate how religious myths can provide people with some sense of meaning and control over nature, but they also show how longstanding is man's debate regarding the intrinsic nature of mankind. This debate still continues within the field of religious ideas but could be assumed not to exist within the 'human sciences'. However, a brief review of the vast literature on the origins of human violence in the next chapter reveals similar conflicts to those which took place between Augustine and his opponents, a conflict which centres round the intrinsic 'goodness' or 'badness' of human nature. We will see how the importance of guilt and Augustine's pessimistic view of human nature and sexuality re-emerges in a modified form in the psychoanalytic and social theories of the early part of this century.

Another reason for dwelling on Augustine's beliefs is that they suggest that our perception of the world alters in relation to our personality. Augustine saw life very differently from his opponents and, from the little we know, he was a man who could not endure loss and death without experiencing these as personal attacks: death is seen as the 'last enemy', grief as a test set by God. Such a personal experience of life's vicissitudes correlates with a character formation which, as we will see later, may well be linked to a fragile sense of self which needs to resort to power and control in order to survive.

What we also learn from these theological battles is how, during certain periods of history, an individual's ideas and attitudes may become popular by their very capacity to respond to the particular needs of a social group or of society in general. This appears to have been the case with the adoption of Augustine's views and the rejection of Julian's in the fifth century. It is of interest to note that the demise of the early Christian beliefs in free will and the goodness of God's creation coincides with a period of history when the Roman world met with terrible epidemiological and man-made disasters.

In his illuminating book *Plagues and Peoples* (1976), William McNeill reveals how the impact of diseases has profound consequences on the cultural and social life of people throughout history. In his study of the Mediterranean populations, he describes a series of devastating epidemics spreading throughout the Roman empire from AD 165 onwards. These new infections brought from the east inflicted severe casualties on people with no previous immunity. In some places as much as a third of the population died in the first epidemic. From then on, subsequent epidemics led to a process of continued decay of the population of the Mediterranean that lasted for more than 500 years.

This population loss was made worse by simultaneous civil wars and barbarian invasions spreading across the empire and often followed by famine and further epidemics. The city of Rome bears witness to this devastation, as it is only in the second half of this century that it has outgrown its old Roman walls.

During these so-called Dark Ages of man-made and natural disasters, McNeill observes the simultaneous rise and consolidation of Christianity taking place, which was to alter world views fundamentally. Stoic and other systems of pagan philosophy, to which we will also add early Christian beliefs, with their emphasis on impersonal process and natural law, were ineffectual in explaining the apparent randomness with which death descended suddenly on old and young, rich and poor, good and bad. The Christian teachings had the merit of making life meaningful even in the midst of such calamities. McNeill quotes a

Syrian bishop of Carthage celebrating the plague that was raging at the
time:

> Many of us are dying in this mortality, that is many of us are being freed
> from the world. This mortality is a bane to the Jews, the pagans and ene-
> mies of Christ; to the servants of God it is a salutary departure. As to the fact
> that without any discrimination in the human race the just are dying with
> the unjust, it is not for you to think that the destruction is a common one
> for both the evil and the good. The just are called to refreshment, the unjust
> are carried off to torture …. How suitable, how necessary it is that this
> plague and pestilence which seems so horrible and deadly, searches out the
> justice of each and everyone and examines the mind of the human race …
>
> *(1976, p.118)*

As McNeill says, 'Christianity was therefore a system of thought and
feeling thoroughly adapted to a time of troubles in which hardship, disease, and violent death commonly prevailed' (1976, p.118).

Though the author cautiously reminds us that such speculation
remains to be proved, it does strongly suggest that the development of
human culture is quite closely linked to the environmental conditions
of its people and that belief systems such as religions serve an important function in providing traumatised communities with a meaning for
their existence and their disasters.

We are left wondering if similar processes may not have been at work
during this century: Freud's 'death instinct', like Augustine's concept of
original sin, is appealing because it also clears mankind of personal
responsibility for the cruelty and destructiveness of the last two terrible
world wars. Freud postulated the existence of the 'destructive instinct'
in opposition to the 'life instincts' or Eros. He describes this instinct as
the manifestation of the 'needs of the id', representing 'the somatic
demands upon the mind'. (The 'id' refers to our unconscious impulses
or drives.) The destructive instinct has as its final aim 'to lead what is
living into an inorganic state. For this reason we also call it the death
instinct' (1940, p.148).

'In biological functions the two basic instincts operate against each
other or combine with each other …'. For example, for Freud:

> The sexual act is an act of aggression with the purpose of the most intimate
> union … Modifications in the proportion of the fusion between the instincts
> have the most tangible results. A surplus of sexual aggressiveness will turn a
> lover into a sex murderer, while a sharp diminution in the aggressive factor
> will make him bashful or impotent.
>
> *(1940, p.149)*

We will explore later why Freud chose to build his psychological theories on the drive theory, but we can note how significant his 'death

instinct' is in terms of re-establishing the old belief in man's inherent destructive tendencies with all the therapeutic, social and political implications such a belief system entails.

There can be little doubt that Sigmund Freud lived during one of the most violent periods of Western history covering the First World War and ending with the beginning of the Second World War in 1939. He was also alive during the early and middle phases of the Jewish holocaust. Being a man devoted to understanding the psychology of mankind, he could not fail to think about humanity's capacity for violence. How he chose to address this issue may to some extent be related to his own personal experience of loss and destruction. Indeed, what is striking is that it was not until 1920, when he was 64 years old, that he introduced the concept of the death instinct in his book *Beyond the Pleasure Principle*. Freud himself expresses his surprise for such an omission when he writes 10 years later that he cannot understand how he left out of his study of life such an important phenomenon as human aggression or destructiveness (1930).

Hamilton suggests that Freud's personal experience of death and, in particular, the death of his younger brother Julius may have played an important part in his thinking about the death instinct (1976, p.152). Freud himself was to write about sibling rivalry as follows: 'Many people, therefore, who love their brothers and sisters and would feel bereaved if they were to die, harbour evil wishes against them in their unconscious, dating from earlier times ...' (1900, pp.250–251). In a later footnote written in 1914, he adds: 'Deaths that are experienced in this way in childhood may quickly be forgotten in the family: but subsequent research shows that they have a very important influence on subsequent neurosis' (quoted in Hamilton, 1976, p.152).

As Peter Reder points out in his paper 'Freud's family', by the time Sigmund was 17 months old, he had lost in quick succession his paternal grandfather, his mother's favourite brother and then his younger brother. His grieving parents may well have become emotionally unavailable to Freud during this time (1989).

For Hamilton, the reason for Freud's failure to deal with human aggression is linked to his failure to have worked through the loss of Julius, which was complicated by the later departure of his maternal-surrogate nanny. Hamilton believes these events left Freud burdened with intense survivor guilt and fear of retaliation, which in turn would account for his constant, almost daily, preoccupation with death. He also suffered from migraine, chronic sinusitis and mucous colitis or what we now call the 'irritable bowel syndrome' (1976, p.152). Freud's use of somatic symptoms to deal with his anxieties may have helped to delay his appreciation of his own aggression.

Whatever the cause for Freud's failure to address the aetiology of man's destructiveness, when he did do so it was in the form of the death instinct as illustrated earlier on. With considerable insight, Freud then suggests that such a mechanism offers some consolation,

> ... it is easier to submit to a remorseless law of nature, to the sublime Ananke (necessity), than to a chance which might perhaps have been escaped. It may be, however, that this belief in the internal necessity of dying is only another of those illusions which we have created to bear the burden of existence.
>
> *(1920, p.39)*

Can we not recognise the Augustinian approach to life's calamities?

Once Freud had created the death instinct, he was able to explain 'moral masochism' or guilt, not as a defence against impotence and vulnerability as suggested earlier, but as an expression of the death instinct which has failed to be deflected onto the outer world (1924).

Negative therapeutic reactions, the phenomenon of repetition compulsion, whereby we repeat the destructive experiences of our past, and all instances of mental conflict are to be seen as a struggle between our 'libidinal' impulses and destructive impulses. In this way Freud also satisfied his inclination to think in dual terms, replacing the previous conflict between the sexual instinct and life instinct by one that involved the death instinct and the life instinct. By sticking to this model he kept up with the physiological theories of his time, which saw the nervous system as seeking to rid itself of all tension. One of the consequences, however, of his inventing the 'death instinct' was to dispose of the fear of death. As Ernest Becker points out,

> the fiction of death as an 'instinct' allowed Freud to keep the terror of death outside his formulations as a primary human problem of ego mastery. He did not have to say that death was repressed if the organism carried it naturally in its processes.
>
> *(1973, p.99)*

In Otto Rank's view, Freud magically transformed death from 'an unwished-for necessity to a desired instinctual goal'. Freud thus disposed of the death problem by making it a 'death instinct'. Rank also believed though that 'the comfort-giving nature of this ideology could stand neither logic nor experience for long' (1945, pp.116–122).

His prediction turned out to be wrong, for, though the death instinct has been repeatedly discredited in scientific circles, it is still of fundamental importance in the psychoanalytic literature, as will become apparent in the next chapter. It clearly still has an important role to play in the psyche of many psychoanalytic thinkers. In Britain, the death instinct was to prove particularly popular with one of Freud's followers, Melanie Klein. She worked with children and, as a result of her play sessions, she came to the conclusion that we are aggressive from the moment we are born. Our innate aggression takes the form of envy, a hatred directed against good objects such as mother's breast. She states that the infant's 'dominant aim is to possess himself of the contents of the mother's body and to destroy her by means of every weapon sadism can command' (1930, p.236).

She seemed to see children very much as Augustine did when he concluded that the rage, weeping and jealousy of which they are capable was proof of original sin. For Klein, as for Augustine, loss is also experienced as the result of one's own destructiveness rather than as an external event (1930, p.249). The infant's envy leads to a phantasised destruction of the good object and then to a terrible paranoid anxiety about having destroyed her only source of sustenance and love. We can detect here the 'magical thinking' described by Jean Piaget earlier on. In fact, though Melanie Klein attributed these feelings and phantasies to the infant during the first two years of life, her youngest child in psychoanalysis was two and three-quarter years old and most of her other patients were older. Her theories are therefore based on the extrapolation of data acquired from older children whose perception of the world is probably quite different from that of a younger infant.

For Klein, feelings of inferiority arise from an unconscious sense of guilt, from a fear of not being able to love truly and particularly of not being able to master aggressive impulses towards others (Klein and Riviere, 1937). As a result, negative therapeutic reactions and other evidence of destructiveness are attributed to the lingering manifestation of our death instinct.

Jay Greenberg and Stephen Mitchell point out that Klein could have built up her theory without believing that early envy derives from constitutional aggression. It could derive from other factors: the frustration of the child's unmet needs; the frequency of intense anxiety or inconsistency in the mothering figures and the primitive nature of the child's cognitive capacities, as was demonstrated by Piaget. They conclude that 'the condition of intense needfulness and dependency upon an anxious and inconsistent caretaker, when living a moment-by-moment sensory-motor existence seems to make early aggression unavoidable, apart from any presupposition of innate aggression'(1983, p.129).

Nevertheless, Klein stuck to her belief in the death instinct as firmly as Freud had done. It is possible that they both shared Augustine's need to see man as the victim of his intrinsic wickedness. It is only after looking more closely at the implications of this belief system that it may be possible to understand why Freud and his followers have held to it with such conviction.

Ian Suttie addresses this polarisation in attitudes between various religious thinkers and the parallel within the psychoanalytic movement. As he saw it, neither Augustine nor Freud had the trust in mankind expressed by Julian of Eclanum or himself. He ascribes their difference in religious temperament and attitudes to a corresponding difference in the child's relation to his or her mother which is culture-bound. If she can successfully and naturally wean her child and help him attach himself to father and society, it means that satisfactory relationships have been built up in the growing individual with a resulting basic trust in humanity and life (1935, pp.120–121).

Suttie thought that both Augustine and Freud had not had such a satisfactory early relationship with their mothers or substitutes, but that they had in fact suffered as infants from intense separation anxiety. This had left them very vulnerable to loss of any kind. As for the rage they had felt on being exposed to such threatening experiences, this had been dutifully repressed only to be re-experienced as a deep pervasive sense of guilt, the source of both the concept of 'original sin' and the death instinct.

Although the spirit of Augustine appears to have found a foothold in the teachings of Freud and Klein, there are numerous psychologists and psychoanalysts who reject the death instinct and what it implies; like Julian of Eclanum, they are concerned to clear man of the burden of his apparent evil nature. These researchers make use of an ever-growing body of evidence to highlight man's need for social relationships. Thus, what becomes clearer when reviewing the relevant literature on human destructiveness, is that a belief in an instinct-driven humanity implies with it a constellation of other attitudes: these will be described in the next chapter.

What appears to be at stake are two very different 'gestalts' or visions of life and of the nature of human experience. The interesting question which remains to be answered is as follows: how much are these two different attitudes related to the personal life experiences and character formation of their protagonists? For, if theories about violence are based on subjective and cultural assumptions, can the phenomenon of human destructiveness ever be the subject of a more scientific and objective enquiry? Recent research in the field of attachment and child development does seem to suggest that man can finally begin to determine his potentials and limitations. As a result of these findings, human violence may be on the way to being understood outside the context of our religious cultural traditions. However, it remains to be seen whether scientists and psychoanalytic thinkers are ready to take on board research findings which could be threatening to some of their belief systems regarding human nature: like the belief in original sin, these theoretical assumptions may well protect people from feelings of helplessness and responsibility they would rather avoid.

A brief review of the literature on human destructiveness may give the reader a clearer idea of what people believe to be at stake when discussing this issue and what the difficulties are in establishing a theoretical foundation for a less violent society.

Chapter 3
Aggression and Violence

'Nature, red in tooth and claw.'

Alfred, Lord Tennyson, 1809–1892

The study of man's potential for human violence can only be carried out successfully when researchers in the field become aware of the cultural and emotional pressures they are subject to when thinking about human nature. Clearly, one of the first steps that has to be taken is to acknowledge the intrinsic difficulties and pressures such an enterprise involves.

When looking back at the establishment of Augustinian Christianity over the last 15 centuries, we can begin to see how cultural and historical events come to influence the development of ideologies. If an ideology is defined as a system of beliefs about the nature of man which is held by a group of people and which also gives rise to a way of life, Marxism and Christianity certainly qualify. Although few would consider modern psychology an ideology, it can also be seen to have a very important influence on the legitimisation of current beliefs about human nature, particularly as we now know that many writers in the psychoanalytic field share the same basic assumptions about human nature as do Christian believers. So, though perhaps not an ideology in itself, Ludwig von Bertalanffy may well be correct when he maintains that 'psychology today is a social force of the first order, moulding man's self-image and directing society' (1967, p.12).

In Leslie Stevenson's book *Seven Theories of Human Nature,* she outlines how people continue to believe in different ideologies despite valid objections to their theories (1974). They do so either by ignoring any evidence against their theory, or by disposing of criticisms by analysing the motivation of their critics in terms of the theory itself. When these two devices are used to silence objectors, Stevenson describes the theory as being held in a 'closed system', impervious to outside information and hence to modification. As she points out, when a belief system underpins the way of life of a social group, it will always be difficult for its members to consider it objectively.

> There will be strong social pressures to continue to acknowledge the belief, and it will be natural for the believers to maintain it as a closed system. People will feel that their belief, even if open to objections, contains some vital insight, some vision of essential truths. To abandon it may be to abandon what gives meaning, purpose and hope to one's life.
>
> *(Stevenson, 1974, p.16)*

In this manner Christians see their critics as 'blinded by sin'; Marxists dismiss their opponents as 'deluded by their false consciousness' which they ascribe to their critics' economic class. Similarly, psychoanalysts deal with criticisms by attributing them to their opponents' 'unconscious resistance'.

The use of one's own theory to undermine the validity of the other's arguments is, however, fundamentally irrational. Objections to a theory have to be replied to on their own merits regardless of the motivation of those who question it.

These points are worth bearing in mind when carrying out an overview of the current literature on the nature of human violence. Clearly any such study is fraught with difficulties. There is the problem of what is meant by violence as distinct from aggression and why these two terms are so often confused, a topic broached in the introduction. In addition, as will soon become apparent, the opinions expressed in the literature on human violence or aggression are often very extreme and authors can often be quite denigrating of those who do not share their views. It is interesting how scientists, who normally express themselves with detachment and objectivity, become passionate when writing about human destructiveness. If we bear in mind that such a study cannot be divorced from the debate about human nature, such extreme views should come as no surprise. Indeed, the very manner in which the subject is presented is in itself revealing: human violence by definition implies an alternative state of non-violence, possibly even of cooperation or, dare one say, of love, yet few study the possible links between these two different forms of behaviour.

Suttie is one such author to make this link in his book *The Origins of Love and Hate:*

> Love of mother is primal in so far as it is the *first formed and directed* relationship. Hate, I regard not as a primal independent instinct, but as a development or intensification of separation-anxiety which in turn is *roused* by a threat against love.
>
> *(1935, p.25; italics are Suttie's)*

He ascribes Freud's death instinct to a theory based on hate – a denial of love.

> It is ... from an affective point of view, the supreme expression of hatred, elevating this, as it does, to the status of a primal, independent, purpose in life – a separate appetite which like hunger requires no external provocation and is an end-in-itself ... Indeed I hold that the theory is not only as I say an expression of unconscious rage, but what empirical evidence can be adduced in its support *can only be so interpreted* by shutting our eyes to the existence of love. It is therefore doubly perverse since it is scientifically unjustified.
>
> *(1935, pp. 182–3)*

Suttie's views as to why Freud and his followers held onto their belief in the 'death instinct' have already been discussed: what he also invites us to observe is that the result of such an attitude is a marked 'taboo on tenderness' in the scientific literature on human violence; this has had the effect of divorcing hate from affection and thus denying the possible links between the two. Suttie is of the opinion that love, if frustrated, can 'turn into' hatred (1935, p. 207).

The same 'taboo' appears to exist in the media, where the vast majority of writers, politicians and 'experts' on human behaviour see hate and love as opposites, as the expression of conflicting interests where one 'wins' over the other. The result of such a polarised approach to the subject is the failure to make any connections between violence and our need for one another.

We are fed on such a regular diet of violence on our TV screens, in our newspapers and books that we have come to see it as part of our way of life and, in a sense, this may well be so. Our Western culture may need violence to maintain itself and, as long as this is the case, the pressure to focus on man's destructiveness will remain. However, people are beginning to realise that the price of violence is perhaps more than we can bear, that our survival and that of our planet are in danger. There is therefore a real need to find out if our species is capable of other forms of social interaction. What if violence is but one of our options? What if we human beings have the potential for far more cooperative forms of behaviour? What if the study of child development were to confirm our need for one another? And what if violence and hate, cooperation and love were the reciprocal aspects of the same human needs and behavioural patterns?

The implications of such revelations could be threatening to our current view of ourselves and of our culture, but they may also be the early manifestations of a new scientific paradigm. In his study of scientific revolutions, Thomas Kuhn makes it quite clear that we may be about to witness a new approach to the study of human behaviour: 'Today research in parts of philosophy, psychology, linguistics, and even art history, all converge to suggest that the traditional paradigm is somehow askew' (1970, p. 121). It is tempting to see in Kuhn's observation an encouragement to explore what has hitherto been avoided by so many experts in the field of human behaviour, the links between our capacity to be violent and our need for one another. Research in this area is very difficult and requires us to establish as objectively as possible what factors are conducive to the full development of our affective and cognitive potential, even if these findings may threaten our current way of being and seeing ourselves.

A brief survey of the writings on human aggression and violence may give the reader some insight into the difficulties involved in studying our own behaviour without subjecting our findings to our deeply held assumptions about human nature. It is important to stress that this review does not attempt in any way to sum up the arguments relating to human violence, for this has been done effectively by several authors. The reader is advised to look at Erich Fromm's book *The Anatomy of Human Destructiveness* (1974) and Anthony Storr's work *Human Aggression* (1968) to have some idea of the psychoanalytic debate in the field. Jo Groebel and Robert Hinde's book *Aggression and War* (1989) and Konrad Lorenz's best-seller *On Aggression* (1966) cover the ethological arguments in the debate about human destructiveness. John Gunn's book *Violence in Human Society* provides a clear survey of the subject in all its complexity (1973).

What I hope to do here is to demonstrate, through examples in the literature, the possible mechanisms and pressures at work in the minds of those who, like the author, have made it their task to expound on the nature of human violence. Although it is important to have some understanding of the social and personal factors which may be involved in the literary debate about human violence, it is also essential to stress that the evidence given by the different authors taken from the fields of biology, ethology (the study of animal behaviour), anthropology and sociology will be duly addressed and discussed later in this book. What we are involved with now are the individual and social contexts in which views on human violence are being elaborated, presented and received. No scientific study of human nature can afford to ignore the psychosocial context from which it derives.

A common finding when reading the literature on human violence is the confusion that appears to exist between words referring to aggression and words referring to concepts such as violence or cruelty. Many authors slip from one to the other without attempting to define their terms or the difference between them. I have already addressed this issue in the Introduction and will briefly re-examine the implications of this confusion. In his book, *Biological Bases of Human Social Behaviour*, Robert Hinde makes the point that, though he is writing about animal behaviour, he has to discuss the prevalent value judgements about human aggression because of the false arguments used in this context. He stresses that to accept them uncritically is very dangerous. Having defined aggression as behaviour directed towards causing physical injury to another individual, he writes:

> There is of course no dispute that aggressive behaviour has been selected as an adaptive characteristic in the great majority of species of higher animals, and that individuals who show it to a reasonable degree are more likely to survive and leave offspring than individuals who do not. But it is a completely different matter from the implication that aggressiveness in man may be a characteristic valuable for human society. There is no need to emphasize that aggressiveness can be a vice, and our concern must be with means to reduce it. It is sometimes argued that we do not know what repercussions a reduction in individual aggressiveness might have on the structure of human personality, but it seems unlikely that a reduced tendency to injure others could have deleterious effects. In any case the question can justifiably be postponed in the face of the urgency of the present situation.

(1974, p.275)

This quotation clearly illustrates some of the difficulties any writer has in attempting to cover this topic. The author takes a biological definition of aggression as his baseline and naturally stresses its important adaptive function in higher species. However, in man, he redefines aggression as a 'vice' and, in so doing, makes a value judgment about a particular form of human aggression, similar to the value judgments made in defining violence which we referred to in the introduction. This is because the word 'aggression' covers all sorts of behaviours from rough-and-tumble play in toddlers to the sadistic torture of political victims. As Hinde concludes, the bases of human behaviour resemble in many ways those of aggressive behaviour in animals, but language and the human level of cognitive functioning introduce new dimensions of complexity which are only just beginning to be addressed and which will be the focus of much of this work.

There is a need to differentiate between various forms of aggressive behaviour in human beings. Authors like E. Durbin and John Bowlby (1939) define as 'simple' aggression the behaviour common to both animals and humans, and as 'transformed' aggression the repressed and converted feelings of aggression which are so specific to humanity. The conversion of one to the other could be assumed to have taken place in Mr Brown when he tormented and murdered his child (see Chapter 1). For the time being, suffice it to say that 'transformed aggression' is what is here described as violence. It can take different forms such as 'hatred', a mixture of aggression and revenge, or 'cruelty' which attends to the delight or callousness we can feel in relation to someone else's pain. 'Torture' and 'persecution', the wilful infliction of pain onto another, are just some of its many presentations. Humans have devised endless different ways of hurting one another, some more obvious than others.

All these interpersonal forms of behaviour can be defined as forms of violence which, we will recall, the *Oxford English Dictionary* describes as 'behaviour tending to cause bodily harm or forcibly interfering with personal freedom'. Implicit in this definition is the concept that humans are entitled to a certain degree of freedom, which is an idea intrinsic to our species, derived from our capacity to think and to speak and which is therefore linked to our cultural environment. The psycho-analyst Patrick Gallway highlighted this when speaking on human violence: 'It is defined not so much by behaviour but by meaning' (personal communication, April 1984). The meaning given to destructive behaviour is therefore intrinsic to the study of violence, both for the victim and for the perpetrator. This important aspect is all too often ignored.

The modern debate on human 'aggression' took off following Darwin's discoveries on the nature of evolution by natural selection. Social Darwinism was born out of his ideas; it extended the concept of 'warfare' in nature to 'warfare' in the market place. The 'law of battle', a term used by Darwin to describe the rivalry between male birds and mammals in relation to their females, was used to justify the free unregulated competition of the Industrial Revolution. Human society was seen as the outcome of a violent struggle between competing males. Such concepts as the 'warfare of nature' or the 'survival of the fittest', allowed the successful to justify the highly competitive struggles of the Industrial Revolution with their resulting class divisions, poverty and exploitation.

What is interesting, is that in reading Darwin's book, *The Descent of Man,* there is no reference in his index to human aggression, violence or war but there are many to the 'social instincts' of mankind. These, as we shall see later on, involve 'love and the distinct emotion of sympathy' (1871, p.610).

Darwin's emphasis on the importance of the social instincts and the role of upbringing in their development is rarely referred to in the literature on human violence. This culturally induced 'blind spot' may reflect a current need to emphasise man's cruelty at the expense of what Darwin calls his 'sociability'. Central to the debate on human violence is the issue as to whether it is 'innate' or not, whether it derives from an instinct such as Freud's 'death instinct' or whether it results from external pressures or a combination of the two.

In the field of ethology, those who believe human violence to be innate are essentially followers of Konrad Lorenz (1966). As he is an ethologist of considerable repute, his views on human aggression are still accepted by many as scientific truths. He sees aggression as an instinct which helps to ensure the survival of both the individual and the species. However, in man, this same instinct becomes destructive because our cultural evolution has, so to speak, outstripped our biological evolution. Rapid technological development, particularly in the field of weapons, has given man a destructive power which is no longer kept in check by appropriate inhibitions. Our future thus depends on how we can channel our dangerous and redundant aggressive drives. Interestingly, Lorenz makes the point that he discovered that Freud's theories of motivation revealed unexpected correspondences between the findings of psychoanalysis and behavioural psychology. He goes on to equate his instinct of aggression with Freud's 'death wish' (1966, p.210).

Konrad Lorenz's views were taken up by a group of scientists and popular writers such as Robert Ardrey and Desmond Morris. Their approach to the issue of human violence is interesting because it is so extreme. Robert Ardrey was a follower of Raymond Dart, a professor in anatomy and an expert on the 'Australasian africans'. The latter's views regarding man's origins are often quoted:

> The blood-bespattered, slaughter-gutted archives of human history from the earliest Egyptian and Sumerian records to the most recent atrocities of the Second World War, accord with early universal cannibalism, with animal and human sacrificial practices or their substitutes in formalized religions and with the world-wide scalping, head hunting, body mutilating and necrophiliac practices of mankind in proclaiming this common bloodlust differentiator, this predacious habit, this mark of Cain that separates man dietetically from his anthropoid relatives and allies him rather with the deadliest of *Carnivora*.
>
> *(1954, pp.207–208)*

The trend, for those who believe in man's innate violence, is to deride those who do not agree with their point of view. Howard Evans, an American professor of zoology, concludes that: 'If man is basically aggressive then the continued mouthing of platitudes about brotherly love is clearly no solution' (1966, pp.107–108). This is a clear example of what Suttie referred to as 'the taboo on tenderness'.

Lionel Tiger takes a similar stance in relation to human violence: in his book *Men in Groups* (1984), he sees male bonding as the predominant instrument of organisation in aggression and violence; for him these are features of a social or group process characteristically composed of men and maleness itself is associated with violence: 'Typically, maleness involves physical bravery, speed, the use of violent force ...' (1984, p.182). He sees these characteristics as reflecting a genetically programmed inherited disposition handed down from the days when men were involved in hunting to survive. His conclusions reflect very much the view of all those who believe mankind to be innately destructive: there is little hope for change for, as he says,

> If aggression is profoundly connected with sexuality – which is important to individuals – and also connected with social groups – which nearly all of us

need and like then dealing wisely with aggression and the potential for violence is very difficult. It is just as well that this be fully realised.

(1984, p.193)

Clearly the author is referring to men rather than women and this highlights another characteristic of those who believe in the innate origins
of human violence: they tend to be men who perceive women as different in terms of their 'brain processes'. For Tiger, this means that
women cannot participate effectively in male group activities and hence
in the political and economic functions of society; they have been
mothers for so long that they have been selected to be closely attuned
to their young, a characteristic which could be a disadvantage for men
involved with political and economic activities. Though such attitudes
towards women may sound very prejudiced, they are nonetheless
widespread among those writers who believe in the innateness of
human violence.

The quest for the deep-seated roots of violent behaviour has produced another school of thought called 'human paleopsychology' highlighted by Paul MacLean's work (1987). He describes the brain 'as a
hierarchy of three brains-in-one' and ascribes our 'will-to-power' to our
primitive reptilian brain. This part of our brain plays a primary role in
instinctually determined functions such as establishing territory, finding
shelter, hunting, homing, mating, breeding, forming social hierarchies,
selecting leaders and the like. Altruism and empathy are seen as more
recently acquired forms of behaviour. Thus, human violence is ascribed
to a regressive expression of our reptilian brain. Hitler and Stalin are
seen as 'superreptiles' trampling upon millions of innocent victims.
This phylogenetic regression is believed by some to expose the original
'hunter–gatherer' within us, otherwise labelled the 'reptilian man'. We
are all 'hunter–gatherers at heart' since 99% of our evolution took
place during that period of our evolution. This theory implies that violent acts like rape and Nazi propaganda are explained away as being
examples of such a phylogenetic regression; so is the current situation
of the world, poised as it is for its own destruction.

Although the paleopsychologists admit to man's capacity to manufacture lofty rationalisations and justifications for every sort of inhu-
manity imaginable, they do not consider the possibility that this may be
what they themselves are doing. Having stated that provocation and
threats are bound to make us regress to some aspect of our primitive
brain function, the message yet again is one that suggests that there is
little hope of change since our existence is, on the whole, fraught with
such experiences.

Psychoanalysts have also contributed to the debate on the hereditary
nature of our destructiveness. Storr is one such a psychoanalyst who
uses his professional experience to reinforce the views of popular

writers and scientists such as Robert Ardrey and Desmond Morris. However, though Storr does agree with the innateness of human aggression, he appears to be less certain when it comes to understanding wanton cruelty. He points out that man's tendency to be cruel is rooted in his biological peculiarities, which are the human infant's longterm dependence and helplessness, as well as his intellectual ability to project unwanted feelings onto others (1968, p.135). He concludes:

> There is little doubt that increasing the understanding of the needs of small children will in time lead to more concern about meeting these needs, and will therefore lead to some diminution of the hostility which, in adult life, derives from childhood deprivation.
>
> *(1968, p.149)*

However, despite acknowledging the importance of deprivation in understanding human violence, Storr remains wedded to the instinctual theory of human destructiveness.

Like Tiger and Darwin before him (1871, p.564), Storr sees women as inferior to men and he links this male superiority to masculine aggression. 'It is highly probable that the undoubted superiority of the male sex in intellectual and creative achievement is related to their greater endowment of aggression' (1968, p.88). No wonder 'aggression' must be preserved if it is at the core of 'manhood'. This is a revealing association, for it shows that, for Storr and like-minded men, male social superiority is justified by innate differences in aggression between the sexes. The belief in such an association is a belief that justifies the current social supremacy of men. If the link between male aggression and male superiority is shown to be false, then these writers and their followers have to find other reasons as to why women do not have the same socio-economic status as men.

This need to see woman as inferior is often accompanied by the belief that it is important that other 'different' human beings are also perceived as 'less human'. For instance, Storr maintains that members of a pariah caste, such as the Untouchables of India, serve a valuable function in human communities for the discharge of aggressive tension (1968, p.43).

The latest theoreticians to support the view that our violence is innate are the sociobiologists from the USA, whose premises and conclusions are very similar to those we have so far mentioned. One of their main writers, Edward Wilson, defines his speciality as: 'the scientific study of the biological basis of all human behaviour in all kinds of organisms, including man' (1978). In *On Human Nature* (1978), he examines the impact a truly evolutionary explanation must have on the social sciences and humanities. He does admit in his introduction that he might easily be wrong because his book is essentially a 'speculative essay'. However, his subsequent chapters show no such modesty and references to this supposedly 'speculative essay' are often given as definite truths by his followers, particularly in the field of human destructiveness.

Wilson has an effective formula for presenting his arguments: first he defines his topic, often in a very simplistic way, and then he gives ethological and anthropological evidence that supports his particular point of view. Having shown the phenomenon in question to be widespread, he infers that this can be accounted for by the fact that

> natural selection has probably ground away along these lines for thousands of generations ... To put the idea in its starkest form, one that acknowledges but *temporarily bypasses the intervening developmental process,* human beings are guided by an instinct based on genes.

> *(1978, p.38; my italics)*

So, when it comes to looking at aggression itself, Wilson is quite clear about his beliefs. He begins his chapter on the subject by asking whether we are in fact 'innately aggressive? His answer is simply 'Yes'. When faced with the fact that some societies do appear to be very pacific, Wilson writes:

> Innateness refers to the measurable probability that a trait will develop in a specified set of environments, not to the certainty that the trait will develop in all environments. By this criterion human beings have a marked hereditary predisposition to aggressive behaviour.

> *(1978, p.100)*

How Wilson measures such a probability remains a mystery.

He does, however, admit that forms of human aggressive behaviour have features that distinguish them from aggression in all other species. He goes on to replace Lorenz's drive–discharge model by what he refers to as a more subtle explanation, based on the interaction of genetic potential and learning. (1978, p.105). Wilson maintains that, on the one hand, the more dangerous forms of aggressive behaviour, such as military action and criminal assault, are learned, but he also believes that we have a predisposition to slide into deep, irrational violence under certain conditions:

> The particular forms of organized violence are not inherited. No genes differentiate the practice of platform torture from pole and stake torture, headhunting from cannibalism, the duel of champions from genocide. Instead there is an innate predisposition to manufacture the cultural apparatus of aggression, in a way that separates the conscious mind from the raw biological processes that the genes encode. Culture gives a particular form to the aggression ...

> *(1978, p.114)*

The irrational aspects of human behaviour are characteristically attributed to the genetics of these 'raw biological processes' and the possibility that unconscious psychological defence mechanisms might have an important role to play is denied. Wilson rejects any idea that human aggression could be the pathological symptom of an upbringing in a depriving or abusive environment. Instead, he writes:

> Our brains do appear to be programmed to the following extent: we are inclined to partition other people into friends and aliens, in the same sense that birds are inclined to learn territorial songs ... We tend to fear deeply the actions of strangers and to solve conflict by aggression. These learning rules are most likely to have evolved during the past hundreds of thousands of years of human evolution and, thus to have conferred a biological advantage on those who have conformed to them with the greatest fidelity.

> *(1978, p.119)*

None of these so-called rules have in fact proved to be inherited as we shall see in our review on the development of attachment behaviour, but what we do know is that this inclination to partition people into 'them' and 'us' is of fundamental importance to Wilson's theories. He believes man is innately programmed to see the 'other' as different, a trait he attributes to:

> the powerful urge to dichotomize, to classify other human beings into two artificially sharpened categories. We seem able to be fully comfortable only when the remainder of humanity can be labelled as members versus non-members, kin versus nonkin, friend versus foe.

> *(1978, p.70)*

The psychological and cultural factors involved in this process are denied, thereby laying the foundation for a biological basis for human oppression, exploitation and abuse. Without any scientific evidence whatsoever to support this assumption, Wilson presents his observations as a scientific fact. This approach and its underlying premise is clearly illustrated when he studies the phenomenon of female infanticide.

Wilson points out that in India and pre-revolutionary China, female infanticide was commonly practised by many of the social classes, with the effect of promoting a

> socially upward flow of women accompanied by dowries, a concentration of both wealth and women in the hands of a small middle and upper class, and near exclusion of the poorest males from the breeding system. It remains to be seen whether this pattern is widespread in human cultures.

> *(1978, p.40)*

If it is, then infanticide and female 'hypergamy' (defined as the female practice of marrying men of equal or greater wealth), which as he says are not rational processes, can best be explained 'as an inherited predisposition to maximise the number of offspring in competition with other members of society' (1978, p.40).

Before we consider the implications of such conclusions, it is important to note how Wilson assumes that, if behaviour is 'both irrational and universal', it is more resistant to the effects of cultural deprivation and also less likely to be influenced by the higher centres of the brain and, therefore, more likely to function at the level of the instinct, through the limbic system. By a clever and subtle choice of words, the author links the 'irrational' with the 'instinctual'. In this way, he bypasses the possibility that both cultural and unconscious processes might be operating in the human mind and he ignores all the relevant psychological research evidence that is available to him in the field of developmental psychology.

This approach allows Wilson to draw his personal conclusions about women, whom he sees as instinctively driven towards 'hypergamy'. The practice of infanticide is no longer an example of deplorable human violence but more likely to be the expression of an inherited biological predisposition which makes evolutionary sense when combined with hypergamy, because it excludes poor and therefore 'unsuccessful' men from the breeding system.

As Wilson himself admitted earlier on, his deductions are scientifically untenable, for nowhere in his book does he explain how a complicated series of behaviours and associated social perceptions, such as would be involved in both in hypergamy and selective infanticide, are translated into our genes, let alone genetically selected for.

However, it is not difficult to see how such conclusions could be used to justify certain coercive practices implemented by some societies to maintain power and wealth in the hands of a select few. Hitler used similar arguments to justify his ruthless quest for Aryan racial purity, with the backing of the medical and scientific opinion of the day. It is of interest to note that Lorenz himself helped to provide the Nazi regime with the scientific backing it needed to carry out its genocidal policies.

> Konrad Lorenz, then an ardent Nazi and also a recipient of a prestigious chair, was able to attack those fellow Nazis who refused to accept the Darwinian view of evolution, arguing that it should be the core of the Nazi creed. At the same time, Lorenz used his Darwinism to extend and legitimate the Nazi biomedical vision, and declared that the racial hygiene project should, in effect, take over the evolutionary process to bring about 'a more severe elimination of morally inferior human beings' and 'literally replace' the natural forces of elimination of prehistoric times.
>
> *(Lifton and Markusen, 1990, p.100)*

In this way, the killing of millions was made legitimate.

Wilson also uses Darwin's evolutionary theories on the survival of the fittest to explain social phenomena. 'Societies that decline because of a genetic propensity of its members to generate competitively weaker cultures will be replaced by those more appropriately endowed' (1978, pp. 79–80).

Like most believers in an instinct theory of human violence, Wilson focuses on the individual and has little time for theories which stress the importance of human relations or society.

> The psychology of individuals will form a key part of this analysis. Despite the imposing holistic traditions of Durkheim in sociology and Radcliffe-Brown in anthropology, cultures are not superorganisms that evolve by their own dynamics. Rather, cultural change is the statistical product of the separate behavioural responses of large numbers of human beings who cope as best they can with social existence.
>
> *(1978, p.78)*

In a few lines, Wilson dismisses all the work of those who stress the importance of society for the individual, with all that this implies in terms of our understanding of group and social phenomena. Mrs Thatcher reflected a similar outlook when she said: 'there is no such thing as society only individuals'. By focusing on the individual, theoreticians can thus deny the importance of the 'other', except as an object for the satisfaction of the individual's needs and frustrations.

Like other believers in the primacy of the instincts, the sociobiologists attempt to validate scientifically current social inequalities between the sexes. For example, referring to reproductive strategies in the two sexes, Wilson writes:

> It pays males to be aggressive, hasty, fickle, and undiscriminating. In theory it is more profitable for females to be coy, to hold back until they can identify males with the best genes .... Human beings obey this biological principle faithfully.
>
> *(1978, p.125)*

Once again, as argued by Tiger and Storr, male aggressivity provides the biological basis for male dominance over females and the running of society by men. Thus the sociobiologist R. Dawkins argues in his much publicised book, *The Selfish Gene*: 'The female sex is exploited, and the fundamental evolutionary basis for the exploitation is the fact that eggs are larger than sperm' (1976, p.158). Such an astonishingly simplistic conclusion derives from the biological observation that since there are fewer eggs available for fertilisation than there are sperm, competition among males for females is inevitable.

Like many other writers who believe in the instinctual origins of human violence, the sociobiologists do not only see the female 'other' as different, they also find genetic evidence that justifies differences between human populations. The way Wilson goes about providing such evidence is quite an eye-opener. Having first agreed with most scientists that 'it is a futile exercise to define discrete human races', he goes on to say that: 'Almost all differences between societies are based on learning and social conditioning rather than on heredity. And yet perhaps not quite all'! (1978, p.48). He proceeds to review the results of certain selected studies on the behaviour and temperaments of infants and children of several racial origins such as Chinese–American, Caucasian–American and Navaho Indian. He concludes after only two pages of extrapolations from some very limited data that: 'Given that humankind is a biological species, it should come as no shock to find that populations are to some extent genetically diverse in the physical and mental properties underlying social behaviour.' (1978, p.50). What is extraordinary is that Wilson does not refer at all to the enormous literature on child development which clearly shows how different cultural rearing practices influence maternal behaviour and thereby affect infant behaviour. (These studies will be the subject of another chapter.)

Once again, Wilson foregoes all scientific standards to leap to a conclusion which enables him and us to ascribe biological differences to our fellow men. The scientific sanctioning of the 'other' as different enough to have 'innate' physical and behavioural differences can be used to justify racial or sexual discrimination, with all that this may imply. By misusing his authority as a scientist, Wilson gives politicians and those whose interests they represent the backing they need to exploit and abuse foreigners and immigrants.

From what has been reviewed so far, clearly, the controversy between those who see man as innately evil or cruel and those who see his violence as secondary to some form of psycho-social or physical deprivation, is as alive today as it was in Augustine's time.

In Ashley Montagu's careful review *The Nature of Human Aggression,* he attributes our belief in ourselves as killers to the doctrine of original sin (1976). He believes, as Elaine Pagels does, that the doctrine of original sin has been one of the most powerful and influential principles of Hebrew–Christian belief. To illustrate this further, he gives us the example of Edward Glover, a one-time 'doyen of English Psychoanalysts', describing the nature of the infant as follows:

> The perfectly normal infant is almost completely egocentric, greedy, dirty, violent in temper, destructive in habit, profoundly sexual in purpose, aggrandizing in attitude, devoid of all but the most primitive reality sense, without conscience of moral feeling, whose attitude to society (as represented by the family) is opportunist, inconsiderate, domineering and sadistic. In fact judged by adult social standards, the normal baby is for all intents and purposes a born criminal.
>
> *(Glover, 1960, p.8)*

It seems almost unbelievable that a modern psychoanalyst could perceive the human infant in this way. We are left wondering where do such feelings come from?

Storr speaks for those who believe that we are innately violent: 'We know in our hearts that each one of us harbours within himself the same savage impulses which lead to murder, to torture and to war' (1968, p.9).

There will clearly have to be some very convincing evidence to challenge such firmly held beliefs, for, as Montagu says, the two opposing views of human violence represent 'not only two ways of looking at human beings – important enough in itself – but also two ways of being human. And that has implications for us as individuals, as societies, and as survivors' (1976, p.11).

At this point, we can observe with Montagu how few have been the references to man's 'sociability' despite Darwin's interest in this form of social behaviour. The reason for this is also made clear by Storr when he states: 'Men learn to cooperate and communicate because they would destroy each other if they did not' (1968, p.52). For those who believe us to be innately violent, there appears to be little interest in human cooperation. This need to deny the importance of human beings for each other is characteristic of those who believe in the instinctual nature of human destructiveness. The emphasis is on the individuality of man. The 'other' is just seen as the recipient of our various innate needs. What is perhaps the most interesting feature of this particular way of seeing mankind is the concurrent need to minimise the impact of loss, trauma and death.

What we are in fact describing is a 'gestalt', a way of perceiving and thinking about our species and our interactions; it incorporates a constellation of features and ideas but its fundamental assumption is the belief that we are instinctively or innately violent and 'evil'. Believing in our innate destructiveness and 'wickedness' allows us to deny the importance of the care and affection we have not had. Like the 'bad child' of Fairbairn, we use our culturally sanctioned 'moral defence' to make sense of our bad experiences. For those of us who do not obtain real gratification from our relations with others and who experience loss and death very much as attacks on our integrity, the belief in our innate violence makes sense of a 'bad' world. It also makes sense of our need to see the 'other' as less than human and facilitates the expression of our violence on our children, our wives and our fellow-men, particularly those we perceive as 'different' because of their skin colour or their customs. The denial of our 'sociability' and of the importance of others for our well-being minimises the importance of loss, of deprivation and of trauma both for ourselves and for others.

The opposite way to understand our behaviour is to acknowledge that we are essentially social animals with a great need for the 'other', both to provide for us and to validate our personal existence. This implies recognition of the impact of loss, of psychological trauma and of death. Relationships take over from instincts and, as a consequence of this, we have to accept how vulnerable we are in our dependency on the 'other' and on 'life events'.

The capacity to form nourishing relationships and feel the pain of loss and hurt without feeling destroyed does not come easily to all, and perhaps even less so in a culture that focuses on the individual, his material gratification and on the denial of death and loss. This may explain the need to cling to the 'death instinct' or to a genetic theory of violence even though such a model is quite misleading (Hinde, 1974, p.264).

Jeffrey Goldstein roundly attacks the belief that we are innately violent but he also thinks that such a belief does in fact make a contribution to the maintenance of conditions conducive to violence. As he reminds us, we are the only species capable of being aggressive because of the beliefs we hold (1989, p.19).

There is clearly a need to abandon a model of linear causation when attempting to understand the origins of violence (Bateson, 1989, p.45). To explain the occurrence of aggression or war, a multidimensional approach is necessary that emphasises the interplay between developing individuals (with their genetic heritage) and their environments. No modern biological theory, including sociobiology, can ignore the fact that the forms of behaviour patterns that develop in an individual and the frequency with which they become manifest depend heavily on external conditions.

This is clearly shown by stimulation experiments on the amygdala, the neurological centres which are involved in attacking behaviour observed in mammals. What has been found is that the stimulation of this part of the brain only elicits attacking behaviour if a 'safe' object is present. For example, a rhesus monkey will not attack a social superior or even a subordinate monkey, if another dominant monkey is present. The animal evaluates the situation and responds with the appropriate behaviour. Jose Delgado notes that, while aggression and violence are patterns of responses that are related to specific brain areas, their expression does depend on previous sensory inputs and experience (1971, pp.27–35). This is of crucial importance in terms of our understanding of both affiliative and violent behaviour. It underlines the complex biological and environmental interactions that are involved in primate social behaviour; in humans such interactions will be even more complex since they also involve our cultural environment. We therefore agree with Groebel and Hinde when they conclude that 'The abolition of violence and war demands a systematic analysis of their causes, a falsification of the myths surrounding them and especially an efficient search for non-violent alternatives to conflict resolution' (1989, p.228).

What we have found in studying the different authors who believe in an instinctual theory of human violence, is that they tend to share some fundamental assumptions about human nature and society. The first is the belief that our aggressive behaviour is to a great extent attributable to inherited predispositions and that this is particularly important for the male sex. The second is the belief that the individual's need for the 'other' is essentially materialistic and that if this 'other' is either female or foreigner, or both, he or she is genetically programmed to behave differently from the white male. Sexual inequality, racism and violence are the inevitable outcomes of these forces of 'natural selection'.

It is interesting to note that Darwin's social conclusions are as useful today as they were during the Industrial Revolution: they are still being used to justify the current 'status quo' with its social inequalities and inevitable exploitation. Although this does not mean that the assumptions underpinning Darwin's theories are correct in terms of ensuring our future survival, what they do clearly address is our need to assume that what we are doing is at best justified and, at worst, inevitable.

For some men in particular, like Lorenz, Storr, Tiger and Wilson, there appears to be a real need to believe in an innately destructive human nature, even if this means flouting normal scientific criteria. Their warning is clear: tampering with our aggression-cum-violence is not only extremely difficult but might be dangerous for 'man'kind. Most of these men also deny the existence or the importance of meaning and of unconscious processes in the aetiology of human violence. It is simplistically relegated to a series of innate behavioural manifestations.

Of course the same cannot be said of Freud, whose study of the human psyche was phenomenal. However, what we shall discover as we review his work in more detail is how, by choosing to dwell on the instinct theory, he also had to cut himself off from psychological observations pertaining to man's need for the 'other'. He shares with other believers in an instinctual theory of human violence the view that every individual is essentially here for his own personal gratification; the 'other' is here to either satisfy or frustrate our needs; we do not need the 'other' for our very sense of being, let alone for comfort, support or affection. In this way Freud could also deny the importance of trauma and abuse in the development of cruel and self-destructive behaviour. Similarly, if aggression is 'innate' then, like original sin, it is here to stay and there is little to be done both individually and socially. The 'status quo' is maintained by both Freud and his followers.

The preservation of the instinctual theory of violence has meant that a vast amount of current research on human development has been ignored, particularly in the field of attachment theory. In Wilson's book

Sociobiology, published in 1975, there is not one reference to Bowlby or to the attachment theory. The latter is only briefly mentioned when Wilson writes *On Human Nature* in 1978. This is all the more surprising since attachment behaviour is in a sense the instinctual manifestation of affiliative behaviour, and hence of crucial importance to any serious analysis of the genetic origins of aggressive behaviour. But it may be precisely the fact that there is a genetic predisposition to form attachment bonds that makes this particular theory so unpalatable to those of us who believe in our innate destructiveness.

Clearly the need to deny man's inherent sociability runs very deep, but such an attitude needs to be changed if the new findings in the field of infant development and psychological trauma are to be taken seriously. What is beginning to emerge is that it is within a psychoanalytic framework of understanding that these findings can be most usefully integrated. This will become evident as we look at how attachment theory and self-psychology have provided us with ways of understanding human violence. This has been possible because an increasing number of psychoanalytically trained people have been reviewing Freud's theoretical premises and adapting these to current findings on human development, with its emphasis on the human need for the 'other'.

Chapter 4
From Attunement to Attachment and the Trauma of Loss

'When we are dead, seek not our tomb in the earth, but find it in the hearts of men.'

Jalaludin Rumi

The origins of attachment theory

For as long as people believe in the 'death instinct' they need not really envisage the existence of trauma- or pain-induced aggression. The belief in an 'innate' self-generated form of destructiveness enables us to blind ourselves to the possible links that may exist between the experience of pain and the expression of violence. As long as such a connection could be 'scientifically' ignored, those who subscribed to a link between trauma and aggression could also be dismissed as misguided idealists.

But the realisation that trauma, be it through war or disaster, can and does elicit forms of violent behaviour can no longer be disregarded. (The evidence for this will be the subject of the second part of this book.) Similarly, the ever-increasing literature on child abuse shows just how vulnerable humans are as infants and children to all forms of physical and psychological abuse; the abused not only fill doctors' clinics but, time and time again, they become the victims of their own violence and occasionally become violent abusers themselves.

However, even these findings have not convinced those who believe humanity to be innately violent that there are links between pain and violence. Some sociobiologists would like to ascribe child abuse to heredity and natural selection rather than to the individual's psychological and biological reactions to their own traumatic experiences. Some psychoanalysts continue to attribute their patients' destructiveness to the enactment of their innately sadistic or seductive fantasies. The reality of their patients' experience of abuse or pain is thus easily dismissed and, as we shall see later, in its very dismissal, the abuse is often recreated in the consulting room. The need to perceive ourselves as victims of our genes or of our instincts is, as we observed earlier on, a very deep one which goes hand-in-hand with a constellation of other beliefs about our independence and individuality and a denial of the inherent importance for us of the 'other'.

If we are to begin to acknowledge that pain induced through deprivation or abuse can elicit violence, we have to be able to prove two things:

1. That we are fundamentally in need of one another or, as Suttie (1935) put it, we have 'an innate need for companionship'.
2. That there is in human beings a psychobiological mechanism or a process whereby psychic trauma can be converted into destructive behaviour.

In the next two chapters, we will be focusing on findings which confirm our fundamental need for one another. In Chapter 6 we will look at how the experience of deprivation of our basic attachment-related needs leads to destructiveness. Indeed, in the last 20 or so years, biologists, psychologists and psychoanalysts working in the field of developmental psychology and 'attachment' have begun to realise that just such a process does and must exist to account for their findings in the field of psychic trauma. One of its manifestations is the conversion of pain into violence. One of its implications is, yet again, the importance of the 'other'.

Thus, 'attachment', once seen as a theoretical construct used to describe certain forms of infant behaviour towards the caregiver, is now known to have a biological substrate which is affected by experience at a biochemical and physiological level. Such psychobiological evidence is providing an increasing understanding of how trauma, in the form of abuse, deprivation or loss, affects the way we behave.

These studies are also forcing us to realise that we matter deeply to one another for our very well-being. It is not just that we need each other to satisfy our hunger or our sexual needs as Freud saw it; it is not only that we need to feel good with one another to feel good about ourselves. What is becoming clearer is that our social interactions play an important role in the everyday regulation of our internal biological systems throughout our lives, such an important role that we cannot do without significant 'others' and remain in health.

As a result of research on separation in both primates and humans, writers in the field are beginning to view attachment as a kind of psychobiological attunement that occurs in multiple relationships throughout life. What is meant by 'attunement' is what we will be focusing on as we attempt to discover how our innate need for companionship becomes validated within the four walls of a laboratory.

In the meantime, outside the centres of research, within the field of psychoanalytic thinking, an increasing awareness of our need for the

'other' has also led to changes and, in some circles, to the abandonment of the old 'instinct' theories of psychoanalysis for theories based
on the primacy of relationships.

These parallel developments in the field of ethology, biology and
psychology, as well as in psychoanalysis, call for integration and yet the
task is an arduous one, particularly as we live in an age where fragmentation is of the essence. Specialists abound and yet the specialist is in a
sense prisoner of his or her own speciality; not only does it require a
considerable amount of time to explore other fields of research but it
can also lead to considerable criticism from those who want to protect
their speciality. My credentials as a biologist, doctor, psychiatrist and
psychotherapist with a multicultural background may not be up to the
task in hand; however, since integration is important, and since our
need to understand the origins of human violence are also urgent, this
is but another small step in this direction.

It is unfortunately through the experience of separation that we usually
become aware of how much we matter to one another. This may well
explain why we 'needed' the terrible experience of the First World War
for British psychoanalysts to begin to question the Freudian belief that
infantile sexuality is important in the genesis of neurosis. Such a belief
implied that the infant or toddler is unconsciously subject to ideas and
feelings centring around the wish to possess the parent of the opposite
sex. Described as the Oedipus complex, Freud saw it as a universal
phylogenetically built-in phenomenon, responsible for much of our
unconscious guilt. For the Kleinian psychoanalysts, the Oedipus
complex is still recognised as the central conflict in the human psyche,
with its cluster of conflicting impulses, phantasies, anxieties and
defences. It is at the centre of Kleinian psychoanalytic work (Segal,
1989).

For other psychoanalysts more involved with issues of loss or trauma, the Oedipus complex no longer has the same significance: this
change dates to the 1930s. In their paper 'Britain between the two
wars: the historical context of Bowlby's theory of attachment', Nora
Newcombe and Jeffrey Lerner show how then, as now, the social and
intellectual climate of the day made it possible for people to think
anew about human development.

> The war produced several changes crucial to the development of attach-
> ment theory: diminution of all insistence on the biological causation of
> mental illness, more widespread recognition of the existence of neurotic as
> well as psychotic disorders, revision of Freud's emphasis on infantile sexual
> trauma as a necessary component of neurosis, and most important,
> increased recognition of the role of 'object relations' in development. The
> experience of treating cases of 'shell shock' both during and after the war
> was an important factor in bringing about these changes. Another important

factor was the postwar atmosphere of bereavement and the changes in mourning custom [which put an end to the old mourning rituals].

(Newcombe and Lerner, 1982, pp.1–2)

It was in this context that John Bowlby, a one-time supervisee of Melanie Klein's, began to observe the responses of children who had lost their mothers and found them to be similar to those seen in adults after the loss of a loved one. His preoccupation with separation anxiety and loss is tentatively attributed by Newcombe and Lerner to the widespread effects of the death of 750 000 British young men during the First World War, leaving behind them as many as 248 000 widows and 381 000 children.

In what appears to be a socially induced form of psychological defence, patriotic stoicism was encouraged, with the result that pre-war funeral and mourning customs were abandoned. The psychological need for that British 'stiff upper lip' and the more material need for massive civilian employment both militated against such 'morbid practices'. The process of mourning was no longer socially sanctioned nor culturally supported. This attitude persisted into the Second World War and its aftermath.

In my therapeutic work with British elderly men who have had leg amputations for vascular insufficiency, I have often witnessed the psychological pain of a one-time soldier reliving some of his terrible memories of fear, violence and loss on the battlefield. What is most striking is that, often, the telling of their painful story to me or to their nurse, is the first opportunity these men have had to share their nightmare. Again and again, the patient explains how no one, not even their loved ones, ever wanted to know what they had been through. 'It just wasn't done.' Their memories were repressed to be reawakened possibly by the experience of their own loss of a limb or of that of others on the same ward.

Prior to the First World War, it was widely believed, as it still is in some medical circles, that the causes of mental illness were essentially physical. Whilst grief was acknowledged by psychiatrists, like Henry Maudsley, as being a 'natural phenomenon', it was not seen to have any links with 'melancholia', the state we now know of as depression.

Before going any further it is necessary to define what is meant by grief, mourning and bereavement, because these terms are often confused. They are clearly described by Stroebe and Stroebe in their book *Bereavement and Health* (1987). Grief is the emotional response to loss, which includes a number of psychological and somatic reactions (Lindemann, 1944). Mourning refers to acts expressive of grief, shaped by the mourning practices of a particular culture; it is a duty imposed by the group. Bereavement refers to the objective situation an individual is in when he or she has recently experienced the loss of someone significant through death: it is therefore the cause of grief and mourning.

Returning to the possible links between normal grief and pathological depression, Freud himself was to write in 1917 an essay on 'Mourning and Melancholia' where he compared the process of grief (mistranslated as mourning) with that of depression. Though grief involves a grave departure from normal life, Freud points out that it has a remarkably similar presentation to melancholia: in both there is dejection, loss of interest in the outside world and apathy. In melancholia, however, there is also a severe loss of self-esteem: these patients are continually reproaching themselves.

Freud argues that both sets of people are in fact reacting to the loss of an object or person, though in the melancholic, it is not a conscious loss. In this case, Freud suggests that the loss is accompanied by the identification of the ego with the lost object. For example, a denigrated wife can only cope with her husband's loss by continually denigrating herself.

In this seminal paper, Freud was to lay the foundations for an understanding of ourselves based on the internalisation of human relationships. But his need to remain wedded to the 'instinct' theory prevented him from systematically following through the concept of internalised relationships and the study of loss. This should come as no surprise, since bereavement cannot make sense unless we understand the fundamental importance of the 'other'.

Ian Suttie and his wife Jane were two of the first psychoanalysts to emphasise the importance of love and companionship in both human development and adulthood. In so doing they felt they broke with a longstanding 'taboo' regarding the importance of loving behaviour. They were well ahead of their time in recognising the significance of the mother–infant relationship in child development. Long before Bowlby had formulated his 'attachment theory', the Sutties wrote:

> In the course of evolution of the higher animals, the highly specific and discrete instincts lost their differentiation and integrity and became very largely merged in ontogeny into a formless, aimless attachment of the infant to the mother. We considered that, by this evolution three advantages accrued:
>
> 1. A plastic, adaptable, educable interest became available.
> 2. The helpless infant will do everything within its powers to preserve itself, e.g. to maintain its close association with the mother.
> 3. The infant will acquire an *associative need*, which will supply the basis both of the social habit and of the rearing impulses when the infant matures in turn.
>
> *(1932, p.209; Sutties' italics)*

Not only did Ian Suttie recognise the importance of the attachment relationship between mother and infant, but he maintained the view that: 'our dependency on others is never completely outgrown, but persists as a need for companionship, *apart from the organic satisfactions that may be derived therefrom*' (1935, p.206; Suttie's italics).

Inspired by the work of Ian Suttie, the psychoanalyst Bowlby was to become a leading figure in the validation of the importance of affiliative relationships in our species. He formulated his theory by integrating his psychoanalytic work with concurrent studies in ethology (particularly the work of Lorenz on imprinting), systems theory, cybernetics and cognitive psychology.

The impetus for his work came from the findings of studies on postwar infants who for one reason or another had been separated from their parents and put into hospitals or institutions. After only three months, these babies would often die from intercurrent infections and, if they survived, they would be markedly underweight and mentally handicapped despite having been physically well cared for.

R. Spitz, the psychoanalyst who initially carried out these studies, described these infants as suffering from 'hospitalism' (1945). He and his colleague K. Wolf also observed a less severe, though similar, phenomenon in infants left in a nursery for the second half of their first year which they called an 'anaclitic depression'. These babies were withdrawn, appeared depressed and also showed less resistance to infections (1946). Spitz was to interpret these findings as due to the loss of the mother but not in terms of the loss of a loved object. In keeping with Freud's instinct theory, he attributed the infants' pathology to the fact that this loss interfered with the discharge of their 'libidinal' and 'aggressive' drives (Eagle, 1984). Bowlby, however, had serious reservations about such an explanation. He did in fact part company with the Kleinians because, as he said,

> I held that real-life events – the way parents treat a child – are of key importance in determining development, and Melanie Klein would have none of it. The object relations she was talking about were entirely internal relationships …. The notion that internal relationships reflect external relationships was totally missing from her thinking.

> *(Karen, 1990, p.44)*

Because of his different approach, Bowlby's study on infants who had been separated from their mother led him to formulate conclusions which were quite different from Spitz's (Robertson and Bowlby, 1952). Bowlby described how the infant becomes acutely distressed when her mother leaves her; she attempts to get her back by every means at her disposal: she cries and screams or throws herself against her cot. Bowlby called this the 'protest' phase. After a while, which varies from baby to baby, he observed that the infant appears to feel hopeless: she no longer cries and scarcely moves; she shows no interest in her environment. This phase, he described as one of 'despair'. In some cases it was followed by a phase of 'detachment' which to an observer might seem like a period of recovery, because the child begins to interact with her environment once again. However, it is when she is returned to her mother that something appears clearly to be wrong. The infant will ignore or even snub her mother. (Throughout this book I will usually refer to the primary caregiver as the mother though it can be the father or an unrelated adult, and I will use the female pronoun for the infant.)

Bowlby was perplexed by what he observed: what is it about the loss of mother that affects infants so much? Are infants also affected by other losses?

These very questions were to be explored in the primate laboratories of Harry Harlow: he studied the behaviour of rhesus monkeys separated from their mothers (Harlow and Mears, 1979). Harlow's primary purpose was, as he admits, to dismantle Freud's drive theory. Like Suttie, Harlow believed in the importance of love. In the second edition of his book *Learning to Love* (1974), he was also to deplore the lack of scientific interest in the phenomenon of affection. Having scanned the psychological literature of the preceding 20 years, he concluded that there were no experiments or scientific essays on the development of love. For Harlow, love was to be defined by the affectional feelings we have for others and he claimed that there are at least five basic kinds of love. 'These are maternal love for the infant, the infant's love for the mother, peer or age-mate love, heterosexual and paternal love.' He then adds that: 'any complex behaviour or behaviours, such as those characterising each of the five love systems, is produced and maintained through multiple variables. For the most part these are some combination and integration of primary unlearned and primarily learned factors' (Harlow, 1974, p.viii). 'In order for each successive love system to develop adequately', he continues, 'the earlier system or systems must have been experienced in satisfactory fashion' (1974, ix–x).

> Thus the maternal and infant affectional systems prepare the child for the perplexing problems of peer adjustment by providing him with basic feelings of security and trust …. By the same token, age-mate experience is fundamental to the development of normal and natural heterosexual love …. In all primates the heterosexual affectional system is hopelessly inept and inadequate unless it has been preceded by effective peer partnerships and age-mate activities.
>
> *(1974, p.3)*

In his now-classical dual mother–surrogate studies, Harlow was to measure the relative importance of body contact for rhesus monkey infants as opposed to the satisfaction of nutritional needs. He exposed the infants to both a surrogate soft cloth mother and a surrogate wire mother. Even though the latter had a nursing bottle attached to it, Harlow was able to demonstrate that 'contact comfort' was the primary factor in the formation of mother–infant affectional bonds. The infants spent most of their time clinging to their cloth mother. 'She' was even able to give infant monkeys a sense of basic security. When placed in a strange environment, the infants would cling to their cloth mothers before venturing to explore their surroundings. As in the wild, they would often return to their surrogate mothers for a reassuring clasp to allay their anxiety before resuming their exploratory behaviour. Subsequently, Harlow and his team discovered that many other variables affected the infant monkey's attachment to its mother once the contact comfort was held constant: nursing activities at the breast were significant in the first 90 days of life; rocking as opposed to non-rocking surrogates were preferred for the first 160 days; warm as opposed to cool surrogates were preferred for the first 15 days of life. The natural mother attends to all these needs and many more, such as training her infant to communicate with others, playing and encouraging separation, which all go towards the development of peer interaction.

Harlow believes that the formation of strong affectionate peer bonds is at the root of aggression control in all primates. As he says, we are all born with an aggressive potential; the fact that it develops relatively late enables us to control it through the earlier normal development of infant–mother love. For Harlow, there appears to be no possibility that violence and love may be reciprocally related (Harlow and Mears, 1979).

Bolstered by Harlow's findings on the comforting nature of infant attachment to the mother, Bowlby was able to discard what he called the 'cupboard-love of object relations' which stipulated that the child attached herself to the mother because she provided her with certain physiological needs such as food and warmth (Bowlby, 1969). It was and still is a basic common assumption for both learning theorists and some Freudians. Bowlby was to create a new

> conceptual framework ... designed to accommodate all those phenomena to which Freud called attention – for example love relations, separation anxiety, mourning, defence, anger, guilt, depression, trauma, emotional detachment, sensitive periods in early life – and so to offer an alternative to the traditional metapsychology of psychoanalysis ... .
>
> *(1988, pp.25-26)*

He describes attachment behaviour as 'any form of behaviour that results in a person attaining or maintaining proximity to some other clearly defined individual who is conceived as better able to cope with the world' (1988, pp.26–27). It is through this attachment behaviour that the first attachment bond with mother is formed.

Although this behaviour is most obvious in childhood, it can be observed throughout life, especially at times of crises. Attachment behaviour is seen as an integral part of human nature and one we share with many other species. For Bowlby its biological function is to ensure care and protection of the young. The relatively long period of infantile dependence, together with a lack of fixed predetermined action patterns in humans, provides our species with the capacity for flexibility and learning which ensures us a great adaptability to a wide range of environments. However, a long period of immaturity also makes us very vulnerable and in need of protection. For Bowlby the attachment behaviour provides us with a behavioural system geared to ensure proximity to our caretaker. A complementary form of behaviour has evolved in the infant's caregiver.

The theory of attachment behaviour is thus an attempt to explain both attachment behaviour and the enduring attachment bonds that are formed between people. This chapter will focus on the first aspect, that of attachment behaviour and its underlying brain mechanisms. Subsequent chapters will attend to the formation of attachment bonds or relationships and their internalisation as 'working models' in the mind.

The trauma of loss

For Bowlby, the discovery of the attachment system and the creation of an attachment theory, was an act of integration, the bringing together of psychoanalysis, ethology, behavioural psychology and cybernetics. As he states:

> The key concept is that of a behavioural system. This is conceived on the analogy of a physiological system organised homoeostatically to ensure that a certain physiological measure, such as body temperature or blood pressure, is held between appropriate limits. In proposing the concept of a behavioural system to account for the way a child or older person maintains his relation to his attachment figure between certain limits of distance or accessibility, no more is done than to use these well-understood principles to account for a different form of homoeostasis, namely one in which the set limits concern the organism's relation to clearly identified persons in, or other feature of, the environment and in which the limits are maintained by behavioural instead of physiological means.
>
> *(1988, p.29)*

Although Bowlby only used the analogy of a homoeostatic system as a metaphor to describe better the attachment behavioural system, more recent studies suggest that attachment behaviour does probably also fulfil a physiological homoeostatic function. Indeed, it appears that the attachment system, with its different behavioural and physiological manifestations, achieves many more functions than Bowlby initially suspected. In his eyes and those of his colleague Mary Ainsworth, the

attachment behaviour initially observed between a mother and her
infant was there to provide protection for the infant and the provision
of a 'secure base' to which the child could return while exploring her
surroundings. The provision of such a 'secure base' promotes in the
infant a sense of self-reliance and autonomy and so lays the foundation
for subsequent peer relations and later adult relationships, whether
sexual or parental.

Ainsworth's important study of mother–infant relationships will be
examined in detail in the next few chapters. It reveals that the earliest
and possibly most damaging psychological trauma is the loss of a
'secure base'. When infants are securely attached to their caregiver,
they grow up into children who are self-confident and successful in
their interpersonal relations. However, children can become 'anxiously' attached to their caregiver when their only source of support and
affection also becomes their main source of distress, either through
rejection or neglect. In some cases these infants behave like Harlow's
monkeys: the more their surrogate mothers frighten them, the more
they cling to her (Harlow and Mears, 1979). The human infant, however, can develop a more complex response: Bowlby describes it as a pattern of behaviour where avoidance competes with the desire for
proximity and care, and during which angry behaviour is likely to
become more prominent (Bowlby, 1973, pp. 46–47). An example of
this 'avoidant' behaviour was seen in the 'detached' behaviour of some
of the infants reunited with their mothers, which was briefly referred to
earlier. These 'anxiously' attached children usually turn out to have
personal and interpersonal difficulties later in life.

Thus, social attachment does achieve a very important psychological
function in primate development, with longterm implications both in
terms of interpersonal behaviour and personality. However, social
attachment is not only a psychological event; it is also related to the
development of core neurobiological functions in the primate brain. As
Kraemer points out, as long as society and social phenomena could be
considered as epiphenomena that occur when members of our species
happen to live in close proximity, it could be assumed that individuals
would survive quite well on their own (Kraemer, 1985, p.137) However,
if the human and other social primate species are viewed as biological
organisms that need to develop, to survive and procreate, the importance of social affiliative relationships becomes apparent. Referring to
mother–infant separation studies which show that in many cases
infants die, even though able to feed themselves, Kraemer writes: 'This
is survival failure of the first kind, and it is an indication that a core
neurobiological function has been interfered with by separation from
an attachment object, but not one that is directly related to physical
maintenance of the infant by the mother' (Kraemer, 1985, p.139).

Referring to the social isolation studies carried out on monkeys (which will be described later in more detail), Kraemer also points out that the resulting abnormal social, sexual and maternal behaviour leads to survival failure of the second kind, the absence of procreation. This provides us with a further demonstration that a central neurobiological function has been altered by the disruption of social attachment during development. As a result, he concludes that social attachment is not optional for primates – it is a motivational system: feeding, fighting, fleeing and sexual behaviour are all considered as independent motivational systems in their own right but are so intimately integrated with the development of social attachment that they are not expressed in an organised manner without it.

Having established the importance of social attachment systems, Kraemer then acknowledges how little is known about the underlying neurobiological systems mediating this behaviour. A brief review of some of the findings in this field will help to demonstrate the importance of relationships to humankind.

Paul McLean (1985) pointed out how family behaviour in mammals made it necessary for certain evolutionary changes to occur in the brain, associated with both communication and affiliation. He highlighted the role of the limbic system in the control of emotions which trigger off the various behaviours used for self-preservation. It is also in the same limbic system that most of the neurological mechanisms involved with attachment behaviour have been located.

The psychobiology of attachment behaviour has been derived mainly from studies on primate infants separated from their mothers. Since in most mammals dependency on the mother has become so important, separation alone produces intense distress in infants. Many researchers have considered the infant's 'separation call' as a classical manifestation of the infant's distress. Accompanying changes in heart rate, temperature and levels of arousal have also been measured during these periods of separation.

It was Coe and his colleagues who were to show that the link between the separation call and the infant's distress is not so straightforward (Coe et al., 1985): brief half-hour separations with infant squirrel monkeys produced highly elevated plasma cortisol levels which continued to be raised long after the calling behaviour had stopped. (Cortisol levels were used as a measure of adrenocortical activation, which is a traditional measurement of stress.) They concluded that vocalisations are part of the signalling behaviour designed to elicit proximity on the part of the mother; they do not accurately represent infant distress. What these authors do confirm is that the markedly high levels of plasma cortisol after separation from mother show that even temporary maternal loss is extremely stressful for this particular species of monkey, more so, they believe, than that induced by physical trauma.

As with other primate separation studies, Coe and his colleagues also recorded several changes in the infants' immune response after prolonged cortisol elevations. They found that although short-term adrenal activation is very important in mobilising the organism to deal with stressful situations, the long-term effect is to produce varying degrees of immunosuppression. These results help us understand why the babies in Spitz's and Bowlby's studies died so frequently from intercurrent infections.

One very important finding arising from Coe and his colleagues' study is that if the infants were separated from their mother but left in the company of other familiar squirrel monkeys, whether adult or peers, these infants showed markedly less stress and immunosuppression. 'Thus, just as the response to loss indicates the importance of a mother-infant bond, we can also state that fear and stress reduction is an important benefit and function of social relationships in general' (Coe et al., 1985, p.196).

One issue in this study remains unresolved, that of the infant's depressive behaviour. Unlike many other studies on infants separated from their mothers, Coe and his colleagues found little evidence of depressive behaviour. They suggest many factors to account for this difference.

For instance, some researchers interpret the absence of calling and movement as sufficient evidence of despair or depression.

Genetic and/or 'socio-cultural' differences can also account for this result: for instance, pigtail macaque monkeys are prone to depression whereas bonnet macaques are not; interestingly, bonnet macaques also have a different social structure whereby their infants spend a lot more time with other members of the group and the general behaviour of the group members is more permissive and responsive than it is in many other primate species. It is perhaps even more interesting to note that a much stronger despair response can be produced by depriving a bonnet infant of these alternative relationships during his early development (McKinney, 1985, p.208). Different rearing practices clearly do have an important effect on the attachment behaviours of primates, effects that become even more obvious in different human societies and which will be explored later on in this book.

A third factor that may account for the variation in depressive behaviours across mother–infant separation studies is the way in which the infants are separated and reunited with their mothers. If subject to repeated separations or if reunited in disturbed social groups, the infants are more likely to be depressed. Similarly, a change in the mother–infant relation upon reunion is also important, such as a mother being in oestrous when her infant is returned to her.

One other important factor is that many of the infants used in these studies were more vulnerable to depression because they were themselves reared without their mothers.

The final and no less important contributor to the variation in responses is the infant's own genetic predisposition to develop depressive reactions to separation (Suomi and Ripp, 1983, p.69). Clearly the causes and manifestations of depression in primates are still far from clear, but what is striking is how similar our affective life is to that of our primate cousins.

Jaak Panksepp and his colleagues take us one step further in the study of the attachment substrate by involving us with the brain itself (Panksepp, Siviy and Normansell, 1985). Panksepp's basic assumption is that all secondary processes by which attachments are expressed depend both on an organism's ability to experience distress following separation from social companions and on its ability to experience comfort upon reunion. He therefore focuses on neural circuits that mediate separation distress and contact comfort.

What he finds is that the vocalisations produced by separation in young animals are inhibited by the administration of opiates. Inversely, the use of opiate antagonists greatly increases the need for attachment, so much so that Panksepp describes social bonding as an 'opioid addiction'! Indeed, the distress symptoms produced by separation are similar to those seen in narcotic withdrawal states. If this is so, emotions are at the root of social bonding: pleasure is the outcome of attachment, mediated no doubt in part by endogenous opiates; separation produces distress, irritability and aggression. This leads Panksepp to postulate that: 'It seems likely that the mechanisms underlying helping and antagonistic behaviour are reciprocally related, and both could be critically linked to brain opioid activity in limbic circuits .... Such reciprocal innervation may be a general property of emotive circuits in the brain' (Panksepp, 1984, pp.42–43).

The possibility that affiliation and aggression may be reciprocally linked at a psychobiological level is of crucial importance in our understanding of violence: love and hate may well be the reciprocal expression of the same phenomenon. In support of this theory, Panksepp and others have found that the areas of the brain with the highest levels of opiate receptors are those involved in social bonding, pain perception and separation distress, so that all these different behaviours could be mediated, at least in part, by the opiate system. The fact that so many social processes have been demonstrated to be especially sensitive to opiate effects is only to be expected because, as Panksepp points out, social processes affect practically everything an animal does (Panksepp, 1984, p.43).

The psychobiology of attunement

Endogenous opiates are probably involved in attachment behaviour, and cortisol secretion and immunosuppression are the products of separation; but many more biochemical phenomena are being brought to light in relation to our attachment systems. Those which are of particular relevance to our study have been highlighted by Myron Hofer (1984). This researcher in the field of psychobiology was struck, as Bowlby was, by the similarities between infant–mother separation reactions and bereavement reactions in adults.

Like Lindemann (1944), Hofer emphasises that in adult bereavement there are two forms of disturbance: the acute recurrent waves of distress which last only minutes, and the chronic slowly developing background disturbance seen over weeks and months. Similar symptoms are present in the separated infants, except that in the human infant the acute distress does not occur in waves, as it does in adults, but precedes the more slowly developing chronic changes. Whilst the acute and chronic symptoms are assumed to be part of the same process, for Hofer this is not to be taken for granted, either in the adult or in the infant.

Hofer takes us through the different phases, showing how the acute phase of bereavement in adults and the 'protest' phase in infants is characterised by a series of similar behaviours such as agitation, crying, aimless activity and inactivity, all of which are attempts to regain the lost 'object'. In the adult there is also a preoccupation with the image of the deceased. Physiological changes such as tears, sighing and muscular weakness also occur in adult and infants with the hormonal and physiological changes referred to earlier.

The chronic changes in the adult also resemble the 'despair' phase seen in infants. The adult shows social withdrawal, decreased attention and concentration, restlessness and anxiety, decreased or variable food intake, sad expressions, illusions or hallucinations and a depressed mood. The infant also shows a decrease in social interactions and play, mouthing and rocking activities, similar changes in appetite, hypo- or hyperresponsiveness, postures and facial expressions of sadness.

The physiological changes in the adult are those of weight loss, sleep disturbance, muscular weakness and cardiovascular changes. The same are seen in infants, who also show a reduction in body temperature and a reduced oxygen consumption. Bowlby made the assumption that these changes in the infant were an evolutionary strategy to allow for the conservation of energy until reunion with mother becomes possible.

Hofer, however, questions this interpretation. By providing infant rat pups with 'placebos' such as a littermate or an anaesthetised mother, the 'protest' phase could be eliminated but the slowly developing changes still continued to occur, suggesting that they arose independently of the isolation-induced distress. Hofer believes these two different phases might be caused by quite different processes, particularly as he found that, on further study, each physiological change was attributable to a single aspect of the mother–infant relationship. For example, some interactions with mother maintain some functions at relatively high levels during normal conditions, such as the heart rate and oxygen consumption. Others normally down-regulate their systems, such as those underlying arousal during sleep and sucking.

Thus the pattern of slowly developing changes is in fact an assemblage of different processes, all activated by the simultaneous withdrawal of all the regulatory aspects of the mother–infant relationship. These results show that even though a 2-week-old rat pup can feed itself, its homoeostatic system, which is seen as a relatively 'open' one, is still intimately connected to its mother. 'These biologic regulators may constitute an early stage in the development of what we believe to be *psychologic* regulators within early social interactions, as infants get older and as species evolve' (Hofer, 1984, p.187; Hofer's italics).

If we now return to the bonnet macaque infants, we discover to what extent the environment can affect attachment relationships. If the mother is obliged to forage for food instead of receiving food *ad libitum,* the mother–infant relationship becomes more tense with increased maternal rejection and earlier infant independence. When separated from their busy mothers, these infants showed the normal 'protest' behaviour of the acute phase but became markedly 'depressed' in their second week of separation. This does not occur in their usual environment (Rosenblum and Sunderland, 1982).

This study, like the ones referred to earlier, shows how the nature of the mother–infant relationship prior to separation can have marked effects on the infant's response after separation. Hofer suggests that it is the presence of regulators within the interaction that determines the form of the response after withdrawal by separation. If these regulators are jeopardised in some way, either through deprivation or trauma, the response of the organism to separation may well be altered.

Hofer believes that such regulatory activities may continue to be important throughout life. We are reminded of the study that shows how women living together for some time develop synchrony in their menstrual cycles. Research into the effects of sensory deprivation and chronobiology (the study of circadian and other rhythms) also shows how dependent we are on everyday environmental stimuli for the proper functioning of our minds; without these stimuli we develop symptoms that are markedly similar to those seen in chronic grief! These findings suggest that the same regulating activities may well be going on in close human relationships; if this is the case, bereavement would also produce a set of withdrawal responses.

Hofer's ideas have been extensively presented because they are indicative of how recent findings in the psychobiology of the attachment system illustrate only too clearly how important we may well be for one another, not only at a psychological level, as we shall find out in subsequent chapters, but also at a physiological level. The fact that we appear separated by our bodies may at some level be more of an illusion than a fact, at least when we are dealing with significant 'others' in our lives.

Such findings have led Reite and Capitanio to wonder if attachment behaviour is actually the manifestation of some type of psychobiological synchrony between individuals (Reite and Capitanio, 1985, p.235). Not only does the mother or caregiver act as a metabolic regulator to the infant's own system but, in addition, researchers like Sander, Stern and Brazelton have shown that one of the main components of the mother–infant bonding is the development of rhythmicity in the infant and of synchrony between the mother's and the infant's rhythms (Reite and Capitanio, 1985, p.239).

For Tiffany Field, these results show that attachment behaviour, as assumed from studies on separated infants and children, is far too limited; she quotes Bowlby's work which showed that in some cases attachment disturbances remained, even though mother and child were reunited, the stage he labelled 'detachment'. Similar behavioural changes have been seen to persist after reunion in primates. Field concludes that these data suggest that separation may be a sufficient condition for behavioural disorganisation, but not a necessary condition (Field, 1985). Not only is the relationship that occurs before the separation important, as Hofer and others have stressed, but so are changes in the relationship that take place after the separation. Field and Reite's study on preschool children's responses to their mother after the birth of another child showed that some remained depressed after mother's return; various factors made it difficult for mother and child to 'tune in' with each other (Field and Reite, 1984).

Field also reminds us that the disorganising effects of separation are not limited to mother–infant dyads. They also occur when monkey infants and children are separated from their peers even though the attachment behaviour between them is quite different from that seen between a mother and her infant. For example, prior to separation, primate infants do not cry, nor do they cling to one another when reunited. However, their separation produces similar physical and physiological effects to those seen with infants separated from their mothers (Field, 1985, p.425).

A fascinating account by Anna Freud and Sophie Dann provides a vivid example of how important peer attachment can be, even for very small children (Freud and Dann, 1951). Their study reports on how six 3-year-old German–Jewish orphans, rescued from the concentration camps, were brought up as a group in a country house in England, staffed by nurses trained in the Hampstead nurseries. Right from the beginning they avoided forming any attachment bonds with the adults.

The children's positive feelings were centred exclusively in their own group. It was evident that they cared greatly for each other and not for anybody or anything else. They had no other wish than to be together and became upset when separated from each other even for short moments.

(1951, p.131)

Four of them had lost their mothers at birth or immediately afterwards, one boy before the age of 12 months and another boy at an unspecified date. They had always lived in a group setting and had formed very close attachments with one another: these bonds essentially saved their lives, providing them with all their psychobiological and emotional needs. Their behaviour puzzled their adult caregivers:

The children's unusual emotional dependence on each other was borne out further by the almost complete absence of jealousy, rivalry and competition, such as normally develops between brothers and sisters or in a group of contemporaries who come from normal families .... They were extremely considerate of each other's feelings.

(1951, pp. 133–134)

They shared all their possessions, lending to each other with pleasure. On walks, they were concerned for each other's safety in traffic. When playing, they assisted one another and admired each other's productions. At meal times, handing food to their neighbour was more important than feeding oneself. There was no sign of envy. 'Behaviour like this was the rule, not the exception' (1951, p.134).

No doubt the children safeguarded their relationships by expressing their anger against the adult staff. Only one child was soon behaving more 'normally' since she was moved by feelings of 'envy, jealousy and competition'; the authors point out that she was the only child in the group who was known to have had a passionate attachment to a mother substitute. Freud and Dann make the point that in English society, the child's relations to her brothers and sisters is subordinated to her relationship to her parents: siblings are normally the accessories to the parents so that their mutual relations are usually marked by jealousy, envy and competition. What these six orphans show is that such behaviour is not inherited: it is the result of a particular form of upbringing. Perhaps of greater importance still, are the implications of this report on the established beliefs of the day regarding maternal care: many experts believed that every disturbance of the mother–child relationship during this vital phase was always pathogenic (1951, p.168).

All forms of disturbance have been ascribed to 'rejection' by the mother, a term which includes every disturbance within the mother–child relationship. Freud and Dann point out that these six children, who were without doubt 'rejected' infants in this sense of the term,

were neither deficient, delinquent nor psychotic. They had found an alternative placement for their libido and, on the strength of this, had mastered
some of their anxieties and developed social attitudes. That they were able
to acquire a new language in the midst of their upheavals, bears witness to a
basically unharmed contact with their environment.

(1951, p.168)

These results invite Field to discuss the highly controversial issue of
'alloparental' care. Contrary to Bowlby's assertions, the mother can be
replaced by a father or another adult as primary caregiver and siblings
do play a major part in the infant's attachment system. For Field:

Attachment is basically a relationship that develops between two or more
organisms as their behavioural and physiological systems become attuned to
each other. Each partner in the attachment relationship provides for the
other a source of stimulation and arousal modulation. Loss or separation
from the partner or a change in the relationship would then understandably
lead to behavioural and physiological disorganisation. Separation may simply be an extreme example of the attached pair being unable to provide for
each other optimal levels of stimulation and arousal modulation.

(1985, p.431)

When Field refers to 'stimulation and arousal modulation' she is
describing a series of behaviours that originally occur between mother
and infant which ensure that the infant is kept optimally aroused.
Arousal modulation is very obvious for example when, while the infant
is busy exploring, she makes repeated contacts with mother.
Something takes place between the two which allows the infant to separate again and which is reflected in a reduction of the infant's cortisol
levels. Infants can provide both of these effects for their mothers, too.
Field and others believe that the arousal-reducing properties of the
mother may be an important factor in the infant's attachment to her.
Fathers may often be inducted to serve more of the infant's stimulation
needs, as may older siblings.

All of these attachments to mother, father and siblings appear to
develop in the very early months of life, though Bowlby and others
believe that attachment behaviour only becomes manifest after the seventh month or so. At this stage the infant has reached Piaget's 'phase of
object constancy', which means that she has the capacity to hold the
image of her parent in her mind. This is a crucial phase which is
marked by the infant's obvious distress on separating from the primary
caregiver and the triggering of attachment behaviour.

However, as Field points out, recognition of the parent occurs in
the first days of life and this allows for the process of attunement to
occur between the caregiver and infant. One could therefore conclude
that, in a sense, this early process of attunement is the precursor and
instigator of the attachment bond which becomes fully developed in

the human infant at about the age of 7 months.

Stern (1985) describes very well this early phase of development and the parallel evolution of the infant's various senses of 'self'. He believes that when the process of attunement works between the mother and the infant, it can lead to 'affect attunement', a state of mother–infant interplay where the mother mirrors her infant's behaviour, either directly or by using a different sensory modality. Thus, for example, to her child's excited jiggling movement, she may respond with excited jiggling sounds which match the movement in shape, intensity and timing: in so doing she both resonates emotionally with her child and recasts the child's experience into another form of expression. For Stern this sophisticated synchronised behaviour produces a matching of inner states between mother and child, an attunement at the level of affect (1985, pp.140–142).

Whilst the caregiver–infant dyad may provide the first such attunement experiences, studies on peer interactions show that preferred playmate pairs showed high correlations between verbal fluency, extraversion–introversion ratings and a propensity to engage in fantasy play. While at school, kindergarten children also appear to develop synchronous circadian rhythms. These change to their parents' cycle during the weekends or holidays. It seems therefore that when children interact frequently they also become attuned to each other's behaviours and physiological rhythms (Field, 1985, p.445).

Adults, too, can become attuned to one another: Hinde refers to this as 'behavioural meshing' (1976, p.11). It describes the interfacing of two adaptable systems where each partner has attuned his or her behaviour to the behaviour pattern of the other. One manifestation of our capacity for attunement can best be demonstrated in the act of love-making between two adults: Erik Erikson sees it not only as the climax of attunement but also as a counterforce to our potentially destructive experiences. 'The total fact of finding, via the climactic turmoil of the orgasm, a supreme experience of the mutual regulation of two beings in some way takes the edge off the hostilities ...' (Erikson, 1950, p.256).

Returning to the dry language of science, the term 'synchrony', which describes the matching of rhythms in physical or physiological activities, could also be seen as a form of attunement: it has been observed in movements between therapists and clients. Byers produces evidence for an underlying rhythm of 10 cycles per second during human interactions which, if matched by the partner, suggests that the individuals are on 'the same wavelength', so to speak (1976). A study by John Mason on the B-52 bomber crews concluded that the individuals all tended to show similar levels of adrenal cortical output when working together (1959). The psychobiological importance of human interactions can no longer be denied.

The doctor–patient relationship illustrates this all too clearly when comparing outcomes of treatment using medication as compared to a 'placebo': the latter form of treatment has no specific objective effect but still produces therapeutic results in about one-third of cases, including side effects in some of these! Levine, Gordon and Fields found that by administering naloxone (an opiate antagonist), they blocked the analgesic effect of a placebo used to relieve pain after a tooth extraction (1978). They hypothesised, as Panksepp would have done, that the placebo acted in this case as an endorphin releaser, thus reducing the patient's perception of pain.

Conclusion

In conclusion to all these various studies, Field writes:

> Multiple relationships for the adult (spouses, friends, children) may differentially serve the adult's stimulation and arousal–modulation needs .... Termination, temporary or permanent separation due to disruption of attunement, may lead to physiological disorganisation, depressed behaviour, and, in some cases, vulnerability to disease due to changes in the immune system.
>
> *(Field, 1985, p.449)*

She naturally suggests that to understand fully the underlying dynamics of attachment or attunement, we need to study the overt and physiological behaviours of those attached individuals both together and apart:

> Only then will the disruptions of attachment, as they occur during separation or loss, be understood. Large numbers of attachment disruptions and disturbances, as manifested in child abuse, spouse abuse, divorce, psychopathology, loneliness, depression, suicide, homicide, disease, death, mandate a deeper and broader understanding of the psychobiology of attachment.
>
> *(Field, 1985, p.450)*

In this chapter, we have seen how our need for 'significant' relationships is being established at a psychobiological level: we are interacting organisms, albeit thinking individuals too; we need one another to maintain ourselves physiologically as well as emotionally. Separation and loss can, when they result in deprivation of essential needs, produce long-term effects such as depression and disease: in some cases, we have had an inkling as to how long-term deprivation of attachment-related needs can result in apparently irreversible changes in an organism's capacity to form satisfactory attachment bonds. What still needs to be explored is how failures in attunement and deprivation resulting from poor attachment relations can result in violence to the self or to the 'other'. This will be very much the focus of the next chapter.

Chapter 5
Violence as 'Attachment Gone Wrong'

'The greatest hate springs from the greatest love.'

Penguin Dictionary of Proverbs (p.119)

Development and working models

Research on the attachment bond and its underlying behavioural systems provides us with increasing evidence of our intrinsic need for one another. Through the process of psychobiological attunement, we have seen both infant and caregiver become what Sander describes as an 'interactive self-regulatory system'. He writes: 'The infant and the caregiving environment show an organisation of their interactions almost from the outset, but one which undergoes a process of change in ensuing weeks and months, shifting from a more prominently *biosocial* to a more clearly *psychosocial* level' (Sander, 1977, p.133; Sander's italics).

For Sander the fundamental concept of regulation in biology is central to the understanding of any living organism. We cannot consider an infant without taking into account her surroundings and the exchanges going on between her and these surroundings. Nor can we consider any life process taking place without integration or synthesis. This ensures a maintenance over time of individual identity or unity. The adaptive process required to achieve this needs both organisation and regulation. As Piaget put it, regulation is the internal aspect of the cycle of which adaptation is the external aspect.

Development therefore begins with a state of dyadic physiological regulation which is characterised by coordinated sequences of behavioural interactions. It is this coordination which appears essential in the early structuring of the infant's inner organisation. By 7–9 months old, she begins to show some initiative and it is around this time that babies tend to show fear towards strangers and to express emotions such as anger. It is also around this stage that the infant will react to separation from her caregiver in the way Bowlby described in the 'protest' response. Depending on the circumstances, more prolonged separations can produce a phase of 'despair'.

64

Infants younger than 7 months do not show any of these reactions, suggesting that something changes for the infant during this period. The reaction to separation is seen by Bowlby as evidence that attachment has taken place between the infant and her caregiver. This means that the infant has developed the capacity to internalise the interactive experiences she has with those who look after her. Such an explanation concurs with Piaget's view that at around this age infants have achieved 'object permanence'. This means that they know that an object which disappears from view still exists. It can be looked for and it can be missed.

Equipped with internal models of organisation, the infant reacts to 'strangers' who fail to correspond to these internal 'working models' as Bowlby called them. Alan Sroufe describes this phase as one where 'the organised caregiving matrix begins to become part of a core of emerging inner organisation. A particular relationship and a self are emerging' (Sroufe, 1989, p.77).

By the end of the first year, the infant is mobile and the caregiver functions increasingly as a 'secure base' around which the infant carries out her exploratory activities. The 'self' has come into being. In Bowlby's words:

> It is plausible to suppose that each individual builds working models of the world and of himself in it, with the aid of which he perceives events, forecasts the future, and constructs his plans. In the working model of the world that anyone builds, a key feature is his notion of who his attachment figures are, where they may be found, and how they may be expected to respond. Similarly, in the working model of the self that anyone builds, a key feature is his notion of how acceptable or unacceptable he himself is in the eyes of his attachment figures.

(Bowlby, 1973, p.236)

> As a result, the model of the attachment figure and of the self are likely to develop so as to be complementary and mutually confirming. Thus an unwanted child is likely not only to feel unwanted by his parents but to believe that he is essentially unwantable, namely unwanted by anyone.

(Bowlby, 1973, p.238)

If provided with a 'secure enough base', the toddler develops more autonomy and develops a sense of being as an independent actor. With the rise of symbolic capacity between 18 and 36 months she then moves to a new level of awareness, that of 'shared awareness' with the realisation that the 'other' can be aware of what she is aware of inside herself. This sense of 'oneness' with the other in addition to a positive sense of self, help to form a basis for empathy. Similarly the toddler moves towards what Bowlby calls a 'a goal directed partnership' whereby she recognises her caregiver's intentions as separate to her own and can act to coordinate her own goals with the other's.

As the child's relationships change, so does the self. This process of emerging inner organisation formed through complementary models of the self and the 'other' is mainly concerned with the maintenance of basic regulation and positive affect, providing a continuity of experience despite developmental and external changes.

Through this briefest of developmental summaries, we can see that, while attachment bonds are being formed involving different behavioural systems and their psychobiological infrastructure, other no less important developments are taking place in the infant's mind. Through the 'internalisation' of repeated interactions with her caregivers, the infant appears to create psychic structures which in some way recreate the experiences lived through her important relationships. These 'working models' are seen by Sroufe and his colleagues as internalised whole relationships and not simply roles played. This means, for example, that role reversal can take place: an abused child can later become the abusing parent. This illustrates another important characteristic of the self, which is the tendency to form new relationships which are congruent with earlier ones and so preserve the sense of continuity of experience alluded to earlier.

Bowlby's 'working models' are very similar to the 'evoked companions' described by Stern (1985, pp.111–122) and to the 'internal object relations' of psychoanalysis. The first two are seen as internalisations of real lived-through relations whereas 'object relations', as we shall see in the next chapter, are more the psychic creations of a rich inner world of phantasy in interaction with the outside world.

Though we may seem to be far removed from the physiological processes of attunement and separation referred to in the previous chapter, this may well not be the case. Following his study on the psychobiological effects of bereavement, Hofer reminds us that:

> Human relationships are conducted at the mental or symbolic level as well as at the sensory motor levels. Our lives are lived as much within the internal world of mental representations as among the actual people themselves. This enables us to endure temporary separations without full-scale bereavement responses ... Could these elements of our inner life come to serve as biologic regulators, much the way the actual sensorimotor interactions with the mother function for the infant animals in our experiments? And could this link internal object relations to biologic systems? I think this may be possible.

> *(Hofer, 1984, p.192)*

Referring to the process of grief, he reminds us how multiple representations of the lost person appear to exist, which then tend to fragment in grief and are dealt with separately by the grieving individual. These units of representation could be related to particular biological responses and, in older children and adults, act as symbolic surrogates that prevent the release of withdrawal responses after separation through their connections with biologic systems. The mind–body link is evidently not as remote as it appears. In fact the connection between the two is vividly illustrated by some research carried out in Professor Beard's department (St Mary's Hospital Medical School, London) on women suffering from pelvic pain. These patients have been found to have enlarged pelvic veins. After a period of both medroxyproges-terone treatment and psychotherapy, a significant number of the women showed a reduction in pain at 9 months, compared to those who had been treated with placebo alone, placebo and psychotherapy, or medroxyprogesterone alone. Parallel venogram studies showed a correlation between an improvement in pelvic congestion and reduced pelvic pain (Farquhar et al., 1989).

On looking back at the psychobiological changes that take place during separation reactions in young children, we learnt that when the separation is short-lived the reactions are usually reversible and adap-tive. However, depending on the circumstances, separation reactions can also involve a failure of attunement with far more serious effects, which we will henceforth refer to as 'deprivation' effects. Similarly, a failure of 'attunement' in the infant can also occur without an experi-ence of separation but with equally severe long-term psychobiological disturbances.

In this chapter we will initially focus on the studies done by Hinde and Harlow on infant monkeys brought up in isolation, deprived of all maternal care. These show just how important the caregiver is in pro-moting normal attachment behaviour, not just in infancy, but also in terms of later behaviour with peers, heterosexual behaviour and mater-nal behaviour. Our study will focus on any links which may emerge between developmental failures and subsequent violent behaviour.

In the second half of this chapter, we will look at how deprivation, whether derived through loss or the disruption of attunement, pro-duces changes at both a biological and a psychological level: the resul-tant behavioural changes are often destructive and very important in terms of our understanding of violent behaviour.

Maternal deprivation

It was again in Harlow's laboratories that some of the first studies on maternal deprivation were carried out on rhesus monkeys (Harlow and Mears, 1979). Infant monkeys were separated from their mothers immediately following birth and placed in total isolation chambers which denied them any social contact with any social agents. The cages were lit and the infants were fed regularly. The results of these studies were of crucial importance for Bowlby in his formulation of the attachment theory.

Harlow demonstrated that maternal deprivation produced gross behavioural abnormalities in infants, a syndrome now described as the 'primate deprivation syndrome' (Mason, 1971). The degree of impairment of social behaviour depends in part on the amount of time spent in isolation and in part on the age at which the infants were isolated.

If only isolated for the first 3 months of life and then placed in a nurturing social environment, the infants appeared to behave normally. However, if isolated for the first 12 months, these monkeys showed a devastating loss in social competence greater than that seen in 6 or 9 month isolates (Sackett, 1972). Those isolated for the first 6 months of life developed a series of qualitatively abnormal patterns of behaviour when placed in social situations. These are described as:

- 'self-orality' which involves digit sucking or, in males, penis sucking;
- 'self-clasping', which typically involves an animal grasping with its hands and feet various parts of its body;
- rocking movements;
- other 'stereotypies' or repetitive whole body movements.

As Capitanio points out, most of these behaviours are related to the absence of particular types of experience. Thus, in the absence of mother's nipple to suck, the primate infant will suck parts of its own body. In the absence of something to cling to, the primate will grasp itself (1986, p.423).

Harlow's monkeys were maintained in partial social isolation for 3 years and then tested.

> Their social efforts were plaintive and their sexual efforts were pitiful. Practically the only social behaviours that seemed to have matured were fear and aggression, and the animals showed these inappropriately and often explosively. Six month isolates aggressed against infants – an act no normal monkey would consider – but before, during and after aggressive acts, they were frozen with fear even though the infants they faced were only half their size. In addition, several isolate monkeys attempted a single suicidal sortie against very large adult males – an act no normally socialised animal would be foolish enough to try.
>
> *(Harlow and Mears, 1979, p.288)*

If previously isolated females were artificially impregnated, they were grossly inadequate mothers. Harlow and Mears describe their behaviour in vivid terms:

> Very soon we discovered we had created a new animal – the monkey mother-less mother. These monkey mothers that had never experienced love of any kind were devoid of love for their infants, a lack of feeling unfortunately

shared by all too many human counterparts .... Most of the monkey motherless mothers ignored their infants, but other motherless mothers abused
their babies by crushing the infant's face to the floor, chewing off the
infant's feet and fingers and, in one case, by putting the infant's head in her
mouth and crushing it like an eggshell. Not even in our most devious
dreams could we have designed a surrogate as evil as these real monkey
mothers.

(1979, p.289)

We will return to this study and others on motherless mothers when
we review the work on child abuse.

In addition to the duration of the isolation, the degree of social
impairment is also related to the age at which animals are isolated.
Animals isolated after 3 or 6 months are not so damaged, though they
still show abnormal social and sexual behaviour. Monkeys isolated after
6 months show very high levels of aggression once reintroduced to
other monkeys. In Kraemer's review of these studies, he makes the
point that it is the perception of social cues that is so severely impaired
in these isolates (1985). Although they do not suffer from physiological
or nutritional problems, they fail to respond to social cues such as the
submission gestures of another monkey during an aggressive attack.

As the effects of early social deprivation persisted into adulthood, it
was believed that they were irreversible. However, by providing these
isolates with 3-month-old socially normal 'therapists', Harlow and his
team saw that their social behaviour improved so remarkably that they
appeared nearly indistinguishable from their socially reared counterparts (Suomi, Harlow and Novak, 1974). The 'therapists' were chosen
at this age because they had not yet developed the normal aggressive
behaviour towards strangers seen in 7 month olds. Their predominant
behaviour was to cling to the surrogates: in this way they provided
them initially with warmth and contact and later with age-appropriate
play behaviour. To the researchers' delight the social isolates developed
their social repertoire in parallel to their 'therapists'. Harlow and his
team saw this as evidence that social deficiencies developed in impov-
erished environments early in life are not necessarily permanent and
irreversible, although they also acknowledged that the 'therapy'
requires considerable time and effort. However, subsequent studies
have shown that previously isolated subjects do in fact manifest their
latent deficits when they have to face socially stressful situations or
carry out tasks requiring complex social discrimination (Anderson and
Mason, 1978). In these circumstances, the social isolates either withdraw or become inappropriately aggressive as well as showing the old
stereotypical behaviour. It also appears that deficits in sexual behaviour
may persist when all else seems normal.

One common feature in these studies is the close link between the
degree of maternal deprivation and the levels of aggression shown by

the social isolates, be it directed towards the self or against others. This is particularly so for males in many of the macaque species which have been studied: this tallies with other studies showing that males do in fact appear to be more vulnerable than females to deprivation rearing procedures.

Some authors, like Harlow, attribute this hyperaggressiveness to the animals' failure to develop the control mechanisms provided by the development of affiliative or loving behaviour, in addition to the isolate's failure to respond appropriately to social cues. However, other authors, such as Capitanio, point out that there is an increasing trend of behavioural disturbances resulting from social privation as we move from monkeys to apes to humans: this escalating vulnerability may be related to the increasingly complex behavioural repertoire seen in higher primates, reflecting more 'open' behavioural schemes and greater plasticity in the underlying behavioural organisation (1986).

The psychobiology of deprivation

These various studies show how far-reaching and similar are the effects of maternal deprivation in primates. For Kraemer, the above findings suggest that the effects of maternal deprivation are the result of damage to the behavioural organisation underlying the specific set of social behaviours which mediate social attachments. He ends up stating that: 'Early social isolation is a treatment that can be viewed as selectively "lesioning" social behaviour ...' (1985, p.145). He compares the effects of sensory deprivation on the visual system with the neurophysiological effects of social deprivation and demonstrates many striking parallels. Given these similarities, there is a strong suggestion that lesions of the social attachment system are similar to those changes produced by deprivation of the visual system (1985, p.149).

Kraemer proceeds to review the neurophysiological effects of isolation in primates. He comes to the conclusion that deprivation of early social experience may produce changes in the central nervous system's neurochemical processes; these are later translated into altered behaviour either in challenging situations or in response to treatment with drugs acting through neurochemical pathways.

For example, socially isolated but rehabilitated monkeys who were given low doses of amphetamine became hyperaggressive compared to their socially reared partners. (Their levels of spinal fluid noradrenaline, a hormone, were also higher.)

Antidepressant treatments also appear to indicate that the central nervous system receptors of socially deprived animals show an increase in sensitivity and thus a heightened response to such pharmacological

agents. Kraemer reminds us that in people, too, there is a great variation in response to drugs such as amphetamines or antidepressants.
These differences could be related not so much to genetic variation,
but to possible neurobiological changes associated with social deprivation in early development.

Kraemer admits that his conclusions are at present only speculative,
particularly as variations in social experience are much less severe in
humans than the total social isolation to which the primates were
exposed, but then he points out that we may also be more vulnerable.
He also reminds us that in non-human primates

> Even brief periods of social deprivation during sensitive periods of develop-
> ment are one of the most serious insults the organism can sustain in terms
> of degree and persistence of disrupted behaviour. This potency of effect
> suggests that, in combination with other factors, even graded levels of social
> deprivation are likely to have an important impact on neurobiological devel-
> opment and later behaviour in primates.

(1985, p.155)

These findings tally with recent evidence in the field of post-traumatic
stress disorder which will be reviewed in later chapters (Perry, 1991).

For Kraemer and other like-minded psychobiologists, primate social
behaviour is seen as a biological mechanism with a specific behaviour
function which is represented in a neurobiological substrate involving
brain mechanisms. This outlook is very similar to that expressed by
researchers like Hofer (1984) and Field (1985) in the field of 'attunement'. From their point of view, the marked increase in aggressivity
observed in these social isolates may well be understood as the reciprocal manifestation of a damaged attachment system, the result of a failure of 'attunement', of a deficiency in the provision of attachment-
related psychobiological regulation and its associated emotional stimulation and arousal modulation.

Before exploring the impact of such failures in attunement between
caretaker and infant, it may be helpful to realise that abnormal behaviours similar to those described in monkeys who have been reared in
isolation or separated from their mother, do also occur in the wild.
Most of the studies have been done on chimpanzees, a species that is
now known to share 99% of our genome. Apparently far more linguistically competent than had been assumed (Rumbaugh and Gill, 1977),
the chimpanzee can be seen as very similar to ourselves both emotionally and intellectually, albeit without our cultural influences. This too is
an oversimplification, for primates also have 'cultures', and links
between their external environment, their social behaviour, rearing
experiences and cultural contexts are beginning to be explored
(Rowell, 1972)

Attachment in the wild

Jane Goodall's research on chimpanzees in the Gombe National Park has been invaluable in providing us with information on the lives of apes in the wild (1988, 1990). Through lengthy studies of mothers and their infants, Goodall began to see links between chimpanzee infant behaviour and different types of mothering. She found that, as with humans, a secure childhood is likely to lead to self-reliance and independence in adulthood.

> A disturbed early life may leave permanent scars. In the wild almost all mothers look after their infants relatively efficiently. But even so there are clear-cut differences in the child-raising techniques of different individuals. It would be hard to find two females whose mother treated them more differently during their early years than Flo's daughter Fifi and Passion's daughter Pom ... .
>
> *(1990, p.27)*

Fifi had a carefree and wonderful childhood. Flo was a highly competent mother, affectionate, tolerant, playful and protective. Figan (her second child) was an integral part of the family when Fifi was growing-up, joining her games when Flo was not in the mood and often supporting his young sister in her childhood squabbles. Faben, Flo's eldest son, was often around, too. Flo, who held top rank among the females, was a sociable female. She spent a good deal of time with other members of her community, and she had a relaxed and friendly relationship with most of the adult males. In this social environment Fifi became a self-confident and assertive child.

Pom's childhood, in comparison to Fifi's, was bleak. Passion's personality was as different from Flo's as chalk from cheese. She was a loner. She had no female companions, and on those occasions when she was in a group with adult males her relationship with them was typically uneasy and tense. She was a cold mother, intolerant and brusque, and she seldom played with her infant, particularly during the first two years. And Pom, being the first surviving child, had no sibling to play with during the long hours when she and her mother were on their own. She had a difficult time during her early months, and she became an anxious and clinging child, always fearful that her mother would go away and leave her behind, which is indeed what Passion had done repeatedly during her infancy (1990, pp.27–28).

The quality of Fifi's and Pom's early attachment relationships was reflected in their response to their first experience of loss during weaning. This is a time when all chimpanzees become upset and depressed and it normally occurs in their fourth year. The mother, usually pregnant by this stage, prevents her child from suckling or riding on her back; she does this with increasing firmness and frequency. When she was weaned, Fifi became markedly less playful and would spend her time sitting next to mother looking hunched and sad. However, by the time her brother Flint was born she was back to her old self.

Pom's depression, however, seemed to go on endlessly. Strangely, Passion's behaviour towards her daughter had improved remarkably during her third year and Pom had appeared more self-confident. However, these signs of improvement disappeared during the trauma of weaning, despite the fact that her mother was far more attentive to her other needs. 'Pom's inability to cope with weaning was almost certainly due to the harsh treatment she had received as an infant' (1990, p.28).

Flo's mothering skills were reflected in the success of her children: her sons rose to the top of the social hierarchy and her daughter became a loving and competent mother in her own right, having acquired most of her skills from her mother and siblings. Passion bore a son called Prof and, though she was not as harsh with her second child, he ended up a social misfit. His weaning experiences were, as for his sister, times of despair during which he threw violent tantrums: he would scream, tearing at his hair and throw himself on the ground. Tantrums usually elicit an immediate response from a chimpanzee mother: Flo would pick up her son and hold him in her arms however violent his rage. Passion, on the other hand, would usually ignore her son's tantrums, making him feel even more rejected and distressed. However, he too recovered before his next sibling was born, but his lack of self-confidence made him unable to separate from his mother, who died when he was eleven.

However, it is through poor old Flo's maternal failure that we discover the importance of weaning for chimpanzees. Worn out by age and endless reproduction, she failed to get her last son Flint through this crucial stage. She repeatedly gave in to his tantrums, so that by the time her last infant was born Flint was still suckling. He then became very depressed and continued to cling to his mother. He was eight and a half when she finally died and should have been able to look after himself. Goodall records very movingly the last moments in his life:

> Never shall I forget watching as, three days after Flo's death, Flint climbed slowly into a tall tree near the stream. He walked along one of the branches, then stopped and stood motionless, staring down at an empty nest. After about two minutes he turned away and, with the movements of an old man, climbed down, walked a few steps, then lay, wide eyes staring ahead. The nest was one which he and Flo had shared a short while before Flo died.

> *(1990, p.165)*

As a result of his mother's death, Flint sank into a deeper depression despite his sister Fifi's attentions: he refused most food and, with his immune system weakened, he fell sick.

The last short journey he made, pausing to rest every few feet, was to the very place where Flo's body had lain. There he stayed for several hours, sometimes staring and staring into the water. He struggled on a little further, then curled up – and never moved again.

(1990, p.165)

Judging from what happened to Flint, we get the strong impression that in chimpanzee life, weaning represents the first negotiated experience of loss, an experience that is crucial in terms of later separation from mother. This may be all the more so since, amongst chimpanzees, the fathers, who in other cultures help their child to leave mother, are scarcely involved in rearing of young chimpanzees: in fact they do not know which male is responsible for siring which child. Mothers go on having an important role in the life of adolescent males and females.

Hunter–gatherers like the !Kung appear to go through the same temper tantrums and distress as chimpanzees do when they are weaned at around the same age of three. In Shostak's (1990) book *Nisa, the life and Words of a !Kung Woman* Nisa gives a vivid account of her own experience of being weaned as a !Kung child but, in her case, her father could help her by giving her his attention and hunting small game for her to compensate for the loss of mother's breast.

Weaning from mother's milk is no longer such an important milestone in Western child development because milk and bottles are now easily available. We do not know whether this has longterm effects in terms of a child's later capacity to separate from his or her parents.

Though Fifi could not save her brother Flint when Flo died, other young chimpanzees do care successfully for their orphaned siblings and young males are as efficient caretakers as females. Following Passion's death, Pom and Prof and little 4-year-old Pax stayed together and the older ones cared for the youngest. One year after their mother's death, Prof was left alone with his little brother and cared for him as a mother would. It is interesting that he could do this since he had himself been unable to separate from Passion prior to her death. Was he resorting to what Bowlby termed the 'compulsive caring' defence in relation to his own loss?

Goodall gives several other examples of successful adoption of orphans by older siblings. To her surprise, she also witnessed the adoption of a 3-year-old orphan by an unrelated 12 year old, an orphan himself whose mother died in the same epidemic. The older monkey allowed the infant to cling onto him both in the ventral position and on his back, and he took care of him for a year thus ensuring his survival: the young one subsequently attached himself to a childless female.

Merlin's tragic life story is perhaps the one that is most likely to remind us of Harlow's 'primate deprivation syndrome': he was four when his mother died and he was adopted by his 6-year-old sister Miff. Despite her care and attention, he lost weight and became increasingly lethargic. His behaviour began to change too; he started approaching full-grown males, paying no heed to their warning signals of impending aggression. This was strange as he had always responded appropriately to signals of this sort. He also became very aggressive towards other infants in his group. A year after his mother's death, his behaviour had become very abnormal: he would hang upside down for hours on end and, hunched up with his arms clasped around himself, he would rock from side to side staring into the distance. He also pulled his hair out while grooming himself. Gradually Merlin became thinner and more exhausted until he finally died at the age of five. Goodall suggests that he died because his caregiver was too young to provide him with the care he needed. She rightly suggests that a lot more research needs to be done on persistent abnormalities following traumatic experience such as these.

Goodall's account of chimpanzee life in the wild makes it quite clear that our primate cousins are very similar to us in the way they respond to separation, loss and inadequate mothering. Other than the account of Merlin's bizarre aggressive behaviour, we have not yet had much evidence of violent behaviour which could possibly be linked to early deprivation or trauma. However, as Goodall found out with time, there was quite a considerable amount of violence among the chimpanzees in the Gombe National Park.

Passion provides us with the first evidence of such destructive behaviour: as we may recall, her mothering of Pom was less than optimal, showing little or no sensitivity for her infant's needs and being often quite rejecting and perhaps at times abusive. What we also learn is that at one point in the colony's life, Passion and her daughter were savagely to attack, kill and eat more than half a dozen newborn chimpanzee infants which they tore away from their desperate mothers.

Goodall has no idea why the two monkeys behaved in this manner. The interesting point is that at least as far as Pom is concerned, her inadequate early attachment experiences may have something to do with it. We know that they made her more vulnerable to loss during weaning and later affected her capacity to mother: could they be in some way related to her violent behaviour towards the other infants? Was her own mother, Passion, subject to a similar upbringing? The evidence presented above suggests that such links are possible.

Long-term effects of loss and deprivation

Most of what has been said in terms of loss and the resultant deprivation has been written about by Bowlby in the last volume of his extensive work *Attachment and Loss*. In this book he views loss as a trauma which implies that the processes of mourning can be compared to the process of healing that follows a severe wound or burn (1980, p.43).

Similarly, the restoration of function can often hide a further sensitivity to further trauma. Having reviewed most of the literature on the effects of loss, Bowlby, like Kraemer after him, is of the opinion that not only does separation or loss engender neurophysiological changes such as are seen in grief, but that some of these changes can be permanent, particularly if they occur in childhood. As a result, individuals may become more or less sensitive to further stressful conditions. He refers in particular to the study by George Brown and Tirril Harris, *Social Origins of Depression* (1978). Though this work on depressed women does not directly link loss with violence, it shows how loss can contribute to depression by being both a provoking agent and a vulnerability factor if the loss of mother occurs before the age of 11. Loss can also influence the severity and the form of the depressive illness.

Recent research shows that those adults who both suffer from psychopathology of some kind and have lost a parent in childhood, do develop significant biological and immunological changes, as would be predicted on the basis of Kraemer's findings (Breier et al., 1988). The authors conclude that early parental loss (which is a traumatic event) accompanied by the lack of a supportive relationship subsequent to the loss is related to the development of adult psychopathology.

Perhaps, the link between loss and violent behaviour is most clearly illustrated when studying suicidal behaviour in the young: this form of self-directed violence has been very much on the increase during the last few years in the UK. Every day, at least one person under the age 25 commits suicide. Ten to twenty per cent of these individuals have a history of violent behaviour. Herbert Hendin believes that most of these young people conceive of death as a response to loss, separation or abandonment (Hendin, 1991). Research findings also show that in a study of young suicides, significantly more frequent parental abuse or rejection had been experienced by the suicidal young people compared to the control group (Shafii et al., 1985). Other studies show that loss from divorce or separation, or severe family instability on its own, are all important factors contributing to suicidal behaviour (Adam, 1982).

Conclusion

What these different studies appear to show is a strong correlation between loss, as a form of deprivation and trauma, and violent behaviour. The latter can increasingly be seen to be the manifestation of attachment behaviour gone wrong. This becomes all the more evident when we look at the research on mother–infant attachment behaviours and on caregiving behaviours in families with child abuse. It is in the light of all these recent findings that Bowlby began to connect violence with attachment behaviour. As he stated, a great deal of the maladaptive violence seen in families can be understood as distorted and exaggerated versions of behaviour that is potentially functional, especially attachment behaviour on the one hand and caregiving behaviour on the other (Bowlby, 1988, p.81).

Chapter 6
Secure and Insecure Attachments in the Formation of the Self

'And much it grieved my heart to think what man has made of man.'

William Wordsworth, 1770–1850

Measuring the quality of attachment relations

The last two chapters on attachment, attunement, loss and deprivation bear witness to the importance of those researchers and psychoanalysts who, like Bowlby, have based their work on the fundamental assumption that relationships are of prime importance throughout our lives. Not only is this hypothesis being confirmed by many research findings, but it has considerable social and therapeutic implications.

One of the most important outcomes of these studies on attachment behaviour is the emerging link between psychological trauma, such as loss and deprivation, and destructive or violent behaviour. Not only does there appear to be such a link between these two forms of behaviour, but it may be, at a psychobiological level, a reciprocal link: violent aggression may be the reciprocal manifestation of a damaged attachment system.

At a more behavioural level, it has also been shown that children who show 'avoidant' or 'detached' behaviour following separations tend also to display high levels of aggression. This finding has been corroborated in a series of experimental studies carried out by one of Bowlby's most enthusiastic and successful colleagues, Mary Ainsworth. She both pioneered studies on attachment behaviour in humans and further developed his theories. After working with Bowlby on parent–child separations and observing unweaned infants and their mothers in Uganda, Ainsworth returned to the USA where she carried out some naturalistic observations on 23 middle-class infants in Baltimore. Her findings inspired her to devise a laboratory to see just how much these 12-month-old infants tended to explore in the presence or the absence of mother. The 'Strange Situation' test was born (Ainsworth et al., 1978). This test goes as follows:

> A mother and child are put together in a room full of toys under observation (Episode 1 & 2). A stranger is then introduced to see how the infant responds (Episode 3). Then the mother leaves the room unobtrusively so that her infant is alone with the stranger (Episode 4). How does the infant respond to the mother's first departure? Mother returns greeting and comforting the infant, encouraging her to play again. Mother then leaves the room again saying 'bye, bye' (Episode 5). The infant is alone for the second separation episode (Episode 6). The stranger returns (Episode 7) and then the mother and infant are reunited (Episode 8).

In the Strange Situation the chief behaviour systems to be activated are the exploratory behaviour, wary or fearful behaviour, attachment behaviour, sociable behaviour and angry/resistant behaviour.

The first infants to undergo this test were divided up into three main groups and eight subgroups depending on how they reacted to being separated from mother. Group-B infants were defined as 'securely' attached to their mothers in comparison to their 'insecurely' attached group-A or group-C counterparts. Ainsworth and her colleagues describe the main behavioural features of these three groups of children.

The typical group-B infant represents about 63% of the infants tested, all of which came from middle-class American homes. She is more positive in her behaviour to her mother than are the infants of the other two groups. Her interactions with mother are more harmonious and she is cooperative and willing to comply with mother's requests. At home, the mothers of these children are observed to be sensitive in response to their infants' signals and communications; they show tenderness and care when holding and touching their children.

Both at home and in the Strange Situation, the group-B infant uses mother as a 'secure base' from which to explore. Whereas at home she would not cry when mother leaves the room because she probably knows from experience that mother is accessible, she does cry or protest when left in the test situation for the second time. Even if she does not cry during the first separation (Episode 4), Sroufe and Waters have shown that the infant's heart rate increases and her exploratory behaviour decreases, both of which indicate that her attachment behaviour has been activated (1977b).

When the group-B infant is finally reunited with mother, she greets her with pleasure, her arms extended for a cuddle during which she moulds her body into her mother's. She seems to need a minute or two of close contact before the attachment behaviour is deactivated.

Main points out that these infants often show anger in the strange situation (1981). This takes the form of angry crying upon separation, an outraged cry upon reunion and an irritated batting at the toys if mother tries to play rather than hold her infant. Such angry behaviour is seen as promoting proximity and is therefore considered adaptive.

As a result of this secure attachment to mother, group-B infants are not only more readily socialised but they are also more positive and out-going with unfamiliar adults. They are more competent in their explorations than anxious group-C and group-A infants; they are also more enthusiastic and persistent with problem-solving tasks, during which they are able to elicit mother's help when these are too difficult. As preschoolers, these toddlers are significantly more flexible, curious, socially competent and self-reliant than their anxiously attached counterparts, who also do less well in their development tests.

The group-C infant represents about 12% of the sample of infants from middle-class American homes. She is typically anxious in her attachment to mother. In the Strange Situation, she is clingy from the beginning, afraid to explore the room on her own. She is characteristically very distressed on being separated from her mother but, when reunited, she appears to show a lot of angry ambivalence, both wanting to be close to her parent and, at the same time, arching away from her and resisting her mother's efforts to soothe her. When observed at home, the mothers of these infants are seen to be much less responsive both to crying and to communications in general than group-B mothers. However, they are not rejecting like group-A mothers and they do not show any aversion to physical contact, nor are they compulsive in their behaviour or lacking in emotional expression.

As a result, the group-C infants cry more and show more separation anxiety after the age of 12 months, as if they are not confident about mother's reliability. Their mothers do not seem to provide the 'secure base' that group-B infants have. The group-C infant is distressed from the beginning of the Strange Situation (Episode 2) and even more so when the stranger is introduced (Episode 3). Mother's departure also activates intense attachment behaviour. These high levels of separation anxiety make it difficult for this group of infants to explore and learn through their discoveries. As a result, their cognitive development lags a little behind that of group-A or group-B infant.

However, what amazed Ainsworth most was the 'avoidant' response seen in group-A infants, who represent 20–25% of infants from middle-class American homes. Such a child appears indifferent to mother's comings and goings, even to the point of snubbing her on reunion and thus appearing very independent. If the mother is not ignored, the baby may approach her only to suddenly turn away. She may even greet mother but then avert her gaze so as to discourage any further interaction. If picked up, the infant indicates, in an emotionless way, that she wants to be put down. She is usually more friendly to a stranger than to her own mother.

Throughout the Strange Situation, group-A infants generally attend to their toys or to the other objects about them. Unlike other infants, they show no distress, no fear and, most importantly, no anger when they are reunited with their mother.

However, Blanchard and Main (1979) found that infants who avoided their parent when reunited in a daycare setting were also more likely to attack or threaten to attack their caregivers. Similarly, these infants physically avoided their playmates and averted their gaze from them to the same degree that they avoided their mother upon reunion. (Interestingly, there is no relationship between the avoidance behaviour shown towards father and that shown towards mother, a finding which has been replicated and has important implications in terms of the infant's internal models of her parents.)

Avoidance behaviour is also related to a reduced emotional response: these babies show less positive affect and enthusiasm (Matas, Arend and Sroufe, 1978). Sometimes, too, avoidance behaviour is found to be related to odd behaviours and stereotypies rather reminiscent of those seen in maternally deprived monkeys. For example, one baby rocked repeatedly, uttering odd vocalisations: her face showed no feelings and she seemed attached to objects and the environment more than to people (Ainsworth et al., 1978). This tendency to avoid people makes the group-A infants also far less able to engage in fantasy play than their securely attached counterparts.

In the laboratory, the heart-rate measurements taken during the separation and the reunion episodes showed that, despite appearances, the group-A infant's attachment behaviour was in fact strongly activated (Sroufe and Waters, 1977b). The infant's tendency to continue playing with the toys in the room during these episodes is therefore seen as a form of defence called a 'displacement activity' because the high heart-rate observed in these infants is incompatible with any true interest, such as is found in really non-anxious separations.

The home studies on group-A infants showed them to be quite insecure since they manifested a lot more separation distress than the group-B infants. Main (1981) also points out that the avoidance behaviour at 12 months was related to a number of aggressive attacks against the mother in the home and also to a number of inexplicable angry episodes, suggesting that these emotions are in some way repressed during the Strange Situation test.

The mothers of 'avoidant' infants are described as interfering, neglectful and rejecting, particularly of close body contact. They are also more angry and threatening with their children than other mothers. They often mock their children or speak about them sarcastically. Ratings showed a strong association between avoidance and maternal anger in the sample studied (Main, Tomasini and Tolan, 1979).

In another study, Main and her team hypothesise that infants of abusing mothers should show a similar pattern of behaviour to infants who strongly avoid their mother. They found that battered infants in daycare settings did in fact behave towards other children and to their caregivers in the same aggressive manner (George and Main, 1979).

We may conclude that frequent hostility, unprovoked aggression and generally negative peer interactions seem to characterise the 'avoidant' children. These findings were confirmed by a study Troy and Sroufe (1987) carried out on 19 pairs of children at play. They found that in pairs in which one or both partners were group-A children, there was victimisation. Five of these pairs were seen to be involved in an exploitative relationship, where one partner continually abused his or her partner both physically and verbally. In all these couples, the abuser had a history of 'avoidant' attachment (type A) and the partner was anxiously attached (type C or A). Children with a secure attachment relationship were not observed to be either abusers or victims. This is an extremely important finding in terms of the study of human violence. It is also of particular interest in understanding the development of 'internal working models' or 'object relations', because the fact that a group-A child can be both a victim and a victimiser suggests that it is indeed the relationship, the 'self' in relation to the 'other', which is internalised.

Another study carried out by Egeland and Sroufe (1981) shows that maltreated infants at 12 months tend to be more insecurely attached than well-treated infants. Fifty per cent of children with a history of neglect were found to be group-C infants. The infants who were physically abused tended to be group-A infants.

On the basis of the above evidence, Main sees the infant's 'avoidant' behaviour in the Strange Situation as a way of coping with the conflict between her feelings of anger in the face of probable rejection and her strong attachment needs stirred up by the experience of separation. 'Cutting off' is a way of maintaining some form of relationship with mother without experiencing anger (Main 1977).

In a later paper, Main (1981) reconsiders the function of avoidance behaviour. Having noted the suffering that the group-C ambivalent infant undergoes as she clings and then withdraws only to cling again in a vicious cycle of frustration, the 'avoidant' child appears far more in control. When a caregiver has unwelcome power over an infant, the infant can retain some degree of control over her own behaviour by focusing her attention away from her parent. This is necessary for a child who is subjected to threats from an attachment figure who simultaneously rejects physical contact. Such a child is placed in an insoluble and self-perpetuating conflict situation: threats from any source arouse tendencies to withdraw from the source of threat and to approach mother; what can such an infant do if the mother is both threatening and forbids contact? She can displace her attention elsewhere and thereby 'cut herself off' from feeling angry and fearful in relation to her mother.

In the field of psychology itself, Ainsworth's research interests were eagerly taken up and successfully repeated by people like Main and Sroufe. However, there has also been strong resistance to the concept of attachment and its implications. Behaviourists believe that man's actions are best understood in terms of environmental conditioning: if rewarded, a behaviour will persist and, if punished, it diminishes. Intrinsic to this framework is the view that attachment is a 'trait', a manifestation of the infant's genetically derived temperament which is being reflected in the classification differences seen in the Strange Situation (Kagan, 1984).

As Sroufe points out, such a viewpoint trivialises the differences found in attachment classification and it does so by denying the fact that what is being measured is a relationship. For Bowlby and Ainsworth, attachment, the affective/organisational bond between infant and caregiver, is inherently a relationship concept. Sroufe and Waters defend this point of view very strongly (1977a). As they say, it is important to establish that the Strange Situation produces assessments of the qualitative aspects of the relationship between infant and caregiver, rather than an inborn disposition for separation distress or some other endogenous characteristic. There are several reasons for the Sroufe and Water stance: not only can relationships be assessed in developmental psychology with all the research implications this has, but these assessments can also be used to predict later individual functioning outside the care giving context.

> This has important theoretical consequences. The most obvious implication is that qualities that arise in relationships ultimately lead to qualities of individuals – an old idea, but one that has proved difficult to demonstrate empirically. Very important process questions automatically follow. With attachment assessments trivialized as temperamental variation, all of this is lost.
>
> *(Sroufe, 1985, p.2)*

Once again, we are facing a conflict between the exponents of two different 'paradigms', between those who see us as genetically predisposed to behave in certain ways and those who think that our early personal experience has a lot to do with the way we later behave. The latter point of view recognises the intrinsic importance of relationships and the possibility of unconscious processes, such as Bowlby's 'internal working models', in human development. It also has social and moral implications for, as Sroufe states:

> As a member of society one shares a responsibility with respect to the quality of care available to all children. If responsibility for the child's well-being does not reside in his or her inborn variation, then it is ours.
>
> *(1985, p.12)*

This is a message perhaps some of us would prefer not to hear. In *The Nature of the Child,* Jerome Kagan writes disparagingly that

> contemporary views of human development contain equally idealistic assumptions. One is that a mother's love for her infant is necessary for the child's future mental health. A second is that the events of infancy seriously influence the future mood and behaviour of the adolescent.

(1984, p.xii)

Sroufe takes Kagan and his other critics head on by pointing out that the main assumption for Bowlby is that the quality of attachment reflects the quality of care. This is what Ainsworth discovered when she found that a sensitive response to the infant's communication in the first year is related to secure attachments in the Strange Situation at 12 months. Her findings have been replicated all over the world despite her critics. What has emerged from these studies is that factors influencing the quality of care have shown very clearly how, for instance, maternal behaviour affects mother–infant attachment patterns.

One such study by Susan Crockenberg (1981) shows how socially supported mothers have securely attached infants and how this support is particularly important for mothers with irritable infants. This means that a hereditary predisposition may well exist but that it can be overridden by the quality of the infant–caregiver relationship.

A study of poor families under stress by Sroufe and his colleagues illustrates how such environmental conditions can produce a greater proportion of group-C infants at 12 months than has been found in the middle-class sample (22% as compared with 9%). Changes in the Strange Situation classification between 12 and 18 months also took place with greater frequency, and were found to relate to an increase in stressful events in the mother's life and therefore clearly not to changes in temperament (Vaughn et al., 1979).

These findings tie up with those referred to earlier which show that physical neglect of the infant's basic needs leads to an elevation in group-C attachment patterns, whereas physical abuse and emotional unavailability leads to an increase in group-A attachment patterns (Egeland and Sroufe, 1981).

The studies which show most clearly that what is being assessed in the Strange Situation is a relationship pattern, are those which reveal different attachment classifications depending on whether the child is seen with his father or his mother. This finding cannot be explained on the basis of differences in temperament (Main and Weston, 1981). Similarly, security with a first-born indicates a likely security between a mother and her second-born irrespective of the infant's temperament (Matas, Arend and Sroufe, 1978). Finally, another study shows how poor maternal care actually precedes infant maladaptive and anxious patterns of attachment. The study showed that some mothers of

3-month-old normal babies were uninvolved in their maternal care and showed little affect when interacting with their infants: by 18 months, 86% of their infants were classed as 'avoidant' (Egeland and Sroufe, 1981). These data show yet again how important the caregiver–infant bond is for the child's future relationships.

Despite strong opposition to the implications of research on the attachment bond, the evidence does seem to indicate that what takes place between the infant and her early caregivers is of paramount importance in how she develops and interacts later on in life. This does not mean that genetic influences do not matter for they do, but only insofar as they are integrated within the interactive process occurring between mother and child and their socio-cultural environment. As a result, maladaptive genetic traits can be ironed out if the relationship is a secure one, just as they can be enhanced if the relationship is insecure. This is shown in a study by Lewis and his colleagues (Lewis et al., 1984) which illustrates how insecurely attached males at the age of one are more prone to psychopathology at the age of six than their securely attached male counterparts. No such relationship between quality of attachment and later psychopathology was observed in females. In the case of the males, other factors were also involved, such as family life-stress events or demographic variables. The authors therefore conclude that although the infant–caregiver attachment relationship does play an important role in the development of psychopathology in males, it can not always protect the child, nor does an insecure attachment necessarily always produce psychopathology.

Bearing in mind our particular interest in destructive behaviour, we have seen how 'avoidant' behaviour with the mother in the Strange Situation is indeed linked with frequent hostile behaviour and unprovoked aggression towards mother, other caregivers and peers in other contexts. We have also learnt how this 'avoidant' behaviour appears to function as an unconscious psychological defence mechanism which allows the infant to be able to stay within her mother's reach at a point in time when he both needs her and fears her rejection.

As with most forms of attachment behaviour, the 'avoidant' behaviour involves both mind and body: this is beginning to be confirmed by endocrine studies, one of which shows that insecure-avoidant infants have low cortisol excretion levels (during a 1-hour separation period) whereas secure infants manifest the opposite (Capitanio, Weissberg and Reite, 1985, p.81).

Capitanio and his colleagues point out that the mother of the 'avoidant' infant shows aversion to physical contact and little emotional responsiveness, a bit like the monkey surrogate mother in Harlow's experiments. Some 'avoidant' infants also show odd behaviours and stereotypies reminiscent of the socially deprived monkeys. These findings suggest that:

> Early experience-induced variations in biological (i.e. neuroanatomical, endocrine) systems may be related to variations in parental competence. Poor parenting, in turn, might adversely affect the development of the particular biological system in the offspring, setting up a biologically related, experience-induced generational transmission of poor parental behaviour, such as is typically seen in cases of child abuse.

> *(Capitanio, Weissberg and Reite, 1985, p.81)*

These tentative conclusions correlate with findings which show that in samples of abused or neglected children, avoidant infants are disproportionately represented (Gaensbauer and Harmon, 1982).

Attachment relations and the formation of the self

Main and her team provide important evidence as to the links between an infant's attachment patterns, the formation of internal working models and the development of the self (Main, Kaplan and Cassidy, 1985). By defining individual differences in attachment organisation as individual differences in the mental representation of the self in relation to the attachment figure, Main and her colleagues were able to study not only infants but also older children and even adults. They suggest that the secure versus insecure types of attachment are best understood as terms referring to different types of working models of relationships, models that direct not only feelings and behaviour but also attention, memory and cognition insofar as these relate to attachment (1985, p.67). They deduce that individual differences in these internal working models would relate not only to non-verbal behaviour but also to patterns of language and structures of the mind. This ties up with a view of the self which Sroufe conceives as an inner organisation of attitudes, expectations and meanings which arise from an organised caregiving matrix: 'That is, the dyadic infant–caregiver organisation precedes and gives rise to the organisation that is self' (1989, p.71).

In their study, Main and her team had a sample of 40 mothers, fathers and their 6-year-old children. Each family had been assessed in the Strange Situation when these children were 12–18-month-old infants: at 12 months, involving the mothers, and at 18 months involving the fathers. Once again, it was found that fathers and mothers differed in terms of the attachment behaviour they elicited in their children.

The authors also found a third category, describing another type of insecurely attached infant, the 'insecure–disorganised/disoriented' infant. These infants appeared dazed when reunited with their parent and would often stop moving, adopting postures suggestive of depression; they also seemed confused and would display simultaneous and contradictory behaviour patterns such as keeping their gaze averted whilst in contact with mother. Their parents had apparently a history of unusual trauma within their own attachment histories.

The outcome of Main and her colleagues' study was to show that individual differences in the early relationship to mother, but not father, significantly predicted the 6-year-old's response to a separation interview. The authors suggest that this discrepancy results from the working model for the father being lower down in the hierarchy of internal working models of attachment figures. What they found with mother was a very strong stability in the child's apparent security on reunion with mother, after a 5-year period, and a weaker one with father.

This stability in the child's reunion behaviour is attributed to the fact that once established, patterns of attachment are self-perpetuating. This is in keeping with psychoanalytic thinking and with Sroufe's emphasis on the self-preserving nature of human relationships. In order to preserve our sense of self-identity through a sense of continuity over time. Main believes that we need actively to restrict and in some cases even distort information that is made available to us. This is achieved by the development of internal working models which include both affective and cognitive components. Once formed, these internal models tend to exist outside consciousness and to resist change in order to preserve a sense of continuity of experience of the self.

In keeping with recent developmental theories on the formation of 'internal working models', Main and her colleagues also assume that they evolve out of real events, from the generalised representation of experienced events, from actions and their outcome. As a result:

> The working model of the relationship to the attachment figure will reflect not an objective picture of 'the parent' but rather the history of the caregiver's responses to the infant's actions or intended actions with/toward the attachment figure.

> *(Main, Kaplan and Cassidy, 1985, p.75)*

The authors assume, as do Stern and Sroufe, that even a young infant will have a working model of a relationship, a knowledge of self and 'other', which is the outcome of event-based relationships right from the beginning of life.

Whilst emphasising the self-perpetuating aspect of attachment behaviour, it is also important to point out that our internal working models are in fact potentially subject to review particularly in adolescence. With the onset of the cognitive stage of formal operations described by Piaget during adolescence, the capacity for abstract thinking will enable the individual to think about her relationships and hence to alter her internal working models.

This conclusion was highlighted by the discovery by Main and her co-workers that parents rated as securely attached not only valued attachment relationships, but were ready to recall and to discuss their own attachment relationships, even if these had been unfavourable. In such parents their responses indicated considerable reflection over their past which usually included rejection and loss. This is in marked contrast to parents rated as insecure in terms of attachment: the parents of insecure–avoidant children (group-A) tended to dismiss the importance of attachment relationships: when they did talk about their parents, they often contradicted themselves, presenting on the one hand an idealised picture of the parent, and on the other, memories of severe loneliness and rejection. They would also insist that they could not remember some period in their childhood. As for the parents of insecure–ambivalent infants (group-C), these still felt dependent on their own parents and tried to please them. The parents of the newly classified insecure–disorganised/disoriented infants had experienced the death of a parent before reaching maturity. When they spoke of their childhood they were often incoherent and contradictory, often refusing to remain within the topic of the interview.

As a result of these findings, Main and her colleagues concluded that it is not so much the experience of rejection and trauma that determines how secure we feel as adults, but the capacity we have to gain access to information about our childhood and how coherently we organise such information. This has very important implications in terms of therapy as well as infant care. If unable to integrate information relating to her attachment experience, a mother is likely to be insensitive and unresponsive to infant signals. For Main, the parent's insensitivity to infant signals may in fact correspond with the parent's need to preserve a particular organisation of information or state of mind.

> The need to restrict or reorganise attachment-relevant information, whether it originates internally or externally, may result in an inability to perceive and interpret the attachment signals of the infant accurately and, in some cases, in an active need either to alter infant signals or to inhibit them.

(Main, Kaplan and Cassidy, 1985, p.100)

Ann Frodi describes just such a phenomenon in her study on parental responses to the infant signals of crying and smiling (1985, p.363). She found that the baby's cry automatically elicits autonomic arousal in mothers, fathers, adolescents and children, a pattern related to a readiness to aggress. This was even more pronounced with babies the experimenters had purposely labelled as 'premature' or 'difficult'.

In fact, all subjects watched a video of the same 'normal' infant, but the experimental manipulation created different cognitive sets that affected the parents' perception and autonomic arousal as well as their subjective feelings. This is very important evidence of how cultural values can literally alter the psychobiology of our attachment relations. Such a cultural impact takes place via the self, which, as has been stressed before, is a social creation, defined, maintained and transformed in relation to others (Sroufe, 1989, p.71).

It is fascinating to learn that the infant crying elicited in all these studies a response pattern similar to that shown when subjects were asked to imagine the most anger-provoking scene they could, or when they were repeatedly insulted or given an electric shock! Infant smiling, however, elicits, in most people, a positive emotional reaction with few physiological changes.

The evidence is quite different when we deal with the response patterns of abusive mothers. They not only reacted to the infant cry with more annoyance and less sympathy than non-abusive mothers, but they also responded negatively to the smiling baby: according to their heart rates, both signals were equally aversive to these mothers.

These results show clearly how both biological and psychological interactions are involved in our attachment responses. We are discovering that deprivation and loss can affect the psychobiological substrate of our attachment behaviour, turning it into aggression; the responses of these abusive mothers show that, at the same time, our 'internal working models' appear to affect the way we perceive our environment, leading to the recreation of familiar self-affirming patterns of experience in our attachment relations.

This has important implications in terms of maternal behaviour. Judith Crowell and Shirley Feldman found similar evidence showing that the behaviours of mothers and their children were related to the mother's internal model of relationships. They also found that the meanings and interpretations given to their childhood experiences contributed as much to parental behaviour as did actual experiences (1988, p.1283). As was seen earlier, it seemed to Crowell and Feldman that in the construction of the working model of the self, one parent, probably the principal attachment figure, may be much more influential than the other.

Ricks' evidence (1985) from intergenerational studies seems to point in the same direction. The mothers' recollections of childhood acceptance by their own mothers were linked with high levels of self-esteem and were particularly important in terms of their capacity to bring up securely attached infants. Their children had higher ratings of positive emotions than their anxiously attached counterparts.

In the case of the 'avoidant' children, their mothers reported rejection by their mothers in childhood, although at the same time they would tend to idealise these parents and to insist that they had few if any memories of childhood events, no doubt in an attempt to avoid painful memories which would conflict with their idealised view of their mothers. As for those mothers who reported a history of disruption and rejection but who still managed to bring up secure infants, these had supportive marriages and good self-esteem. The mothers of anxious/resistant (group-C) infants were more likely than group-B mothers to be defensive and idealise their mothers.

Changes in 'internal working models'

Lest a hasty conclusion be drawn regarding the immutability of 'internal working models', there is now increasing evidence that this is not the case. Ricks's study shows that maternal problems with child-rearing related not so much to separation experiences in childhood but to serious disruptions in their family of origin such as death, divorce or separation. Ricks emphasises that the evidence she gives only shows that the infant attachment classification is linked more to the parent's current 'internal working models' of attachment relationships than to past representational models. This would concur with the Piagetian view that the past is continuously reorganised according to present needs and present structures. This does not mean, however, that early 'internal working models' are not highly influential. Indeed, as Ricks points out, the anxiously attached child will seek to recreate similar experiences because these would confirm a major basic assumption in this person's conceptual system and her view of reality. Quoting Epstein, she writes that an unpleasant but predictable world is preferable to a chaotic one.

However, though there may be resistance to changing 'internal working models', as we have seen earlier, this does not mean that change cannot occur, particularly if our subsequent attachment relations continuously disconfirm our earlier experiences. This can happen in the context of a loving supportive relationship, through changes in our relationship with our parents, or in therapy.

Theodore Gaensbauer and Robert Harmon (1982) provide us with observations on just how such changes may take place. They looked at a group of children who had experienced disturbed parenting, including physical abuse and losses (and at another group of premature infants). Many of these children were sent to foster parents with whom they appeared to form very rapid and strong attachments. These children also saw their parents for weekly supervised visits. On such occasions they would soon be behaving like securely attached infants during a modified Strange Situation test. The authors question whether such results do in fact reflect optimal development. They give an example of a 15-and-a-half-month-old infant who had been so badly abused that he had had his skull fractured and had been fostered for 5 months. Though he appeared securely attached, he cringed and cried in response to one of the examiner's gestures when he was being tested and he appeared hypervigilant and inhibited.

Another 12-month-old infant showed secure attachment behaviour with his foster parent after only 2 weeks but, at the same time, he also showed clear evidence of depression during the test. Gaensbauer and Harmon conclude that the attachment behaviour they observed reflected the relatively recent quality of infant–caregiver relationship as opposed to the remote past. They also believed that such an attachment relationship provides the vehicle for developmental recovery, undoing or changing the effects of earlier difficult experiences in different areas. That such a recovery takes time and that the children may still be vulnerable to stress is also shown by the behaviour of the depressed infant referred to earlier. After 3 months, his foster father became very ill and his foster mother was unable to give her fostered infant the special care he needed. On testing, he was seen to be 'avoidant' whereas a similar aged granddaughter of the foster mother, who also lived at home and who had not experienced such trauma, was not affected. As the family situation improved, the little boy emerged from his 'avoidant' withdrawal: this child reminds us of Harlow's deprived monkeys and their persistent vulnerability to stress despite their improvement in 'therapy'.

The issue of potential change in our 'internal working models' can also overlap with our interest in understanding the possible links between trauma and destructive aggression. Main points to the repeated finding that in infants and children, 'avoidance' behaviour upon reunion occurs, not only after brief separations as seen in the Strange Situation, but also after major separations from their parents. In her eyes, both responses represent the infant's state of mind or 'internal working model' of the infant–caregiver relationship. As Main concludes, this implies that the 'internal working model' is not simply a sample of interaction pattern with the caregiver since it can change in the absence of any such interaction (Main, 1977).

This is clearly illustrated in the study of a 2-year-old boy separated for 10 days from his mother and looked after by a couple called the Robertsons during her absence. They describe the child's relationship with mother prior to separation as a good, secure one. During the separation, Thomas was regularly presented with a photo of him and his mother (Robertson and Robertson, 1971). He initially kissed it and held it lovingly. A few days later, he stood back from the photograph, with his eyes downcast and fiddling with something in his hand. At the end of the separation period, Thomas actively avoided the photograph by turning his back to it and looking anxious, insisting on putting it away from him. Thus the child's response to the pictorially represented reunion with mother had changed from one which sought closeness to one of avoidance over a 10-day separation. The authors point out that since the behaviour of the photograph had not changed, they are led to conclude that what had changed was the child's internal representation of the relationship.

This means that the 'internal working model' will include the psychic outcome of the infant's attempt to gain access to the caregiver in his or her absence. Such an outcome is important enough to produce a noticeable change in the child's 'internal working model' with very real implications in terms of how she behaves upon reunion with her caregiver. In terms of the permanent loss of the parent, such an internal development could lead to the de-activation of the whole attachment system if the child's emotional needs are not attended to.

We may recall here Main's explanation of the avoidance behaviour as a way for the infant to retain some control of her behaviour when both under threat and yet unable to make contact with a rejecting mother (Main 1981): the infant has to 'cut herself off' from her parent. Such an explanation also accounts for the 'avoidant' behaviour seen after prolonged separations. The child's need for her attachment figure is repeatedly frustrated, so much so that her extreme feelings of anger and pain become psychologically intolerable and attention must be shifted away from the attachment figure. In this way, the child is no longer distressed and appears to have 'adapted' to her loss. However, at a deeper level both thought and behaviour are being actively reorganised away from the parent and from the memory of the parent. From a psychoanalytic point of view the attachment relationship is being 'split off' and repressed from conscious awareness. This form of 'dissociation' is extremely common, as we shall find out, following severe psychological trauma. What needs to be understood is that it has its roots in the simple experience of prolonged loss even in the context of what was a good attachment relationship.

A young 29-year-old man in psychoanalytic treatment illustrates this phenomenon very clearly: he lost his mother through illness when he was only nine. Her death was followed by a series of severe family disruptions and losses. These experiences appeared to have led him to forget everything to do with his relation to his mother, including any memory of her.

After several years in therapy, this patient, Mr Jones, is now able to form a close relationship with his therapist, though not without marked ambivalent feelings particularly when faced with separations. However, he no longer needs to 'cut off' as he used to do and memories of mother are beginning to appear in a semi-disguised form in his dreams.

One day, he announced that one of his last remaining relatives, a grandfather whom he has idealised and clung to emotionally, had betrayed him for someone else. The impact of the grandfather's experienced rejection and loss of love was such that, though Mr Jones knew he was angry, he did not realise to what extent he had been hurt. It was not long, however, before his therapist was made aware of the extent of this young man's hidden pain: Mr Jones spent most of the session trying to convince him that he needed to stop treatment, for perhaps a year or so; he found many good reasons why he should do so and all feelings of loss and sadness about losing his therapist were temporarily suppressed.

His grandfather's rejection had brought back his biggest fear of all, the threat of losing yet again a person he both loved and needed. Faced with the terrible pain and rage of this past and new experience, he had to 'cut himself off' from his therapist, the one person he later admitted would keep him in touch with feelings he feared so much. He became the 'avoidant' child of his past, regaining some degree of control over his painful sense of rejection and loss. With insight, he later admitted to giving his therapist a taste of the treatment he had just been subject to. In fact, the 'cutting off' was short-lived. Supported by an empathic therapeutic relationship, he soon realised what was happening and experienced considerable regret at having dismissed his therapist and his treatment.

On looking back at his 'avoidant' behaviour this same patient often reports considerable relief and satisfaction at having been able to annihilate his mother so effectively. Thus, though he successfully dissociated himself from his relation to his mother, the destructive rage persisted with all that this implied in terms of violent behaviour towards himself and towards those he needed.

Conclusion

Our brief foray into the psychotherapist's consulting room provides us with a timely reminder of the role psychoanalysis can play in our understanding of human destructive behaviour. Though much of the research we have referred to in child development has been carried out by American psychoanalysts such as Stern and Sroufe, most psychoanalysts appear to remain impervious to these findings and their implications. Such blatant 'selective inattention', as Bowlby would define this defensive process, is in fact essential if old-established psychoanalytic premises are to be preserved, with all that this implies in terms of protecting the psychoanalytic 'group self'. However, despite the entrenched views of some thinkers in the field, psychoanalysis has developed considerably since Breuer and Freud wrote their first work *Studies on Hysteria* (1893–1895). The evolution of these psychoanalytic ideas will be the subject of our next chapter.

Chapter 7
Self and Other

'The Mulla walked into a shop one day. The owner came forward to serve him. "First things first," said Nasrudin, "did you see me walk into your shop?"

"Of course."

"Have you ever seen me before?"

"Never in my life."

"Then how do you know it is me?"

The subtleties of the incomparable Nasrudin

Theory and practice in psychoanalysis

From psychobiology to the internalisation of relationships, the developmental pathways are complex and the implications of these studies are still far from clear. However, an understanding of attachment behaviour as both the product of attunement and its vehicle of expression appears to be necessary if researchers are to begin to understand some of the psychobiological effects of separation, loss and deprivation, including the destructive behaviours often associated with a disruption of the attachment system.

In parallel, and of no less importance, are the psychological processes which enable us to adjust to these changes and to preserve our sense of self, a self we are discovering to be the product of our multiple relations with significant 'others' and guarantor of our sense of unity and continuity.

The conceptual tools which contribute to the understanding of the psychological processes involved in the day-to-day running of our lives derive from the psychoanalytic work of Freud and his followers. The patient–therapist relationship which develops within the psychoanalytic setting of the consulting room provides unique possibilities for

understanding human reactions within the context of a fairly controlled environmental setting. It is probably for this reason that so
much more information seems to be forthcoming when reading the
clinical papers written by psychoanalysts rather than their theoretical
works. In the latter, the need to remain loyal to the psychoanalytic tradition of their teachers and of their institution can influence the psychoanalysts' perception of their patients' difficulties. This is clearly
illustrated in the presentation of two analyses of the same patient by
the well-known American psychoanalyst Heinz Kohut. It illustrates
what Erik Erikson so wisely said: 'The trouble with followers is, they
repeat what their leader said fifty years ago and they think they are following him, but they are not following him anymore' (Konner, 1991,
p.19).

In 1979, Heinz Kohut produced a paper entitled 'The two analyses of
Mr Z'. It contains the summaries of an analysis of the same young man
carried out in two instalments of 4 years each, separated by an interval
of about 5 years. The paper is to be commended not only for its honesty
but also because of its implications for psychoanalysis as a whole.

In the first period of psychoanalytic treatment, Kohut thought and
spoke with his patient along the traditional lines of a Freudian analysis.
By the second instalment, however, Kohut had considerably altered his
theoretical outlook, so much so that he both perceived and addressed
his patient's difficulties in quite a different way which 'enabled me, to
the great benefit of my patient, to give him access to certain sectors of
his personality that had not been reached in the first part of his treatment' (1979, p.3).

Kohut's patient was a handsome young man in his mid-twenties
who first presented with vague somatic symptoms and who complained of feeling lonely and being unable to form any relationships
with girls. He masturbated frequently and his masturbation fantasies
were of a masochistic nature. He was an only child who still lived with
his mother. His wealthy father had died 4 years before. The latter had
had a serious illness when his son was three and a half years old, during which he had fallen in love with his nurse whom he had then lived
with for over a year. Though his father had then returned home, his
parents' marriage remained an unhappy one. Mr Z, on the other hand,
appeared to be the apple of his mother's eye.

During his analysis, this patient clearly wanted his analyst to attend
to his narcissistic needs for admiration and understanding. However, in
keeping with his Freudian training, Kohut would only interpret these
'insatiable narcissistic demands' as attempts on the part of his patient
to control him as he imagined he had exclusively controlled his mother
during his father's absence. The patient would react by blowing up in a
rage, accusing his analyst of not understanding him. This went on for
about a year and a half. Then Mr Z rather suddenly became calmer. He

ascribed this change to the analyst saying: 'Of course, it hurts when one is not given what one assumes to be one's due' (1979, p.5). Kohut did not understand the significance of this statement and simply assumed that his patient was giving up his narcissistic demands because he had 'worked through' these particular infantile needs.

From then on the analytic work was carried out along conventional Freudian lines, in the area of Mr Z's 'infantile sexuality and aggression, his Oedipus complex, his castration anxiety, his childhood masturbation, his fantasy of the phallic woman, and, especially his preoccupation with the primal scene' (1979, p.5). This was not difficult since Kohut's patient had often witnessed his parents having sexual intercourse. In talking about his childhood and adult sexual fantasies, he described himself as being treated like a slave by a mistress who would force him to carry out humiliating tasks such as, for example, having to take care of her excrement and urine. His masochism was interpreted as being due to his guilt about his pre-oedipal possession of his mother and about his unconscious oedipal rivalry with his father, all in keeping with classical psychoanalytic theory. By the end of his first analysis Mr Z no longer spoke of his masochistic preoccupations; he had successfully left his mother's home and was making sexual relationships with women.

This vast improvement was attributed by Kohut to the structural changes that come about as a result of bringing unconscious conflicts into consciousness (1979, p.9). However, five and a half years later, Mr Z was back in treatment with Kohut. He complained that his sexual relationships were giving him no real satisfaction and that his work felt a burden. It appeared to Kohut as if his patient's masochistic tendencies had only been repressed and had now shifted to his work and life in general. What seemed important, too, was the information that around this time, his mother had become a social recluse who suffered from paranoid delusions. This suggested to the analyst that she might have been far more disturbed than he had originally assumed.

During the first part of this second analysis, Mr Z established what Kohut describes as an idealising transference: the patient's resulting sense of well-being and confidence then subsided to be followed by a period during which he became self-centred and demanding, insisting on perfect understanding or empathy and being 'inclined to react with rage at the slightest out-of-tuneness with his psychological states, with the slightest misunderstandings of his communications' (1979, pp.11–12). This phase resembled the early part of the first treatment but Kohut's reaction was quite different. He focused on it 'with the analyst's respectful seriousness vis à vis important analytic material' (1979, p.12), looking upon it as the replica of a childhood condition revived in the session.

This change in attitude had two good results: one was that Mr Z had far less aggressive rages against his analyst; the other was the exploration of a part of the patient's life which had hitherto remained hidden. What became clear is that Mr Z's mother had always been an intensely possessive woman who would become pathologically jealous whenever her son showed any sign of independence. Like the mistress in his fantasies, she would involve herself with his faeces when he was little and then with the blackheads on his face when he grew older. It became clear that she was not interested in him but that she needed him as a permanent 'selfobject', in other words as an object fulfilling a homoeostatic function, which in this case appeared to be a misplaced parental function similar to the functions Bowlby describes as having been taken on by 'parentified' children.

In discussing this part of his work, Kohut wonders why the crucial material about Mr Z's mother never came up in the first analysis. The fact is that it did come up but only to be re-enacted or recreated without this being acknowledged in the transference relationship. His own reply is a self critical one:

> My theoretical convictions, the convictions of a classical analyst who saw the material that the patient presented in terms of infantile drives and of conflicts about them, and of agencies of a mental apparatus either clashing or co-operating with each other, had become for the patient a replica of the mother's hidden psychosis, of a distorted outlook on the world to which he had adjusted in childhood, which he had accepted as reality – an attitude of compliance and acceptance that he had now reinstated with regard to me and to the seemingly unshakable convictions that I held.
>
> *(1979, p.16)*

What Kohut is telling us is that, armed with the Freudian belief system centred around the drive theory, he unconsciously re-enacted the abuse perpetrated by Mrs Z on her son. Deaf to his patient's cries of rage and deaf to his criticisms, Kohut would impose his interpretation of the Freudian truth, thus unwittingly but nonetheless actively denying the reality and the pain of Mr Z's early life experience. This is extremely important in understanding why Freud and his followers failed to see the link between trauma and violence. Indeed, as long as Kohut saw his patient from a classical Freudian perspective, his attacks of rage could easily be dismissed as anger at being made to give up his childish selfish demands. It took Kohut another few years to realise that what Mr Z was expressing was his 'narcissistic rage', the rage of the child wounded by the repeated denigration and denial of his needs, first by his parents and then by his analyst. This repetition of the early abuse in psychoanalytic treatment is to be expected if the therapist does not conceive of rage and anger as being potentially connected to experiences of loss and psychic trauma. For such a psychoanalyst the 'death instinct' can come between him and his patient.

For those who may wonder why Mr Z put up with this psychoanalytic abuse and why he became so compliant, we could enumerate countless examples of patients undergoing similar experiences in treatment, recreating with their therapists the very tragedy they seek to put right. Like Mr Z, they bring with them the internalised relationships of their past, the only interpersonal reality they have known. And like Mr Z, they recreate these attachment patterns with their therapist. What happens next depends on how the experience is perceived both by the patient and by his therapist. Looking at the first analysis, Kohut's patient may well have picked up an unconscious empathy on the part of his analyst which helped him to put up with Kohut's more overt denigration of his pain. However, what happened subsequently in Mr Z's second analysis may give us a better idea as to why both patients and analysts stick to Freud's instinct-based formulations and their resultant interpretations, however invalidating these may be.

Having been helped to understand what had gone on with his mother, Mr Z then began to remember good things about his father. However, these memories were interrupted by recurrent attacks of severe anxiety, which included a number of very frightening quasi-psychotic experiences during which he felt he was disintegrating both mentally and physically. He also had some awful dreams of war and dead bodies. It seemed that in getting close to his father he was beginning to face the loss of his internalised mother, hitherto his main acknowledged source of love and identification. She appeared to him once in a dream, standing with her back to him. This prompted him to recall her icy withdrawal from him when he attempted to step towards independence, particularly towards independent maleness. In former times, he had always responded to this warning signal by an emotional return to his mother, like the deprived monkeys in Harlow's experiments. Now, held by the idealised transference with his father-analyst, Mr Z allowed himself to undergo the pain of losing her and what she had represented to him. He thus abandoned his internalised 'bad-object', an object he had clung to all his life and made part of his own self, rather than face the annihilating terror of total loneliness.

This clinging to the 'bad object' was for the psychoanalyst Fairbairn the expression of the 'moral defence'. Countless patients, driven by the guilt of their own wickedness, the badness of their internalised 'bad object' parent, have said to me: 'Better the devil you know than the devil you don't.' When faced with the loss of this fundamental part of their own self-identity in treatment, many choose to remain as Mr Z originally did, a little better but safely the same, with their 'infantile drives and conflicts' under somewhat greater control. Similarly, their analysts too, in their own training analysis, may well prefer to remain 'instinct-bound' than to face the very real anxieties of their narcissistic vulnerability. As Kohut states:

> Decisive progress in man's knowledge of himself is, in my opinion, not primarily a cognitive feat, but achieved mainly as a consequence of what, expressed in everyday language, must be called an act of courage. Pioneering studies in depth psychology require not only a keen intellect but also characterological strength, because they are in essence based on the relinquishment of infantile wishes and on discarding the illusions that have protected us against anxiety.
>
> *(Kohut, 1985, p.210)*

I have chosen to present Kohut's case in such detail because it highlights so many of the issues we are grappling with here. It shows how much psychoanalysis has changed over the last century. As Kohut takes us from the old Freudian perspective centred round the conflicts of 'infantile sexuality' towards his 'psychoanalytic psychology of the self', he covers the development of psychoanalytic thinking from a theory based on the instincts to one based on relationships. In so doing, he shows us just how much psychoanalytic theories can influence both the therapist's perception and his behaviour towards his patients.

In Kohut's experience, to believe is to see: as long as he believed his patient to be struggling with his Oedipus complex, he could not see what effects his relationship with his mother had had on him. It was only when, as an analyst, he could acknowledge the effects he was having on his patient, that he could also see what effects others had also had on Mr Z.

The recognition of the importance of our 'objects', particularly of our 'selfobjects', goes hand in hand with the recognition of the importance of the self, its formation, maintenance and vulnerability. It is also striking how much the Kohutian 'self–selfobject' relationship resembles Field's concept of attunement; this similarity becomes particularly obvious when he describes his second analytic relationship with Mr Z as one of 'empathic consonance with another human being'.

Thus, people tend to see what they have been taught to see. They elicit what they expect to find: it is as if they only understand what they can bear to understand.

From Freud to Kohut

As a result of these difficulties, the journey from Freud's theories regarding 'infantile sexuality' and the 'life and death instincts' to the recognition of our fundamental need for one another, is a long and tortuous one. However, it needs addressing since it is the shift from these instinct-based theories to those centred on the importance of relationships and the parallel formation of the 'self' which has provided researchers with the possibility of understanding the origins of human violence. This psychoanalytic development can be followed by tracing the development of 'Object Relations Theory'. Clearly any such attempt is full of pitfalls since an account of such brevity is bound to oversimplify the complex issues involved.

However, the aim here is only to illustrate how the basic assumptions underlying Freudian psychoanalytic theory evolved to produce two different theoretical perspectives, one founded on man's need for relationships and the other centred on man's need to discharge his instinctual impulses. As has already been pointed out in earlier chapters, the fact that there are still psychoanalysts who believe in the Freudian instinctual theory of man, despite the fact that it is scientifically untenable, is an indication that it does play an important function for us which needs to be acknowledged and understood.

In keeping with the central theme in this book, this review will remain focused on the causes of violent behaviour as proposed by different psychoanalytic schools of thought.

Sigmund Freud

Though Freud came to believe in an 'instinct theory', his early work reflects a very different view of human nature: like Darwin and other truly original thinkers, Freud developed theories which embodied more than one basic assumption. As will be seen in more detail, in the study of child sexual abuse, Freud was to take up his 'drive theory' when he abandoned his 'seduction theory' at the turn of the century.

One of his earliest publications was a seminal paper Freud wrote with Breuer 'On the psychical mechanism of hysterical phenomena' (Breuer and Freud, 1893). Both authors were interested in the effect of trauma in the aetiology of hysterical illnesses: Freud had in fact recognised that many of his hysterical female patients had been sexually abused in childhood.

Breuer and Freud ascribed the symptoms of their hysterical patients to the 'memory of the trauma' which acts like a foreign body permanently at work in the unconscious. Such memories 'are not at the patient's disposal'. It is only when these traumatic memories are acceded to, in these cases through hypnosis, that they reappear:

> The memories which have become the determinants of hysterical phenomena persist for a long time with astonishing freshness and with the whole of their affective colouring ... [But] these memories, unlike other memories of their past lives, are not at the patients' disposal. *On the contrary, these experiences are completely absent from the patients' memory when they are in a normal psychical state, or are only present in a highly summary form.*
>
> *(1893, p.9; Freud's italics)*

This phenomenon is in keeping with recent psychological research which shows that the retrieval of information is, in part, dependent on reinstituting the brain context that was present when the to-be-remembered event was encoded and stored in the memory (Weingartner, Miller and Murphy, 1977). It is also in keeping with the postulated existence of a variety of 'memory banks' in the brain: this means that different sets of memories and their affective components can coexist in the mind, one being unavailable or unconscious to the other (Gazzaniga and LeDoux, 1978).

In the same paper, Breuer and Freud also described the phenomenon of 'splitting of consciousness', a tendency to dissociation which is characteristic of hysterical conditions: it allows painful thoughts and memories to be cut off from the rest of consciousness to varying degrees. The authors emphasised how severe trauma can bring about such splitting off of ideas and feelings even in people 'who are in other respects unaffected', and that this would be the mechanism of psychically acquired hysteria. They went on to link this capacity to split our consciousness with the existence of focalised areas of 'insanity' in our psychic activity, such as we experience during our dreams.

Though he was to abandon most of these insights on the psychological effects of trauma, Freud did not forget them altogether. This capacity of the human mind to split itself was taken up when dealing with the effects of loss in his paper on 'Mourning and melancholia' (1917). Here, he described the ego of the melancholic as being split to form a 'critical agency or conscience' which he later renamed the 'super-ego'. The remaining ego he saw as identified with the lost object. As a result of this process, he concluded 'In this way an object-loss was transformed into an ego-loss and the conflict between the ego and the loved person into a cleavage between the critical activity of the ego and the ego as altered by identification' (1917, p.249). He also notes that these patients still succeed

> by the circuitous path of self punishment, in taking revenge on the original object and in tormenting their loved one through their illness, having resorted to it in order to avoid the need to express their hostility to him openly. After all, the person who has occasioned the patient's emotional disorder, and on whom his illness is centred, is usually to be found in his immediate environment.
>
> *(1917, p.251)*

This is a fascinating account from Freud's point of view for several reasons. First, in this text he actually relates the individual's psychopathology to an external person. The second important point is that in admitting that interpersonal relations are important, he finds himself postulating the existence of internal objects. The result is that he is once again referring to internal conflicts which have more to do with internalised relationships within the 'ego' than with any instinctual forces.

With his usual acumen, what Freud was in fact describing is a failure to mourn that is manifest in some people whose close relationships are so ambivalent that their loss does not produce grief but a nagging sense of guilt: this arises from their unconscious anger towards their rejecting object. They thus become victims of their own super-ego. In terms of attachment theory, such a description could pertain to the depressive behaviours seen in people who would have been classified as 'avoidant' children. Freud did in fact go as far as postulating the existence of internalised relationships when he described the 'super-ego', otherwise known as our conscience, as a 'successful instance of identification with the parental agency' (1933, pp.63–64).

By proposing the idea that there is a psychic world of internalised relationships, Freud was to open the way for Melanie Klein's work on the internalisation of object relations, which in its turn led on to the appearance of the British Object Relations theorists such as Balint, Winnicott, Guntrip and Fairbairn. It is the latter who was finally to reject Freud's 'instinct' theory.

By this time, Freud had long since abandoned the seduction theory. In 1905 he wrote that 'obviously seduction is not required to arouse a child's sexual life: that can also come about spontaneously from internal causes' (1905, pp.190–191). In this manner Freud waved aside the importance of childhood abuse in the aetiology of mental disturbances. In his new model of the psyche, the object only really exists in relation to the drive whilst the latter is itself subject to the 'principle of constancy'.

Freud was a follower of Helmholtz, believing that all rational phenomena are explicable in terms of physical or chemical forces. Freud therefore transposed the popular hydraulic model used by scientists at the time to his findings in psychology. Thus, in *Beyond the Pleasure Principle* (1920) he writes: 'the mental apparatus endeavours to keep the quantity of excitation present in it as low as possible or at least to keep it constant' (1920, p.9).

As instincts, in particular the sexual ones, became more and more important for Freud, he formulated 'repression' in terms of a need to keep out unpleasurable increases in excitation rather than as an attempt to split off the memories of traumatic experiences, which is what he had originally suggested. We can thus begin to see the emergence of a theory which has as a central belief the view that we are driven by our instincts, and, as result of such a belief system, the individual becomes of central importance, social ties and external reality are of secondary importance and the 'object' or 'other' is seen mainly in terms of drive satisfaction.

In keeping with the views of others who believe we are driven by our instincts, Freud had a tendency to deny women their importance and he attributed their poor social standing to the fact that they presented to society the 'reality of castration', since they do not have a penis (1933, p.134). As a result, women are governed by the castration complex and penis envy and have a weaker super-ego than men. For Freud, the boy's development consists in freeing himself from his sexual urges towards his mother in the face of the paternal threat of castration. This is how he moves from dependence to autonomy.

For Ian Suttie, Freud took up the 'instinctual' point of view because of his own developmental failure in relation to his mother. Suttie writes:

> The social environment, mankind, takes for us the place once occupied by our mother, and if we have been deprived of this place by *violence* this will engender bitterness and repressed longing, (for mother and for tenderness), which will make the 'world' seem hateful to us and lead us to deny the very existence of the objects of our disappointed longings. This pessimism, I maintain, constitutes a taboo on tenderness... .
>
> *(1935 p.203; Suttie's italics)*

The fact that Freud and his followers continued to believe in the 'death instinct' forced Ian Suttie to defect. For him, the most important aspect of psychological development to be elucidated was the idea of others and of one's own relationship to them. Unfortunately he died too young to present us with a coherent alternative theory, but his emphasis on interpersonal relations was to be taken up by the 'Object-relations' school in this country and by the 'Interpersonal psychoanalysts' in the USA.

Melanie Klein

Meanwhile, as we saw in our chapter on aggression and violence, Melanie Klein was to take up the theory of the 'death instinct' with as great a conviction as Freud. However, although her underlying belief in man's innate aggression does have serious therapeutic and social implications, her positive contribution to our psychological understanding of the human mind has also been profound and deserves further consideration.

First of all, her concept of instinct or drive is quite different from Freud's. He saw instincts as tensions arising from the body. For Melanie Klein the body is used to express our drives, which are passionate feelings of love and hate directed towards others. As Jay Greenberg and Stephen Mitchell point out, drives for Klein are relationships and libidinal and aggressive phantasies are from the outset the mental expression of both life and death instincts (Greenberg and Mitchell, 1983, p.146). The result was her greatest contribution to our psychological understanding, the conception of a subjective world of internalised or self-created relationships, an internal world of 'object relations'.

In the most general sense, these psychic structures arise through a more or less complex process of 'internalisation' whereby external object-relations are modified in terms of subjective phantasies to become incorporated in our minds and to form the templates of our future relationships. Their importance in influencing our subsequent relationships will depend on how early they are formed and how representative they are of our life experiences with our caregivers.

According to Klein's view of the development of 'object-relations' in the infant, the contribution from the internal world of instincts and phantasies is as great as, if not greater than, that from the external world of relationships. This allowed Klein and her followers to maintain their belief in the 'death instinct' which is manifest right from the beginning of life in the form of envy. For example, in his book *The Tyranny of Malice* (1989), Joseph Berke defines this feeling as follows: 'Envy is an inborn, destructive motivating force, opposed to love and antagonistic to life' (1989, p.57). He also makes it quite clear that

> Envy may be associated with real events, but it is more than a reaction to them. Envy is both the tension and the hostile reaction to this tension in the envier, a tension that is not dependent on, or necessarily related to, anything actually happening.
>
> *(1989, p.61)*

This need to deny the importance of external reality is, as we now know, characteristic of those who believe that we are driven by our instincts; the intensity of this belief is often matched by a similar need to denigrate those who see the need to stress the importance of environmental experience. Interestingly, Berke goes on to say with considerable insight: 'Envy can be seen as a mechanism of defence at the service of the death impulse' (1989, p.62). Its function is even more clearly revealed when the same author also acknowledges that 'the death instinct seems ominously close to original sin' (1989, p.58). Berke believes that this makes the death instinct difficult to accept, especially on ethical grounds. However, he also dismisses any scientific criticism of the 'death instinct' and does not refer to the psychological literature on aggression or, for that matter, on attachment, though he claims his purpose is to: 'develop a detailed understanding of our capacity for destruction as well as for making good' (1989, p.13).

I have dwelt on the importance of the Kleinian assumptions underlying the concept of envy, because of the social and therapeutic implications of such a belief system. However, Berke's study of envy itself rather than its origins is excellent and far reaching, especially when he points out how difficult it is for us to acknowledge our own envy when it means acknowledging our inferiority with respect to another. This is very true and remains of paramount importance whatever the origins of envy.

Whilst Klein and her followers continue to uphold the 'death instinct' as a primary motivating force, for other psychoanalysts, such as Fairbairn and later Bowlby, the contribution of the external world becomes far more important. The concept of an internal world of object relationships based more, though never totally, on external experiences, allowed them to formulate another theory of motivation which is essentially based on the human need to relate with others. This enabled some psychoanalysts finally to reject the concepts of the 'life' and 'death' instincts and to begin to develop a theory of man's development and self-esteem based on the nature of his relationships with the outside world.

Interpersonal psychoanalysis

One American psychoanalyst stands out for having put interpersonal experiences at the heart of human development. He is Harry Stack Sullivan who, with his colleagues Erich Fromm, Karen Horney and Frieda Fromm-Reichmann, felt that the drive theory as elaborated by Freud and his followers was wrong in terms of human motivation and the difficulties in living. It also ignored the cultural dimension of human experience with its effect on human development.

He never espoused the model of 'object relations theory' as such, being keen to choose words suggestive of process and function rather than fixed structures. However, his assumptions are the same as those of his colleagues Fairbairn and Winnicott in Britain. In terms of the study of violence, what is of particular interest is Sullivan's theory of child development which he elaborated after many years spent in treating schizophrenic patients.

Persons, he said, are motivated by two types of 'needs': for satisfaction and for security. The first are fairly straightforward: needs for food, warmth, human contact and for increasingly complex forms of play and self-expression (1953, pp.37–40). Through the infant's needs, a successful integration is achieved between the mother and her infant. Some of the needs for satisfaction change as the infant matures, particularly the emotional needs, and failure to meet them results in loneliness, which is seen by Sullivan as the most painful of human experiences.

The second type of need, for security, is the search for the freedom from anxiety, anxiety which the infant catches, so-to-speak, from her caregiver (1953, pp.41–44). The fear it arouses is such that the infant learns to discriminate between her anxious mother and her non-anxious mother and, later, to control this anxiety by a set of processes which are designed to block the unwanted experiences from her awareness. In this process the 'self' is formed, which Sullivan defines as 'what one takes oneself to be' and which is largely the product of what others take one to be. 'The self is made up of reflected appraisals.'

The 'personality', on the other hand, describes the entire functioning of the person. So those other experiences which are incongruent with the appraisals of significant others, form part of this personality as the 'extra self'. Components of the self are those behaviours and experiences that meet with mother's approval and thus make the child non-anxious and hence feeling like a 'good me'. Through a series of what Sullivan calls 'security operations', not only is anxiety reduced by controlling awareness, but it is also reduced by distracting attention from the source of anxiety onto other thoughts or feelings which feel more secure, often imparting an illusory sense of power, stature and specialness.

One way in which the self bolsters itself in the face of potential anxiety is to create illusory relations with others, based on actual experiences with others in which the self has experienced some sense of security or control such as: the self as special/the other as admiring or the self as victimised/the other as powerful and tyrannical. In this way, the self distorts actual relations with others. The central aim of most people becomes the need to bolster the self to reduce anxiety, leading to a conflict with the need to pursue one's satisfactions. Sullivan's 'self' is very much in keeping with the 'False Self' as described by Winnicott (1960).

For Sullivan, the reciprocal relationship with other people is fundamental. He describes it as the 'concept of communal existence':

> Everything that can be found in the human mind has been put there by interpersonal relations, excepting only the capabilities to receive *and elaborate* the relevant experiences. This statement is also meant to be the antithesis of any doctrine of human instincts.
>
> *(1950, p.302; Sullivan's italics)*

Recognising the importance of the self and acknowledging its relation to the 'other' is characteristic of all psychoanalytic theories founded on a relationship model rather than an instinct model.

When it comes to understanding how and why we become malevolent, Sullivan rejects the view that man is essentially evil or sadistic. In keeping with the views of others who focus on the importance of human relationships, he believes children become 'malevolent' as a result of their early experiences. When looking at envy in particular, he writes:

> A child may discover that manifesting the need for tenderness towards the potent figures around him leads frequently to his being disadvantaged, being made anxious, being made fun of, and so on, so that, according to the locution used, he is hurt, or in some cases, he may be literally hurt. Under those circumstances, the developmental course changes to the point that the perceived need for tenderness brings a foresight of anxiety or pain. The

child learns ... to show something else; and that something else is the basic malevolent attitude, the attitude that one really lives amongst enemies.

(1953, p.214)

This description may remind the reader of Ainsworth's 'avoidant' infant whose life circumstances are very much those of the 'malevolent' child.

For Sullivan, envy is one of the outcomes of this malevolent attitude and it pertains to personal attachments or attributes. It involves a two-group or two-person situation whereas jealousy involves a three-person situation. Envy betrays an unsuccessful organisation of the self-system which Sullivan attributes to early life experiences. Some very envious people were once children who simply did not meet their parents' expectations. Others were led to believe that they were more gifted than they really were and this led to a personal experience of repeated failures to match up with their parents' extravagant ideals. As a result, the envious person has come to invest with importance all sorts of things which carry prestige and approval, to feel on an equal footing with others (1956, pp.128–132). Thus envy poisons our lives and our capacity to relate to others, but what envy is not, for Sullivan, is an instinctive impulse that afflicts us all indiscriminately. However, what he does also believe is that the American culture, centred round the gratification of the individual, makes envy more widespread.

This emphasis on the development of an internal world of relationships, created in response to external life experiences of relationships with significant others, was also taken up by the followers of Melanie Klein in Britain.

W.R.D. Fairbairn

Fairbairn, the Scottish analyst, to whom we owe the concept 'moral defence', stands out among his colleagues for his rigorous theoretical approach and his resulting rejection of Freud's 'instinct theory' (1952). Whilst many psychoanalysts agreed with his criticisms of Freud's theories, few had the courage to dispense openly with the instinctual theory. Fairbairn did so on the grounds that he saw man as essentially 'object-seeking', that is to say relationship-seeking and not pleasure-seeking.

Like Sullivan, Fairbairn saw the infant as enmeshed in his relations with others, discovering himself in the process of interaction. He believed that all early object-relationships are based on identification. This explains why children feel ashamed and bad when they have bad parents; the latter are not only internalised but they are so intolerably bad as internal objects that they have to be repressed. For example, children who have been victims of sexual abuse do not want to recall the event or the intolerable relationship they had with the 'bad object'.

The main reason why the child internalises her parents as bad objects is because she needs them. In fact, the more her parents neglect her, the more she needs them. As Fairbairn states: 'It is because this need remains attached to them in the unconscious that he cannot bring himself to part with them. It is also this need for them that confers upon them their actual power over him' (1952, p.68).

It is at this point that the 'moral defence' comes into play: the child would rather see himself as bad, which makes Fairbairn believe that the child makes himself the 'bad' one in order to make his objects 'good': 'The phenomena of guilt must be regarded ... as partaking of the nature of a defence.' As he puts it on behalf of his patients: 'It is better to be a sinner in a world ruled by God than to live in a world ruled by the Devil' (1952, p.66). To abandon this defence is to have no security and no hope of redemption. The only prospect is one of death and destruction. He points out, as Kohut was to do many years later, during the second analysis of Mr Z, that,

> The deepest source of resistance is fear of the release of bad objects from the unconscious: for, when such bad objects are released, the world around the patient becomes peopled with devils which are too terrifying for him to face.
>
> *(1952, p.69)*

However, this has to happen if the patient is to abandon his identification with his bad objects and his resulting self-destructive behaviour. What then becomes essential is that the analyst establishes himself as a sufficiently 'good object' for his patient to hold on to when going through this living nightmare.

Aggression, for Fairbairn, results from the failure to achieve satisfactory relationships. This reactive origin of aggression does not in any way diminish its importance, but it does mean that there is no longer any need for the 'death instinct'. As Fairbairn points out, a relationship with a bad object can hardly escape being of either a sadistic or a masochistic nature.

> What Freud describes under the category of 'death instincts' would thus appear to represent for the most part masochistic relationships with internalised bad objects. A sadistic relationship with a bad object which is internalised would also present the appearance of a death instinct.
>
> *(1952, p.79)*

For Fairbairn, violence is therefore the outcome of our unmet needs. He also believed that our culture increases our potential for violence by disrupting the mother–infant relationship and their much-needed mutual contact: in a state of nature the infant would never normally experience that separation from his mother (or other caregivers) which is imposed on her in this culture. Fairbairn believes this results in the development of intense aggression in our infants struggling to maintain a good relationship (1952, pp.109–110).

The development of the internal world of object relations is a complex one for Fairbairn. Having internalised the bad mother, there is a need to split her into a luring tempting object and a bad rejecting object. The individual's relationship to these internalised and opposite versions of mother are made more complex by further splits in the ego and subsequent repression: the final outcome of this psychic drama is the recognition that the individual clings to his original hate as he clings to his original childhood objects (1952, p.117).

No other British psychoanalyst of the Object-relations school was able to break away from Freud's instinct theory in the way Fairbairn did. Though many became increasingly aware of the importance of human relationships in the development of the psyche, most psychoanalysts tried to accommodate their clinical findings with Freud's theoretical assumptions. The resultant confusion of ideas can be quite exasperating for those of us who seek conceptual consistency, but this same confusion reflects two important human phenomena.

The first is the importance we all attach to remaining within our chosen group and the fear we experience at being marginalised or thrown out of it. Paradoxically perhaps, it is those who maintain the overall importance of the individual and of his or her instincts who illustrate this group phenomenon most clearly.

The second phenomenon is simply the recognition that in our present intellectual climate, it is still far easier to stick to an instinctual theory of man with all that it implies than to acknowledge the importance of what Darwin termed our 'sociability', our need for one another.

Donald Winnicott

Winnicott is an example of an outstanding paediatrician and psychoanalyst whose observations of mothers and children made him only too aware of the importance of mother for the infant. Indeed he is famous for his comment that there is no such thing as a baby, only a nursing couple. He criticised Melanie Klein for neglecting to study child care (1959, p.126), but when it came to discussing the function of aggression he implied that aggression for Klein was really the result of frustration, 'frustrations that inevitably disturb instinctual satisfactions as the child begins to be affected by the demands of reality' (1958, p.22). This description simply bears no relation to Klein's descriptions of the 'death instinct'. Winnicott also often maintained that aggression did not entail anger or hate; he saw it as a general expression of vitality or activity, which is correct but ignores the problem of human destructiveness and its origins (1950, p.204). In this way Winnicott never openly dissociated himself from either Freud's or Klein's 'death instinct' but simply modified it to suit his own theories of human development.

Otto Kernberg

Kernberg, an American psychoanalyst, openly maintains that he believes in the drive theory. However, he sees man as social by nature with a mind composed of internalised relational experiences. For him, the 'object' exists in its own right and not just as a recipient of our instinctual needs. The aggressive drive results from the accumulation of bad experiences or as he puts it: 'The developmental stages of libidinal and aggressive drive derivatives depend upon the vicissitudes of the development of internalised object relations' (1976, pp.185–186). The latter come first.

Greenberg and Mitchell are very critical of Kernberg's need to remain wedded to the instinctual theories of Freud. After pointing out that he views man as inherently social by nature right from birth and that he sees our mind as 'forged from relational experience', they remind us that:

> Drives are not a *discovery* of psychoanalysis, they are an *á priori* statement asserting a particular view of man's basic nature. Changing this assumption necessarily changes the theory; merely asserting that one believes in drives does not make one a drive model theorist.
>
> *(1983, p.340; Greenberg and Mitchell's italics)*

They insist, with Kernberg, that 'of the earlier psychoanalytic conception of irreducible, biologically determined drives, *nothing remains but the terms*' (1983, p.341, Kernberg's italics). What is highlighted so strikingly here is the intellectual contortions to which Kernberg subjects himself in order to remain within the Freudian fold, so to speak.

Heinz Kohut

His other American colleague, Heinz Kohut, was faced with the same dilemma. Like Sullivan, he attached a lot of importance to the 'self', which he describes even in infancy as 'a centre of initiative and a recipient of impressions' (1977, p.99). It takes shape from within the matrix of selfobjects (1985, p.218).

> Self psychology does not work with a framework of biological drives and a mental apparatus. It posits a primary self which, in a matrix of empathic selfobjects that is held to be as much a prerequisite for psychological existence as oxygen is for biological life, experiences *self*object greatness (assertiveness; ambitions), on the one hand, and self*object* perfection (idealisation of one's goals; enthusiasm for one's ideals), on the other. Drives are secondary

phenomena. They are disintegration products following the breakup of the primary complex psychological configurations in consequence of (empathy) failures in the selfobject matrix.

(1985, p.74; Kohut's italics)

Kohut's theory rests on two important assumptions: the first is the importance of the 'selfobjects': these are usually people carrying out caregiving functions, most of which will be taken on later by the growing child's psychic structure through a gradual process of internalisation.

This gives rise to the development of the 'self', a permanent psychic structure which consists of two 'poles' derived from early modes of relationship, either of which can function as the core of a healthy and cohesive self. The personality can be organised round a 'grandiose exhibitionist trend', expressed as healthy ambition and derived from a 'mirroring' or empathic selfobject, usually the mother.

But, if 'mirroring' does not achieve the sense of being grand, we have another chance: we can identify with an admired figure and feel grand by association with them. This 'idealising selfobject relationship' which, for Kohut, is usually with the father, particularly in boys, is expressed in terms of healthy ideals and values.

For Kohut, as for Fairbairn before him, the formation and maintenance of 'selfobject' relationships is the motivating force. However, these selfobjects are not sought for themselves in infancy but because they perform functions for the infant an adult person normally performs for himself. They have therefore a homoeostatic function, very much in keeping with the concept of 'working models' proposed by the 'attachment' theorists and by Hofer, whose ideas we referred to earlier. Kohut claims that, as a result of the attachment bonds, which develop between the infant and her caregivers, homoeostatic functions are initially achieved via interactional regulatory processes or what Hofer calls 'biologic regulators'. Then, as the infant develops a capacity for symbolisation, internal representations begin to develop which appear to have regulatory functions and which therefore lead to increasing self-regulation in the child: these would be described by Hofer as 'psychologic regulators'. It is important to note that Kohut maintains, as do Bowlby, Hofer and other attachment theorists, that selfobjects remain necessary throughout life. 'There is no mature love in which the love object is not also a selfobject' (Kohut, 1977, p.122). Even when husband and wife are psychologically healthy, there is a need for mutual mirroring and idealisation. Their need for what Kohut calls a 'symbiotic merger' can be gratified within their sexual relationship.

Kohut's second basic assumption is also in keeping with current attachment theory: just as Kraemer, Reite and Field stressed the importance of 'attunement', so does Kohut believe in the importance of empathy, which he believes is essential for normal development (1985, p.166). It was defined by Kohut as an experience of: 'resonance of the self in the self of others, of being understood, of somebody making an effort to understand you' (1985, p.222).

Such a definition of empathy is strikingly similar to the concept of attunement described by the attachment theorists. In keeping with their recent views, Kohut stresses that this empathic experience does not need to be provided by the child's biological mother and can be provided by more than one person (1985, p.167).

For Kohut, psychopathology results from a chronic failure in empathy due to the parents' character pathology. Specific traumatic events and memories of them serve as pointers of more general disturbances in relations with the parents. When a child is faced with parents who fail to respond empathically to her emerging self, her original search for selfobjects breaks down into either aggressive or sexual drives, depending on the family dynamics.

As with Kernberg, Greenberg and Mitchell argue that once Kohut had deduced that 'drives' follow relational failures, he had embraced the fundamental premise of the 'relational' model. And yet Kohut refuses to break with Freudian instinctual theory.

> Self psychology does not deny the validity of this conception of man – how could it? It is not only Freud's conception but also that of such widely divergent viewpoints which jointly shaped the basic convictions of the Western world as Christianity (which teaches sin and redemption) and Darwinian evolutionism and its biological applications (which teaches development from the primitive to the progressively mature).

> *(Kohut, 1980, pp.539–540)*

This insistence on not rocking the boat is very important for Kohut, who writes about 'the need for gradualness in theory change if the psychoanalytic "group self" is to be preserved' (1977, p.85).

And yet the same Kohut is far more outspoken on the nature of human violence, which is what interests us. In 1972 he wrote:

> The hypothesis that a tendency to kill is deeply rooted in man's psychobiological makeup and stems from his animal past – the assumption, in other words, of man's inherent propensity toward aggression (and the correlated conceptualization of aggression as a drive) – protects us against the lure of the comforting illusion that human pugnacity could be easily abolished if only our material needs were satisfied. But these broad formulations contribute little to the understanding of aggression as a psychological phenomenon.

> *(1985, p.140)*

Referring to the horrors of the Nazi phenomenon, Kohut writes:

> The truth is – it must be admitted with sadness – that such events are not bestial, in the primary sense of the word, but are decidedly human .... So long as we turn away from these phenomena in terror and disgust and indignantly declare them to be a reversal to barbarism, a regression to the primitive and animal-like, so long do we deprive ourselves of the chance of understanding human aggressivity and of our mastery over it.
>
> *(1985, p.141)*

For Kohut, the answer to the problem of human violence lies in understanding the phenomenon of narcissistic rage. His colleague, Ernest Wolf, describes its origins:

> The origin of narcissistic rage must be sought in the childhood experience of utter helplessness vis à vis the humiliating selfobject parent .... Such experiences of helplessness are unbearably painful, because they threaten the very continuity and existence of the self and they therefore evoke the strongest emergency defence of the self in the form of narcissistic rage.
>
> *(1988, p.80)*

As Kohut states, narcissistic rage is at the origins of some of the most gruesome aspects of human destructiveness, often in the form of well-organised activities in which 'the perpetrators' destructiveness is alloyed with absolute conviction about their greatness and with their devotion to archaic omnipotent figures' (1985, p.141).

Narcissistic rage can occur in many forms but they all have one feature in common: the deeply held need for revenge, for undoing a hurt by whatever means, and a deep unrelenting compulsion in the pursuit of those aims (1985, p.143). One classic example of narcissistic rage is given to us by Captain Ahab in Melville's novel *Moby Dick*. It is also at the root of Hitler's destructiveness (Miller, 1983, pp.142–195).

As Kohut says, it is clear that this destructive tendency arises when self and object fail to live up to the expectations directed at their function, be it 'the unconditional availability of the approving-mirroring selfobject or the merger-permitting idealized one'. The result of this developmental deprivation is an adult whose maintenance of the self requires this twofold experience if she is not to experience feelings of intense shame or violent forms of narcissistic rage (1985, p.149).

The American psychoanalyst Graeme Taylor points out that Kohut's contributions to the understanding of aggression invite a reconsideration of the role of aggression in health and in illness (1987, pp.256–257). His advice has gone largely unheeded in Britain, where the need to cling to Kleinian assumptions is still much in evidence.

Conclusion

Throughout this all-too-brief review of the development of object relations in psychoanalytic theory, it is possible to discern the now-familiar polarisation of views between those who favour a drive model and those who favour a relational model.

For Greenberg and Mitchell, the difference between these two theoretical approaches reflects two profoundly 'incompatible visions of life, of the basic nature of human experience' (1983, p.406). For the first, the search for individual pleasure and the need to discharge our instincts is seen as fundamental to human existence. Such an assumption has profound political and philosophical implications and is in tune with our predominant cultural belief system.

For those who favour an object-relations model, the need for the 'other' is seen as of paramount importance for our psychological and physical well-being. Human beings cannot exist outside society. Unsatisfactory relations are what lead to frustration, self-destruction and violence, because we are essentially sociable animals.

Whilst the two conflicting psychoanalytic models clearly reflect an analogous philosophical and political dichotomy based on incompatible premises, it can be questioned whether they must continue to do so. Clearly, if psychoanalysis can only be seen as the intellectual manifestation of its practitioners' political and personal visions of life, then there is little hope of any real exchange of ideas or of conceptual integration because what is being addressed are two opposing belief systems rather than an understanding of human behaviour such as violence. However, what is also remarkable when studying the psychoanalytic literature is the witnessing of a coming together of both concepts and research evidence in the field of child development and psychological trauma; these new ideas and findings are clearly derived from an integration of psychoanalytic theory with current studies in biology, ethology and psychology. This integration is particularly evident in the study of the 'self', in our understanding of how it develops and how it survives. By acknowledging the importance of the 'self', human beings have had to come face to face with both their sense of vulnerability and their desperate need to deny it. This is the subject of the next chapter.

Chapter 8
In Defence of the Self

'Cruelty, persecution and humiliation of one's fellow men, are all expressions of that will-to-power functioning in every phase ... of human life.'

George Riley Scott (1938)

Preserving the self

Few of us realise just how much we depend on our psychological defence mechanisms simply to get through the day. The reason people are not aware of their existence is that they operate on an unconscious level, protecting us from experiences and feelings which are too threatening or painful.

As Anna Freud points out in her book *The Ego and the Mechanisms of Defence,* the term 'defence' occurs for the first time in Freud's study *The Neuropsychoses of Defence,* published in 1894, where it was used to describe the 'ego's struggle against painful or unendurable ideas or affects' (Freud, 1894, p.42).

When Freud later lost interest in the traumatic origins of hysteria to take up the 'drive theory', the defence mechanisms took on the role of controlling the instincts. This was necessary or else every instinct would simply aim for gratification.

As can be seen in this chapter, the function of the defence mechanism varies according to the theoretical approach an individual adopts. Because defences are usually referred to in relation to clinical work, they tend to be seen as associated with mental pathology and, indeed, Freud defined them as 'all the techniques which the ego makes use of in conflicts which may lead to neurosis' (Rycroft, 1968, p.28).

However, any idea I may have had that the gross manifestation of defence mechanisms tends to belong to the realm of mental illness was soon dispelled when I took on a post as consultant psychotherapist to a surgical team specialising in cardiovascular surgery, such as limb salvage and amputations. Many of the patients in their care were old men and women who had lived through the last war, but there were also young patients. Most of them had to face chronic disorders, some of which were life-threatening. One such patient was Mr Smith, a 32-year-old man who suffered from Buerger's disease, a vascular disorder which affects relatively young men and is one of the lethal complications of smoking. It leads to the gradual clogging up of the small vessels of the hands and feet and its development can be arrested by the cessation of smoking. Unfortunately, many patients suffering from Beurger's disease do not appear able to give up smoking, an addiction which could be related to a history of early deprivation, trauma or abuse.

This man had been on the ward for several months before my arrival. He had clearly not been able to stop smoking and kept himself to himself. He also would not let any one touch, let alone amputate, his gangrenous foot. When the nurses tried to clean the putrid flesh on his toes, he shouted abuse at them, complaining about the pain he was in. The atmosphere in his room was a grim and fetid one. There was also a question as to whether he had become a 'junkie' since he now took such huge doses of opiates.

By the time I was consulted very few nurses could bear to go near him. Day after day, the surgeons would visit this young man and recommend that he have his foot amputated before the gangrene spread up his leg but he persistently refused to have an operation. Clearly, for Mr Smith the staff were experienced as bad; he behaved as if they were out to get him. He seemed to feel he must protect himself by not giving in to their wish to remove his foot. He appeared unaware of the danger he was in, only of the need to fight the staff: in this way he felt in control of his fate.

On my first visit, I tried to talk with him but he refused to have anything to do with me. I was seen as 'one of them'. It seemed to me that this young man would rather die than lose all control. I wondered if he, too, had learnt to survive by avoiding dependence and all its terrors, whatever the cost. What did seem clear was that in his desperate attempt to maintain his sense of self-control, Mr Smith had unconsciously adopted a psychological defence Klein described as the 'paranoid–schizoid' defence. It is a psychic configuration whereby the individual deals unconsciously with his rage by splitting his ego and his internalised objects into 'good' and 'bad' parts: then, whilst identifying with the good object, he projects his destructive and bad feelings onto the 'other'. This produces a 'psychological boomerang' effect whereby the 'other' is then re-experienced as persecuting.

Another patient who had been in psychoanalytic psychotherapy with me would, during a certain period of his treatment, move in and out of this paranoid–schizoid position during a session. Though this took place unconsciously and made him experience me as a persecutor, he was also able to explain how it enabled him to cope with his over-whelming feelings of dependency towards me: 'By seeing you as an experimenter needing me, I could forget about my fear of depending on you so much', he explained.

Returning to Mr Smith, it seemed clear that he was using the same defence mechanisms. As a result, he had regained some control over his life but at the cost of denying his real needs. We needed to act urgently if his leg was to be saved. My second intervention involved the team in its relationship with the patient. It seemed that Mr Smith had in a sense recreated his internalised object relations with the staff, a relationship that mirrored the one he still had with his parents, the two silent non-communicative visitors at his bedside.

I prescribed a series of measures which were designed to change the relationship between this man and the ward staff, thereby altering the psychic configuration of his object relations. The surgeons were asked to increase the patient's sense of responsibility by giving him the information he needed to make an informed decision about his amputation. The nursing team were invited to voice their feelings and concerns about this man in a staff meeting and to let him take charge of the dressing of his foot.

The results were rapid: an amputation was carried out at the patient's request. He was seen by the drug addiction consultant to discuss the best way of coming off his opiates. I saw him to discuss his worries. His reaction during this visit was to jokingly accuse me of having manipulated all this, a 'manipulation' I confessed I did not regret.

It was not long before Mr Smith left the ward, following a remarkably rapid rehabilitation period on his new prosthesis. By this time he had established a good relationship with all the staff and had a job as a guitarist in a musical band.

Psychologically, he had moved into what Klein described as the 'depressive' position. It implies a recognition by the individual that he or she can feel both loving and angry feelings and cope with the sadness this engenders: it is an essential psychological phase for mourning to take place.

It is important to realise that patients are not the only ones who need to defend themselves against such fears of helplessness and death. Staff, too, need to protect themselves from similar anxieties as well as deal with the feelings their patients project onto them. A considerable number of medical and nursing staff do in fact cope with such feelings by unconsciously enacting the role of the 'compulsive carer', a defensive and often well-established way of coping with unmet personal needs: these are projected into the 'other' who then becomes the subject of our ministrations. (Bowlby, 1980, p.206). This powerful defence, otherwise called 'projective identification', was originally described by Klein and has been invaluable in understanding human interactions between medical staff and their patients. It is also a common experience in therapy, particularly with patients who have been abused. This defence can help us to understand what took place between Kohut and Mr Z in the first analysis, when Kohut re-enacted with his patient the controlling and abusive relationship with his mother. Mr Z not only projected his 'bad mother' onto his psychoanalyst, he also got him to enact this mother's controlling insensitivity in the session.

Unlike projection, which simply represents putting into the 'other' some of the disowned aspects of the self, projective identification has been described as a threefold process: the ridding of unwanted aspects of the self, the depositing of these unwanted parts into the other person, and finally the recovery, through the 'other', of a modified version of what one has projected (Ogden, 1979, p.357). What is important in this relation is the sense of 'oneness' with the 'other' rather than the sense of 'otherness' that characterises pure projection. The two defences often occur simultaneously.

Projective identification is believed to be of crucial importance in normal infant development, allowing the caregiver to contain and process feelings too intense for the infant to handle on her own. No less important in development is the caregiver's use of projective identification in the raising of children: disowned aspects of the self are put into the infant or child, who is pressurised into enacting them or else face the threat of annihilation, of 'not being there'. This is what takes place in cases of child abuse, where the victim becomes the hated vulnerable aspect of her parents which then has to be controlled and 'brought into line' very much as we saw happening with Mr Brown and his daughter. We shall find out how important this particular defence mechanism is in the differentiation between the sexes and what this implies in terms of violence in the family.

Meanwhile, if we now return to the ward, we can see how the same phenomenon of 'projective identification' was taking place between Mr Smith and the ward staff: it began with the staff desperately attempting to 'treat' a man who became desperately less and less 'treatable' the more he felt infantilised. This led to a sense of failure in the nursing and medical staff with the gradual withdrawal of caregiving behaviour and an increasing sense of resentment and anger towards the patient. In this way he unconsciously manipulated the staff into feeling the hopeless and bad caregivers of his paranoid–schizoid internal organisation. Once nurses and doctors became aware of what was happening through group discussions with the psychotherapist, they could own their own feelings of despair and anger and regain their warm and caring feelings towards Mr Smith.

Institutions have, like individuals, inbuilt psychological defences to cope with the anxieties engendered by the nature of the work in which they specialise. In a seminal paper on 'The Functioning of Social

Systems as a Defence against Anxiety' (1970), Isabel Menzies illustrates the defensive techniques used by the nursing profession. Her work has led to important changes in patient care. For example, the splitting of the nurse–patient relationship is no longer the norm: whereas different nurses used to deal with different aspects of the same patient, now each patient is assigned a key nurse who gets to know his patient in his totality. Similarly, emotional detachment and the denial of feelings about our patients are no longer advocated in many institutions, where staff are encouraged to discuss their work, often in a group setting. However, such staff discussion groups are still far too rare, which makes any hope of providing better patient care without the provision of support for the staff quite unrealistic. We all need to hold onto our defences, particularly in treating the very ill and dying as well as the mentally disturbed.

One of the most established of institutional defences is the split between medical and nursing staff: it enables surgeons, for instance, to feel that they carry out the 'real, important treatment work' whilst nurses are made to feel that they are there to 'pick up the pieces', particularly the emotional pieces. This institutional split also makes it easier for patients to deny their feelings by splitting doctors against nurses.

One patient, on the same surgical ward as Mr Smith, illustrated this most clearly. Mr Thomas appeared as an incredibly resilient man of 70, who prided himself on having been with the Gurkha regiment at the end of the war. His tough attitude seemed to derive from a sense that he had to survive, whatever the cost. His early life story was in fact a sad one, since he had become an orphan early on in childhood: his father had apparently died on the battlefield when Mr Thomas was only an infant and his mother died when he was seven. A tough though idealised upbringing with his grandparents had made him determined never to show any emotional weakness or vulnerability, both physical or emotional. His main defence appeared to be a manic narcissistic one which involved both the denial of loss or vulnerability as well as a sense of invincibility or omnipotence.

As a result of his and his surgeon's wish to preserve his limbs at all costs, he endured at least seven major operations to improve the blood supply to his legs. I saw him at death's door on more than one occasion but he pulled through, physically and emotionally, in a most extraordinary fashion by both denying any fear or grief and by idealising the medical staff, particularly his surgeon.

Following one of his later operations, a very difficult one which nearly killed him, his key nurse noticed that she was finding it difficult to look after him. She found Mr Smith's 'chirpy' behaviour quite intolerable nor could she stand stand his 'gluey niceness' as he lay on the brink of death riddled with drains. His endless idealisation of his surgeon made her feel that, as far as Mr Smith was concerned, she had played no part in looking after him throughout what had been for her a very frightening and difficult few months. She had in fact seen him close to death and had feared for him. His denial of any such feelings and anxieties made her feel rejected. In a sense he was making her enact what he felt was being done to him in his internal world, a world from his childhood where males were seen as idealised and powerful, and where women were hard and ungiving.

This example of 'projective identification' illustrates yet again the power of this particular defence mechanism which, if not understood by the medical team, can lead to the destructive situation seen with Mr Smith, aggravated in this case by the additional rivalries Mr Thomas stirred up between nurses and doctors.

A few days after having survived yet another 8-hour operation, I found Mr Thomas in tears and, for a moment, I wondered if he was finally in touch with his feelings of loss and pain. However, I soon realised that his tears were not those of sorrow but due to guilt and fear: he had noticed that his surgeon had an eye infection and he was sure the surgeon's infection was the result of a spurt of blood from a patient in theatre. It became clear that he was also convinced that the patient was himself and he was terrified lest his consultant should die. 'I cannot bear to see him ill – he is my life!' Mr Thomas moaned. He felt he had infected and put at risk the very man on whom his life depended.

I felt that, despite his attempts to split off his destructive anger in order to protect his potential 'saviour', his anxiety at being so terribly dependent and so close to death had broken through his earlier defences. He was now 'psychotic' in the sense that he was losing touch with reality: the destructive anger he felt had become his actual contaminated blood which threatened to kill his potential saviour. He felt guilty about having brought this about. The projection of his split-off angry feelings manifest in the contaminated blood he imagined had infected his surgeon is an example of a delusional projection.

In my view, Mr Thomas's anxieties arose from reliving the terrifying feelings of disintegration and helplessness which he had possibly experienced as an infant, and then later when he had lost his mother. Such feelings would be even more powerful if, as an infant, he had not experienced the containing effect of a relationship with a 'good enough' mother or, in Bowlby's terms, a secure attachment relationship. For the Kleinian psychoanalyst however, such as Isabel Menzies, what Mr Smith and his nurses are believed to be experiencing, is the reliving of their most primitive infantile phantasies stirred up by the objective situation that confronts them, a situation that 'bears a striking resemblance to the phantasy situations that exist in every individual in the deepest and most primitive levels of the mind .... The elements of these phantasies may be traced back to earliest infancy' (1970, pp.5–6).

This is a time when the infant is believed by Kleinians to experience the effects of the opposing 'life and death instincts' which she projects on to her external objects, to then internalise them again in the creation of an inner world which, because of the operation of her aggressive forces, contains many damaged, injured, or dead objects: 'The atmosphere is charged with death and destruction' (1970, p.6). The resulting inner world thus owes its existence to the activities of the 'death instinct'.

For Klein and her followers, the 'death instinct' obviates the need to understand why some of us are more prone to experience these terrifying and infantile anxieties than others. What is also glossed over when fears are explained in terms of the 'death instinct', are the very real anxieties and phantasies which death evokes in all of us and how we attempt to cope with them.

Some analysts do address this all too human dilemma; Earl Hopper describes this terrible fear as 'annihilation anxiety', which he sees as being caused by an experience of absolute helplessness and failed dependency (1991, p.608). Such an experience elicits a defence against this fear of annihilation, a defence Hopper describes as 'encapsulation'. In this process the lost or abandoning object is introjected and fused with the self to produce a 'split off' encapsulated 'foreign body in the psyche'. Hopper believes that this phenomenon has been largely ignored because therapists have colluded with their patients in order to avoid the analysis of defences against the terror of annihilation and all the overwhelming feelings such a process arouses. His conclusion is of considerable importance for, as he states:

> The study of encapsulation and the fear of annihilation leads to the study of 'trauma'. I have the impression, both from my own practice and from private discussions with colleagues about their's, that *most patients have had traumatic experience* [my italics] … . This topic continues to raise the most contentious issues in psychoanalysis. Our current views about the nature, causes and consequences of traumatic experience are diverse, confused and curiously nascent. In fact, our views have been encapsulated, perhaps in connexion with a basic fault in the development of our theories.

> *(1991, pp.619–620)*

The psychoanalyst Harry Guntrip, one of Fairbairn's closest followers, touched on this same phenomenon when discussing the origins of guilt, the guilt Mr Smith was expressing and which is for Klein a consequence of our innate destructiveness.

> The core of psychological distress is not *guilt* but *fear*. Guilt is a form of fear, but it arises at the stage when the child is becoming socialised and capable of realising the effects of actions on other people, and the nature of their reactions of anger and condemnation … . There are much more primi-

tive fears than that, fears not of the effect of our *strong* and dangerous needs and impulses, but of our infantile *weakness*, littleness, and helplessness in the face of an environment which either fails to give the support we needed as infants or else was positively threatening. Human beings all prefer to be bad and strong rather than weak. The diagnosis of guilt allows us to feel that the source of our troubles with ourselves and others is our possession of mighty and powerful instinctive forces in our make-up, which take a great deal of controlling and civilising

(Guntrip, 1969, p.31; Guntrip's italics)

As he stresses, such a view of ourselves goes hand in hand with our competitive Western culture where contempt is felt for weakness.

A diagnosis which traces psychological troubles to our innate strength supports our self respect and is what is today called an ego-booster. A diagnosis which traces our troubles to deep-seated fears and feelings of weakness in the face of life has always been unacceptable.

(1969, p.31)

Erikson, too, acknowledged the importance of infantile fear throughout our lives, a fear that springs from our early experience of being small, dependent and vulnerable (1950, p.394). We also know from a personal confession of Freud's, the inventor of the 'death instinct', that helplessness was one of the two things he hated most, the other being poverty, which in our society is another form of helplessness (Becker, 1973, p.115).

Returning to Guntrip, it becomes clear that for him the 'death instinct' is a 'moral defence' against terrifying feelings of helplessness and fears of annihilation. It is a defence which we will encounter with increasing frequency in patients suffering the psychological effects of trauma as well as in psychoanalysts seeking to make sense of these patients' deep feelings of guilt. What perhaps has become clearer, thanks to the work of Klein with very young children, is how early in life this defence mechanism comes into being. We may recall that, according to Piaget, the child begins to make sense of the world through the use of 'magical thinking' from the age of about one and a half years to two years, until the age of about seven. 'The most primitive forms of causality found in the child seem, in fact, due to confusion between reality and thought, or, more accurately, to a constant assimilation of external processes to schemas arising from internal experience' (Piaget, 1929, p.157). Piaget stresses that this means that if the child believes in the all-powerfulness of thought, it is because, at certain levels of cognition, she does not distinguish her thought from that of others nor her self from the external world. He adds that such a conception of the world is reinforced by the parents' prompt response to the infant's needs.

At this stage, for example, a child can perform an action or a mental operation (such as counting) and believe that this action can influence a particular event she desires or fears. In the same way, a child can believe that reality can be modified by a thought, a word or a look. Piaget stresses how magical thinking is often used by children to avoid misfortune: 'This happens particularly often with those children – a much greater number than would be supposed – who are haunted every night by fears of death, either for themselves or their parents' (1929, p.161).

He gives the example of a boy who from the ages of six to eight was terrified by the thought of not waking up in the morning. He developed a ritual to overcome his fear of death, counting fast between the loud rattles emitted by his radiator at night. 'If I passed a certain number, I was saved. I used the same method to know whether my father, who slept in the next room, was on the point of death or not' (1929, p.161). Piaget adds: 'The relation of these facts to the manias of the insane and their defensive gestures is clearly brought out' (1929, p.161).

One of the examples Piaget gives links up very clearly with the concept of guilt in relation to magical thinking in childhood. Mademoiselle Vé was a little girl of four or five when her mother became very ill. She was told by a servant that she would die in a few days. Mademoiselle Vé had a little toy horse she treasured.

> A curious thought came into my head: I must give up my horse in order to make my mother better. It was more than I could do at once and cost me the greatest of pain ... . I know that in the greatest distress I ended by smashing my horse to bits, and that on seeing my mother up, a few days later, I was convinced it was my sacrifice that had mysteriously cured her, and this conviction lasted for a long while.
>
> *(1929, p.163)*

Anyone familiar with the Catholic religion knows only too well how steeped in magical thinking is the belief in the power of the sacrifice.

Indeed, as Piaget points out, traces of magical ideas found in children are present among normal civilised adults. Who has not made a recoiling movement when he sees two bicycles or cars about to collide in the street? We act for a second as if we could prevent the collision by some form of magic participation. Piaget describes a man about to give a lecture, who goes out for his daily walk. He was about to turn back when he caught himself feeling compelled to go right to his usual end point in order for his lecture to be a success. Such rituals are essential to people who suffer from obsessional disorders, but they are also intrinsically linked to most religious practices for the same reasons: they give people a sense of magical control which protects them from the unspeakable terrors of existence and death.

The defence mechanisms we have so far highlighted occur in

so-called 'normal' people when under severe stress. As Vittorio Guidano points out in *Complexity of the Self*, once we can begin to see the self as an organiser of inner and outer experiences which ensures us our sense of perceived identity, then we can understand how the maintenance of this sense of identity becomes as important as life itself (1987, p.3). 'Any interruption of our personal identity is invariably experienced as a loss of the very sense of reality, undoubtedly the most disrupting and devastating emotion that any human being can feel' (1987, p.87).

We know from reading Kohut's work that just such experiences lead to violent attacks of narcissistic rage: feeling helpless, mortified, paralysed with fear leaves us in a state that is so unbearable it must be changed: the offending selfobject or the totally denigrated self must disappear even if the whole world goes up in flames.

The greater the threat to our sense of who we feel we are, the more powerful the defence processes we use. Some of these, such as splitting and denial, projection and projective identification, are sometimes referred to as 'primitive' defence processes. They are very much in evidence during psychotic episodes when we lose the capacity to test reality against our internal representations. Threatened by the fear of psychic death or disintegration, the psychotic will use every defence at his or her disposal in order to survive.

My first psychotic patient illustrates this very clearly. He was an intelligent man of 35 called Mr Davies, diagnosed as suffering from paranoid schizophrenia. He had spent a great part of his adult life in the back wards of a psychiatric hospital, sedated with huge doses of tranquillisers. When he first presented to the psychotherapeutic team who took over his care, Mr Davies spent most of his time talking about the voice of a man from the British Broadcasting Corporation (BBC), who was constantly commenting on his activities in a most critical and persecuting manner. His consultant, a psychoanalyst of considerable repute, interpreted these delusional ideas about the BBC as a desperate and unconscious attempt on his part to feel important when he really felt so small and helpless. After all, it was pointed out, not many British people are important enough to be hounded by the BBC.

With time and much care and attention from nurses and doctors, Mr Davies began to show more interest in the outside world. His medication was considerably reduced and he began to take classes in mathematics. Whenever he referred to being persecuted by the BBC, both staff and patients would ask him what was troubling him and attempt to respond to some of his needs. The paranoid delusion and the accompanying hallucinations would cease, only to reappear when Mr Davies felt threatened. This happened in therapy, particularly towards the end of our relationship. Through the medium of his 'voices' he could let me know about his angry and contemptuous feelings.

The mechanisms involved in this man's psychotic defences involved the repression of past painful experiences with massive splitting of his 'good' and 'bad' feelings, the latter being then projected into his auditory hallucinations. His was a permanent 'paranoid–schizoid' state with all that this means in terms of how he experienced the world and his feelings. He had, in all probability, never really been able to reconcile his angry destructive feelings with his caring loving feelings. This crucial psychological development referred to earlier as the 'depressive position' can only take place within the safe and containing environment of a 'secure' attachment relationship. It is what object-relations theorists define as a prerequisite for the formation of real and satisfying relationships with others. Although Mr Davies had no access to such feelings, he could, with the help of the BBC man, feel that he was never quite alone and that in a strange way he mattered, however unpleasant the persecution.

This need to matter to someone, be it even a delusional 'other', seems at the core of human psychic existence. For those individuals who cannot be valued for being 'good', being 'bad' is preferable to not being at all. For those individuals whose hold on life is even more precarious because of early failures in attunement or genetic predispositions, salvation can lie in the creation of a psychotic world in the image of their internal world. In this way psychologically damaged human beings can survive, but at what costs? The costs are revealed both in how they perceive the world and in the hidden rage that throbs beneath their defences.

As we have seen in the examples above, the use of psychological defences, particularly the so-called 'primitive defences', can profoundly alter the individual's perception of both internal and external reality and often compromise other facets of cognition. This observation raises an extremely important point, highlighted by Guidano: 'Our way of seeing reality – and ourselves inside reality – essentially depends upon how we see and conceive of ourselves. In this way our models of reality are provided with stability and coherence in an ever-changing world' (1987, p.90). He adds: 'Idiosyncratic problem-solving strategies also permit ane to actively manipulate environmental situations so as to produce events that are in keeping with one's perceived identity' (1987, p.91).

In this way, people can create, both in their own minds and in their environment, a social reality that effectively confirms the very conceptions that direct their mental processes.

This phenomenon was clearly illustrated in the two analyses of Mr Z by Kohut and is extremely relevant to any discussion on the origins of human violence. If human perception is relative to the psychic structures of the self, individuals will tend to create a world in the image of these same psychic structures.

Returning to the origin of human defence mechanisms, what is now clear is that when subject to deprivation, loss or abuse, people can only survive by doing violence to their feelings. Pain and rage must be suppressed or denied in order to remain close to those on whom our lives depend. Such feelings can be 'cut off' in order to remain in control, like the 'avoidant' infant of the Strange Situation. These destructive feelings can then also be projected and subsequently attacked in the 'other' as Mr Smith did or, as with Mr Davies, the reality of the past is 'lost' only to be recreated in the image of the psychotic's inner world of paranoid persecution.

If it is realised that the infant's and the child's most pressing and overriding need is to be loved, all else falls into place: she will do anything for her parents' approval and affection, even if it means sacrificing her own sense of who she is and what she feels, in favour of a 'false' but approved 'self'. Sullivan and Winnicott both referred to this developmental process.

One such a 'false self' is the 'compulsive carer' who deals with his own needs by repressing them and then splitting them off to project them into the 'other' whom he can care for in the form of a baby, a partner or a patient.

Stern gives us an example of a child who learns in the first few months of her life how to 'dissociate' in order to avoid a conflict with her mother. This adaptive defence could well turn out to be the beginning of the development of a false self (Stern, 1985). Molly was a small infant whose mother was very controlling. She decided what toy her daughter was to play with, how Molly should play with it and when Molly was to finish playing with it. The mother controlled the interaction to such an extent that it was hard to trace Molly's own interests and excitement. But, she found an adaptation.

> She gradually became more compliant. Instead of actively avoiding or opposing these intrusions, she became one of those enigmatic gazers into space. She could stare through you, her eyes focused somewhere at infinity and her facial expressions opaque enough to be just uninterpretable, and at the same time remain in good contingent contact and by and large do what she was invited or told to do. Watching her over the months was like watching her self-regulation of excitement slip away .... When playing alone she did not recover it, remaining somewhat aloof from exciting engagement with things. This general dampening of her affectivity ... was still apparent at age three years.
>
> *(Stern, 1985, pp.196–197)*

These dissociative processes provide the individual with the possibility of remaining in contact with his or her attachment figure whilst repressing the feelings of destructive rage which arise from narcissistic injuries, the pain of which can, in cases of loss and abuse, be so intense as to be associated with the neurophysological changes referred to earlier.

These 'split off' feelings of rage and destructiveness, and their associated painful memories, become unconscious and remain so for as long as the individual's psychological defence structures can maintain the split. In certain conditions, either the defences 'break down' as happened with Mr Thomas under severe stress, or destructive feelings can be indirectly expressed, usually through displacement onto a culturally approved object. 'Displacement' is one of the most commonly used defences in the maintenance of the self.

Thus, when faced with the reality of a fatal cancer, many patients will attempt to avoid their fears by unconsciously presenting with other apparently more treatable symptoms. In this way they obtain some relief from their terrifying anxieties.

Similarly, the insecurely attached individual who cannot experience the real satisfaction of ever feeling 'at one' with the 'other' will, when faced with threats to his sense of identity, resort to displacing his violent feelings on to 'safe' culturally approved targets such as women or Jews, or he will project what he disowns about himself on to 'others'. As Durbin and Bowlby (1939) point out, this is particularly common in groups whose members project their violent feelings on to some minority which ends up carrying the 'sins of the people'. For these authors, it is because of our fear of loss, that our aggression is repressed to be 'transformed', through mechanisms such as displacement and projection, into group violence. The structure of the 'group-self', like that of the hospital institution mentioned earlier on, can be used to bolster the defences of the individual self, albeit at the expense of the 'other'. At this point it seems important to note, with Erikson, that there is therefore a danger in abandoning prejudices particularly for the 'unbalanced and neurotic individual'.

> As he abandons all prejudice, he forfeits the mechanism of projection: his danger becomes introspection and 'introjection', an over-concern with the evil in himself. One may say he becomes prejudiced against himself. Some measure of this must be tolerated by men of good will. Men of good will must learn to fear accurately and to cope judiciously with the anxiety aroused by a renunciation of prejudice.
>
> *(1950, pp.406–407)*

The link between self and other is intrinsic to the whole concept of the self and to our sense of identity. Erikson defines it as: 'the immediate perception of one's self sameness and continuity in time, and the simultaneous perception of the fact that others recognise one's sameness and continuity' (1946).

George Mead, as early as 1934, was well aware of the fact that if the individual possesses a sense of self, it is only in relation to other selves.

He, too, saw it not as a structure but as a process of interactions between one's organism and others (1934, p.179). As for the development of the self, Mead saw it taking place in two stages:

> At the first of these stages, the individual's self is constituted simply by an organisation of the particular attitudes of other individuals towards himself and toward one another in the specific social acts in which he participates with them. But at the second stage in the full development of the individual's self that self is constituted not only by an organisation of these particular individual's attitudes, but also by an organisation of the social attitudes of the generalised other or the social group as a whole to which he belongs.
>
> *(1934, p.158)*

If we focus on the first stage, we may recall that the development of the self is inextricably linked to the development of internal working models within the context of attachment relationships. The outcome of such an approach is the conception of the self as an inner organisation.

The implications of this organisational view of the self are essentially twofold. The first is that the developing self will reflect the quality of the relationships between the infant and her caregiver; in most cases this is the mother but need not necessarily be so. If attuned to her baby's needs, the mother has the empathy required to sustain a secure attachment with her infant, who will then develop a sense of high self-esteem. If, however, mother is unable to empathise with her baby's needs, the insecure attachment relationship that develops will make it hard for the infant to feel good about herself. Thus, children with histories of 'avoidant' attachments, will have feelings of low self-worth, isolation and angry rejection, which they sometimes turn inwards.

These two possible outcomes lead us to the second implication of an organisational view of the self. Once formed, the self will tend to perpetuate itself in an attempt to preserve its integrity in the face of environmental changes. This tendency for continuity is ensured by the active structuring of experience by the self via the internal working models which unconsciously predispose us to form relationships congruent with our earlier ones and with our view of oneselves. 'The core of self lies in patterns of behavioural and affective regulation, which grant continuity to experience despite development and changes in context' (Sroufe, 1989, p.83).

However, we will recall that evidence given in Chapter 6 showed that some women could, in the context of a caring supportive relationship, look back at their early relationships with their parents, and see them for what they were truly worth. Such an insightful acknowledgement, similar to what takes place in therapy, appears to lead to changes in the internal working models with a resultant improvement in self-esteem and an associated capacity for empathy (Main, Kaplan and Cassidy, 1985; Ricks, 1985; Crowell and Feldman, 1988). Internal working models can change but they tend not to do so because of the organisational function of the self in the preservation of its integrity.

The development of empathy

Thus, the first stage in the development of the self has important implications for the study of human violence, for, as we have seen in previous chapters, children with 'avoidant' attachments are prone to be aggressive. Similarly, they also show low empathy scores, unlike their securely attached counterparts who appear to have internalised their parents' capacity to tune into the needs and feelings of others. This is an extremely valuable social attribute, for not only is empathy an important source of altruism, but it is also a possible inhibitor of aggressive behaviour (Staub, 1984).

Indeed, whilst there appears to exist an early primitive emotional responsiveness to others, the feeling of empathy we are referring to is dependent on a parallel cognitive elaboration of the sense of other people as separate.

According to Stern, empathy begins with the realisation of a sense of oneness with the other, in a feeling of identification with the other which he describes as 'intersubjective relatedness' or 'affect attunement' which begins to take place around the age of 9 months. This sense of oneness in the infant with respect to her mother goes hand-in-hand with a positive evaluation of the other. Both can only evolve in the context of a warm, loving infant–caregiver relation and not in conditions of parental hostility and rejection.

The fact that a high self-esteem and empathy are linked is not surprising, since empathy is in part an extension of the self to other people. As Staub points out, 'a poor self concept makes it more difficult to extend the boundaries of the self in benevolent ways' (1984, p.142). Racism, nationalism and prejudice are the inevitable consequences.

As Stern acknowledges, if this affective attunement turns out to be a basic psychological need, the implications will be momentous for clinical theory and very much in keeping with Kohut's theories. It also throws doubts on the established psychoanalytic view of development promulgated by Mahler, Pine and Bergman (1975). The latter describes the infant as starting life in an undifferentiated state of fusion with her mother, from which she emerges to establish a separate and individuated self. Stern thinks that, as a result of this theory, theoreticians failed to notice that it is the state of affective attunement that paradoxically allows for the creation of mutually held mental states and for 'the reality-based joining (even merging) of inner experience'. So, in his view, 'both separation/individuation and new forms of experiencing union (or being with) emerge equally out of the same experience of intersubjectivity' or affective attunement (Stern, 1985, p.127).

So whatever else happens at this time in an infant's life, much depends on the caregiver's capacity to tune in to the infant's affective state. Thus, by selectively resonating to some of their infant's states and not to others, parents unconsciously mould their child's subjective and interpersonal life. In this way a 'false self' can begin to develop.

> We are describing the first step in that process, the exclusion from intersubjective sharing of certain experiences. Whatever happens next, whether the experience excluded from the interpersonal sphere becomes a part of the 'false self' or a 'not me' phenomenon, whether it is simply relegated out of consciousness, one way or another, or whether it remains a private but accessible part of the self, the beginning lies here.
>
> *(1985, p.210)*

What Stern is describing here is the necessary repression and splitting off of feelings and memories which could threaten the infant with the loss of her parent's love. This process is of the utmost importance in the understanding of human violence. It can mean, as with the 'avoidant' child, the splitting off of important internal working models. This is particularly pronounced in abused children.

For example, a father presents for therapy because he finds himself becoming increasingly enraged with his young son, whom he ends up beating, much against his principles. After some months in treatment, it becomes clear that it is at times when this man feels particularly needy, for instance when his therapist is away, that he becomes abusive towards his child. At other times, father and son appear to have a good caring relationship.

This man initially described his parents as good enough parents, though he had few recollections of his childhood. It became clear from the transference relationship that, because of a severe chronic illness, his father to whom he had been very close became unable to give his son, then aged seven, the support and understanding he had needed, especially as his mother was far more involved with his younger siblings. So now, when this man felt 'needy', he would not recognise such feelings, having learnt to deny and repress them throughout childhood. Thus, dissociated from consciousness, this state of neediness would be projected onto his own son, whose natural demands would then be experienced by the patient as quite unbearable. He would then, like the father of his childhood, shout and hit out at his child, recreating within their present relationship the split off, unconscious and painful relationship of his past.

Similar processes of dissociation can also mean the splitting of a parental figure into idealised and denigrated internal objects, resulting in incongruous descriptions of early relationships, such as that of an abusing parent being described by his child as a very special parent. As Kohut was to emphasise, the need to idealise a parent stems from a need to feel 'good' by being part of an idealised relationship. This is often a desperate attempt to make up for the absence of empathy or, as he puts it, of 'mirroring', in the infant–caregiver dyad: idealisation provides a second opportunity to make good a potentially deprived childhood experience.

The verbal self   *real self*

This process of splitting into various selves becomes even more obvious during Mead's second stage in the development of the self, when it becomes increasingly subject to the pressures and attitudes of the group. This is the period of the formation of the verbal self, a time when the language process becomes essential to the self. Through the experience of learning how to talk, the infant and her caregivers find new ways of being with one another, for the child to individuate within the new context of language, with all the additional skills and dimensions it can contribute to these developmental experiences.

However, as Stern says 'language is a double-edged sword', which can, not only reinforce splits that already exist, but also be a source of splitting in its own right. Understanding how these processes take place gives us new insights into other forms of defences used to maintain the integrity of the self.

On turning our attention back to the child who is learning to talk in her second year, we are reminded of the fact that experience lived is not the same as experience verbally represented. Similarly, we become aware that, through language, parents can so easily ratify the split between their baby's 'true self' and 'false self' by simply verbally endorsing aspects of their child's behaviour that they like and ignoring those which they do not. As a result, the true self tends to become an amalgamation of sensations which are often not linguistically represented. This allows for personal and emotional meanings to remain inaccessible both to the self and to the other. In this way self-deception and the distortion of reality begins to take place in the service of the self. This is because through the use of language and symbolic thinking children can modify and transcend reality. For example they can symbolically represent a parent as 'bad' or 'good'. They can create their own 'life narrative', one that is dissociated from the 'true self'.

We can begin to see how language does indeed cause a split in the experience of the self. However, this should come as no surprise for, if the self is an organiser of experience, as it has been defined earlier on, it is in great part through the activities of the 'verbal self' that this organising activity takes place. Bearing in mind that, in the language of the neurosciences, the verbal self is referred to as a language system which exists in relation to other systems and subsystems, we can join

Michael Gazzaniga and his team in trying to understand the different activities of the two human hemispheres. In their attempt to investigate the workings of the right hemisphere in a split brain patient whose *corpus callosum* had been cut, what they could not fail to note was 'that our sense of subjective awareness arises out of our dominant left hemisphere's unrelenting need to explain actions taken from any one of a multitude of mental systems that dwell within us' (Gazzaniga and Le Doux, 1978).

These systems, which coexist with the language system, are not necessarily in touch with the language processes prior to a behaviour. Once actions are taken, the left speech hemisphere, observing these behaviours, constructs a story as to their meaning, and this in turn becomes part of the verbal system's understanding of the person (Gazzaniga, 1983).

This does not mean that language is identical to 'subjective awareness' or 'consciousness' but as they state:

> it would seem more prudent to think that the left language system is intimately linked to a cognitive system that strives for consistency and order in the buzzing chaos of behaviours that are constantly being produced by the total organism.
>
> *(Gazzaniga, 1983, p.536)*

These neuropsychological findings have important implications. The first is the recognition that the self is a conglomeration of selves – a sociological entity – and that the essential task of our verbal self is to construct a reality based on our actual behaviour.

What these authors are also saying is that these multiple mental systems of behaviour in the brain, each with the capacity to produce behaviour and each with its own impulses for action, are systems which are not necessarily conversant internally, In other words, one system can be 'unconscious' or 'split off' from the other and, in particular, from the verbal self. The function of this verbal self then appears to be that of giving meaning and consistency to behavioural manifestations derived from these other selves. In so doing the verbal self invents a plausible explanation.

For example, a split brain subject is given a command like 'rub', which is presented to his right hemisphere (which in this rare case has some capacity to understand speech). He immediately proceeds to rub the back of his head. When asked what the command was, he said 'itch'. This is the conclusion his verbal left hemisphere came to after it had 'noticed' the patient's behaviour, not having any direct knowledge of what message was actually projected to the right hemisphere since communication between the two hemispheres had been cut off (Gazzaniga and Le Doux, 1978).

We have here our first neuropsychological evidence of a defence mechanism at the service of the self in its need to preserve its sense of consistency. As we can see, neuropsychology is re-discovering what Freud and many of his followers have made so clear, the need for defences in the preservation of the self, even if this involves splitting of the self itself.

This brings us back to the phenomenon of dissociation and splitting in the formation of the self and its links with language. We have seen how this process takes place within the context of the infant–caregiver dyad. The latter is itself a subsystem of a larger social system or group which, through the process of language, imposes further distortions and splits in the self. As Mead pointed out: 'What we have here is a situation in which there can be different selves, and it is dependent upon the set of social reactions that is involved as to which self we are going to be' (1934, p.143).

But there is another effect of the use of language in the formation of the self. As long ago as the 1920s, two anthropologists called Sapir and Whorf became famous for introducing the concept of 'linguistic relativity'. Their hypothesis was that language determines to a great extent the way we perceive the world about us.

> Human beings do not live in the objective world alone, nor alone in the world of social activity as is ordinarily understood, but are very much at the mercy of the particular language which has become the medium of expression for their society .... The fact of the matter is that the 'real world' is unconsciously built up on the language habits of the group .... We see and we hear and otherwise experience very largely as we do because the language habits of our community predispose to certain choices of interpretations.
>
> *(Spier, Hallowell and Neuman, 1941)*

Other anthropologists have suggested that the grammatical structure of the language is in itself an important way of delineating how aspects of 'reality' are related (Dell, 1980).

For example, Western languages divide phenomena into subjects and predicates, which leads us to believe that this does indeed reflect the 'real' structure of the world. However, the language of the Hopi Indians has quite a different grammar which describes the world in terms of processes, the continuing flow of events one in relation to the other.

The concept of 'linguistic relativity' is not a comforting one for those of us who would like to believe that there is such a thing as an absolute 'Truth'. The idea that our perception of the world is structured by the language we use is in fact all too easily ignored. However, recent evidence from the field of psychiatry and psychology has not only confirmed the idea that language determines our view of reality but that it is also intrinsically linked with our sense of identity: through the study of bilingual patients both in psychotherapy and in psychiatry, it is becoming clear that our sense of self is very closely bound up with the language we speak. This was made very clear to the author when treating a 19-year-old English man, who was diagnosed as hypomanic with a recurring history of manic–depressive illnesses. He was studying languages and had recently learnt Spanish.

One day, whilst still severely disturbed and suffering from hallucinations and thought disorder, he picked up my office phone and began to talk to me in Spanish, knowing that I spoke the language. Then something quite inexplicable happened. As he talked to me, he became quite coherent: all evidence of his thought disorder disappeared. He repeated the telephone call twice and then he remarked, still in Spanish: 'Isn't it strange but when I speak to you in Spanish my mind is quite clear and then, when I talk to you in English I become all confused again.'

Following this extraordinary experience, I proceeded to search the literature and discovered just how important are the links between our sense of self and the language we speak (Zulueta, 1984, 1990). Our maternal and group language determines not only how we experience the world outside but also how we experience ourselves.

It was Erikson (1950) who stressed how the deprivation of a sense of identity can lead to murder. Recent events in the countries of Eastern Europe seem to confirm this, for they are making us painfully aware of how important the issue of cultural and linguistic identity still is for all of us. After years of oppression and trauma, faced with the loss of all their old beliefs and threatened with material insecurity, people seem to long for a sense of certainty. Belonging to a common language and culture may become the only certainty in society, the only value beyond ambiguity and doubt.

If our mother tongue can and does give us a sense of security, so can a second language, if learnt after puberty, act as a 'linguistic defence', protecting the self from memories and feelings which are too painful or overwhelming, as was the case with the young linguist in my care. This discovery has important implications both for our understanding of the links between violence and our sense of self, and for the psychotherapeutic treatment of bilinguals: a second language can act as a defence in the protection of the self or it can become another manifestation of the 'false self'.

Conclusion

We can conclude that the defence of our sense of self is clearly of crucial importance to mankind. Indeed it is striking how intertwined are both our sense of self and our capacity for destructive aggression. A weak sense of self and a low self-esteem, with their origins in deprivation, loss and abuse, all contribute to human violence. When cultural and parental conditions fail to give us a sense of worth, the self knows only how to survive. The 'other' must become the 'object' of a self that needs to be in control. Reminders of inner weakness and pain must be banished, even at the cost of destruction of the self or dehumanisation of the other.

When cultural and parental conditions allow, the self develops self-esteem and empathy, a capacity to relate that bridges the differences, tunes into the other and makes of this affective attunement another source of self-esteem.

We can begin to see how the self, with its roots in the psychophysi-ology of attachment relations, can be both the instigator and the con-tainer of our destructive feelings. What needs to be studied further is just how the self survives when subject to severe trauma, be it in child-hood or in later life. This will be the subject of the next section.

Part II
The Psychology of Trauma

Chapter 9
The Unspeakable: Child Sexual Abuse

'Don't tell, don't think. Don't what ever else you do, don't feel. If you feel, the pain will be there again. Don't.'

Elly Danica (1988)

The traumatic origins of 'functional physical disturbances'

The study of psychological trauma began when Sigmund Freud discovered that his first 18 hysterical patients had all been sexually abused during their childhood. He rightly felt he had made a momentous discovery but, as it turned out, the psychiatric world of his time was not ready to hear him.

It was in April of 1896 that a young and keen Dr Freud gave his paper entitled 'The aetiology of hysteria' to the Society for Psychiatry and Neurology in Vienna. Krafft-Ebing, the distinguished professor of the Department of Psychiatry, was chairing the meeting. As Freud was to subsequently write to his friend Wilhelm Fliess (Schur, 1972, p.104):

> A lecture on the aetiology of hysteria at the Psychiatric Society met with an icy reception from the asses, and from Krafft-Ebing the strange comment: It sounds like a scientific fairy tale. And this after one has demonstrated to them a solution to a more than thousand-year-old problem, a 'source of the Nile'!
>
> *(Schur, 1972, p.104)*

What he had revealed to his illustrious male audience was that:

> At the bottom of every case of hysteria there are one or more occurrences of premature sexual experience, occurrences which belong to the earliest years of childhood but which can be reproduced through the work of psycho-analysis in spite of the intervening decades.
>
> *(1896a, p. 203)*

139

Freud continues:

> Our view then is that infantile sexual experiences are the fundamental pre-
> condition for hysteria ... and that it is they which create the hysterical symp-
> toms, but that they do not do so immediately, but remain without effect to
> begin with and only exercise a pathogenic action later, when they have been
> aroused after puberty in the form of unconscious memories.
>
> *(1896a, p.212)*

Having pre-empted all possible objections as to the genuineness of his
patients' accounts, he continued:

> Sexual experiences in childhood consisting in stimulation of the genitals,
> coitus-like acts, and so on, must therefore be recognised, in the last analysis,
> as being the traumas which lead to a hysterical reaction to events at puberty
> and to the development of hysterical symptoms.
>
> *(1896a, pp. 206–207)*

The abuser, he discovered, was unhappily all too often a close relative

> Who has initiated the child into sexual intercourse and has maintained a
> regular love relationship with it – a love relationship moreover with its men-
> tal side developed – which has often lasted for years.
>
> *(1896a, p.208)*

He found that the sexual experiences dated back to the fourth or third
or even the second year of life. He was also convinced that if sexual
relationships took place between two children it implied that one of
them had previously been seduced by an adult and that he was repeating the same procedures he had been subjected to.

In this extraordinary paper Freud also addresses the issue of childhood vulnerability to traumatic experiences of this nature: 'Injuries sus-
tained by an organ which is as yet immature, or by a function which is
in process of developing, often cause more severe and lasting effects
than they could do in maturer years' (1896a).

Towards the end of his paper, Freud affirms that the aetiological role
of infantile sexual experience is not confined to hysteria but holds
good equally for the remarkable neurosis of obsessions, and perhaps
also, indeed, for the various forms of chronic paranoia and other functional psychoses. He was to rename these the 'neuroses and psychoses
of defence'. Freud ended his lecture with a challenge:

> The new method of research gives wide access to a new element in the psy-
> chical field of events, namely, to processes of thought which have remained
> unconscious...Thus it inspires us with the hope of a new and better under-
> standing of all functional psychical disturbances. I cannot believe that psy-
> chiatry will long hold back from making use of this new pathway to
> knowledge.
>
> *(1896a, p.221)*

His hope has not yet been fulfilled. Freud himself was to formally turn
his back on his patients and the reality of their traumatic experiences.

Much has been written as to why Freud later denied the importance of childhood seduction and why psychoanalysts still tend to underplay its importance (Masson, 1984). The reasons are many and have already been partly addressed. However, in my view, it is only when reliving the horrors of childhood seduction with a patient that we may begin to understand why the psychoanalytic world clings to the importance of childhood sexual 'phantasies' at the expense of reality.

The treatment of sexual abuse

The account* that follows describes the brief therapy of a young woman who was sexually and physically abused during her childhood. Rachel will soon be writing her own story, an intensely personal account of a harrowing childhood during which she was abused both physically and emotionally by both her parents, and sexually by her father. Hers is a living testimony of how much pain and violence parental abuse can engender in children. It is also an example of how psychiatrists tend to remain blind to the traumatic origins of their patients' emotional disturbances.

Rachel was born in England 24 years ago. She was apparently a quiet child who never cried. Her mother was a housewife whom her daughter described as a highly emotional person who suffered from 'nerves'. She had a very low self-esteem and seemed to be unable to give her daughter the love and support she needed. As a result, separation from mother was always difficult for Rachel, who became very distressed when she had to go to school. This attachment relationship was not helped by the fact that, when only 18 months old, she had to spend 2 months in hospital, separated from her mother while being treated for the effects of a fall.

Her father was a businessman with a strong character who would at times become aggressive and violent, particularly when drunk. Rachel lived in fear of him. She also had an older brother and a younger sister but they have scarcely figured in her account of her life. Hers was always a lonely existence. At school, she had no friends and was desperately unhappy, so much so that at the age of nine she was referred to a psychiatrist. She saw him for a long time, during which they would play with puzzles together. As she said, this did not help her to make friends and her life at home remained a well-kept secret.

By this stage, Rachel's father had been abusing her sexually since she was only six. He would visit her at night, when her mother was out, in her little room where she slept with her rag doll Lucy. He came to 'teach her to be grateful', grateful to 'it' for making her a woman. She was forced to kiss his penis, on her knees, and later to have sexual

---

* This patient, who wishes to remain anonymous, gave the author permission to publish extracts of her writing and this account of her treatment, which she corrected and commented on.

intercourse with him. This went on for 7 years, two or three times a week. Mother never seemed to notice anything. She was for a quiet life and never stood up for her children, specially not for Rachel whom she seemed not really to care for.

The psychiatrist was unaware of what nightmares his little patient carried inside her, what feelings of disgust and pain she felt. Her father had always said: 'No one will ever believe you if you tell them'. She did try and tell her brother but he would not hear of it and told her she was disgusting. She tried once to tell a teacher at school, but father was right, no one would believe her.

The atmosphere at home was terrible. Her father would often go out drinking and would come home and beat her and her sister. This led to the parents separating, but by the time Rachel was 17 her father was back and had resumed sex with her as before.

Not long after, she was admitted to a psychiatric hospital where she was diagnosed as suffering from depression and treated with anti-depressants. A year or so later she was admitted to a psychotherapy in-patient unit but she was soon discharged because she was seen as such a 'difficult patient'. Attempts were made to work with her family but with no success. From this time on, until the age of 22, Rachel was a 'psychiatric patient'. She would be seen by a series of different psychiatrists who gave her a wide variety of diagnoses, depending on how she presented to them. She began her psychiatric career as someone who was perceived to be suffering from a 'personality disorder'; this was later changed to a diagnosis of 'borderline personality disorder' when she was admitted after taking an overdose. At this stage a psychologist tried to work with Rachel by meeting with her on a regular out-patient basis. She was asked if she had been sexually abused but she denied it. The therapy came to an end. During this frightening period of her life, Rachel took several overdoses, and as a result, nearly died from liver damage. She also suffered from a variety of eating problems all centred round the conviction that she was fat and ugly. She would binge and vomit.

By the age of 21, Rachel had been in and out of hospital several times and was finally diagnosed by her psychiatrist as suffering from 'paranoid schizophrenia'. She was treated accordingly with powerful tranquillisers such as fluphenazine decanoate (Modecate), a pheno-thiazine which is injected regularly and which she says made her feel disoriented and worsened her depression. She also had repeated courses of electroconvulsive therapy amounting to a total of 42 treatments in all.

She writes of these times:

My recollections as an in-patient are mostly horrendous. I have faced quite terrifying experiences in hospital, each terrifying experience feeling like a punishment I was due to receive. It was as though this is what I deserved for becoming ill.

Of the medication she writes:

All these drugs made me feel unreal, my depression increased and the voices in my head tormented me even more. I had now turned into a vegetable, standing still and lifeless. I was a certified nothing.

Of the voices she writes:

The voices were my only company, my only reliable companions. Maybe in some strange way I needed them. I knew deep down that I wanted and needed them to go away ... otherwise I would never stand any real chance of leading any real life.

As she grows older, Rachel becomes increasingly aware of feelings and memories she has had to repress:

My feelings seemed to be rising and reaching nearer to the surface, and thoughts and feelings that had been repressed for up to ten years now wanted to burst and explode and most of all wanted to be heard. But I could find no psychiatrist who had time to listen; they didn't want to hear. My determination and need to be heard led me into the world of therapy, the fascinating experience that psychotherapy can bring. The day I embarked on analytic psychotherapy was the first day of the coming to realisation of my true self identity. It is a day that was very profound for me because I had at last found someone who wanted to work with me, wanted to hear me, even with the risk that both myself and the therapist involved knew that a very painful and bumpy road lay ahead of us.

Rachel's first therapeutic contract lasted 18 months. She began to trust another person but she never talked about her sexual experiences with her father lest she lose her therapist. When this treatment was over she once again felt alone and rejected. She finally got her psychiatrist in another hospital to arrange for her to be assessed for psychotherapy. She was accepted for treatment with a female psychoanalytic psychotherapist.

We drew up a contract of six months therapy on a once a week basis, but the ultimate rejection came when our last session of six months finished and we could no longer meet in a therapeutic relationship together again.

When Rachel first met Dr King, she had not told anyone that she had been sexually abused by her father. However, she had suffered from many of the symptoms suffered by women who have been sexually abused as children. Their past suffering is reflected in their self-destructive behaviour, their repeated experience of further abuse, their mixed eating problems and their inability to have satisfactory sexual relationships. Most telling perhaps was Rachel's confused psychiatric history. Many sexually abused girls end up with a diagnosis of so-called 'borderline personality disorder', a diagnosis which is now accepted in most psychiatric circles, though by no means all (Tarnapowlsky and Berelowitz, 1987). The disorder appears to be associated with a history of abuse, particularly verbal and sexual abuse; it is also associated with a history of neglect, particularly emotional withdrawal and early separation experiences (Herman, Perry and van der Kolk, 1989; Zanarini et al., 1989; Schetzky, 1990). People with this diagnosis are chronically unstable individuals with stormy and difficult relationships, poor self-control and low sense of identity. They often present with brief psychotic episodes and feelings of being unreal or that the world about them is unreal (described as 'depersonalisation and derealisation') whilst paradoxically appearing to function quite well in society. Their psychotic experiences make them liable to be diagnosed as suffering from schizophrenia, particularly if their assessor does not believe in the diagnosis of the 'borderline personality'.

What struck Dr King when she first spoke to Rachel was the quiet and sad way in which this dark-haired young woman presented herself. When she spoke of her past therapeutic relationship, she cried gently and was clearly very distressed over having lost her first therapist. When Dr King pointed this out, Rachel acknowledged that before going into therapy, she used to become very aggressive and still did so, but she was now more often sad than angry. This meant that, in her earlier therapy, she had acquired the capacity, albeit tenuous, to grieve. She could feel sad rather than split and project her feelings as she used to do. This important finding gave Dr King the confidence to offer this keen and determined young woman another chance at understanding and working through her feelings about her parents, in particular her father. Their harrowing therapeutic journey together had begun.

Dr King was to learn that not only had Rachel's father had sex with her in her teens, but that she became pregnant by him and had to abort their baby secretly. This baby became an important figure in their therapy. Though dead, she was far from dead for Rachel who invested her with a lot of the hope and love she could not yet own for herself. She felt a murderous guilt about killing her baby; the product of a sexual relationship with her own father, the baby was in a sense her potential brother or sister. Again and again, her little baby Julia would be brought back to the session.

To Dr King it seemed that Rachel had to split and project a good part of herself into the baby, a part which had not been destroyed and which the therapist had now to hold.

At times Julia was her special friend, the only person Rachel had come to love never to be parted from. This idealised image of the little girl contrasted starkly with Rachel's own horrific sense of guilt and badness. The need to defend herself against her own feelings of destructiveness and guilt by believing in this idealised and concrete projection was overwhelming, since Rachel naturally expected to be hated for what she had done.

During one of their sessions, Dr King expressed her view that for Rachel to see herself as 'wicked' was the only way of making any sense of the way her mother and father had treated her and of explaining what she had done in both having and then destroying the child of her father. She also pointed out that Rachel would need to test out her therapist to see if she could indeed be seen as different from the 'wicked' child of her past.

This promptly led to the revelation that Rachel feared she might well kidnap a child. As with so many of her threats, it was difficult to know how seriously to take this warning. Holding on to any anxiety she may have had, Dr King asked: 'To replace Julia?' Rachel said yes; she often had this thought, but she also realised she could have abused a child in her care. 'Like your mother abused you?' asked Dr King.

Rachel then told her the story of the doll called Laura. She used to take her everywhere with her. She was the only 'person' she could talk to. Her mother would take the doll away when she was naughty and then get her to kneel down in front of her and say the things she wanted to hear, like 'I am very wicked because I disobey my mother ...'. Then, with a smile of triumph on her face, Rachel disclosed how her mother had finally burnt the doll, when her daughter at last refused to get on her knees.

Working in the transference relationship between herself and her patient, knowing that it reflected the internalised relationship between Rachel and her mother, Dr King said: 'I feel you are talking about us, the session with your friend which I am about to take away from you like your mother took and burnt Laura.' She agreed with this as she was aware of the ending and then bursting into tears, she cried: 'I wish you hated me'.

Again and again, Rachel was either to express this wish or to attempt to provoke these feelings in her therapist: she could then have given up her painful struggle, convinced herself that therapy did not matter and that the ending, already in sight from the beginning, mattered even less.

Indeed, this internal struggle became manifest as she spoke of how much she also felt she had to control herself so that Dr King would not think ill of her and reject her. Dr King reminded her that any such control of her feelings was at the expense of her wounded angry self. Rachel's reply was to warn her therapist of the suicidal thoughts she had: she wanted to hang herself, such was her despair and loneliness.

Dr King pointed out that these suicidal thoughts were telling them that she was leaving a side of herself out of the session, her angry destructive side that wanted to express her rage and her pain. These feelings she was now turning against herself. Her patient's reply was to speak of her anger as having poisoned her mind. Then, she asked her therapist for something which she was aware her therapist might not like, 'a kind of ritual': she wanted to end the sessions by both of them eating a piece of chocolate.

In the face of her intense dependency needs and the unbearable pain of having to do without, this young woman copes in the only way she knows: she twists the relationship into one where the therapist becomes the person who is seductively invited to pretend that an ending is not an ending, just like her father showered her with gifts and sweets to make her feel that his abuse was not abuse. 'I will teach you to be grateful ...' he used to say, forcing her to do what gave him pleasure.

By the seventh session, 2 weeks before the first break in treatment, Rachel appears to have acted out her destructive feelings by cutting herself and having to go to casualty. She comes to the session with her arms in bandages, grinning triumphantly; she readily admits that it gives her great pleasure to do something she feels she is good at, which is harming herself. The triumph is about the power to control and abuse her own body as her mother and father once did: it is an act of revenge in which her body becomes the object of her hatred, just as she felt the object of her parents' perverted hatred.

In the same session, she also brings a piece she has written. The patient reads and her therapist reads it with her; in this matter the therapist has complied with Rachel's repeated need to share in a fairly concrete way the poems and writings she brings to the sessions. On this occasion, the poem is about Julia and it reveals Rachel's desperate wish for fusion: the child sits on her mother's bed and asks her why she left her. Her mother replies that she is now here for her. Rachel writes:

> I felt her warm breath and I felt in tune with her heartbeat as though she were once again inside me ... I complimented her on her pretty dress and she said: 'Mummy, you chose it for me.' She shed a tear and I felt her presence disappearing. I felt alone again and she had gone.

Glasser (1979) describes this deep pervasive longing for fusion with the other, for this state of oneness with another which characterises perverse relationships: he calls it the 'core complex'. Whilst some Kleinians would describe it as a defence against envy, Estella Welldon, for example, sees it more as a defence against the terror of being helpless and annihilated (1988, p.65). In some sense, one could see the patient's desperate clinging to her idealised therapist in much the same way as we saw Harlow's terrified monkeys clinging to their surrogate mother or 'therapist' in the face of danger. The presence of a reliable attachment figure or of its internal representation is essential if threatening and painful feelings and memories are to be confronted. However, if no real good internal object exists to fulfil such a need, the available object is idealised, made special and the beginnings of a very fragile trusting relationship are set up. It is precarious, however, because it is maintained at the expense of all the real destructive feelings the patient has to repress and split off.

This was made manifest when, faced with her first separation from her therapist, Rachel asked Dr King to look after her small rag doll Lucy which was with her when her father raped her. This doll represented the patient, for not only had she witnessed the abuse but, as yet unbeknown to the therapist, she too had been sexually 'played with' by her mistress. By giving her to Dr King to look after, she was yet again trying to deny the fact that separation was in fact taking place.

Rachel turned to her therapist and told her how much she wanted to remain close to her and how unbearable was the thought of the ending, particularly as she felt a lot for her therapist. Then, faced by the enormity of the separation ahead, Rachel suddenly changed: her face lit up into a cruel smirk and she talked of the pleasure of killing herself, something she could do so well and which would show her mother that she was not such a failure.

Dr King pointed out that there were two sides of her expressing themselves: a side which, like Julia, wanted to be looked after in a caring relationship but feared fatal rejection, and another side which was terribly angry and got pleasure from self-destruction. This enabled Rachel to voice both her need for Dr King and her fears that everybody would leave her, as her first therapist had done. The only caring she had known was from the man her therapist and others would call her 'abusing' father. Caring and abuse had become intimately linked for this young woman.

Later in the session, when Dr King was interpreting her patient's need to attack her, she was to be suddenly silenced by an outburst of rage. It was clear that the therapist had become the object of her patient's destructive projection, described in the second poem of that session entitled 'My psychotherapist: electric lady', the same name she had given to the lady who administered her electroconvulsive therapy. 'You poke and pry, and painfully explain to me the punchline of my sick joke. While gradually I'm killing myself laughing.'

There is a sickly quality to this joke, a twisting of all that is caring into something deadly, a perversion of therapy into the re-experiencing of abuse, so vividly re-enacted by the psychiatrist in the administration of electroconvulsive therapy to her patient.

Unfortunately, it was to be re-enacted here, too, in the psychotherapeutic relationship. With the best will in the world, Dr King could not get away from the fact that she was offering her patient the support and empathy that Rachel had scarcely known, only to take it away after an arbitrary time limit of 25 sessions. Some could indeed describe this as an abusive experience for the patient, a professionally condoned re-enactment of the earlier abuse now taking place between therapist and patient.

It was with this worrying possibility in mind that both Dr King and her supervising team embarked on this particular therapy. Her patient was probably also well aware of the possibility and of the guilt it could engender in her therapist. This, too, had to be borne in mind. So, following this session, Dr King's supervision group pointed out to her that her patient was unconsciously and understandably trying to avoid the pain of working on her abuse: it was in fact being re-enacted in the session.

The struggle around her intense need to merge with her therapist and the rage at having been used and abused persisted throughout the therapy, reflecting both the damage due to her emotional deprivation and that caused by her physical and sexual abuse.

However, also central to this treatment was the vivid and, at times, almost unbearable experience of the perversion within the patient–therapist relationship. Once believed by Freud (1905) to be a manifestation of sexuality, perversions are now increasingly recognised as being related to other 'instincts' or motivational systems. Welldon, in her recent book *'Mother, Madonna and Whore'* (1988), is perhaps the first psychoanalyst to point out that scarcely any mention is ever made of the perversion of the 'maternal instinct'. We could describe this as a perversion of the attachment relationship. It implies the distortion of relationships and of their underlying internal object-relations, such as to produce desires to dehumanise the 'object', to take complete control of, and to merge with, the 'other'. When sexualised, as happens in victims of sexual abuse, the perversion is aptly described by Stoller as the 'erotic form of hatred' (1975).

Thus, just as deprivation is the result of a failure in attunement, so is perversion the result of child abuse. Both these effects are often present together in people who have been sexually abused as children.

In the case of attachment relationships, the result of abuse is a distortion of the relationship between self and other. The self is weak, with poor self-esteem, and feels compelled to control and use the 'other' in order to survive; the other thus becomes a dehumanised 'object' at the service of the pathological self. In the case of sexual abuse the damage to the attachment relationship is compounded by the erotic nature of the abuse: all relations are sexualised. But, whatever the type of trauma, 'the hostility in perversion takes form in a fantasy of revenge hidden in the actions that make up the perversion and serves to convert childhood trauma to adult triumph' (Stoller, 1975, p. 4).

Rachel's transference relationship to Dr King was influenced by her relationship to her father. As she said, she had lost her innocence: the result was a therapy carried out in her father's shadow. As Dr King put it, not only had he 'screwed' her but he had also twisted everything else up for her, especially her capacity to love and to trust. As a result, any physical contact that Rachel made in therapy, and she did make quite a few, had to be seen both in the context of her sexual abuse and in terms of her desperate need for comfort and reassurance.

More disturbing was her need to take control of her object, the therapist, and to subject her to a particular form of perverse abuse which became more intense towards the end of treatment. This experience bore traces of both mother's and father's abusive relationships with her which she re-enacted with Dr King. Just as she had been tied up and locked up in a cupboard for being angry towards her mother, so would Rachel refer to the rope in her cupboard, a rope she planned to hang herself with. During a very difficult session, when Rachel was both enraged with her therapist and struggling with having just witnessed the recent death of her 'good' grandfather, she suddenly started to laugh in a hysterical way. Between these disturbing outbursts of laughter, she spoke of the rope, the rope she thought of and held and twisted and finally dressed herself in ... Then back to death, to her grandfather 'slipping through' and of another relative dying before her from an overdose ... From death to the rope she weaved her way, her laughter most painful to bear; by the end of the session she was seductively inviting her therapist to dress with her in the rope ...

To Dr King, it was clear that her patient simply could not contain her pain and terror. The need to take control, to sexualise her destructiveness and make her therapist partake in this defensive orgy was her only way of dealing with the overwhelming feelings of terror and destructiveness she felt. Perversion was manifestly a defence against the unbearable, a defence transmitted to her by her parents, possibly struggling with similar fears engendered by the wounds of their own past abuse.

This session was followed by many more where her rage could be more directly expressed. She would scream her hatred and physically threaten her therapist and her objects. Baby Julia and patient merged into one as she described what father had done to her and with her. Then she would become terrified by the violence of her feelings, by her guilt for having had sexual intercourse with her father and, especially when older, for not having resisted him and even found comfort in it. The triumphant smile and the disguised threats would return, provoking confusion and anxiety in her therapist.

By this time, there was much talk of what therapy Rachel was to have when she finished with Dr King. The ending seemed very close. Rachel continued to express her feelings of rage which became particularly

intense on the day she announced she had lost Julia. She felt that Dr
King did not care and that she had made her a lot worse. In her rage,
Rachel got up and was about to hit her therapist. Dr King put her arm
out to protect herself and made it quite clear that if she hit her, therapy
would have to end. Rachel sat down and began to chant, smiling
strangely at the wall. Dr King felt she had been given a glimpse of the
one-time 'schizophrenic' patient Rachel had once been. Then, at the
end of this session, it was as if a small girl was pleading with her to
touch her cheek. Dr King, still shaken by her earlier experience, heard
herself say 'no', loud and clear. Rachel sat still and refused to move for
a few minutes. As she left, she complained bitterly about having no
control over her therapist.

The next day, Dr King was phoned three times: Rachel made it clear
she was saying goodbye. It was a suicide threat. Her consultant psychiatrist was informed but she was not forcibly admitted. Instead, he
expressed his concern for Rachel and made it clear that he would be
there for her when therapy was over. His constant presence and support was invaluable for the therapy; both he and Dr King provided
Rachel with the caring parental couple she had never known.

Rachel did not kill herself but she did, however, miss her next session, phoning in to say that she felt ill. Later, she told Dr King that she
kept away because she feared she would hit her. The rage had given
way to some sadness and to concern for her therapist's well-being.

The last three sessions followed the therapist's two-week summer
holiday. In the first, Rachel appeared with shining eyes and wearing
jewellery she had previously felt too ugly to wear. She played a very sad
and beautiful goodbye song and then commented on how detached
she felt, a state she had never known before but which she enjoyed.
Rachel then told Dr King of how, during her absence, her mother had
been diagnosed as having cancer of the breast and had refused treatment, preferring to get better by looking after her daughter. (This same
mother had told Rachel only a few weeks before that she had never
really loved her.) It was clear that this poor mother felt considerable
guilt. But what was also striking was how Rachel now spoke of their
relationship; she felt that the illness had brought her and her mother
together. During her account of their time spent together, she turned
to Dr King and said that what was happening between her and her
mother she owed to her and to what they had done together. She now
realised how much she needed therapy and this made the future much
clearer. She felt she had found a friend in Dr King and the fact that she
had not hit her was to her a measure of her love for her. It had also
been very important that on the day she had heard about her mother's
illness, she was seeing another psychotherapist to discuss her future
treatment. He had known her before and was able not only to confirm

the changes she had achieved but also to give her some much needed support.

This session with Dr King was a moving one but it became clear to the therapist that, in order to preserve the good relationship with her mother and her therapist, all Rachel's feelings about being hurt and rejected had gone. Her patient replied that she had put these feelings away in the cupboard with the rope ... The function of her manic denial became clear. Sadly, Rachel noted how tragic it was that she should be able to get close to mother only to see her getting weaker and weaker and then losing her. Perhaps she felt that was all she was entitled to?

Dr King's own feelings of guilt and anxiety about her patient made it increasingly hard for her to end as planned, in only 2 weeks' time. She did, however, experience some comfort at the thought that both knew that they would be meeting in 3 months' time for a follow-up session.

Their next meeting was very painful. Again, Rachel played a beautiful song about a love that remains for ever. As both of them sat listening she sobbed and Dr King felt very sad. Then, her patient told her she had arranged for her mother to be seen in a specialist centre for patients with cancer. Her father could not cope with his wife's illness, nor could he allow his daughter to grow up. 'You will never get better,' he had said. This took her back to those sessions of family therapy, when he had been allowed to take over so that nothing was achieved. Sadly, she commented on how he would never change.

Her therapist noted how, faced with her mother's death, she looked for support and found none. Rachel then expressed her deep fear that no therapist would want her because of the pain she felt; it would be too much. No one had been able to put up with her pain.

The rest of the session was about her anger with doctors, about patients left to suffer in pain, about how she had had to scream so that her mother could get the painkillers she needed, about how no one ever listened the first time. As the phone rang, she said to Dr King that she always felt that people did not want her to have her to herself. She wept and held her therapist's hand as she struggled with the loss of both mother and Dr King.

In their last meeting, pain and perversion, anger and love were all intertwined. It became clear how important her psychiatrist had been to her and how important he was to be in the next few months, while she looked for further therapy. He was the father figure who did not abuse her and who stayed with her throughout. He was the one she could scream her rage to, knowing he would stay.

Like most workers in the field of sexual abuse, both Dr King and her psychiatric colleague had felt themselves tempted to reject the painful truth of their patient's abuse and its horribly destructive effects. Feeling themselves caught up in the vicious and sickly cycle of guilt and abuse, they had wanted to tear themselves away from it and their patient. But they were held by the supervisory experience they shared with their peers and by a genuine wish to give this young woman the chance to voice her pain and to begin to understand the devastating internal manifestations of this pain twisted into violence and hatred.

Rachel came to see Dr King for her follow-up appointment 3 months later. By this time she had been in three-times-a-week subsidised analytic therapy for 2 months with a fully qualified therapist whom she valued. She had written to Dr King telling her this. When they met, Rachel also had a part-time job and was playing the violin in an orchestra. She now felt able to write and paint. However, it was clear that life was not easy as she struggled with her sick mother's demands on her and her refusal to get any outside help. Like so many abused children, Rachel was clearly mother to her own mother. She felt upset and angry about not seeing Dr King again, but her creativity and progress as well as her sadness were a testimony to what she had achieved in the 6 months of psychotherapy that they carried out together.

One month later, Rachel urgently asked to see her ex-therapist. She had began to wonder if Dr King had not really ended therapy because Rachel had neglected her feelings; she feared therapy had ended because her therapist wanted to see her suffer. She thought that her feelings were not rational but that they were important enough for her to check out. Dr King suggested that she still felt considerable anger at having been left in so much pain, as well as remorse for her violent feelings and that this mixture of ambivalent emotions was at times intolerable. She would then find refuge in seeing Dr King as someone who had not really cared for her but as yet another abuser who wanted her to suffer.

Many months later this young woman took her 'A' levels and got a place at a university. She is now married and it feels to her as if her dream has finally come true. She is now glad she saw her therapy through with Dr King and clearly neither will ever forget the painful journey they made together. I think too that both are aware that without real feelings of concern, affection and respect on the therapist's part, the outcome could have been quite different.

It is clearly not possible to do justice to a therapeutic experience of this nature. The above account can only reflect a selection of experiences as they are described by the therapist. But, however limited and simplified the presentation, it does highlight certain key issues in our understanding of trauma and the role of defence mechanisms in the aetiology of violence. In the case of Rachel, it is clear that two types of traumatic experiences were at work in unconscious manifestations of her life, those due to the probable failure of her mother to tune in to her infantile emotional needs, compounded by a long early separation experience, as well as the effects of the sexual abuse perpetrated by her father. The meaning of this latter experience is coloured by the nature of the child's relationship to her mother. Despite and because of the abuse, father gives his daughter a relationship where she can at last feel special and where feelings of triumph over her 'bad' rejecting mother can be enacted to the full. However, as Welldon states:

> Incest gives much and then takes everything away, all at once. The little girl is now supposed to have all she could have dreamt of in her wildest unconscious fantasies, including her father as her lover ... And she is left in utter misery, with a complete lack of trust in anyone. Those who were supposed to look after her, and to keep firm boundaries between her worlds of fantasy and reality, have failed her, and all is now confusion. She has an enormous sense of loneliness. Such girls have difficulties in acknowledging any angry feelings because these feelings are extremely intense. They feel angry with their mother, who they see as having failed to protect them, and angry with their father because he has abused them.

> *(1988, pp.151–152)*

Rachel's history and the therapeutic experience she had with Dr King illustrate very clearly the various characteristics that develop in women who have been emotionally neglected and sexually abused by their fathers from a very early age. As Weissberg stresses: 'Incest is as much a symptom as a cause of individual and familial dysfunction. It results from complex shifts in the family and from the nonempathic, self-centred narcissistic use of children by *both* father and mother' (1983, p.128; Weissberg's italics). As he says, both parents need the family to stay together: the mother often relinquishes the central family role to her daughter and the father sometimes looks to his daughter for the love he did not receive from his wife or parent. Rachel was thus a 'parentified' child. Collusive secrecy is of the essence, which makes it clear to the child that what is happening between her and father is something bad and dangerous. It also makes her feel special and powerful in keeping the family together, but in so doing, she sacrifices her real needs, her childhood and her self.

Like most incest victims, Rachel suffered from depression, low self-esteem and feelings of being damaged. As a result, she could not form trusting relations or have any satisfactory sexual relationships. The fact that she was emotionally and physically abused by both parents as well as sexually abused by her father made her particularly susceptible to suffering from symptoms referred to earlier as those of a 'borderline personality disorder'. She also had a history of somatic symptoms which in some cases of childhood sexual abuse may be the main presenting problem.

As Welldon describes, living in a state of confusion, these women tend to feel exploited, abused and treated as sex objects, not humans.

On the other hand, they feel superior, omnipotent and precious. Their actions are dictated by the intense disgust they feel for their bodies, which they often subject to relentless physical attacks. The defence mechanisms they employ are, as we have seen, those of splitting into good idealised objects and bad objects, denial and dissociation.

Of particular interest to us, however, is this self-destructive aspect of Rachel's behaviour and her violent feelings of rage. As with all trauma victims, Rachel had difficulty in expressing her anger but, when she did, her outbursts could be extremely violent and occasionally uncontrollable, leading to attacks on herself. A history of self-abuse and suicide attempts is a common sequel to severe sexual abuse in non-clinical and clinical populations of adults who have been abused as children.

From a psychodynamic point of view, this is usually understood as the result of an unconscious 'identification with the aggressor' (Anna Freud, 1936). However, we also know that victims of trauma tend to re-enact their abusive experiences and that, in some cases, they engage in self-destructive behaviour because it calms them down through stimulating the release of the body's endorphins (van der Kolk, 1989). These psychobiological phenomena are of great importance in our understanding of the traumatic origins of violence and will be discussed in the next chapter.

What we are beginning to discern is that the study of the effects of child abuse, as indeed of psychological trauma in general, depends on a bringing together of psychodynamic, developmental, biological and social models of psychopathology. However, for the time being it is worth noting how powerful are the purely psychological motives for self-destruction. If we cast our minds back to the 'avoidant' infants described by Troy and Sroufe (1987, p.170), we will recall that these insecurely attached infants could be alternately victim or victimiser depending on the circumstances: this indicated that they had internalised the infant–parent relationship as a whole.

Identifying with the aggressor, even at the expense of her own body, gives the incest victim a sense of control and power which she desperately seeks. But such an identification with the abusing parent also implies a belief that the child is wicked and deserves to be punished, as Rachel believed when subjected to electroconvulsive therapy. Dean and her colleagues found that maltreated children justified their parents' behaviour on the basis of their own misbehaviour (Dean et al., 1986). As Fairbairn points out, the abused child will cling to this belief in her own wickedness because in becoming 'bad' the child makes her objects 'good'. Her outer security is purchased by her taking on the badness of those on whom she depends (1952, pp.65–66).

The child's need for her rejecting abusive parent is thus salvaged but the price is a terrible sense of guilt, a guilt that is as powerful as the need of the victim for her abuser. As Frank Putnam points out, victims of sexual abuse have an extremely low sense of self-esteem (1990). Indeed, in the most severe cases of sexual and physical abuse, the child's repeated need to dissociate from the abusing experiences and their memories leads to a state of fragmentation of the self that Putnam and other American psychiatrists describe as a 'multiple personality disorder'.

This fragile sense of self and the utter sense of helplessness that accompanies it makes the victim of sexual abuse very vulnerable to attacks of narcissistic rage. Wolf points out that it is very common in borderline personality disorders:

> In the latter, the tenuousness of their selfobject ties, including their tie to the therapist, always makes these episodes of narcissistic rage a threat to the treatment process. But even if the treatment continues, it remains a difficult task to achieve amelioration of the rage. Interpretation usually has little effect, because it is not experienced as supportive to the self. Indeed, interpretations are often experienced as criticisms that aggravate the self's vulnerability. What the self needs is to be understood. However, that does not mean that the self needs approval of its rage. It may take a very long period of time during which empathic understanding alone rules before a gradual fading away of the rage takes place.
>
> *(1988, p.81)*

What appears to get left out of the literature on childhood sexual abuse is any reference to the perversion which we described taking place during Rachel's therapy with Dr King. The closest reference to this behaviour is the acknowledgement that incest victims sexualise their relationships with others, which puts them at risk of further abuse even when treated by psychotherapists and psychoanalysts who should know better. This important finding highlights some of the serious emotional difficulties that arise in working with childhood victims of sexual abuse, but we do not really know in any detail how therapists come to partake in this re-enactment of their patient's sexual abuse; like the original incest, it tends to remain a well-kept secret (Kluft, 1990; Fahy and Fisher, 1992).

Perhaps what is most important to note is that the manifestation of perversion in sexually abused patients can have a very real defensive function in protecting the self against overwhelming pain and loss of control. This was clearly illustrated in the sessions when Rachel felt unable to contain her intense destructive feelings and fears of being annihilated. In so doing, she denied the reality of her feelings of dependency and pain, the reality of her therapist's concern and care and she became a powerful omnipotent seducer whose central aims were both fusion with and manipulation of the 'object' in the service of the threatened self. When able to express her rage, pain and dependence in a more direct form, Rachel did not need to resort to such re-enactments of her abuse.

Freud himself appears to have acknowledged the defensive function of perversion when he wrote about a young man whose highly perverse father had obtained sexual excitement by licking the feet of his sexual partners; he had done the same to his son who then repeated it with his sister. Now this young man 'abhors all perversity while he suffers compulsive impulses'. Freud then adds: 'If he could be perverse, he would be healthy, like his father' (Masson, 1984, pp.93–94).

For Welldon, the acknowledgement that perversions occur in women and men means that we need to go back to Freud's early theory of real seduction. As she says, by attributing the incestuous material of their patients to the world of unconscious phantasy, psychiatrists and psychoanalysts have denied the reality of incest and sexual abuse in society (1988). It is my view that this very denial may be an important factor in predisposing therapists to re-enact their patient's experience of sexual abuse.

We have up to this point become increasingly aware of the traumatic effects of loss and deprivation in the formation of insecure attachment relationships and of the self. What we are now seeing is how distorted and disturbing these attachment patterns can become when a child becomes the sexual and physical object of his or her parents' needs. This new dimension was clearly demonstrated in the perversion of the therapeutic relationship when Rachel felt overwhelmed by feelings of pain and rejection she could not contain. What we still do not really understand is why psychoanalysts have had to deny for so long the reality of their patients' traumatic experiences.

The denial of childhood sexual abuse?

The psychoanalytic treatment of people who have suffered childhood sexual abuse raises very important issues in terms of the feelings such patients engender in their therapists. Not only is it extremely distressing to listen to an account of the horrendous experiences of those who as children were subjected to the perverse and often violent sexual demands of an adult, but the feelings and defences used by the victim also affect the therapist in other ways: Dr King would often find herself caught up in a process which could so easily have led to an abusive recreation of her patient's childhood trauma. Freud was well aware of the revulsion such patients often engender in those who attempt to help them. In describing his original cases of hysteria he wrote:

> My thirteen cases were without exception of a severe kind; in all of them the
> illness was of many years duration, and a few came to me after lengthy and

unsuccessful institutional treatment. The childhood trauma which analysis uncovered in these severe cases had all to be classed as grave sexual injuries; some of them were positively revolting.

(1896a)

Freud also describes the mental 'sensitiveness which is so frequent among hysterical patients and which leads them to react to the least sign of being depreciated as though they had received a deadly insult'. He adds:

It is not the latest slight – which, in itself, is minimal – that produces the fit of crying, the outburst of despair or the attempt at suicide ...; the small slight of the present moment has aroused and set working the memories of very many, more intense, earlier slights, behind all of which there lies in addition the memory of a serious slight in childhood which has never been overcome.

(1896a, p. 217)

This insightful account of the narcissistic injuries and rage experienced by his patients reminds us of Rachel's outburst of rage and Wolf's warnings about the difficulties of keeping patients with a 'borderline personality disorder' in treatment. Indeed, if we are to go by Freud's descriptions of what took place between him and his patients, we could be justified in believing that many of his so-called hysterical patients would now be diagnosed as suffering from a 'borderline personality disorder'.

However, having challenged the psychiatric establishment with his important discoveries and new therapeutic techniques, Freud was to find himself out in the cold. It seems clear to me that the extent of Freud's own narcissistic injury has been underestimated. By September 1897 he wrote to his friend Fliess that he no longer believed in his seduction theory and he gave various reasons for this:

The continual disappointment in my efforts to bring any analysis to a real conclusion; the running away of people who for a period of time had been the most gripped [by analysis]; the absence of the complete successes on which I had counted ...Then the surprise that in all cases the *father*, not excluding my own, had to be accused of being perverse – the realisation of the unexpected frequency of hysteria, with precisely the same conditions prevailing in each, whereas surely such widespread perversions against children are not very probable. (The perversion would have to be immeasurably more frequent than the hysteria, because the illness, after all, occurs only where there has been an accumulation of events and there is a contributory factor that weakens the defence.) Then, third, the certain insight that there are no indications of reality in the unconscious, so that one cannot distinguish between truth or fiction that has been cathected with affect. (Accordingly, there would remain the solution that the sexual fantasy invariably seizes upon the theme of the parents) ...

(1897; Freud's italics; quoted in Masson, 1984, pp. 108–109)

And indeed this was finally the solution Freud was to take. It seems hardly surprising that, faced with the very real difficulties, both technical and emotional, which are inherent to the psychotherapeutic treatment of sexually abused patients and feeling absolutely rejected by his professional colleagues, the champion of incest victims took flight. As he so candidly put it at the end of the same letter to Fliess:

> The expectation of eternal fame was so beautiful, as was that of certain wealth, complete independence, travels, and lifting the children above the severe worries which robbed me of my youth. Everything depended on whether or not hysteria would come out right. Now I can once again remain quiet and modest, go on worrying and saving. A little story from my collection occurs to me: 'Rebecca, take off your gown, you are no longer a Kalle [bride]'.
>
> *(1897, quoted in Masson, 1984, pp. 108–109)*

It seems that Freud felt very humiliated by what took place when he presented his paper to the Society for Psychiatry and Neurology. Hoping for recognition and glory, he fell flat on his face before the illustrious father figures of his profession. His letter suggests that in his wounded narcissism, he displaced his anger from those who rejected his views on to his difficult patients who failed to get better, abandoned treatment and, as we know only too well, evoked such horrible feelings of pain, disgust and fear. Many times, during Rachel's treatment, Dr King and her psychiatric colleague would feel they had to check out if what they had heard and experienced with their patient was indeed truth or fantasy. Were they 'being taken for a ride' they wondered, as they would find themselves unconsciously dissociating from the traumatic experience they were reliving with their patient. However, with the backing of current evidence on child abuse and the experience of other colleagues who have treated similar victims, they maintained their belief in their patient. One wonders how Freud could have carried out such a task in isolation, particularly as he would have been a social outcast and, who knows, even penniless, a prospect we know terrified him as much as death.

Freud had to do to his patients what had been done unto him in order to survive. In 1905, he recanted on his 'scientific fairy tale' and wrote that seduction is not required in order to arouse a child's sexual life, for this can come about spontaneously from internal causes. And as for perversions, these are now seen as innate:

> It is an instructive fact that under the influence of seduction children can become polymorphously perverse and can be led into all possible kinds of sexual irregularities. This shows that an aptitude for them is innately present in their disposition.
>
> *(1905)*

In this way Freud accounts for the high incidence of prostitution (now a known outcome of childhood sexual abuse), and concludes that 'it becomes impossible not to recognise that this same disposition to perversions of every kind is a general and fundamental human characteristic' (1905, p. 191).

Freud summed up the meaning of his 'volte-face' when he wrote to Fliess: 'The factor of a hereditary disposition regains a sphere of influence from which I had made it my task to dislodge it – in the interest of illuminating neurosis' (1897, quoted in Masson, 1984, pp. 108–109).

As a result, the effect of trauma and childhood abuse was practically ignored for another 70 years. Only Sandor Ferenczi was brave enough to challenge Freud's new beliefs. In his last paper on 'Confusion of tongues between the adult and the child', he makes it quite clear that trauma, and particularly sexual trauma, is a pathogenic agent and that sexual abuse in children is commonplace (1949). When he delivered this paper to the assembled gathering of psychoanalysts in Wiesbaden in 1932, their response was very similar to that which Freud had encountered 36 years before when addressing Krafft-Ebing and his colleagues: Ferenczi's paper was not published in English until 1949. In the discussion over the therapeutic implications of his findings, he shows a remarkable sensitivity for his patients:

> The analytical situation, i.e. the restrained coolness, the professional hypocrisy and, hidden behind it – but never revealed – a dislike of the patient which nevertheless he felt in all his being – such a situation was not essentially different from that which in his childhood had led to the illness. When, in addition to the stress caused by ther analytical situation, we imposed on the patient the further burden of reproducing the original trauma, we created a situation that was indeed unbearable. Small wonder that our effort produced no better results than the original trauma.
>
> *(1949, pp. 226–227)*

By being able to recognise their mistakes and avoid them, Ferenczi believed that a new therapeutic alliance could be built up, one that brings therapists their patients' trust:

> It is this confidence that establishes the contrast between the present and the unbearable, traumatogenic past, that contrast which is absolutely necessary for the patient in order to enable him to re-experience the past, no longer as a hallucinatory reproduction but as an objective memory.
>
> *(1949, p. 227)*

What becomes apparent when reading the literature on psychological trauma, is that it is a subject that both fascinates and repulses. For example, there was widespread interest in Europe at the end of the century in the phenomenon of 'dissociation' and its relationship to hypnosis; Breuer's treatment of Anna O is an example of this, as was

Freud's early work on hysteria (Carlson, 1986). However, as we have seen with Breuer in the case of Anna O and then with Freud and his hysterical patients, once clinicians actually experienced the emotions aroused by the traumatic experiences of their patients, they either had to flee or defend themselves. Breuer abandoned Anna O when, having ended treatment with her, she developed a phantom pregnancy which he dimly knew related to the intense feelings she had developed for him. The victims of trauma make therapists realise how vulnerable they are; in their empathic identification with their patients lies the frightening realisation that what has happened to these victims could so easily happen to those who attend to them.

This awareness of our mortality and of our terrible vulnerability is one which most of us have spent our entire lives avoiding, as Becker so vividly demonstrates in his book *The Denial of Death*. Reflecting on Pascal's frightening reflection that 'Men are so necessarily mad that not to be mad amounts to another form of madness', he reminds us of our excruciating dilemma, that of being literally split in two:

> Man has a symbolic identity that brings him sharply out of nature. He is a symbolic self, a creature with a name, a life history. He is a creator with a mind that soars out to speculate about atoms and infinity, who can place himself imaginatively at a point in space and contemplate bemusedly his own planet. This immense expansion, this dexterity, this ethereality, this self-consciousness gives to man literally the status of a small god in nature, as the Renaissance thinkers knew.
>
> Yet, at the same time, as the Eastern sages also knew, man is a worm and food for worms ... He goes back into the ground a few feet in order blindly and dumbly to rot and disappear for ever.
>
> *(1973, p.26)*

To cope with this terrible existential paradox, we develop from childhood onwards particular ways of thinking and of reacting to life's events, in keeping with our cultural context, which protect us from the glaring manifestations of our vulnerability. These fundamental defensive postures of the mind become character traits which Ferenczi brilliantly described as our 'secret psychoses' so essential to our psychic survival.

The trauma victim's plight is that he knows that his sense of invulnerability was an illusion. He also cannot make any sense of what has happened to him; since most of us believe we live in a world over which we have some control and which is therefore comprehensible, the experience of total helplessness, which is at the crux of the trauma, shatters this second illusion. Psychological trauma is at one level the outcome of having lost two basic assumptions essential for our psychic survival.

Therefore, what the clinician sees in her patient is just how terrible life can be without such illusions. What the clinician cannot bear to think about is how much she also relies on these illusions for her own survival. To protect herself from 'secondary traumatisation', the reality of the trauma has to be denied or put in second place: thus for most psychoanalysts the world of internal phantasy takes centre stage. Similarly, the psychiatrist must label as 'symptoms' and 'diseases' what are in fact desperate defences on the part of the victim's self to overcome the terror of disintegration.

However, since the 1970s, American psychiatrists have seen the Vietnam war veterans pour into their clinics with all sorts of symptoms and disturbances for which a 'diagnostic category' had to be found: the links between psychological trauma and mental disorders could no longer be ignored; the time was ripe for another look at child abuse and its effects. We will be following these developments and their implications in the next two chapters.

Chapter 10
The Traumatic Origins of Violence in Adults

'Forwith this frame of mine was wrenched
With a woful agony,
Which forced me to begin my tale;
And then it left me free.
Since then, at an uncertain hour,
That agony returns:
And till my ghastly tale is told,
This heart within me burns.'

The Rime of the Ancient Mariner by Samuel Coleridge, 1772–1834

Psychological trauma

Lindemann's definition of psychological trauma as the 'sudden, uncontrollable disruption of affiliative bonds', lies at the heart of our thesis. It is a definition that recognises the importance of attachment relationships and hence their social, psychobiological, emotional and cognitive manifestations. To deny the impact of trauma over human life is once again to deny that we matter to one another; it is a way of dissociating ourselves from human pain and its violent manifestations. What we have begun to see through the lives of Rachel and of Mr Brown, at the beginning of the book, is how their terrible pain did turn into violence, a violence that appeared to carry the very imprint of their own psychological scars.

If we recall the earlier work on the development of our primate cousins and the studies on infant–parent relationships, we may begin to see how those crucial attachment bonds that develop between parent and child and then amongst fellow men and women can be twisted into hatred and violence with all the associated defences and cognitive distortions which are required by a self threatened with annihilation.

Whilst the importance of attachment and attunement in human relationships can scarcely be denied today, we will recall how difficult it was for Bowlby and his followers to be taken seriously by those psychoanalysts who believed that mental illness was the outcome of intrapsychic conflicts rather than the result of abuse or overwhelming life events.

Freud illustrates some of the difficulties engendered by such an approach: when he was asked to explain the symptoms of the 'shell-shocked' victims coming back from the Front during the First World War, he tried to adjust his revised theories to fit with the evidence these soldiers presented. He discovered that infantile sexual trauma was not a predisposing factor in most of these men's illnesses and their battle nightmares could scarcely be explained in terms of wish-fulfilment (Newcombe and Lerner, 1982). Instead, Freud attributed their terrible dreams to ways in which the mind mentally repeats stressful experiences in order to assimilate them, a phenomenon he termed 'repetition compulsion'. Linking this with patients' similar tendencies to repeat the past in psychoanalysis, Freud came to speculate that such a compulsion was in fact 'instinctual'. He then concluded: 'It seems, then, that an instinct is an urge inherent in organic life to restore an earlier state of things ... or, to put it another way, the expression of the inertia inherent in organic life' (1920, p.36). Eight pages later, Freud gave this urge the name of the 'death instinct' which he linked with the phenomenon of 'masochism'. And so the death instinct was born in what seems a desperate attempt of Freud's to disown what he had once made so clear, the link between mental symptoms and the experience of psychological trauma. Instead, by relying on the assumed existence of certain biological instincts, Freud re-established the importance of our hereditary disposition, very much in line with the scientific theories of his day.

As a result, the reality of the soldiers' personal experiences and torments was denied and the subject of psychological trauma was effectively buried for another 20 years, when Fairbairn (1952) and Kardiner (1941) studied the war neuroses and Bettelheim (1943) wrote about the concentration camp survivors. However, it was not until after the Vietnam war in the 1970s that psychoanalysts in the USA began to work with traumatised war veterans. In the UK, psychoanalysis tends to have little to say about the effect of external events because the main focus of treatment still remains the inner phantasy life of the individual.

Mainstream psychiatrists have also shown a limited interest in the effects of psychological trauma on mental health, despite the important work of Pierre Janet on this subject over 100 years ago (van der Kolk and van der Hart, 1989). Like Breuer and Freud, he was to study the psychological phenomenon of 'dissociation'. He described it as a process whereby feelings or memories relating to frightening experiences are split off from conscious awareness and voluntary control to show up later as 'pathological automatisms'. These intrusive images, somatic experiences or anxiety reactions are reactivated by conditions similar to those experienced at the time of the original trauma. Such a formulation implies that Janet conceived of memory in very modern terms, that is, as capable of storing either all or only a portion of the emotional and physiological concomitants of certain life events; Janet suggests that this would happen because the traumatic experience engenders in the victim such intense emotions that these cannot be stored into existing schemas, but have to be split up and their component parts organised on a non-linguistic level in the form of somatic sensations, behaviour re-enactments, nightmares and flashbacks. This crucial phenomenon, now called the memory of 'states', lies at the centre of our current understanding of what is now termed the post-traumatic stress disorder or PTSD. However, Janet's ideas were not popular amongst his colleagues and he was to pursue his studies in increasing isolation as French psychiatry fell in step with the prevailing medical interests in biology and genetics. Unlike Freud however, Janet did not alter his views to save his reputation and he continued with his studies and the treatment of his patients.

Psychiatry's need to maintain its position within medicine had and still has unfortunate consequences in terms of understanding human behaviour and psychopathology. Not only has psychiatry had to remain within the framework of conventional biological psychiatry to justify its position but, as Alvin Pam points out, it also colludes with the current socio-political ideology. If personal problems are seen as a biological destiny they are therefore the problems of no one. He writes:

> By the mere assumption that the locus of psychopathology lies within the body, both family and society are not deemed to inflict psychopathology, and even the symptom-bearer becomes a passive victim ... The majesty and mystique of biological psychiatry resides in determining personal problems to be tantamount to medical problems.
>
> *(1990, p.25)*

In this way no major adjustments need to be made by society to reduce the psychological distress of individuals.

However, few present-day psychiatrists would subscribe to such an extreme form of 'biologism' as Pam calls it (1990). Current theories accept that psychological distress can be precipitated by social or non-biological factors, but they also continue to maintain that biological factors are what make such people vulnerable to such distress. These are ultimately more important than the 'precipitating' social or familial factors and must be the target for prevention or cure. This ensures that psychiatrists continue to have a medical *raison d'être* as well as remaining protected from the potentially disturbing evidence that their patients' traumatic experiences could elicit.

In his paper entitled 'Biological psychiatry: is there any other kind?', Samuel Guze makes this point very clearly. Having acknowledged the importance of the reciprocal interaction between genotype and culture, the importance of ethology and ecology and the understanding that behaviour is part of an interaction, he writes as follows of 'psychological meaningful experiences':

> But even if ultimately it can be showed convincingly that these experiences play causal roles in illness, it is to the specific vulnerability that we must direct our attention if we are to hope for essential scientific understanding and effective therapeutic intervention. It appears highly unlikely that an intervention strategy designed to reduce or eliminate the troubles, disappointments, frustrations, and pressures of daily living will prove feasible or powerful enough.
>
> *(1989, p.317)*

Within such a conceptual framework there can be little scope for the study of psychological trauma, for it is by its very nature interactive and very much dependent on social factors both in its causation and in its outcome.

However, as happened with the development of attachment theory and its implications, a new way of thinking 'biologically' about human needs and behaviour has begun to permeate the field of mental health. Within psychiatry, this new way of thinking is most aptly represented by the work of Bessel van der Kolk, who reminds us that:

> A human being is a biological organism embedded in a social environment from the moment of birth. Disruption of the social matrix, particularly in childhood, has serious long-term effects on both psychological and biological functioning.
>
> *(1987, pp. xi–xii)*

As he points out, mainstream psychiatry continues to study people as self-contained entities, relatively divorced from their social environments despite all the work on families and in social psychiatry of the 1960s.

This author and his colleagues' work on psychological trauma is of particular interest because of its emphasis on the need to understand psychopathology in terms of the human and primate developmental research which was reviewed earlier. Such an approach stresses the close interdependence between the psychological, the biological and the social aspects of human behaviour and experience: it is within such a framework that psychological trauma and its violent derivatives can be most usefully understood.

After defining psychological trauma, there follows a study of its effects, focusing particularly on those that lead to the re-enactment of the traumatic experience with all its violent implications for the self and the 'other'. Though psychological trauma in childhood is very similar to that seen in adults, there are important differences both in the way in which it presents and in the long-term effects it produces. For this reason, it will be reviewed separately and in more detail in the next chapter. However, it is clearly impossible to do justice to the vast literature on post-traumatic stress disorder (PTSD) in these two chapters. Of the countless books on the subject, I can recommend van der Kolk's work *Psychological Trauma* (1987) and Charles Figley's book *Trauma and its wake* (1985). A more psychoanalytic approach is provided by Henry Krystal (1968, 1988).

Post-traumatic stress disorder

People have experienced extraordinarily stressful life events since the dawn of humanity. There have always been natural disasters brought about by earthquakes, cyclones, droughts, floods, volcanic eruptions and disease epidemics. To give an example of the frequency of disasters, it has been estimated that between 1947 and 1973 there were over 836 major disasters reported worldwide, in each of which more than 100 people were injured or killed, or which resulted in more than a million dollars' worth of damage (Green, Wilson and Lindy, 1985, p.54). The psychological effects of these stressful events have always existed and have probably been very important agents in the development of magical and religious practices and beliefs. Indeed, it has been postulated that the devastating experiences of Europeans during the fall of the Roman Empire may have been an important factor in the adoption of the belief in original sin (Chapter 2).

Wars, ethnic strife, slavery and various forms of human abuse have also been part of human existence for many thousands of years, though how widespread and ubiquitous they are to human existence is subject to serious debate.

Ninety per cent of an estimated 101 million war deaths that have occurred since 1700 AD have occurred in this century and more than 70% of these deaths have been civilians (Sivard, 1988). Civilian deaths have increased from 5% in the First World War to 50% in the 1950s, to 84% in current conflicts excluding the Gulf. The bitter fighting in what was Yugoslavia is particularly devastating for Westerners because not only has it brought back the horrors of war to Europe but it also involves so many civilians.

Until the recent Balkan war began there had been about 127 wars and 21.8 million war-related deaths in the world since 1945: indeed, except for 26 days total peace, there has been armed conflict going on somewhere in the world every day since the end of the Second World War. All but two of these armed conflicts took place in Third World countries, often with the backing of the superpowers (Zwi, 1991). In 1987 alone, conventional wars are estimated to have caused at least 2.2 million deaths in the underdeveloped world (Zwi and Ugalde, 1989). If it had not been for the American involvement in Vietnam, these wars and their human casualties would probably have been of little interest either to professionals in the field of mental health or to the general population in the West; indeed for many Westerners the 50 or so years since the last World War have been perceived as essentially peaceful; such a belief has made it easier to deny the traumatic and longterm psychological consequences of modern war. (This denial may be particularly important when military spending on weapons is so high: in 1991 it ran to about $1000 bn (£635bn) worldwide, of which about $830bn was spent by the developed world and $170bn by the developing world (World Development Report, 1991).)

The need to present a sanitised picture of war dates to the First World War when reporters and soldiers were not allowed to describe what really took place on the front-line. One of the main reasons for this is perhaps most clearly spelt out by an American writer called Eugene Sledge who fought in the American Civil War. In the midst of the battle he discovered what all combat troops finally perceive:

> We were expendable. It was difficult to accept. We come from a nation and a culture that values life and the individual. To find oneself in a situation where your life seems of little value is the ultimate of loneliness.

(Fussell, 1989)

It was this realisation, this traumatic moment of truth that had to be denied for as long as possible, if not on the battle field, at least back home among the voters.

Wars are living nightmares of human destruction. On the battlefield itself, all the senses are overwhelmed: sounds of firing, explosions, the screaming of men, the wailing of the wounded; the sight of limbless bodies, disembowelled twisted friends and fellow men and, perhaps most difficult to forget, the stench of death and decay. The senses are assaulted by the unimaginable and the mind and body are galvanised by fear, terror and disgust as well as a triumph of murderous rage. Medical observers have reported that 'there is no such thing as getting used to combat'.

There is little doubt that throughout history some soldiers were psychologically affected by their experience of war, as were the civilian victims. However, the relationship between war trauma and psychopathology received little or no attention until the late nineteenth century (Scrignar, 1988). Affected soldiers were first diagnosed as suffering from 'nostalgia' and then from 'irritable heart syndrome' and 'neurasthenia'. In the First World War, the initial response to mental distress in soldiers was punitive and some men were even shot for being cowards. However, by 1915, there were so many affected soldiers and officers that a more understanding attitude developed towards the afflicted: the syndrome of 'shellshock' began to appear in medical journals, a condition attributed to concussion of the central nervous system. However, after the war, the War Office Committee of Enquiry was to dismiss this condition as mistaken. Doctors were then brought in for the first time to decide upon cases of 'war neurosis' of doubtful character (Gal and Mangelsdorff, 1991).

Even today, despite all that has been learnt about battle-related traumatic stress disorders, British soldiers who fought in the Falklands war, Northern Ireland and the Gulf war are not being given proper health-care and self-help facilities by the Ministry of Defence. A voluntary Crisis Line, set up for these men and their families in the UK provides evidence that there is a large and invisible population of these war-trauma sufferers who present with unusual and sometimes violent behaviour when they return home (Nasmyth, 1991).

As has already been noted, there has been a marked resistance in the field of Western mental health to acknowledge any links between the overwhelmingly stressful nature of the life events reported by our patients and their 'symptoms' and behaviour.

Some of the reasons for this 'blind spot' in psychiatry and psycho-analysis have been explored earlier. It is only because of the resurgence of interest in psychological trauma following the Vietnam war, that mental health workers have become aware that there is a whole spectrum of syndromes to describe the different types of victims, depending on the different traumatic experiences they have been exposed to such as: shell shock, the rape trauma syndrome, the disaster victim disorder or concentration camp syndrome. However, on closer study it has become clear that, on the whole, the human response to overwhelming and uncontrollable life experiences is quite consistent, despite variations due to the age and personality of the victims. For the first time in psychiatry, the traumatic event itself has been causally linked to a psychiatric disorder, irrespective of other vulnerability factors. This in no way denies the importance of personal vulnerability or social factors, but it does underline the fact that overwhelmingly stressful events can have a fundamentally destructive effect upon our sense of self and our attachment relationships. It could now be said that the young Freud who spoke out so bravely in April 1896 has finally been vindicated and, as he said, this is a step towards the 'solution to a more-than-a-thousand-year-old problem, a source of the Nile'. It took a devastating war and the defeat of a world power with all the internal social and political consequences of this disaster for psychological trauma to begin to be recognised for what it is, the wounding of the human psyche during states of terrifying helplessness.

As a result of this finding, a separate category for psychological trauma was introduced in the 1980 edition of the *Diagnostic and Statistical Manual of Mental Disorders* (DSM-III) under the heading of 'Post-traumatic Stress Disorder'. The manual defines a traumatic event as occurring when

> A person has experienced an event that is outside the range of usual human experience and that would be markedly distressing to almost anyone such as: a serious threat or harm to one's life or physical integrity; serious threat or harm to one's children, spouse, or other close relatives and friends; sudden destruction of one's home or community; or seeing another person who has recently been or is being injured or killed as a result of an accident or physical violence.

Most people simply experience the traumatic event as a source of stress but some go on to develop a post-traumatic stress reaction or PTSD. This is essentially a biphasic response, involving on the one hand the reliving of the traumatic events, alternating with a sense of numbness or a reduced emotional responsiveness to the outside world.

Traumatised people find themselves reliving the traumatic event mainly through intrusive thoughts in the form of visual flashbacks, nightmares, recurrent distressing memories or re-enactments of the traumatic situations. In these behavioural re-enactments of the trauma, the subject may play the role of the victim or the victimiser; it is this particular consequence of psychological trauma that is a major cause of violence, one that is still too often neglected or denied, even though it is often at the root of what appears to be cold or unprovoked violence occurring many years after the original trauma.

The 'psychic numbing' response, similar to that seen in grief reactions, is a psychological state during which traumatised people complain of feeling detached, unable to feel close even to those they love and with little interest in sexual relations or pleasure in general. These people become socially isolated and retreat from family obligations. This may be the victim's way of avoiding any feelings or situations that might bring back intrusive memories or emotions associated with the trauma. This emotional withdrawal often leads to marital tensions and divorce.

People who suffer from PTSD also suffer from at least two of the following difficulties: they have problems in concentrating and in remembering things; they can also feel so aroused that they jump at the slightest sound and are constantly on the look out for danger, the latter being determined by the nature of their original trauma; if exposed to any reminder of their traumatic experience, these people relive the entire horrendous event with all the feelings and symptoms which I have just described. They also feel irrationally guilty, a symptom we may well recall in victims of child sexual abuse.

The life of a PTSD victim can indeed be a particularly terrible one, especially in the acute phase. Given time, some people get better but others do not. For instance a recent study of Vietnam theatre veterans shows that 500 000 (15.2% of men and 8.5% of women) still suffered from PTSD 20 or so years after the war (Shlenger et al., 1992). These results are ascribed not only to the nature of the stressful event itself, but to the particular social and political factors surrounding the return of these soldiers from war. In fact it is to these victims of war that we owe the current interest in PTSD and the controversy over the role of personality and vulnerability factors in psychiatry. As we have seen earlier, these personality factors are of fundamental importance to conventional psychiatry but, in the case of the Vietnam veterans (and other victims), studies on possible predisposing features have been particularly difficult to carry out because clinicians often become the advocates of their patients, even to the point of representing their patients' interests in court. As McFarlane states: 'The need for social justice and the prevention of the stigmatisation of victims has been a major concern for some clinicians, aware of how the victims can all too easily be blamed for their disorder' (1990, p.16). In his review of the literature the same author points out, in agreement with many others, that there is no conclusive evidence regarding the importance of personality or other vulnerability factors in the aetiology of PTSD in Vietnam veterans.

PTSD can last many years, even a life time. Prisoners of war from the Second World War and concentration camp victims have been found still to be suffering from symptoms of PTSD, more than 50 years after their terrible experiences. The life of a friend illustrates this all too clearly.

Mr and Mrs Greenbaum were a Jewish couple in their 70s when I first met them. She was a grey-haired lady sculptor who chipped away at her statues, working at the bottom of their garden. Her sculptures were mostly delightful renderings of children in the arms of their mothers, of dancers in graceful poses, of embracing lovers ... But among Mrs Greenbaum's sculptures was one I will never forget, the terrible shaved head of a tormented man: aghast, his features are wild with fear and his eyes stare into space under a brow furrowed with pain; his open mouth seems to gasp with disbelief at what awaits him. In the painful twist of his neck, the terror of his face, he expresses for me the frozen horror of human violence. His name is 'Auschwitz'. He was born of the mind of a woman who suffered three concentration camps and yet survived. Her little book *I Did Survive* is a surprisingly delicate and moving account of what she and others endured in the infernos of the Nazi Holocaust (Elro, 1978). These terrible experiences were to haunt her for many years to come, until she found some solace in the sculpting of the human forms she has left behind with us, testimonies of her deep love of life and the victim's need to give a meaning to the unthinkable. Her death, however, was brought on by the reliving of those same horrors, recreated in her mind by the sight of her poor husband's suffering form as he struggled with the dehumanising effects of advanced dementia. She told me that in his confusion and painful agitation he had become one of those ghostlike semi-naked figures of the concentration camps. Her heart could not take it; she had suffered too much.

Post-traumatic stress disorder develops in anyone who has been exposed to an overwhelmingly traumatic experience. In less extreme conditions, various important interactive factors appear to be involved in determining whether an individual succumbs to psychological stress or not. Clearly, the nature, the duration and the intensity of the traumatic experience are of primary importance. Any soldier will break down if exposed to combat long enough. The stage of development and the age of the person exposed is also very important, children and adolescents being more vulnerable than adults.

Equally relevant, and rightly emphasised by psychoanalysts, is the importance of the meaning that is given to the traumatic event. This may link in with how it is perceived in the first place and whether the individual has a sense that he or she can cope with its effects. It may be recalled that in the discussion on defence mechanisms (Chapter 8), Guidano emphasised that the way human beings perceive reality depends very much on the way they see and conceive of themselves (1987). In other words, if human perception is relative to the psychic structures of the self, the individual will attempt to create the world in the image of these same psychic structures. The meaning that is given to a traumatic event will therefore also relate to the individual's inner world, formed as it is by the interaction of past experiences with feelings, phantasies and his or her genetic predisposition. From my experience of working on surgical wards, psychotic reactions appear to take place when the individual's worst personal phantasies are confirmed by reality.

Related to the importance of meaning is the interesting finding that man-made disasters are more likely to produce PTSD than natural disasters (Scurfield, 1985). This will be seen to tie in with another important finding ,which shows that the nature of the individual's social environment, during and following the traumatic event, is particularly important in determining whether or not he or she develops PTSD, for a common reaction to victimisation is to turn to others for help and support. The sharing in common of danger and loss can bring people together and provide the victims with valuable support and reassurance. Outsiders can also demonstrate considerable good will and help. But, in our current Western society, these basic human needs are not always met: people tend to see victims as responsible for what happened to them, probably in an attempt to maintain that crucial sense of personal invulnerability, or because of a fear of guilt by association; victims are also often depressed and this puts people off. So, at a time when social support is essential, traumatised people can be left to suffer alone.

Cultural characteristics are clearly significant in determining both how a survivor experiences the traumatic event and how her cultural milieu deals with her resulting needs. This was illustrated by a study of

Ugandan war victims. Following the devastation of years of civil war in that country, a team of health workers attempted to investigate how they could best help the victims of this awful man-made disaster, where between 100 000 and 500 000 people had disappeared and many more had suffered torture at the hands of the security services. What Bracken and his colleagues found was that very few people had escaped some degree of suffering: there were no limits to the numbers of victims of trauma. But they soon also realised that:

> War and violence are not new phenomena in Africa and communities have been coping in one way or another with their effects for centuries. Emphasis is placed on the maintenance of very strong family bonds in most African societies and, as Lambo has suggested, 'psychotherapy in Africa, especially in the traditional era, [has] formed part of the social fabric'. This has meant that, as with other effects of social conflict, many of the effects of violence are dealt with within the family group.
>
> *(Bracken, Giller and Kabaganda, 1992, pp.157–158)*

The outcome of their assessment was the provision of initiatives which had the function of integrating and supporting the local reactions and responses which already existed in the community. The team only attended directly to certain victims who did not receive any help, such as the rape victims. Their conclusion is a plea to Western agencies not to impose their models of care on other cultures: therapeutic strategies need to be as diverse as the cultures within which one is operating.

It need hardly be stressed that social attitudes will also affect the recovery environment of the victim: for example, homecoming for some of the veterans of the Vietnam war meant facing the hostility of those who were against the war. This response from friends and family left the Vietnam veteran without the support and understanding he so badly needed; this invalidation of his experiences and the resulting isolation may well be an important factor in producing an incidence of PTSD symptomatology two to three times higher than that found in other groups of trauma victims. It is also very interesting to note that in a study by Wilson and his colleagues, the small sample of rape victims showed the next highest level of PTSD symptoms. This group contained women who had been sexually abused as children. Could it be that the secrecy and denial that surrounds child sexual abuse affected these women in the same way as the Vietnam veterans, making them more vulnerable to PTSD? (Wilson, Smith and Johnson, 1985, p.162).

The social and individual implications of PTSD

The importance of social support in helping a potential victim either to avoid PTSD, or recover more rapidly, has been largely ignored because it does not fit in with the paradigm underlying conventional biological psychiatry. The psychiatrist Caroline Gorst-Unsworth, who has worked with torture victims, makes the very important point that the PTSD classification on its own simply does not take into account either social adjustment or psychosocial functioning, and yet it is through making social links that the tortured person achieves some psychological and social wellbeing (1992, p.167).

Quarantelli refers to this conceptual polarisation from a slightly different perspective when he contrasts the 'individual trauma approach' with the 'social sponge approach' (1985). The latter refers to the community, which he believes has a great capacity to absorb and prevent the initial negative effects of a disaster. He produces evidence of natural disasters, such as the tornado Xenia disaster in the USA, where the community links were preserved and very few people suffered from PTSD. Quarantelli even goes on to stress that a study carried out 18 months after the disaster showed that a large percent of the people had 'extremely positive reactions to the disaster. Eighty four percent of the people claimed that the people found that their experiences had shown them they could handle crises better than they thought' (1985, p.192). For about a quarter of the population close relationships had improved. For only 2% had they got worse.

In stark contrast to the findings following the Xenia disaster, are those reported after the Buffalo Creek disaster. In this case, the catastrophic outcome was due to

> massive corporate negligence in the form of dumping coal waste in a mountain stream in a manner that created an artificial dam, resulting in increasingly dangerous water pressure behind it. After several days of rain, the dam gave way, and a massive moving wall of 'black water' (containing the coal waste), more than 30 feet high, roared through the narrow creek hollow, devastating the mining hamlets along the 17-mile valley ... 125 people were killed and nearly 5000 were made homeless.
>
> *(Lifton and Olson, 1976, p.1)*

Two years after this disaster, 80% of the survivors were diagnosed as suffering from a 'traumatic neurotic syndrome' and changes in character structure (Titchener and Kapp, 1976, p.296). Lifton and Olson were involved in the psychiatric assessment of the victims over 2 years. Their findings were that everyone was affected and that the forms of psychological impairment were strikingly consistent. What was also striking was the persistence of this impairment, which in many cases got worse rather than better over time.

Quarantelli points out that the 'individual trauma approach' taken up by these authors argues that post-disaster negative reactions have longterm effects. He quotes their statement:

> There is, in fact, mounting evidence that the effects of disaster can extend over generations, and that adverse effects of significant proportion can

occur in children of survivors, even when the children are born some years
after a particular disaster...

(Lifton and Olson, 1976, p.14)

This transgenerational effect has indeed been seen in children of concentration camp survivors and of Hiroshima victims. It seemed to Lifton
and Olson that a similar phenomenon could occur with the Buffalo
Creek disaster victims, since many families appeared to be a 'collection
of severely disturbed and traumatised individuals'.

In accounting for the marked difference in findings arising from the
Buffalo Creek disaster compared to those following the Xenia tornado
disaster, Quarantelli makes several points. For him, the two different
outcomes reflect two different responses: as he sees it, in the Xenia disaster, the community was preserved and, because of this, the psychological damage was contained by supportive and effective networks of
people who shared the traumatic event. In the case of the Buffalo
Creek disaster, the community was destroyed, not only by the flood,
but also by what took place after the disaster, when the federal state
and the relief agencies assigned people on a first-come-first-served
basis to trailers in the mobile home parks, rather than placement
according to prior communal patterns; at the same time the high population density of the new trailer park resulted in a further sense of dis-
location and an unrelieved feeling of temporariness (Lifton and Olson,
1976, p.12).

Lifton and Olson are also of the view that such a communal breakdown results in severe stress and contributes greatly to a wide degree
of medical illnesses and psychiatric disorders; this is what the destruction of the community is attributed to. The victims' resulting sense of
despair was not helped by the fact that the cause of their loss and pain
was the very company on whose employment they depended. This is
the crucial aspect of man-made disasters: the victim can but feel violently angry towards those who caused the disaster or who allowed it
to happen through negligence. Unlike a natural disaster, which, however terrible, can be experienced as a challenge to mankind, a chance for
our communities to prove their worth, a man-made disaster elicits feelings of 'dehumanisation' in the victim who sees himself as worthless, a
dispensable object to others. In Buffalo Creek the victims felt that the
company only cared about the coal and the dollars it brought in and
that it viewed the miners as expendable. To quote one of the victims:
'It's like the coal company is bound and determined to take advantage
of people in one way or another' (Lifton and Olson, 1976, p.10).

In a study comparing the effects of a tornado, the Irish famine and
the Nazi holocaust, Luchterhand concludes that 'As the source of stress
shifts from indiscriminate violence by nature to discriminate oppression by man, the damage to human personality becomes less remedia-
ble' (1971, p.47). The reason for this may have a lot to do with the

intensity of the rage experienced by victims of man-made disasters and their sheer inability to express it for personal or social reasons. As we shall see, when a Holocaust victim is provided with an environment where his rage can be legitimately expressed in all its fury and where his past experiences are fully validated for what they really were, considerable recovery is possible. However, this is rarely the case and especially not for the Buffalo Creek disaster victims, who remained financially dependent on the very company that destroyed their lives. For this reason, Lifton and Olson point out that the resulting psychological effect of a man-made disaster like the one in Buffalo Creek, let alone Hiroshima or the Holocaust, 'is that people who feel their humanity violated and unrecognised by others internalise that diminished sense of themselves in ways that impair their capacity for recovery or even hope' (1976, p.10).

Thus, a man-made disaster like the one in Buffalo Creek can be experienced as an act of violent abuse by man against man. The resulting feelings of utter helplessness and accompanying loss of trust and sense of meaninglessness, in addition to the loss of self-esteem which goes with feeling dehumanised, all these experiences combine to shatter any human being's basic assumptions about life. As Janoff-Bulman stresses, the assumption that we are invulnerable, that 'it can't happen to me', the assumption that the world is meaningful, 'that it makes sense' and, in many, a sense that we are worthy, decent people, these are the three unconscious assumptions we use to conduct our daily life. 'The stress syndrome described by post traumatic stress disorder is largely attributable to the shattering of the victims' basic assumptions about themselves and their world' (1985, p.18).

Janoff-Bulman, however, takes a step further in understanding the victim of psychological trauma. As has already been pointed out, people who suffer from PTSD tend to suffer from guilt and it is particularly prevalent after man-made disasters and after the experience of loss, often leading to states of depression. However, in some victims like rape victims, self-blame is a predictor of good outcome (Burgess and Holmstrom, 1979, p.1279). In an attempt to resolve these inconsistencies, Janoff-Bulman points out that there are in fact two different types of self-blame. One he calls 'behavioural self-blame' which implies that the victim, such as the rape victim, blames herself for her own behaviour leading up to the assault, thus restoring a sense of control over her life in the future: she feels she can take measures to protect herself better. The other type of self-blame is more what would be referred to as guilt and is described by Janoff-Bulman as 'characterological self-blame': it involves attributions to one's enduring personality characteristics and it is maladaptive. The victim focuses 'on the past and the question of deservedness rather than avoidability' (1985, p.29). It affects the victim's very sense of self and is often described as an identification with the aggressor, a defence which we have discussed before in relation to child abuse victims in particular.

Returning to the wider effects of disasters, like the Buffalo Creek disaster, there is no doubt that Lifton and Olson were aware of the social implications of this catastrophe: 'The totality of the Buffalo Creek disaster, then, encompasses this communal breakdown as well as the survivor conflicts described earlier. Both in fact merge in a final common pathway of individual suffering' (Lifton and Olson, 1976, p.12).

Quarantelli, however, would like to see a stronger emphasis on the importance of social factors in the aetiology of PTSD, which he believes are minimised because most psychiatrists tend to use biological psychiatry's 'individual trauma approach' when studying the effects of trauma (1985, p.202); this attitude, as was shown at the beginning of this chapter (pp.162–163), emphasises the specific vulnerability of the individual at the expense of social factors (van der Kolk, 1987; Guze, 1989; Pam, 1990; Gorst-Unsworth, 1992).

Quarantelli quotes Golec to make his point:

> By ignoring the social context and by focusing on the causal primary of disaster impact, the medical metaphor leads to a misunderstanding of *at least some of the post-disaster problems* which have important consequences for disaster victims. It also fails to recognise, therefore, that the most efficacious solutions to some disaster problems may reside in changes in public policy and in intervention aimed at changing aspects of the social structure.

> *(1980, pp.162–163)*

The importance of community ties is perhaps even better illustrated by the many studies carried out on Holocaust victims since the Second World War. What these have shown is that for the victims who settled in Israel, and in particular those who were involved in the formation of the kibbutzim, rehabilitation to a more or less normal existence was far easier than for those victims who settled in the USA or in Europe.

In a study of families of Holocaust survivors in the kibbutz, Hillel Klein notes how, after the liberation of Israel, these survivors needed a strong cohesive in-group which would help them rebuild their shattered identities (1971, p.86). They seem to have found it in the kibbutz with the experience of mutuality and the regaining of a positive sense of self. However, several authors including Klein stress that the marked improvement and well-being of the Holocaust survivors in Israel was also due in great part to the open way they could deal with their rage about their experiences in the concentration camps (1971, p.88).

Their feelings regarding the Arabs were (and still are) very ambivalent: on the one hand they did not want to be identified with the aggressor, hence the need to justify their battles, victories and occupation of Arab territories on the basis of self-defence; on the other hand, the fact that their aggression could be victoriously turned against the 'enemy', the Arab, provided them with a legitimate opportunity to put right their feelings of humiliation and terrible helplessness they had suffered under the Nazis (1971, p.90). In addition, as Klaus Hoppe points out, in Israel the suffering in the Holocaust is given a meaning, for it is seen as having given birth to the state of Israel (1971, p.181).

The other factor which facilitated the rehabilitation of the Holocaust victims in Israel is the fact that readaptation was the goal of the new state itself; as a result, the survivor did not feel excluded or different: on the contrary, he felt an asset to his country.

By contrast, in Germany these victims did not reintegrate well because of their feelings of shame and guilt and, in the USA, many still suffer from the debilitating effects of their torture (Rosen et al., 1991). This does not mean that the Israeli survivors of the Nazi Holocaust are free from such effects; this is far from being the case, but what can be said is that since the state of Israel was created because of the horrors of the Holocaust, it tends to provide its traumatised inhabitants with what they need. Unfortunately, the same cannot be said for its Palestinian neighbours who tend to be identified with the Nazis in the eyes of some Israelis, with the result that the violence once perpetrated upon the Jews can now be re-enacted with the Arabs: the one-time victims can and in some cases do become victimisers. As the Israeli writer Amos Oz points out in his book *The Slopes of Lebanon:*

> Begin presented the war in Lebanon as an act of 'settling accounts' with Jew-haters through the ages. And thus a large part of the public perceives the war in Lebanon as a 'worldwide struggle' (and a neurotic one) against all our past and present foes.
>
> *(1989, pp.40–41)*

What Israel shows us is how long term are the psychological effects of a genocide such as the one we witnessed in Europe this century. For example, however well adapted the Jewish Holocaust victims appear to have become in their new country, the effects of their past seem still to be present in the psychobiology of their own Israeli-born children. In a study on PTSD casualties in the Israeli army victims of the Lebanon war, Solomon and his team found that over the 3 years following the war, the children of Holocaust survivors had greater rates of PTSD than did the control subjects whose parents had not been victims of the Nazi genocide. Similar results had already been found in Israel. The authors suggest that this may reflect an enhanced psychological and/or physiological vulnerability to stress in the children of survivors (Solomon, Kotler and Mikulincer, 1988).

All these findings are of particular importance when attempting to understand the current conflicts between the Serbs, Croatians and Muslims in the former Yugoslavia. Theirs is a ruthless struggle rooted in the violent history and culture of some of the different ethnic groups whose very existence has relied on denigration and hatred of the 'other'. This will be discussed in greater detail when exploring the role of culture in the perpetuation of violence and the associated need to sanction the dehumanisation of the 'other'.

The traumatic origins of violence

In this review of some of the literature on psychological trauma, it becomes ever clearer how important are human attachment bonds and social relations; they are of crucial importance in determining both the incidence and the severity of PTSD. It is not surprising to learn that the loss of significant people also affects those who survive a traumatic event: many studies show that bereavement is indeed associated with a prolonged stress response and the more important the dead or lost person is to the victim, the more severe is their PTSD. What has also been established is that as with deprivation, loss and abuse, psychological trauma is also associated with a propensity for violence. This should come as no surprise when we bear in mind that trauma is itself defined in terms of the sudden rupture of our attachment bonds; the psychobiological implications of this phenomenon will be the subject of the next chapter.

Both the importance of loss and the traumatic origins of violence are particularly obvious in Vietnam veterans suffering from PTSD who fought when they were only adolescents and who also lost a close 'buddy' during the war. Not only was the state of 'psychic numbing' very severe and prolonged in these men, but so was their tendency to outbursts of rage and violence. This particular outcome was attributed by van der Kolk to their developmental stage (1985).

Adolescents need to identify with a peer group to make the transition from the state of childhood dependency on the family to that of adult independence. The group gives the adolescent a sense of belonging and being accepted, a great sense of power or even omnipotence: such feelings derive from a sense of being 'us', all in it together and better than 'them' out there. The degree to which an individual identifies with a group depends on the strengths and weaknesses of that person's sense of self and on the degree of external threat. The greater the outside danger, the stronger the allegiance.

The army makes use of this group cohesion, for it is what holds the men when overcome by fear. In the American Marine Corps, for instance, the training is actually geared toward total submergence in the group: all ties with home and girl friends are ridiculed and the drill instructor becomes the soldier's 'mother, father and friend'. Van der Kolk comments that this identification with the combat unit had persisted in the young PTSD victims (1985). Upon the death of their 'buddy' in combat, these young men had experienced feelings of murderous rage and, being clearly unable to mourn their loss, they had only felt driven by a wish for revenge. Fifteen years later these younger men still felt only revenge and no sense of loss, unlike the older soldiers who felt guilt and were preoccupied with their friends' death. Like Richard Fox (1974), van der Kolk ascribes this rage in the younger men to experiencing the death of their 'buddy' not as the loss of a close person but rather to having experienced 'the death of a friend and the concomitant dissolution of the once omnipotent group as a narcissistic injury' (1985, p.368).

From this point on, many of these men are driven by the need to revenge their buddy. Fox points out that prior to the death of the buddy, these soldiers' aggressive behaviour had been 'adaptive', carried out as a team effort and according to the 'rules of warfare'. This aggression worked on group dynamics, with personal motivation and responsibility becoming secondary to the group-directed goals. After the deaths of their 'buddies', these men's feelings of aggression became intensely hostile and in some cases led to outright slaughter of the Vietnamese (1974).

Fox describes a 21-year-old lance corporal who was referred to him for having beaten his 18-month-old daughter. At the time when he beat her she had been crying and he had failed to quieten her.

> He reported intense feelings of helplessness that he equated with an experience in Vietnam when his unit was pinned down in a mortar attack, and he was unable to be of any help to his wounded and dying buddies who were screaming in pain.
>
> *(1974, p.808)*

When talking about his experiences of killing, he said that it was after the death of a friend that he had felt impelled to shoot a Viet Cong suspect in the back of the head which had given him some satisfaction. However, from then on he had developed recurring nightmares of being shot in the back of the head himself.

He confessed that as his 18-month-old daughter was conceived out of wedlock, he now had doubts about his daughter's paternity since she failed to recognise him when he came home after a year in Vietnam. He had also felt murderous towards his wife and wondered if he could kill someone he loved.

This case may remind the reader of the description of my encounter with the father, Mr Brown, who had viciously attacked and killed his daughter (Chapter 1). Was this killing the result of a re-enactment of his earlier abuse? Did this man suffer from post-traumatic stress disorder? Like most psychiatric patients, he was never investigated for this condition but what we do know is that he had the capacity to 'dissociate', a psychological defence mechanism which comes into play to protect the self from the overwhelming experience of trauma. Traumatic experiences which are felt as too painful to bear are split off from ordinary consciousness to be stored as separate units. These isolated sets of interacting affects and memories can be reactivated by perceptions or mood states in the victim that are congruent with the traumatic experience. This is what probably happened to both Fox's patient and Mr Brown: their inability to soothe their child's pain took them back to the overwhelmingly painful feelings of their own past traumatic experiences and the murderous rage of those who feel annihilated by the other.

Van der Kolk gives a vivid example of re-enactment in a traumatised adult. He describes a patient of his who had fought in Vietmam: one night in 1968, this man had lit a cigarette which caused the death of a friend by a Viet Cong bullet: from 1969 to 1986, on the exact anniversary of his friend's death, to the hour and minute, he committed 'armed robbery' by putting a finger in his pocket and carrying out a 'holdup' in order to provoke gunfire from the police. His compulsive and unconscious re-enactment came to an end when he understood its meaning (1989, p.391).

This conceptualisation of the reactivation of traumatic material tallies with the cognitive model of state-dependent memories postulated by Bower (1981). Janet called these new spheres of consciousness organised around memories of intensely arousing experiences 'subconsious fixed ideas'. He emphasised that these memories could be split up into fragments and encoded as such. As a result, traumatic memories that are reactivated can be expressed as sensory perceptions, somatic or affect states and behavioural re-enactments. This tallies with current theories which postulate the existence of a variety of 'memory banks' representing the multiple forms of mnemonic representation existing in the brain.

> The brain has a variety of ways to encode and store information and that given information storage system in the brain is not necessarily accessible to every other network of stored information ... As the motivational state changes access to innate or learned behaviour patterns is allowed expression.
>
> *(Gazzaniga and Le Doux, 1978)*

People who react to stress by carrying on as though nothing has happened dissociate themselves from the reality of their pain, terror or humiliation, but at a price: the self becomes divided and the process of dissociation becomes part of the patient's identity, to be brought back into action when faced with further stress or even situations that are only reminiscent of the original stress. As a result of this repeated dissociative process, the victim becomes emotionally constricted and cannot experience the full range of feelings within the same state of consciousness. This can lead to a progressive narrowing of conscious-ness and an increasing inability to deal with reality.

As Spiegel (1990) points out in his study on dissociation and hypno-tisability in PTSD,

> most of the symptoms associated with post traumatic stress disorder in DSM-III have a dissociative flavour: the re-experiencing of a traumatic event through intrusive recollections, nightmares or flashbacks; emotional numb-ing with feelings of detachment or isolation, stimulus sensitivity (including the avoidance of environmental cues that are associated with recollections of the traumatic events); survivor guilt; and difficuly in concentrating.

(1990, p.250)

As for the 'psychic numbing' and associated social withdrawal, this is seen as a kind of pseudonormality in which the victims avoid such painful memories through dissociation or repression with a constric-tion in their affective response. The author notes that:

> this polarisation of consciousness can be seen in the hypnotic state, in which intense absorption in the hypnotic focal experience is accomplished via the dissociation of experience at the periphery. Like the hypnotic experi-ence, traumatic imagery is either intense or intensely avoided.

(1990, p.253)

Spiegel found that a more frequent use of dissociative defences is observed in PTSD victims compared to controls.

However, it is in childhood that these defences are most accessible to the threatened individual and it is during this stage in human devel-opment that the effects of trauma appear most devastating.

Chapter 11
The Traumatic Origins of Violence in Childhood

'I thus drew steadily nearer to that truth, by whose partial discovery I have been doomed to such dreadful shipwreck: that man is not truly one, but truly two ... and I hazard the guess that man will be ultimately known for a mere polity of multifarious, incongruous and independent denizens.'

Dr Jekyll and Mr Hyde by R.L. Stevenson (1886)

The abused child

The links between psychological trauma and violence are often denied or minimised, particularly in relation to childhood abuse. In some circles, children are still believed to be exempt from the effects of psychological trauma. The reasons for such a denial of psychic pain and its effects on children are many, and have to a great extent been discussed earlier when considering Freud's rejection of the seduction theory. However, research carried out in the last 20 years now makes it clear that childhood psychological trauma does exist and that it is an aetiological factor in a number of psychiatric disorders both in children and in adults, as well as being a powerful cause of human violence.

Following a brief survey of the psychiatric literature on the longterm effects of abuse in childhood, we will attempt to explore in some detail the recent psychological and biological evidence which links up the experience of childhood trauma with subsequent acts of human violence. Clearly, if any links are to be made between trauma and violence, we need to clarify whether what is referred to as childhood abuse is in fact a traumatic event capable of producing, under certain conditions, a post-traumatic stress reaction, with all that this implies in terms of the longterm effects we find in adults.

Defining child abuse is far from easy. In the USA for example, there is only a modest consensus regarding the definitions of childhood abuse and neglect, even though the federal government enacted The Child Abuse Prevention and Treatment Act of 1974 and established a

National Centre for Child Abuse and Neglect. The problem becomes even more acute when studying child maltreatment in different cultures (Gelles and Lancaster, 1987, pp.15–30). Richard Gelles suggests that R. Rohner probably offers the most satisfactory solution by seeing abuse as a specialised form of rejection: he defines rejection as the absence or significant withdrawal of warmth and affection of parents towards their children. Such rejection can take the form of hostility and aggression or indifference and neglect. Acceptance is defined as warmth, affection, and love.

Such a definition is in keeping with the research on attachment behaviour which we reviewed in the first part of this book. We may recall how, in Chapter 4, we were made aware of our need for 'significant' others to sustain ourselves both physically and emotionally with the result that, in their absence, we may become ill or depressed. In Chapter 5, it became clear that at the root of our experience of loss and all its manifestations, is the experience of 'deprivation', otherwise known as a failure of attunement. In infancy, the disruption or absence of this crucial interactive experience between mother and baby is seen to be a key factor in producing the neurophysiological changes which make us and our primate cousins more liable to aggressive or violent behaviour. Such an outcome, due to loss or neglect, can be understood as the reciprocal manifestation of a damaged attachment system, the result of a failure of attunement, of a deficiency in the provision of attachment-related psychobiological regulation and its associated emotional stimulation and arousal modulation. In Chapter 6, the 'avoidant' infant, as classified by the Strange Situation, appears to demonstrate just such a tendency to be hostile in her interactions with others; such behaviour is attributed to the quality of care she had in the previous year. Indeed, the mother of such an infant is judged to be both emotionally unavailable and prone to be physically abusive. It is worth remembering, at this point, the study carried out by Troy and Sroufe (Chapter 6) which showed how an abused child could become either victim or victimiser, depending on the context; this shows that it is the relationship between self and other, in this case mother–infant, that is internalised to become a 'working model' or 'object relationship' of the self in its interactions with others. This explains the repeated tendency of abused people to identify with the aggressor, a role that at least ensures them some control over events and a possibility of revenge. The 'avoidant' child has learnt to 'cut off' from her rejecting mother so as to retain some sense of control when under threat, while at the same time being able to make contact with her caregiver. This same dissociation takes place if mother is away for too long.

The mother of an abused child shows her little empathy: in other words she cannot identify with her child's feelings and needs, a state Stern describes as 'intersubjective relatedness' (Chapter 7). As a result, her child develops a poor sense of self-esteem and, not surprisingly, since empathy is in part an extension of the self to others, such children also show little empathy and an inverse amount of aggression towards their peers. They are essentially egocentric and this predisposes them to maladaptive behaviour with others.

Main and George (1985) found that abused toddlers responded negatively or even aggressively to signs of distress in their peers, whereas nonabused children of the same age showed interest and sadness. This may be because abused children find their peer's distress intolerable, as it can remind them of their own pain and, possibly, the way their parent dealt with their tears.

A battered wife, who was a patient in the author's group, reported that if she cried as a child when she was distressed, her father would beat her up and shout: 'Now you have something to cry about.'

If an abused child has difficulties in empathising, she also has certain cognitive difficulties. In a study on the relation between mother–infant attachment and the emergence of visual self-recognition, Schneider-Rosen and Cicchetti found that maltreated children were developmentally delayed or impaired in their affective reactions to their mirror images (1984). Their conclusions were that these children either hid their feelings or experienced themselves in a negative way. Abused children also tend to interpret peer behaviour as having aggressive intent, which increases their tendency to be hostile.

Recent research carried out by Main and Solomon (1989) on abused or neglected infants exposed to the Strange Situation has identified another category of attachment called the disorganised/disoriented type of attachment. It describes a mixture of avoidant, proximity seeking and resistant reunion behaviours with other bizarre symptoms such as interrupted undirected movements or expressions and strange postures. By the age of six these same infants had developed a controlled form of reunion behaviour either of a punitive nature or of a 'caretaking type' (Main and Cassidy, 1988). The mothers of these children were found to have lost a parent during their childhood and to have been unable to mourn this loss.

Child abuse and psychological trauma

Child abuse now encompasses a vast field of research and embodies all types of maltreatments such as neglect, emotional abuse, physical abuse and sexual abuse.

Neglect is described as the lack of appropriate supervision or provision of basic needs of the child and is believed to be the most common form of abuse, accounting for about two-thirds of identified cases of abuse (Rogers, 1983 p.1).

Emotional abuse refers to a form of child maltreatment which can take the form of consistent negative attention such as repeated criticisms or belittlements, or a lack of attention such as withdrawal or rejection. This type of abuse is the most difficult to measure but it is probably the most common form of abuse in families.

Physical abuse defines all forms of non-accidental injury inflicted on children by their caregivers.

Sexual abuse is now of growing concern and usually involves more than one type of abuse, as was so vividly illustrated by Rachel's childhood experience (Chapter 9). It has been the most difficult form of abuse to recognise, and some people, including therapists, still question whether incest is always a form of child abuse. They argue that some children get pleasure from the experience and collude with it. In response to those who blame children for their abuse, both Finkelhor (1984) and Russell (1984) have argued that it is illogical even to suggest consent in children given the discrepancy in power between the adult and child. Bearing in mind the nature of attachment relations, we can understand how a child made fearful by the secrecy her abusing parent imposes, if not by the physical experience itself, cannot but feel an increased attachment for the abusing parent. She is being abused by the very same person she would normally run to for protection. If we also realise that children of all ages justify their parents' maltreatment on the basis of their own failings and badness and thereby identify with their abuser's view of themselves, one can see how, on purely developmental grounds, such children are not free consenting individuals in their parent's perverse relationship. Indeed, the abused child is for the father a source of all his longings for the love and care he never received from his mother: the little girl is only an object of gratification for her father's needs. As in all perversions, the sexual act is compulsive and infused with power as the father exerts total control over his child; the secrecy only adds to his excitement as does the pain he inflicts on his child. In this way, the attachment bond is twisted into one of compulsive violence to become as Stoller put it yet another manifestation of the 'erotic form of hatred' (1975). This increased attachment in the face of danger is a key feature in understanding why abused children do not want to be separated from their parents and why hostages can become so involved with their captors. Van der Kolk reminds us of how the bond between the batterer and his victim in abusive marriages resembles that between captor and hostage (1989). Having isolated herself from others, the battered victim devotes herself to pleasing her partner, only to rediscover that she has failed again when she becomes the victim of yet another attack. While being abused, these women tend to dissociate themselves, not quite believing what is happening to them. The battering is followed by a state of post-traumatic numbing with feelings of guilt, misery and helplessness. The violence brings victim and abuser together. In the calmness that follows these women will forgive and become reconciled with their partners, so restoring the fantasy of being one again, a state so desperately yearned for by all victims of abuse or deprivation. Unfortunately, as van der Kolk stresses, the battered woman has often no memory of the abusive trauma because it is usually dissociated and 'state-dependent', that is, it can only be 'accessed' or re-experienced when the victim is exposed to external or internal cues reminiscent of the trauma. This means that the victim realistically cannot assess her predicament: this allows her longing for a close attachment to get the upper hand and she remains with her partner. Thus, in this form of maltreatment as in all forms of family abuse, the violence actually consolidates the attachment bond between victim and victimiser (Bowlby, 1984). What happens to the neurophysiological substrate of the attachment behaviour will be discussed further on in this chapter.

Child abuse has been studied in other primates and seems to occur in response to similar conditions as those reported in humans. Suomi and Ripp (1983) report on a study of a colony of motherless rhesus monkeys who became mothers themselves. Their findings are very similar to those of Harlow: the maternally deprived monkeys produced very inadequate and abusive mothers.

Ruppenthal et al. (1976) carried out a study on such mothers and found several factors to be associated with poor maternal care. Early social deprivation, particularly prolonged deprivation, was associated with inadequate mothering. The younger the mother at the first delivery, the more likely she was to be abusive. The female offspring of inadequate mothers were three times as likely to receive adequate maternal care as were male offspring. The latter, in turn, were four times more likely than female infants to be physically abused by their mothers. The maternal care of these deprived mothers improved with parity.

Suomi and Ripp (1983) were to find another predisposing factor to child abuse: the group of monkeys they studied had been separated from their peers at regular intervals during their development to be left in isolated cages for 4 days at a time. What they discovered was that a quarter to a third of the monkeys were badly affected by these separations; they became socially withdrawn and lethargic, a reaction the authors described as 'depressive'. These particular monkeys later became inadequate mothers whereas their counterparts did not: not only did the latter hardly react to the separation but all of them provided adequate mothering to their offspring. These differences are ascribed to different genetic predispositions already present early in infancy, when the potentially depressive monkeys would react with a lot of fear to mild environmental challenges (1983, p.69). Poor attunement for whatever reason appears to be involved in these more vulnerable monkeys.

Suomi points out that there are some strong human parallels with the primate findings. Many abusers were abused or neglected in early life and abuse happens more with socially isolated mothers. Many abusive parents have also a history of depression. Premature infants, especially males, are at risk of abuse.

However, there are also clear differences between the abusive motherless primate mothers and human child abusers, the first being that most of the women involved in child abuse do not grow up in the absence of mother. A great proportion of human abuse occurs after infancy and parity makes no difference to the risk of abuse. Also, unlike humans, primates took good care of their defective infants (Schapiro and Mitchell, 1983, p.42). This last finding points to the role of expectations in human abuse: parents are seen to react negatively to a baby crying if that child has been labelled 'premature' or 'difficult' (Frodi, 1985). Such evidence highlights the cultural and social dimensions of child abuse, factors which will be considered in more detail in the next chapter.

It is important to realise that what all these primate studies show is that the primate infants subjected to abuse and deprivation are likely to engage in aggressive if not violent relationships with their peers when they become adults: this is particularly so for the males and reflects similar findings in humans. In Harlow's study (1974) the females quickly learnt to suppress their aggression whilst the males continued to be violent. The females, however, remained distrustful of any heterosexual contact.

The most important principle to take away from the primate literature is that there is no single factor responsible for child abuse. An interactive model is necessary, where the nature of the abuse, the genetic predisposition and stage of development of the victim, the family and sociocultural contexts all play a part. Such an approach attends to the interactions taking place between the 'type' of abuse and the 'type' of child within the context of the family, community and society at large.

What has become increasingly apparent, is just how much individuals depend on the attachment relationships of their formative years to build up both their self-esteem and their capacity to form satisfactory attunement relationships. These psychological developments are themselves rooted in the psychobiology of the attachment system.

In *Dangerous Secrets,* Weissberg also makes the attachment relation central to his understanding of abuse when he states that defective parental attachment to their children is central to the problem of abuse and neglect (1983, p.98). He believes that 'primary among the long-term emotional effects of abuse and neglect are problems with violence and intimacy, and an inability to modulate strong feelings' (1983, p.101). Such a description resembles very much the effects of post-traumatic stress disorder, which is scarcely surprising since it is the same psychobiological system that is being disrupted by the traumatic event, producing as Lindemann stated, 'a sudden, uncontrollable disruption of affiliative bonds'.

The evidence reviewed so far gives some insight into the many ways child abuse can affect future development, but it is evidently impossible to do justice here to the vast amount of research in this field. What needs to be done, however, is to focus on those aspects of childhood trauma which contribute to violent behaviour in both children and adults. Such an endeavour relies on making the link between abuse and trauma, a link which is now very familiar since it relates to the work on the long-term effects of deprivation (Chapter 4) and abuse (Chapter 9); the noticeable increase in hostility and aggression which was observed as a result of these traumatic experiences was attributed to the manifestation of a damaged attachment system: violence can be seen as the manifestation of attachment gone wrong.

Attempts are now being made to understand how children can and do suffer from post-traumatic stress disorder. What has become clear is that children react to psychological trauma much as adults do. Leonore Terr defines trauma in simple terms, seeing it as: 'the mental result of one sudden, external blow or series of blows, rendering the young person temporarily helpless and breaking past ordinary coping and defensive operations ...' (1991, p.11). For Terr, the trauma begins with events outside the child. Once these have occurred, a number of internal changes take place within the child: these changes last, often to the detriment of the young victim (1991, p.11).

When discussing single blow traumas, Terr points out that these usually meet the criteria of avoidance, repetition and hyperalertness seen in adult traumatic responses (DSM-III). The young victims often have to find reasons for their unexpected suffering and they often feel very guilty, no doubt because many are still in what Piaget describes as the egocentric stage of development. The impact of such a traumatic event is illustrated by Terr's study of the effects of psychic trauma on 25 children of varying ages who were kidnapped in a school bus in Chowchilla; 4 years after the event, every child still exhibited post-traumatic effects, irrespective of their different ages (Terr, 1983).

As for the second type of psychological trauma, the longstanding or multiple traumas, these produce different effects. Massive attempts are made to protect the psyche and the self: this is achieved through denial and psychic numbing, self-hypnosis and dissociation.

Although denial and psychic numbing are often absent in children who suffer from single shock trauma, these defences are usually very much in evidence in those who have been through longstanding and repeated horrific experiences such as have been described by childhood victims of physical and/or sexual abuse. These children can also suffer for years from specific fears, a tendency to 'see things', repetitions of the trauma during play and other forms of behavioural or physiological re-enactments of their traumatic experience. They also tend to change their views about life, about the trustworthiness of people and about the future.

However, some traumatised children do not develop PTSD: they appear to be resilient or they develop depressive illnesses, multiple personality disorders or a tendency to abuse drugs. There is clearly a need to study the development of PTSD in response to varying childhood traumas as well as the factors which affect the severity and pattern of this disorder.

Most important to the study of the traumatic origins of violence, is the child's enhanced capacity to achieve spontaneous self-hypnosis and to dissociate. As was seen with the 'avoidant' infants and then with adult victims of trauma, this defence mechanism plays an important part in warding off the impact of an overwhelming trauma. When left without any external source of protection, the child manages the abuse through internal changes: one such mechanism is that of dissociation. Thus, for example, some sexually abused girls will, when molested or raped, experience themselves leaving their body and looking down at what is being done to them.

Dissociation can subsequently be used to ward off other potential traumas with a resulting constriction of the personality. The resulting 'multiple personality disorder' or MPD is seen by many American psychiatrists as a major defensive strategy to cope with severe trauma that has occurred generally and repeatedly in young children. Braun reports studies which confirm child abuse in more than 90% of the cases (1990, p.228). Spiegel sees 'multiple personality disorder' as a chronic form of PTSD (1990, p.247). It is characterised by the disruption of memory and identity whereby the affected person appears to exhibit more than one personality. There is a lot of research currently being carried out on this particular disorder in the USA (Putnam, 1986).

However, the British reaction to MPD is rather reminiscent of Krafft-Ebbing's response to Freud's paper on the aetiology of hysteria when he said that it sounded like 'a scientific fairy tale'. For instance, Mersky, in a recent review of past cases of MPD, ends up stating that suggestion and prior preparation of the patients are at the root of this condition. He concludes by stating that: 'The concept of MPD should be seen now as, at best, a by-way in the history of ideas' (1992, p.338). He believes that not only does its recognition jeopardise the treatment of other diagnoses but 'the value and good sense of psychiatry become suspect as the wonders multiply' (1992, p.339).

There may be a case for suggesting that, by focusing on the different personalities developed by patients to ward off their traumatic experiences, a therapist might encourage further splitting. However, in his eagerness to protect 'the good sense of psychiatry', Mersky does in fact throw away the baby with the bathwater. He ignores the importance of trauma in producing these dissociative experiences and what this means in terms of our understanding of the human mind.

For instance, the conventional neurophysiological theories of psychiatry have as yet to explain why an English-speaking man, diagnosed to be suffering from active thought disorder due to a recurrent manic-depressive psychosis, should lose all trace of this symptom while speaking in another language. The same phenomenon has been reported in other bilinguals (Zulueta 1984).

The human mind, including the psychiatrist's mind, tends to deny the powerful effects of trauma so as to avoid being a witness to the contortions of our psyche when it is overcome by a sense of overwhelming helplessness. The story of Anna O, Breuer's 21-year-old patient who helped Freud to focus on hysteria, vividly illustrates the phenomenon of dissociation: when sitting by her dying father's bedside, she suddenly saw a black snake coming to bite her father. In her attempt to ward it off, she found her arm to be paralysed and saw her fingers turn into little snakes with death heads. When the hallucinated snake vanished she was so terrified she tried to pray 'but language failed her: she could find no tongue in which to speak, till at last she thought of some children's verses in English and then found herself able to think and pray in that language' (Breuer and Freud, 1893–1895, p.39).

By switching from German to English, Anna O fended off her terror and dissociated herself from feelings and memories stored in her maternal language. She was to use this 'linguistic defence' till the end of her treatment with Breuer when she regained the capacity to speak in German, her mother tongue (Zulueta, 1987, p. 103).

The fact that Anna O hallucinated as she did by her father's bedside makes one suspect that earlier traumatic events in her childhood may have been re-activated by the experienc of her father's illness. This is indeed what Freud was to report in his paper on 'The aetiology of hysteria' (1896a).

A refusal on the part of psychiatrists and therapists to validate the horrors of their patients' tortured past implies a refusal to take seriously the unconscious psychological mechanisms that individuals need to use to protect themselves from the unspeakable. Such a denial is, however, no longer ethical, for it is in this human capacity to dissociate that lies part of the secret of both childhood abuse and the horrors of the Nazi genocide, both forms of human violence, so often carried out by 'respectable' men and women. The Nazi doctor would go home to wife, children and dinner after a day's work in the death and torture chambers of the concentration camps, leaving behind him the horrors of a human hell. The child abuser goes out to work, leaving behind the secret nightmare of his personal torture, a nightmare carried on in the psyche of his child.

In her important work on the unconscious origins of violence, Alice Miller explains the German people's collusion with Hitler as being the result of their authoritarian upbringing (1983). Hitler himself was the victim of severe physical abuse. Together, the Fuhrer and his people recreated a victorious version of the 'split off' aspects of their own traumatic history, projecting on to their Jewish victims all that they hated about themselves and their parents.

This brings us back to the crucial question of how trauma and violence are so closely linked. In attempting to reply to this question it is necessary to take into account the two dimensions involved in the manifestation of human violence: the first is the 'self' derived from a matrix of internalised early attachment relationships bolstered by powerful psychological defence mechanisms such as denial, dissociation, projection and displacement, all commonly used in dealing with trauma; the second comprises the neurophysiological underpinnings of the attachment system and their profound disruption as a result of trauma. Both of these entities are involved in the origins of violence which, at one level, can be seen as an extreme manifestation of human rage due to overwhelming narcissistic injuries, and at another level can be understood as the manifestation of a disrupted attachment system.

The phenomenon of narcissistic rage has in great part been dealt with in earlier chapters. What still needs to be understood are the long-term neurophysiological aspects of PTSD. In van der Kolk's view, the victim's compulsion to repeat the trauma lies at the heart of the traumatic origins of violence (1989).

When exposed to a real or perceived danger, a series of physiological processes take place in the human brain which activates the autonomic 'fight and flight' reactions, the immune system and the hormonal system involved with stress – a system otherwise known as the 'hypothalamic–pituitary adrenocortical axis'. Thus, the initial alarm produces a state of anxiety and hypervigilance accompanied by the activation of the neurophysiological system. These are rapid and reversible responses but they do use up the available stores of neurotransmitters and hormones. If the trauma persists and, with it the associated state of general arousal, the brain changes to produce a 'state memory' (Perry, 1991). This implies the establishment of a new homeostatic set point to regulate the neurotransmitter systems controlling arousal, affect and the functioning of the 'fight flight' system. These 'state memories' are at the root of many PTSD symptoms; indeed, during these states of massive autonomic arousal, memories of the trauma are laid down which will later be reactivated by an internal cue such as a feeling, or an external event reminiscent of the earlier trauma. The result is that the victim feels she is back in the original traumatising situation. In this way, battered women who otherwise live competently are plunged back through their intimate relationship into the violence of their childhood home with all the feelings of terror and helplessness they felt as children.

A trauma victim is therefore likely to be exposed repeatedly to states of high arousal, as if the trauma had returned. Unaware that this is in fact not the case, unaware of her past original trauma, the victim is therefore unable to assess her situation and resolve her difficulties. The somatic experiences accompanying the revival of the old trauma are also extremely unpleasant and are linked to a failure to modulate the levels of arousal. This state of affairs is believed to be due to a dysregulation of the serotonin system which appears to be involved in modulating the activity of other neurotransmitters and in the fine-tuning of emotional reactions, particularly aggression.

Accompanying this chronic state of high arousal, is a reduced ability to use symbols and fantasy to cope with stress. The result is that the trauma victim tends to respond through action rather than thought. This predisposition to repeat the traumatic experiences betrays an inherent vulnerability which has already been touched upon when discussing the effects of maternal deprivation in primates. Though these deprived monkeys appeared to adapt to their social environment, when under stress they were in fact easily aroused and would become socially withdrawn or aggressive. Their levels of aggression were commensurate with their degree of maternal deprivation, particularly in males (Harlow and Mears, 1979; Kraemer, 1985).

Even those monkeys who been less affected by maternal deprivation betrayed their vulnerability when they responded inappropriately to sexual arousal and to social cues. Their responses to stress were a higher than normal increase in catecholamines, the 'fight and flight' neurotransmitters, and a below normal cortisol response.

It may also be recalled how Panksepp and his colleagues described social bonding as an 'opioid addiction' (Panksepp, Siviy and Normansell, 1985). They were able to show how the vocalisations produced by young animals separated from their mothers would stop if they were given opiates and that the symptoms of distress produced by separation do in fact resemble narcotic withdrawal states. Restoring social contact alleviates the separation distress and strengthens the social bonds: it does this partly by releasing endogenous opiates. In addition, the brain areas with the highest levels of opiate receptors are also those involved in attachment behaviour, and the lack of caregiving in infancy decreases the number of these opioid receptors.

Such findings have led to research on the endogenous opiates during stress: what has been found is that high levels of stress, including social stress, activate the opioid system. Using the animal model of inescapable shock which closely resembles PTSD in its effects, it was noticed that animals exposed to stress did in fact develop stress-induced analgesia, an effect mediated by endogenous opioids and blocked by naloxone, an opioid receptor blocker. The same pheno-menon has been observed in humans.

Van der Kolk's team carried out a controlled study where they exposed eight Vietnam veterans with PTSD to a combat videotape which they knew from previous research would reactivate their trauma. During the viewing of the tape, seven of the men showed a 30% reduc-tion in perception of pain, an effect which was reversed with naloxone. The authors calculate that the analgesic effect of 15 minutes of a com-bat movie was equivalent to the administration of 8 mg morphine (Pitman et al., 1990).

Van der Kolk notes that one of the prime functions of the infant–mother relationship is to modulate physiological arousal in the infant. This is probably achieved through the opioid system. However, victims of childhood abuse and neglect fail to modulate their arousal levels and may well need a much higher activation of the endogenous opiate system to feel soothed. 'These victimised people neutralise their hyperarousal by a variety of addictive behaviours including compulsive re-exposure to situations reminiscent of the trauma' (van der Kolk, 1989, p.401).

This important finding casts a new light on the phenomenon of rep-etition compulsion: trauma victims may well become addicted to their trauma, re-creating it in some form or other throughout their lives. The repeated exposure to traumatic stress produces both the need for the activation of the endogenous opioid system and the resultant with-drawal symptoms. This may partly explain the link between childhood abuse and self-destructive behaviour: often these people become self-mutilators; many report finding peace and relief from their pain and arousal in the act of cutting themselves.

It is important to note that, as with all human behaviour, the self is also rooted in the psychobiology of the attachment system: so while the self-mutilator slashes herself and the endorphins she releases calm her down, her sense of self may also find intense satisfaction in the act of controlling and attacking her body, now simply a part-object in the enactment of her self-abuse. Trauma-induced self-destructive behaviour can also be found in veterans who enlist as mercenaries, sexually abused children who become prostitutes (Welldon, 1988), physically abused children who recreate their violent abuse with their partners. It appears that these people often feel apprehensive, empty or sad: the trauma appears to act as the purveyor of the missing endogenous opi-oids: it has become an addiction.

The traumatic origins of 'mental disorders'

Having explored in some detail the relationship between child abuse, trauma and its violent manifestations, it is now possible to look into both the prevalence and the destructive consequences of child abuse. It is particularly in the field of adult psychiatry that such findings are being made and, as will become clear with children too, violent behaviour is an intrinsic aspect of the clinical picture.

Alvin Rosenfeld reported that out of the first 18 of his psychiatric patients treated in one year, 33% reported a history of incest and most had a diagnosis of 'hysterical character disorder' (1979). He was struck by the high incidence of sexual abuse these findings implied.

Judith Herman (1986) looked at the diagnostic summaries of 190 consecutive psychiatric outpatients and found that 22% had been victims of physical or sexual violence: most of these were women who continued to be victims (81%). Out of the 16% who acknowledged having been physically or sexually abusive to others, most of these were men (81%). In summary, 29% of the male outpatient population had been abusive to others. These findings of major sex differences in violent behaviour are quite characteristic, female patients being more commonly victims of violence and men more often offenders. The majority of the reported violence was intrafamilial and the most common type of abuse reported was physical abuse in childhood. Some 13% of the women had been sexually abused; the men denied any history of sexual abuse. The diagnoses of substance abuse and 'borderline personality disorder' were particularly common in women who had been victimised.

Elaine Carmen and her colleagues report that almost half of the 188 psychiatric patients they interviewed had histories of physical and/or sexual abuse; again females were much more likely than males to report a history of abuse (Carmen, Rieker and Mills, 1984). As with previous findings, abused males were more likely than abused females or other males, to have abused others.

> Perhaps the most important characteristic that distinguished the behaviour of the abused males and females was that the males had become more aggressive while the females had become more passive. In some ways the sex role stereotypes seemed to be exaggerated in this sample.

> *(1984, p.382)*

Indeed, one of the characteristics that differentiated between male and female victims was the way they coped with anger: 33% of the men expressed their anger by directing it aggressively towards others, whereas only 14% of the women did so; 66% of abused women turned their anger inwards, a quarter of these becoming actively self-destructive.

George Brown and Bradley Anderson came up with similar results on a sample of 1040 consecutive psychiatric admissions where 185 reported childhood abuse (1991).

These studies concur with the studies on people suffering from 'borderline personality disorder' which we referred to when discussing the victims of child sexual abuse (Herman, Perry and van der Kolk, 1989; Zanarini et al., 1989; Schetzky, 1990). Studies of adult rape victims and battered women also show that many were physically and sexually abused as children and that they tend to be abused or raped by spouses or others in adulthood (Browne and Finkelhor, 1986).

In her excellent book, *Mother, Madonna and Whore*, Estela Welldon emphasises the role of neglect and abuse, both physical and sexual, in the psychogenesis of these disorders (Welldon, 1988). She also emphasises the three-generational or 'transgenerational' nature of this process.

> From being victims, such people become the victimizers. In their actions they are the perpetrators of the victimization and humiliation previously inflicted on them. They treat their victims in the same way they felt treated themselves: as part-objects who are there only to satisfy their [parents'] whims and bizarre expectations. Such apparent sexual acting-out is a manic defence against formidable fears related to the threat of losing both mother and a sense of identity.
>
> *(1988, p.9)*

Welldon makes the point that the abuser is often the mother (Welldon, 1988). She stresses that the person who suffers from such a perversion is aware of the compulsion to repeat the action but is not aware of the underlying rage and hatred. 'The perverse individual has been prevented, from a very early age, from achieving sexual emotional maturity (that is genital sexuality), and consequently has difficulties in forming satisfactory heterosexual relationships' (1988, p.11).

Ken is a young homosexual man who asked to be assessed for psychotherapy and recounted the following story: his father had left home before Ken was born but he would reappear from time to time, get drunk and create violent incidents when he would hit the children and then be thrown out by his wife; the patient's mother was described as a terribly dominant woman who beat Ken and the other children regularly; he also had several brothers and sisters, one of whom was his twin, the one person he says he was close to.

Ken cannot remember ever being cuddled; on the contrary, he recalls his mother washing his hair and then, in a fit of rage, bashing his head against the sink. She would also dress him and his brother in girls' clothes. However, he is grateful to his mother for providing for them.

Ken spent most of his youth in a drug-induced dream world, that is, until he discovered plastic surgery. This destructive passion followed an accident which led him to have surgery to his face. He was delighted by this as he had always hated the way he looked. Since this period, Ken has had more than 30 operations to his face: before the operation, he used to feel terribly excited at the thought of being 'knocked out' and cut up. But, now that he no longer responds to the anaesthetic, the pain during surgery is so intense he has to be held down and, as a result, he can also no longer find surgeons willing to operate on him. Though he is aware that the operation will not change how he feels about his face, he is 'addicted' to the surgery itself which makes him quite 'euphoric'.

Though Ken said he had no interest in sex, he had a relationship with a man, the first long-term relationship he had ever had. This relationship appears to have made him feel increasingly insecure and tearful. He had also become aware of being very violent, so violent that his friend had ended up in hospital on numerous occasions. Driven by the fear of being abandoned, Ken would wind up his partner so as to have a fight.

Ken's sad story does illustrate the constellation of perversion, sexual identity problems and violence which Welldon describes. He also reminds us of the addiction to trauma which so often takes over the life of child abuse victims.

As with aggression in other victims of sexual and physical abuse, there is a difference in the aim of the perverse act between men and women: men aim their act at an outside 'part-object' whilst women aim it at their own bodies or at objects they see as their creation, such as their babies; both their bodies and babies are perceived as part-objects, with no other function than that of satisfying the woman's compulsive perverse activities (Welldon, 1988, p.72).

In her study of female perversion, Welldon puts an end to the idealisation of motherhood: she shows how children who have been subjected to mothers who use them for their own personal gratification, will themselves be vulnerable to repeating such perverse behaviour on others or on themselves and their own children: the latter manifestations are characteristic of women.

> While man pursues his perverse goals with his penis, woman does so with her whole body, since her reproductive organs are much more widespread and their manifestations are more apparent.
>
> The power of the womb distinguishes women from men and leads to the power of motherhood – truly as potent as, and usually more far-reaching and more pervasive than, the power of money or law or social position ... It is a power which is normally used in a beneficent way, but the same instincts that produce love, fulfilment, and security can, if things go wrong, produce their opposites. The power of the womb can lead to perversions ...
>
> *(1988, p.40–41)*

What Welldon is referring to is the perversion of what she refers to as the 'maternal instinct' and which we would describe as the attachment bond: this can result in the distorted type of object-relationships seen in other perversions which involves dehumanising the 'other' and using 'it' to satisfy a compulsive desire for complete control and fusion. The resulting mother–infant relationship brings with it the deprivation and abuse with all the inevitable distortions in the formation of the self. Childhood abuse is very much at the root of sexual perversions.

Another area of increasing social concern is the plight of adolescents who commit suicide: their rate of suicide has risen considerably throughout Europe and particularly in the UK. For instance, in England and Wales alone, the youth suicide rate rose by 90% between 1974 and 1988 (Pritchard, 1992). This means that in the south of Britain every day one person under the age of 25 commits suicide: 80% of young suicides are male; 80% of young attempted suicides are female. Some of the factors known to be associated with suicide may be relevant, such as unemployment, family breakdown, alcohol and drug abuse, AIDS and the availability of methods of committing suicide. It is suggested that changes in society may have resulted in men feeling less integrated and therefore more vulnerable to other stresses, a view derived from Durkheim's work. However, what is rarely mentioned in the psychiatric literature is that there may also be an important link between adolescent abuse and suicide rates. The American National Centre on Child Abuse and Neglect reports that adolescent abuse is twice as prevalent as abuse of children under six. In 1980, 192 000 adolescents were recognised as having been abused in the USA but the actual incidence is much higher. Girls are twice as likely to be abused in this age group. The fact that men are more likely to kill themselves than women may well link up with earlier findings showing a greater degree of violent aggression in male victims compared to women.

Most abused adolescents show signs of depression and self-destruction. Herbert Hendin reports how, in young black urban male subjects, suicide was the outcome of intense feelings of rage and murderous impulses originating in early personal exposure to violence (1991). These young men felt that they would not be able to control their murderous rage. Just under half of young suicide victims had a history of aggressive behaviour.

In their review of the literature on child abuse and violence, Lewis and her colleagues found that a high proportion of violent delinquents and criminals have been severely abused. They conclude that there is an association of childhood abuse and subsequent antisocial, aggressive acts (Lewis, Mallouh and Webb, 1989). In their study of 15 death row inmates waiting for execution for murder, 8 had been themselves the victims of 'potentially filicidal' assaults, which suggests that there may be a relationship between the parental brutality towards a child and the severity of that child's subsequent behaviour. Another four were subject to extraordinary abuse.

> For example, one mother shot at her son with a gun as he tried to get away from her. She threatened him with a knife, kicked him and whipped him all over his body with horse whips, ironing cords, sticks and belts. When she tied him to a water heater and horsewhipped him, police were called to intervene.

> *(1989, p.712)*

Of the 12 who had been physically abused, 4 had also been sexually abused. 'One mother forced her son to sleep with her throughout his childhood and forced him to stimulate her orally and to fondle her breasts' (1989, p.712).

The authors note that in three of these sexually abused victims the murders they committed included sexual assaults. The man whose father had inserted objects into his rectum and forced penetration when he reached adolescence, was found guilty of having locked up a girl, inserting objects into her vagina and rectum and performing a number of bizarre sexual activities with her (1989, p.712).

These findings suggest that in some murders and crimes there appears to be a considerable degree of re-enactment of the victim's own traumatic experience.

However, it is important to stress at this point that most abused children do not become violent delinquents or murderers. It is therefore necessary to identify other factors that contribute to an abused child's likelihood of becoming violent. Lewis and her colleagues found that many of the violent men who had been abused also had some form of neurological or cognitive abnormality. This may be secondary to abuse in infancy, but whatever its origin, it interferes with a child's capacity to make the best of his social or academic life, thereby reducing further his self-esteem and increasing his narcissistic rage (1989, pp.713–714).

The same authors found that one other very important factor that makes it more likely for abused children to become violent is the effect of witnessing violence between parents. For example, most of the death row victims witnessed appalling levels of violence between their parents, including attempted murders (1989, p.715).

Finally, many of the parents of violent criminals are psychiatrically disturbed, which makes their children vulnerable to suffering from distorted thought processes themselves whereby they misperceive their environment and feel terribly threatened.

These findings confirm what these authors found in an earlier study on nine murderers (Lewis et al., 1985). Lewis and her team conclude their article with a moral question which is all too relevant for the American men facing execution on death row: 'To what extent is a violently abused individual responsible for his or her own violent behaviours?' We can reply for the time being with yet another question: 'To what extent is our society responsible for the abused individual's violent behaviour?' This is a question that will be indirectly addressed in the next chapter which focuses on some of the ways culture interacts with our attachment relationships.

Chapter 12
Cultures and Violence

'The tradition of all the dead generations weigh like a nightmare on the brain of the living.'

Karl Marx, 1878–1883

Environment and cultures in interaction

Gazing across the blue waters at the bare Greek islands of Symi and Kos and the bald flanks of the neighbouring Turkish coastline, the traveller could be forgiven for thinking these lands are as they always were: rocky outcrops, dry and burnt by the sun, once the homes of ancient fishermen and sailors. And yet, the sleepy town of Symi was once famous for the fast and graceful ships she built for the Greek and Ottoman fleets. The puzzled traveller may well wonder how those wooden ships were ever built, for there is not a forest to be seen in this scorched Mediterranean landscape. One warfaring empire after another built her vessels from the trees that once covered these islands and the mainland, cool shady forests watered by streams, teaming with animals and flowers long since vanished.

The Mediterranean as we know it is a man-made environment, the product of the agricultural revolution that took seed to the east. Only 50 miles from this same sea are the ruins of Catal Huyuk, one of the oldest cities in the world built around 4800 years ago with a population of some 6000 people. They could build such cities because they had discovered how to sow grain and farm, making the land produce more food for human consumption. Small family settlements grew into villages and villages into towns. The growth in human population led to the development of new relationships between communities and within communities, affecting men, women and children as roles changed to adjust to the increasingly complex social structures of city and country life.

As one civilisation took over from the previous one, it would bring

200

with it a new cultural outlook and a new power structure, a new set of relationships with the world, be it with nature or with its gods. It is said that ancient goddess-worshipping cultures once governed these lands. In her book *The Civilisation of the Goddess: the World of old Europe* (1992), Marija Gimbutas describes a culture that was essentially peaceful, agricultural and respectful of the earth and which lasted from the seventh to the third millenium BC. Following its decline, the Indo Europeans arrived and the more belligerent patriarchal cultures took over.

One such culture is that of the Romans whose attitude to life was an all-too-familiar one in our society:

> To them it seemed that nature could be ravished and plundered as men wished. Its products were self renewing and inexhaustible. They saw no reason why men should not take what they wanted as often as they wanted it. The state gave legal title to undeveloped land to anyone who cleared it of forest. As the human population around the Mediterranean grew, so more and more of the forests that had once girdled it with green were destroyed.

(Attenborough, 1987, p. 98)

And, though men were aware of the effects of deforestation, the cultural system they had developed required them to continue cutting their forests for fuel, building and war.

Commenting on the denuded hills around Athens in the fourth century BC, Plato is quoted as writing: 'What now remains compared to what existed is like the skeleton of a sick man, all the fat and soft earth wasted away and only the bare framework of the land being left' (Attenborough, 1987, p.98).

Not only did the land change with man's cultural development, so did his whole way of life, including his interpersonal relationships and moral values. Harris is an anthropologist who has paid particular attention to the links between reproductive pressure and environmental depletion in the evolution of our social organisation which, as he points out, not only involves property relations and political economy but also religious beliefs. One example illustrates this approach very clearly: having noted how important the pig was as a source of food to the early neolithic cultures of the Middle East, he explains the demise of pork in the Bible as resulting from the widespread deforestation that took place after 7000 BC. Pigs used to feed in the shelter of the extensive forests that once covered Anatolia but, when these disappeared, the extra food this animal required made it ecologically competitive with humans, hence the need for a taboo against eating pork (1977). Whether this particular explanation is correct or not, Harris's merit is to stress the importance of human interactions with the environment and the bilateral changes that result from such interactions. And yet, there is still considerable resistance to focusing on ourselves as a species whose power to modify the world cannot be divorced from the effects of these changes: we are dependent on this very same world we are so busily destroying. Such an awareness requires a humility which is not in keeping with our current Western way of life and the way of thinking that goes with it, an attitude strikingly similar to that of our Roman predecessors.

There is a similar resistance to recognising that within this interactive process between humanity and the natural world, there is a third invisible and yet everpresent dimension, that of our culture. Though considerable lip service is now being paid to the importance of cultural identity, far less attention is given to what this concept really means for us in terms of human evolution and in terms of the way we relate to the world and to each other in our daily lives.

The concept of cultural relativity was briefly touched upon when looking at the development and maintenance of the sense of self (Chapter 8). George H. Mead divided the development of the self into two stages: the first involved what could be described as the internalisation and organisation of the attitudes and relationships with significant others; the second stage, Mead described as the internal

> organisation of the social attitudes of the generalised other or the social group as a whole to which he belongs. These social or group attitudes are brought within the individual's field of direct experience, and are included as elements in the structure or constitution of his self, in the same way as attitudes of particular other individuals are.
>
> *(1934, p.158)*

The individual self thus becomes

> an individual reflection of the general systemic pattern of social or group behaviour in which it and the others are all involved – a pattern which enters as a whole into the individual's experience in terms of these organised group attitudes which, through the mechanism of his central nervous system, he takes towards himself, just as he takes the individual attitudes of others.
>
> *(1934, p.158)*

More succinctly put, the individual becomes an 'organic member of society'.

This relatively old description reflects very much what object-relations theorists and systemic thinkers in the field of psychoanalysis currently believe. If this theoretical approach is appropriate, it means that, as we evolved from hunter gatherers through the neolithic age to the present day, both our culture and its manifestation in the group and individual self must have reflected these changes: in other words, our individual and social life can be seen to reflect the changing interactions between our society and the biological environment it affects and modifies.

As Humberto Maturana stated when writing about evolution and adaptation:

> The life history of every organism is a history of structural change in coherence with the history of structural changes of the medium in which it exists, as realised through the continual mutual selection of the respective structural changes.

(1987, p.77)

Whilst the theory of biological evolution is generally founded upon the premise that hereditary factors are transmitted through our genes down the generations, there is as yet little evidence as to how cultural interpersonal attitudes and values are handed down the generations. It has been postulated that language plays an important part in this transmission since people perceive the world differently depending on the language they use (Zulueta, 1984, 1990). However, the study of attachment relations make it clear that there is also another form of transgenerational transmission which is of crucial importance in determining how people perceive and relate to each other. The attachment studies of mother–infant relations do in fact show how important this primary relationship is in the development of maternal behaviour down the generations. Primates deprived of maternal care cannot look after their own infants satisfactorily. Women who have been abused often maltreat their children: Egeland and his colleagues found that of the mothers they studied who had been abused, 70% maltreated their children (Egeland, Jacobvitz and Papatola, 1987, p.266).

What these studies show is the importance of the caregiver–infant relationship in the development of the human capacity to relate satisfactorily with others. When the attachment system is damaged through deprivation or trauma, the social behaviour of the individual is affected, as is his or her sense of self with the potentially violent repercussions referred to earlier on.

However, the mother–infant relationship is itself embedded within a complex socio-biological matrix with which it interacts; it is a sub-system of the family system which itself is part of a larger social system and this has direct implications for how both mother and infant interact.

The impact of our environment on the way children are brought up is a contentious issue, as it touches on characteristics people refer to as 'human nature'. It is therefore to our primate cousins that we will turn to compare ways in which similar attachment relationships to ours are affected by different environmental factors.

Upbringing and attachment relations in primates

Upbringing and attachment relations in non-human primates

Hinde points out how the quality of an interaction varies with its context (1976, p.11). In one study, two groups of bonnet macaque mother–infant dyads were used (Rosenblum and Sunderland, 1982, p.111). One group was placed in a 'high' and another in a 'low' 'foraging demand environment'. In the first, the amount of time spent in finding the hidden food was considerable; in the second, the monkeys found their food fairly quickly. After the infants had been reared in these two different environments for 6–7 months, they were separated from their mothers for 2 weeks.

During the first day all the infants showed distress but the 'high foraging demand group' showed significantly more depressive behaviour which got worse in the second week, whereas the 'low foraging demand group' showed less depression in the second week and more normal 'complex' behaviours. These differences were attributed by the authors to the infants having become insecurely attached as a result of living in a high foraging demand environment, a conclusion derived from observing the different interactions between infants and mothers in the two settings.

In the high foraging demand environment there was more aggression between adults and low levels of grooming, both of which are seen as dominance-related behaviours. However, these mothers did not reject their infants. When off their mothers, the infants in this group spent more time at a greater distance from their caregiver than the infants in the low foraging demand environment. In the latter, mothers were more available to their infants and able to respond quickly to their sudden distress calls because they did not have to spend so much time looking for food. It is interesting that the dominant female in the high demand group had the infant who became the most depressed.

This study clearly shows how environmental factors, such as food scarcity, can and do affect the attachment patterns of certain primates, leading to what appear to be insecure attachment relationships with possible repercussions in the next generation. However, it is also important to point out that in the wild this particular species of monkey would rely on alternative or allomaternal supports when going foraging for food which ensures added protection for the infant (Simonds, 1965).

Plimptom and Rosenblum point out that the reproductive strategy for primates is one that is focused on quality rather than quantity (1983, p.106). This requires a fairly stable reproductive environment, that is, a consistent food supply and the presence of a social group.

In many primate species it has been noted that females other than mother play an important role in infant caregiving; this appears to be the case for human hunter–gatherers and, if so, the disruption of the extended family system may well have a lot to do with the high rates of idiosyncratic child abuse in Western society.

This appears to be borne out by cross-cultural studies on child abuse carried out by Korbin (1981, pp.7–8).

Upbringing and attachment relations in humans

If child rearing is the responsibility of a community or the extended family rather than of individual parents, cultural standards of child care are more likely to be ensured and the deficits and failings of parents are likely to be less harmful. Korbin's (1981) studies support the link between social isolation and a lack of support systems, on the one hand, and child abuse and neglect, on the other.

This is clearly illustrated by a study on child rearing in Polynesia where children are very rarely abused. However, when these families move to areas where a Western style of life exists, mothers are forced to bring up their children alone and according to new standards: child abuse then becomes a problem (Ritchie and Ritchie, 1981).

Bowlby noted that Western babies did suffer unnecessarily from maternal deprivation, resulting from traditional patterns of child rearing at the beginning of this century. He proposed a model of care whereby the infant should be provided with almost continuous care until the second year of life (Bowlby, 1969). By implication, it seemed that the mother should be the one to provide this primary care for the infant. From the evidence provided by maternal deprivation studies, ethology and object relations theory, it became evident that the infant relies on an intricate system of psychological and physical attunement to develop satisfactorily. This 'psychobiological state of synchrony' was and is still felt by some to be best provided by the mother in her interactions with her infant. Such a 'monotropic' view of infant care is used to argue that a lack of maternal care or multiple caregiving is detrimental to the infant's emotional and psychological development (Bowlby, 1958). However, although continuous care is required for the early infant, some would argue that this requirement can be provided in different ways: mother can be the exclusive caregiver or she can be the main caregiver assisted by one or a few others; caregiving can also be shared by a few stable individuals (Rutter, 1981, pp. 141–149).

Jay Belsky stirred up a furore in the USA because he suggested that a sample of 176 infants subjected to over 20 hours of non-maternal care per week in the first year of life produced 43% of insecurely attached infants, whereas a sample of 315 infants having had less than 20 hours per week of non-maternal care only produced 26% of insecurely attached individuals (Belsky, 1988). Boys tended to be more affected than girls. He made the important point that since over half the infants in both samples established secure relationships with their mothers, the time the infant spent in non-maternal care was only one of the factors producing insecurely attached infants. What his critics rightly pointed out is that it may not have any relevance at all because other factors such as family dynamics, child abuse and quality of care might be what was actually being measured. In the meantime, 51.9% of American mothers with infants under the age of one who go out to work are being made to feel extremely worried about whether or not they are putting their children at risk of becoming 'aggressive and non-compliant' (1988, p.402).

Tronick and his colleagues presented some detailed evidence on the child-rearing practices of the Efe, a tribe of hunter–gatherers living by the Ituri forests of Zaire (Tronick, Winn and Morelli, 1985, pp.306–319). They showed that the alloparental care given by the extended family and the community provided adequate care for their infants' development. Various caregivers looked after the infant from birth onwards so that the mother could go and work. If the baby was upset, they would try and comfort him or her, putting the infant to the breast, whether they were lactating or not. If the baby remained inconsolable, mother took over. As a result, the infant was always held in close body contact and was never left alone. The authors argued that not only can alloparental care be very good for the infant, it also reflects the needs of people living in hunting–gathering communities.

This ties up with the findings of researchers in the field of attachment who stress that one of the main advantages of a developmental theory based on the attachment system is that

> Attachment theory implies, instead, a basic compatibility between child and society; a disposition to become socialised develops naturally in infants reared in an environment similar to the environment in which the species adapted.
>
> (Egeland, Jacobvitz and Papatola, 1987, p.257)

Upbringing and social relations in primates

Upbringing and social relations in non-human primates

As with humans, differences in social behaviour in primates can also be seen to be linked to different rearing patterns. For instance the pigtail and bonnet macaques have very different social structures. The pigtails tend to be much more aggressive than bonnets, not only towards each other but also towards their infants: after 5 or 6 months during which the mother is quite restrictive with her infant, she will then become highly rejecting.

Bonnet mothers are fairly permissive and consistent with their infants. They will also readily adopt familiar infants from their mothers though they will reject unfamiliar ones. The infants spend much more time interacting with other members of the troop and the general behaviour of troop members is much more permissive and responsive than that of other species.

In comparison, the pigtails may come to the aid of distressed kin but they will ignore or even attack unrelated others. The pigtail's own infant might be injured if he attempts to make contact when the mother is re-establishing her position in her group after an absence. This tendency to behave aggressively becomes more obvious in stressful environmental conditions. Pigtail macaque mothers and infants interact differently in 'rich' and 'poor' laboratory environments: the first was defined by the availability of toys and sources of interest for infants; the second environment was a bare cage in a sound-proofed room. Mothers were less aggressive to their infants when they lived in the 'rich' environment and their infants responded to maternal aggression by keeping their distance, whereas, in the 'poor' environment infants responded by clinging to their mothers (Jensen, Bobbitt and Gordon, 1968). This increase in clinging when punished by the mother is a characteristic of pigtail infants in general: their mothers punish them more than the bonnet macaque mothers and yet their infants are more dependent (Kaufman and Rosenblum, 1967). This should come as no surprise if we recall the paradoxical increase in clinging seen in rejected or abused primates. What is interesting is that this type of maternal behaviour is conducive to the maintenance of a social structure based on strong permanent mother–infant ties, leading to the formation of socially exclusive matrilines. Bonnet macaques live more communally with little social differentiation.

As a result of the different mother–infant relationships, the pigtail infant who loses its mother becomes severely depressed and takes a long time to recover. The bonnet infant, on the other hand, is adopted by other females in the group and, after a period of searching and protest, settles down without any signs of depression (Kaufman and Rosenblum, 1967). This outcome in the bonnet macaque can be reversed by simply depriving the bonnet infant of this substitute social support: the infant then shows far more despair on separation from its mother. Such findings confirm the importance of social bonds in attenuating the effects of loss and trauma (Chapters 4 and 10).

Though these differences in social behaviour are attributed to genetic differences between species, it is evident that the genetic differences in social behaviour that may occur between pigtail and bonnet macaques can be also be reinforced or counteracted, depending on the biological and social environment of the animal (Plimpton and Rosenblum, 1983). Such a potential flexibility in social behaviour reflects the inherent plasticity of primate development: the primate, and even more so the human primate, is, by virtue of its attachment system, subject to the interpersonal manifestations of the community's social structure which is made manifest within the micro system of the mother–infant dyad. This ensures that the infant's social development is in keeping with the requirements of the social structure in which it will live.

Upbringing and social relations in humans

Similar dynamics are known to operate in human beings. By using the Strange Situation test, researchers have been able to show that parents tend to re-enact with their children the patterns of behaviour they themselves experienced as children. Transgenerational transmission of parental behaviour does occur in humans, though it is subject to modification under certain conditions. For example, abused women who have supportive marriages and good self-esteem do not re-enact their abuse (Ricks, 1985, p.224).

But the most important findings arising from the Strange Situation are those that show a clear link between social conditions and security of attachment: poor families under stress produce a greater proportion of group-C babies, that is, 22% as compared to the 9–12% normally found in American samples (Vaughn et al., 1979). It was once thought that the proportions of securely attached versus insecurely attached infants would be more or less the same in different populations. However, cross-cultural studies similar to those carried out by Ainsworth using the Strange Situation test have shown a different distribution of securely versus insecurely attached infants to that found in the USA.

In northern Germany for example, the Grossmans and their colleagues found that one half of the infants were classified as insecure-avoidant (group A) as compared to about one quarter of American infants (Grossman et al., 1985). The authors explained this finding on the basis of the cultural values that were being upheld in northern Germany: people in Bielefeld believed in 'keeping their distance' so that, as soon as infants became mobile, most mothers thought their children should be weaned from close bodily contact.

The ideal in this part of the world is to produce an independent, non-clinging infant who does not make demands on the parents but rather unquestioningly obeys their commands. The Grossmans and their colleagues noted that such attitudes were very similar to those described by Kurt Lewin about the time of the Second World War (1948, p.27). However, the authors were also at pains to stress that the

German infants' avoidant behaviour was not the result of an underlying rejecting attitude in the mother but a reflection of the need to comply with cultural norms. This is true in the sense that the northern German mothers were more sensitive in their responses than the mothers of avoidant infants in the USA. But the fact remains that, in order to comply with their cultural norms, these women did deprive their children of the body contact they still needed for their full and satisfactory development. The needs of the child are sacrificed to produce the ideal north German adult who appears independent, but only at the cost of dissociating herself from her needs and her experience of rejection. As we now know, the unconscious pain and anger associated with this form of upbringing makes of the 'avoidant' infant a potentially more violent person than her securely attached counterpart. Alice Miller would probably go as far as to say that it is the 'avoidant' infant who could make the good Nazi, both obedient and yearning for revenge (1983). Such a view complements the work of Kohut and his followers:

> The origin of narcissistic rage must be sought in the childhood experience of utter helplessness *vis à vis* the humiliating selfobject parent ...
>
> The painful memory lingers on, and so does the slowly boiling resentment. At some point, weeks, months or even years after the insult, the smoldering animosity is likely to break out into open hostility, perhaps a hot fury, perhaps a coldly calculating destructiveness, and find its satisfaction in victimising a substitute selfobject that has given offence.
>
> *(Wolf, 1988, p.80; Wolf's italics)*

In Japan, Miyake, Chen and Campos found that the infants they observed were much more likely to be classified as insecure-resistant (group C) than American babies, that is, 38% compared to 10–20% (1985, pp.276–297). These infants showed extreme crying, difficulty in soothing and moderate levels of resistance on reunion. This apparent cultural difference was ascribed to the fact that Japanese mothers do not separate from their infants at all during their first year: as a result the Japanese infant child is strongly motivated to prevent any separation from mother. Miyake and his colleagues therefore labelled some of these infants (10%) as 'pseudo Cs' since they showed good quality play prior to separation unlike their American equivalent (1985, p.280). This trend continues into childhood, as Japanese mothers have a lot more physical contact with their children than their Western counterparts, including co-bathing and co-sleeping. The other notable finding is the absence of any 'avoidant' group A infants (1985, p.287).

In Israel, a study by Sagi and his colleagues also showed a larger than expected number of insecure infants in the kibbutz, 50% compared to 30–35% found in most American samples (Sagi et al., 1985, pp.257–275). Of these insecurely attached infants, a third of the attachments, be they to mother or to metapelet, fell into the resistant category (group C), that is, three times more than is typical in an American sample. For many infants the Strange Situation test had to be prematurely stopped because they became so distressed. It appears that in these particular kibbutzim, children slept away from their parents and their metapelet who looked after them in the day. At night they were often left in the care of unfamiliar women at the end of an intercom. These sleeping arrangements whereby infants were separated from their attachment figures are considered by the authors as the source of insecurity. It is important to note that a comparison group of city infants in day care showed the American distribution of secure versus insecure infants but the proportion of the insecure-resistant group continued to be high.

For those who, like Kagan, support the 'temperament' position discussed in Chapter 6 (p.81), these differences in attachment patterns are ascribed to inherited character traits. However, further studies show that this is unlikely to be so.

In the case of Germany, a subsequent study done with mothers born some time after the Second World War (and therefore younger than those observed in the Bielefeld sample) revealed proportions of securely versus insecurely attached infants that were the same as those found in the USA (Sroufe, 1985, p.6).

In Japan, subsequent studies have also confirmed the importance of attachment as being crucial in determining subsequent mother–infant relationships. In the case of 'modern' Japanese families where mothers go out to work and leave their infants in the care of others, the ratio of attachment behaviours observed in their babies were the same as those found in the USA, including the proportion of 'avoidant' infants (Sroufe, 1985).

Similar differences have been found with Chinese-American infants where an increase in group C attachment patterns was found. However, in fully acculturated families, the infants presented with a similar classification pattern to that found in Caucasian Americans (Li-Repac, 1982).

What these different studies appear to show is that cultural differences in upbringing may well result in different attachment patterns, with all that this implies in terms of the cultural group's sense of self, interpersonal relations, and psychological strengths and vulnerabilities. We may be able to learn a lot more about 'culture-specific' variations in attachment patterns by comparing groups that live in the same country but that differ widely in terms of their shared belief systems.

If we return to the study of the Efé referred to earlier, Tronick and his colleagues stated that child care practices are really decisions about cultural values: what we want our children to become (Tronick, Winn and Morelli, 1985). They point out that the life of the Efe is one of continuous social contact where individuals know how to avoid disruptive and aggressive conflicts and where cooperation, group identification and attachment are of great importance. Similarly, because people tend to move from one group to another and because death is more of a reality, the individual must not be too affected by such losses. These requirements appear to be met by the alloparental care system of the Efé. Bearing in mind the fact that the process of psychobiological attunement is an interactive self-regulatory system whereby the infants' and caregivers' interactions are organised to ensure the maintenance of the individual's identity (Sander, 1977), we can see that the Efé baby's task is a complex one. This infant is exposed to different entraining stimuli which need to be internally regulated and then internalised. The infant has therefore to develop the regulatory capacity to adjust to these differences and so form multiple adjustments alongside a primary attachment to the mother. Such a pattern of child care is supposed to promote a high degree of group attachment and identification. The paradox is that a more complete self–other differentiation can result from this form of upbringing.

We can thus see with pigtail macaques and Efé tribesmen how cultural continuity is maintained down the generations through the mother–infant attachment system, embedded as it is within the interpersonal matrix of the family and the community. As Erikson stated in his book *Childhood and Society:*

> Every society consists of men in the process of developing from children into parents. To assure continuity of tradition, society must early prepare for parenthood in its children; and it must take care of the unavoidable remnants of infantility in its adults. This is a large order, especially since society needs many beings who can follow, a few who can lead, and some who can do both, alternately or in different areas of life.
>
> *(1950, p.394)*

He goes on to to describe how humanity goes about this task, starting with the creation of a presymbolic or prelinguistic group self:

> While it is quite clear, then, what *must* happen to keep the baby alive (the minimum supply necessary) and what *must not* happen, lest he die or be severely stunted (the maximum frustration tolerable) there is increasing leeway in regard to what *may* happen; and different cultures make extensive use of their prerogative to decide what they consider workable and insist on calling necessary. Some people think that a baby, lest he scratch his own eyes out, must necessarily be swaddled completely for the better part of the day throughout the greater part of the first year; but also that he should be rocked or fed whenever he whimpers. Others think that he should feel the freedom of his kicking limbs as early as possible, but should 'of course' be forced to wait for his meals until he, literally, gets blue in the face. All this depends on the culture's general aim and system.
>
> *(1950, p.67)*

In his study of Sioux rearing practices, Erikson points out how free and easy going is the early development of the infant. But though there is no systematic weaning, the child who suckles must learn not to bite the breast: this is done by thumping the infant on the head so that he flies into a fit of rage and he is then strapped onto a cradleboard. The Sioux mothers would recognise the good future hunter in the strength of their infant's fury. This expression of infantile narcissistic rage and its accompanying sadistic wishes at mother's breast is linked in Erikson's mind with the later self-torture that these warriors carry out when they rip open their own chests in the Sun Dance ceremony, an institution-alised form of atonement. He adds:

> It is hard for our rational minds to comprehend ... that frustrated wishes, and especially early, preverbal, and quite vague wishes, can leave a residue of *sin* which goes deeper than any guilt over deeds actually committed and remembered.
>
> *(1950, p.143 present author's italics)*

This concept of 'sin' is a familiar one in the debate we find ourselves in when we attempt to understand the origins of human violence: we may recall how intertwined is the sense of intrinsic evil with that of human destructiveness. What Erikson appears to suggest is that this concept of original sin may well be the moral and hence cultural translation of the sense of guilt produced by early infantile experiences. He goes on to suggest that such values persist through the child training system, because the cultural ethos continues to consider them 'natural' and does not admit to alternatives. They persist because they have become an essential part of an individual's sense of cultural identity which he must preserve as a core of sanity and efficiency.

But as Erikson states also, these values persist because they work economically, psychologically and spiritually. Anchored as they are in early childhood training, the latter must be embedded in a system of continued economic and cultural synthesis if it is to remain consistent. This synthesis brings together and mutually amplifies both climate and anatomy, economy and psychology, society and child training (1950, p.132).

Cultural traditions of violence

Cultural traditions of violence in non-Western societies

What, we may well ask, may be the link between violence, the wide-spread belief in our intrinsic sinfulness, our upbringing and the partic-ular socio-political and economic system in which we live? The question is an important one, for it acknowledges that human violence needs to be seen within the socio-cultural environment in which it takes place. Any answer to such a question needs to take into account the importance of our attachment system which, in the interplay with its cultural environment, moulds our sense of self, our interactions with others, our very perception of ourselves and of the world about us. It also needs to take into account the inherent vulnerability of this same attachment system when exposed to trauma and deprivation. Indeed, we have seen how certain primate societies exploit the vulnerability of this attachment system to perpetuate certain individual and social characteristics. The pigtail macaques' maternal aggressiveness ensures the maintenance of powerful matrilines; the north German mothers' physical aloofness ensured the development of 'independent' yet obedient citizens. In war-torn Mozambique children are kidnapped and abused by being forced to witness and participate in acts of indescribable violence; these 'instrumentalised' children are then trained for military action under the auspices of the South African government (*New Internationalist,* 1989).

Indeed, throughout the world different communities have ritualised ways of establishing their continuity through the treatment of their young. As Korbin was to find out, even though so-called 'idiosyncratic' physical abuse does not take place in non-Western cultures, other forms of culturally approved child abuse do occur. These can be viewed as legitimate practices by one culture and as abusive or neglectful by other cultures (Korbin, 1981).

Eastern cultures are coercive and punitive but these forms of socialisation, such as spanking, mutilations or ritualised punishment, are culture wide and accepted. They take the form of traditional institutions. Young children are brought up in a permissive way but initiation ceremonies are usually carried out to introduce the child to the world of adults.

The Gusii culture in Kenya practises corporal punishment in the form of canings and the rubbing of hot pepper in the anogenital areas. The aim is to produce an obedient and respectful toddler who automatically does what he or she is told. The initiation rites are harsh, requiring physical and emotional humiliation. Wife-beating is common (LeVine and LeVine, 1981). When exposed to outside influences, Western idiosyncratic child abuse becomes more common (Field, 1983, p.165).

The Machiguenga from South America give their children scalding baths to test their pain endurance and make them into hard workers. Dipping into the river is also used to stop infants from crying. 'The practices are ritually administered, culturally accepted disciplinary devices to overcome the child's reluctance to conform' (Field, 1983, p.165). Wife abuse is also common. All in all, these and other South American tribes have a high incidence of societal violence, too, but not of idiosyncratic abuse.

In peasant societies in rural India, group conformity is so important that children are harshly punished so as to become obedient, particularly the boys. One of these ritualised punishments consists of hanging by the hands. Girls are prepared to adjust to life in a new family, an arrangement which can pose such serious problems that they commit suicide. These practices are regarded as necessary for the continuation of rural society and its values (Poffenberger, 1981).

In Taiwan, filial pity is very much valued and punishments are seen as necessary for the assertion of parental authority so as to gain total submission from the child (Wu, 1981).

Males and females are treated differently in all these cultures: boys appear to go through more punitive rituals and routine punishment. However, the lot of females is not a painless one. In China, millions of baby girls have been killed by their parents following the 1979 one-child family policy. Peasants hated it because only sons can support their old parents and only they can worship the ancestors (Mirsky, 1992). More than 75 million girls have been circumcised in the world, mostly in Africa but also in Indonesia and Malaysia (Vernier, 1988). The most extreme form of circumcision is infibulation, which involves complete removal of the vulval tissue including the clitoris and the labia without anaesthetic. Apart from causing women considerable pain, this practice appears to put these women at high risk of AIDS.

These examples illustrate how important different forms of child rearing are for the maintenance of cultural traditions. They also show us that there is hardly a culture which does not administer some form of physical abuse in the rearing of its children, a process that is clearly considered necessary if people are to become obedient and compliant. These findings show us most clearly that producing obedient children is of primary importance the world over.

However, there remain a few exceptions. One of the cultures where such ritualised forms of punishment or initiation rites do not appear to take place is that of the MaButi pygmies who live as hunter–gatherers in the rain forests of Zaire (Turnbull, 1961). During their life in the forest the children learn the ways of their people by participating in their daily activities. They do get slapped when naughty but others interfere if a parent is too harsh. The male pygmie becomes a 'man' when he kills his first big game: he can then join the other men in a special singing and dancing celebration. The MaButi's god is a benevolent deity they identify with in the forest. Their life and culture are thus intimately linked to that of the forest.

In contrast to the MaButi, the agricultural villagers who live outside the forest, and for whom the pygmies work on a seasonal basis, do have harsh initiation rites for their boys. Their purpose is to fit their sons for adult life by making them full members of the tribe. Magic and superstition are involved in the ceremony, which consists of circumcision followed by a period of fasting and the observation of certain taboos and painful endurance tests. In this way the village boy becomes a man and his ties to his mother are severed for good.

When a girl menstruates for the first time in the village, she is secluded and has to be cleansed and purified whilst the clan has to protect itself from the evil she has brought them. Her incarceration may end with her being given away in marriage in exchange for a dowry.

When a MaButi girl menstruates for the first time, she is joined by her girlfriends in a special house and a long joyful celebration follows with much social intercourse. The girl learns the arts and crafts of adult women. Any interested young man must fight his way through the protecting adults into the house where he can flirt or sleep with the girl who invited him in; in this way couples get to know one another before committing themselves to living together.

Unlike most human societies, there is considerable equality between men and women among the MaButi, who are free to choose their spouses or take lovers or separate. As for child rearing, this is based on the alloparental form of care described for the Efé except that the men also participate. Group hunting with the net is carried out by both sexes, although hunting with bow and arrow or spear is carried out by men only. There is considerable flexibility in the MaButi's division of labour and the lack of exclusive sex roles and punitive child-rearing practices is reflected in the tribe's social structure, where more or less everyone in the small band of about 25 adults takes part in everything: there are no chiefs, no councils, no judges, no jury, no courts, whereas the opposite takes place in the neighbouring agricultural village.

If the MaButi social structure has been described in some detail, it is because it shows that the way children are brought up is intimately linked to the social structure of their community and its relation to its natural environment.

Cultural traditions of violence in Western societies

However, how do such findings apply to our Western societies? What cultural values are we promoting in the upbringing of our children? It could appear to some that we no longer resort to forms of culturally sanctioned abuse in the raising of our children. As Korbin states, our form of child abuse is considered to be 'idiosyncratic', that is, at odds with our cultural norms. However, other non-Western cultures who come into contact with Westerners often view us as unable to care for our children properly or to love them. They condemn the practice of isolating children in rooms or beds of their own at night, of allowing our infants to cry without immediately responding to their needs and, also, of keeping them waiting for available food. These Western traditions are at odds with most other cultures' child-rearing practices.

Interestingly, members of our own society have been highly critical of these forms of upbringing. Fairbairn points out that in a state of nature, the infant would never be separated from mother as happens in our civilisation. The infant would be constantly sheltered in mother's arms and have ready access to her breast until such time as she felt ready to dispose of him or her. He concludes that, in our culture, the infant's relationship with the mother is disturbed from the outset by a considerable degree of frustration which becomes the source of early aggression: this leads to splitting of the maternal 'object' into 'good' and 'bad' objects as a way of dealing with such premature exposure to the outside world (1952, pp.109–110).

In Frodi's study of the parental responses to the infant's crying, he showed that it elicited an autonomic response linked to a readiness to aggress. He pointed out that children in hunter–gatherer societies are not left to cry so their parents are not subject to the long spells of aversive crying which parents in the West have to endure and which can lead to abusive responses (1985, p.366).

Kohut had similar reservations about our cultural values made manifest in the child-rearing practices of the West. As he says, the deeply ingrained value system of the Occident extols altruism and concern for others but disparages concern for ourselves. This denial of our need for narcissistic gratification appears to be producing a culture with increasing numbers of people with disorders of the self.

More to the point, however, is: what kind of upbringing do we really give our children in the West? Starting with infancy and early childhood, we have learnt how different cultural systems appear to produce a certain ratio of securely attached versus insecurely attached infants. Twenty-three per cent, that is, about a quarter of American or Swedish infants, are classified as belonging to the 'avoidant' group A classification (Miyake, Chen and Campos, 1985). This means that these particular infants have been subject to rearing practices that are detrimental to their capacity to 'tune in' to others and form satisfactory relationships. They are also aggressive with their peers and caregivers. Although some of these infants have had long separations from their mothers, many of the mothers of these children are described as being interfering, neglectful, angry and rejecting, particularly of close body contact. Many of them are known actually to have abused their infants (Chapter 6).

Such high numbers of avoidant children in Western societies do suggest high levels of generally neglectful and rejecting parental behaviour. We now know that estimated rates of abuse are of the order of about 6% and rising. In what was West Germany, 1000 children died in 1988 as a result of being beaten up by their parents (Moorehead, 1989, p.7). In Britain, every week, at least four children die as a result of abuse and neglect (Meadow, 1989, p.727) and one child in ten is said to be sexually abused (Moorehead, 1989, p.8).

Possibly less well known are the striking findings of Gelles regarding violence toward children in the USA. In a survey of a representative sample of 2143 American families, he found that violence, 'well beyond ordinary physical punishment', is a widespread phenomenon in parent–child relations (Gelles, 1978). Having reviewed the widely differing figures for child abuse in the USA, Gelles concludes that we simply do not know what the incidence for child abuse really is because of the difficulties involved in both defining it and collecting the evidence. To him it therefore seemed necessary to study the forms and extent of parental violence; this seemed particularly relevant knowing that in the USA (as in the UK), 84–97% of all parents use physical punishment on their children. Through the use of completed hour-long interviews with parents, Gelles was able to make an assessment of what violence did take place in American family life. He defines violence as 'an act carried out with the intention, or perceived intention, of physically injuring another person'.

In many cases, the acts of punishment carried out by parents would have been considered, if done to strangers or adults, as criminal assault. What was striking was how often these acts were seen by their perpetrators as being carried out in the best interests of the victim. As Gelles points out, ordinary 'physical' punishment and 'child abuse' are but two ends of a single continuum of violence towards children. His findings are quite disturbing: out of 46 million children between the ages of 3 and 17 years old living with both their parents in 1975, 46.4% had been pushed, grabbed or shoved, 71% had been slapped or spanked and about 7.7% (3.1 to 4 million) had been kicked, bitten or punched by parents at some time in their lives whilst about 3.2% (between 1.0 and 1.9 million) had been similarly treated that year. About 4.2% (between 1.4 and 2.3 million) had been 'beaten up' while growing up, and between 275 000 and 750 000 (1.3%)had been so treated that year. Lastly, Gelles found that 2.8% (between 900 000 and 1.8 million) of American children had their parents use a gun or a knife on them.

With the exception of these last figures, the above data illustrate patterns of regular violence. It is also important to realise that these figures are low estimates of what takes place, since they are based on self-reports and do not take into account the increased violence that occurs in single parent families. It was also found that mothers are more likely to hit the child with something or slap or spank the child. Interestingly, there was no significant difference between fathers and mothers with respect to other forms of violence. Boys were found to be more likely to be the victims of violence, possibly because it is considered part of their socialisation process. Younger children are more likely to be victims of forceful or violent acts, but all ages are vulnerable to severe types of violence.

The author believes he has only began to scratch the surface of this important topic; in case some of us might find his definition of violence too overinclusive, he reminds us that if one million children had knives or guns used on them at school, we would consider the problem very seriously but, since it happens at home, there is far less concern. And yet, as we know only too well, the consequences of such violence carried out by those held to be the child's loving caregivers, are potentially very serious and a major cause of violent behaviour.

Murray Straus takes up where Gelles left off (1991). He stresses the fact that physical punishment is a universal phenomenon: in the USA, for instance, it involves nearly all Americans either as recipients or perpetrators. This is so because, as he states, this form of punishment is 'central to the primacy and continuity of the socialisation process'. In other words it is a culturally sanctioned form of abuse. This is why Straus also believes that it may also have the effect of legitimising violence, particularly since physical punishment is a legally permissible physical attack on children which fits exactly the definition of violence given by Gelles. Thus physical punishment and capital punishment are similar despite great differences in severity:

> Since physical punishment is used by authority figures who tend to be loved or respected and since it is almost always used for a morally correct end when other methods fail, physical violence teaches that violence can and should be used under similar circumstances. The intriguing question is whether this legitimisation of violence spills over from the parent–child relationship to other relationships in which one has to deal with persons who persist in some wrongdoing, such as a spouse or friends.

> *(1991, p.134)*

Straus attempts to use his Cultural Spillover Theory to show that such a causal connection does exist. The underlying assumption in this theory is that processes which produce criminal behaviour are structurally parallel to processes which produce conforming behaviour, only the cultural content differs. Culture is here defined (as it is throughout the book) as a constellation of norms, values and beliefs shared by the members of society. In his study the author succeeds in demonstrating that his empirical findings are almost all consistent with his theory but they do not use data that can prove the theory in a causal direction.

The evidence shows that parents who believe in physical punishment not only hit more but they also tend to assault their children more, with the risk of inflicting physical injuries on the child. These same children who were physically punished tended to do the same to their siblings and were significantly more likely to engage in street crime. It also appears that the more physical punishment was used by the father, the more he was likely to assault his wife and vice versa.

Interestingly, the more physical punishment was authorised in schools, the higher the rate of assault by children in the same schools. One finding that directly supports the Cultural Spillover Theory is the fact that, in a study of teachers from ten different nations, the more they approved of physical punishment, the higher the infant homicide rate was found to be in that particular country (Baron and Straus, 1987). This does not mean that there is any direct connection between the two, but it does show that cultural approval of physical punishment might create the conditions for the increasing incidence of infant homicide; the combination of early and frequent use of physical punishment, as well as the vulnerability of the infant, means that more babies are at risk in a society that favours physical punishment even though no one favours killing infants. The irony is that physical punishment is meant to make children more socially conforming, certainly not more deviant. Unfortunately what seems to happen is that violence begets violence. A series of studies show that implicit cultural support for killing inherent in war is associated with a higher murder rate (Archer and Gartner, 1984) and a higher rate of child abuse (Shwed and Straus, 1979).

A similar study to Straus's was carried out by the same team on the links between legitimate violence, violent attitudes and rape across 50 American states (Baron, Straus and Jaffee, 1988). It had already been observed by Sanday in a cross-cultural study of 156 tribal societies that there was a strong association between levels of non-sexual violence (such as warfare) and rape (1981). He concluded 'where interpersonal violence is a way of life, violence frequently achieves sexual expression' (1981, p.18). This was also shown to be the case in antisocial teenagers studied by Bandura and Walters (1959).

Baron, Straus and Jaffee finally confirmed the validity of the Cultural Spillover Theory when they found that legitimate violence is indeed directly related to rate of rape across the different states of America. Other factors also related to the incidence of rape are the degree of cultural disorganisation, urbanisation, economic inequality and the percentage of single males.

Legitimate violence was measured by looking at three main indices:

1. The role of violence in the mass media, i.e. what percentage of the population read violent magazines and what percentage of the same population watched the six most violent network television programmes.
2. The government's use of violence whereby socially desirable aims are attained by physical force. The indicators here are: state legislation which allows the use of corporal punishment in schools, race-specific measures of the percentage of prisoners sentenced to death and the percentage of executions over certain years.
3. The rate of participation in violent but legal or socially approved activities such as hunting, National Guard enrolment rates and

National Guard expenditure per capita and finally the percentage of lynching. Cultural support for violence was also measured more directly through the use of questionnaires.

What these authors found was that women in a western State of America were eight times more likely to be sexually assaulted than women in an eastern State. The two tests used to assess cultural support for violence showed that it has a direct and non-spurious association with the incidence of rape (1988, p.100). 'This suggests that legitimate violence tends to be diffused to relations between the sexes, resulting in an increased probability of women being raped' (1988, pp.100–101). These results go hand-in-hand with an earlier piece of research by the same authors which showed that legitimate violence, poverty and social inequality are significantly associated with state-to-state differences in the incidence of homicide (Baron and Straus, 1988).

However, this latest study linking rape with legitimate violence is unique because it was the first to employ a measure of culturally approved violence that was empirically independent of the criminal violence it tried to explain. For this reason the authors claim that such research gives us the strongest support to date for cultural theories of violent crime. They are very much aware that the cultural implications for such research are enormous (1988, p.102).

> The findings suggest that if rape is to be reduced, attention must be paid to the abundance of socially approved violence, not just to criminal violence, and to the structural conditions that underlie a reliance on violence for socially approved ends. This will be a formidable task, considering that economic and racial inequality, corporal punishment of children, violent sports, mass media violence, capital punishment, and other forms of legitimate violence are woven into the fabric of American culture.
>
> *(1988, p.103)*

The task is indeed a formidable one but it needs to be addressed, for violence has become a major problem in the USA. Its citizens kill each other in such appalling numbers that the American homicide rate is the highest in the Western World with 25 000 murders committed in 1991, an average rate of 10 killed for every 100 000 citizens. (In the UK the rate is 5.5 and in Japan it is only 1.3 – Ellis, 1992.) Since 1988, the firearms death rate has exceeded the total for all natural causes of death combined. In addition, 6 million Americans were victims of violent crime. As a result of so much violence, children often witness community violence and, as a result, suffer from PTSD, much as their adult counterparts do (Figley, 1992).

Conclusion

Gelles' evidence on family violence and Straus's Cultural Spillover Theory of crime, backed up by the developmental evidence of cross-generational transmission of violent behaviour, do indeed indicate that our Western way of life is one that relies on the use of violence from infancy onwards. If this is correct the implications are far reaching: not only are we destroying our planet, as our Greek and Roman forefathers did, but we are doing so at the expense of our emotional and physical wellbeing. Violence to the self and to the 'other' seems endemic to our way of life.

And yet, something is still missing in our understanding of human violence, a dimension we could well overlook until we re-read the writings of those who believe in the genetic origins of violence. If the 'status quo' and its current beneficiaries are to be preserved, violence must not be seen as a culturally derived phenomenon. Thus, through the use of government sponsored research, sociobiology and the media, we are being convinced of the intrinsic nature of our violence. This is not difficult to do if we bear in mind how much we tend to see the 'other' as 'less than human', often different and threatening or otherwise 'dispensable'. All political leaders know that they can whip up popular support by appealing to our racist and nationalist prejudices. Although some would see this as evidence of our 'basic instincts', what these leaders are in fact doing is appealing to the injured self and to its associated narcissistic rage which lies dormant in most of us. An example of this is being seen in the horrific 'ethnic cleansing' campaign that is being carried out in what was once Yugoslavia: hidden in the new 'concentration camps', the Bosnian inmates have become the living ghosts of their Serbian oppressors' own wretched past during the Second World War. The Serbs were subjected to 'ethnic' cleansing carried out by their Croatian neighbours, under the auspices of the Nazis. Misha Glenny (1992) reminds us of the history of these Serbian enclaves in the Krajina area, a history which goes back to the seventeenth century. At that time, the Serbs used to fight with the Habsburg forces against the Ottoman army. In the wake of a failed Habsburg attack against the Islamic armies, the Serbs had to flee from Kosovo to escape the wrath of the Ottoman victors. They were allowed to settle in what is Vojvodina and, in exchange, they agreed to populate, as military colonists under Viennese control, many parts of the Vojna Krajina which was mainly Croatian territory.

This strip of land in south-east Europe was to become the boundary between the powers of Islam and the Church, and between the Roman Catholic and Orthodox Christian faiths. It was here, on what Glenny describes as 'the most active and disruptive historical fault line in

Europe', that the war erupted between Tito's partisans and the Croat fascists, the Ustashas, a war far from forgotten in the minds of these different ethnic groups. It is no coincidence that it is here again that the current Balkan war is taking place.

> Settled in the Krajina as fighters and moulded by the Dinaric surroundings, the Serbs developed an extraordinary affinity with weaponry. Of all the region's traditions, this is probably the most enduring to this day. Children are schooled in weaponry at an early age, learning to handle and control first shotguns and latter handguns before they reach their teens. Thus guns are not just a central part of the people's character. A person's standing will be enhanced and confirmed by his or her (there are many female fighters in Krajina) ability to wield a gun... The Krajisnici, as people from Krajina are called, say that the gun was born with this land and will never disappear.
>
> *(Glenny, 1992, pp. 6–7)*

In such a land the cult of the 'enemy' goes hand in hand with the power of the gun. This dehumanisation of the 'other' is fundamental to the perpetuation of violence within society and between societies. How does it come about? This will be the subject of the next chapter.

Part III
The Prevalence of
Psychological Trauma

Chapter 13
The Dehumanisation of the 'Other'

'The most important thing is that disobedience should be crushed to the point of regaining complete submission, using corporal punishment if necessary.'

D.G.M. Shreber, a German authority on education (1858)

Culture and the dehumanisation of the 'other'

John was a 22-year-old American veteran, brought up in a middle-class home in a family characterised by strong family ties and a sense of duty towards the community. After an older brother was killed in Vietnam, John enlisted in the Marines.

From the beginning he 'refused to think of the Vietnamese as people'. He often brutally killed both prisoners and civilians. One day, he was asked to guard a number of high-ranking Viet Cong prisoners. He got to know them, sharing cigarettes and food with them and exchanging family photos. A week later, his commanding officer gave him orders to 'blow them away'. John refused and stood frozen as he watched his officer and the other soldiers kill the Viet Cong (Haley, 1974, p.193). From that moment onwards, he felt a murderer, guilty of war crimes.

All Western societies still uphold the Jewish God's commandment: 'Thou shall not kill' (*Exodus* 20, 13). Yet most Western societies also uphold the right to go to war and to have armies trained to kill the 'enemy'. Many also carry out the death penalty on their own citizens.

This contradiction can only be resolved by the perception of the 'enemy' or the 'criminal' as less 'human' than ourselves. In Western countries where legitimate violence is intrinsic to the system, the potential for dehumanisation must therefore exist. Its expression is most in evidence in the army.

John's story, drawn from the vast literature on Vietnam veterans, illustrates two central ingredients in the genesis of human violence. The first is the importance of obedience, a human trait which is instilled into us from birth onwards through the powerful use of physical punishment. Obedience is clearly believed to be of paramount importance in the running of all societies but, when it is over-developed, its potential can be devastating, as will be illustrated in the next chapter.

The second cause of human violence lies in the perception of the 'other' as a non–human being. All genocides begin with a propaganda campaign aimed at dehumanising a group of people or a nation. Similarly, although most individual acts of violence are not officially condoned, they are often facilitated by the fact that the victims are either seen by the community as 'less than human', such as prostitutes or blacks, or they are perceived by their attacker as only 'part objects' in what, for many traumatised individuals, is the re-enactment of an earlier experience of abuse (see Chapters 10 and 11).

For John, the belated realisation that the Viet Cong were human beings like himself gave him the strength to disobey his commanding officer's orders. In the process, he regained his own humanity and, after being helped to share his awful feelings of guilt with a non-judgemental therapist, he returned to American life. Other veterans who have had to continue believing in a dehumanised view of the Vietnamese are still suffering from PTSD, like this marine sergeant who said: 'How could a person be a person [if his] intention was to bring communism about...' (Laufer, Frey-Wouters and Gallops, 1985, p.85). Perhaps what this soldier cannot countenance is the appalling prospect of how he would feel about himself as a person if the communists he had attacked and killed were actually 'people', too. Following most wars, such a denial of the enemy's humanity is in fact maintained for a considerable period of time, because it is shared both by the returning soldiers and their community of origin. The reason this denial did not work for this sergeant and other Vietnam veterans lies in the peculiar circumstances in which they found themselves when they returned home: the war had ceased to be seen as a 'just war' by a considerable number of Americans. Its injustices and its horrors were not collectively denied as happens after most wars. This meant that the Vietnam veteran found it a lot harder to suppress the reality of what he had been through, an unnecessary war of terrible brutality.

This was clearly illustrated by Lieutenant Calley's trial for the Mai Lai massacre. Half of the population saw his actions as justified in defeating the enemy at any price and the other half saw him as a criminal. Calley's defence was centred on the fact that he was obeying orders and that he did not regard the Vietnamese as human beings; he also claimed to be affected by 'battle stress' (Gunn, 1973, p.89).

Just as war-induced post-traumatic stress disorder can no longer be denied, nor can child sexual abuse: for as long as women had no real power in their community, their voices remained unheard and the plight of millions of abused children was denied. Now that children are beginning to be recognised as human beings, at least in some cultures, their story of systematic maltreatment is beginning to be acknowledged too, both in the present and in the past (Aries, 1962; de Mause, 1974). Whether this will lead to changes regarding child care remains to be seen.

If the principle of obedience can be instilled within the confines of the family through the use of legitimate physical punishment, from where does our propensity to see the 'other' as less than human derive. For many scientists the human tendency to divide the world into 'us' versus 'them' is seen as an inherited biological trait; to others, it is culturally acquired: this represents the familiar polarisation of views that crops up in any debate that touches upon the subject of human nature (see Chapter 2).

After many years studying chimpanzees, Jane Goodall came to the conclusion that they show an inherent fear or hatred of strangers, sometimes expressed by aggressive attacks (Goodall, 1990). In her description of the protracted 'war' that took place between two different troops of chimpanzees in the Gombe reserve, she discovered that the male chimpanzees attacked each other so viciously that they died from their wounds (Goodall, 1990, pp. 86–92). The attacks were not like those seen between members of the same community but more like those seen when chimps kill their prey, twisting off their limbs and tearing off their skin and even drinking their blood. It seemed to their observers that by separating themselves from the original group, the members of the newly formed group had forfeited their 'rights' to be treated as chimpanzees: they were as Jane Goodall puts it 'dechimpized'. She thinks that we have the same disposition to divide the world into 'them' and 'us' (Goodall, 1990, p.176).

Ervin Staub, a serious researcher in the field of human violence, also assumes that: '[The] differentiation between us and them is so basic an aspect of human thinking that it is worth considering its bases in the human genetic makeup' (1984, p. 150). He does, however, believe that we can extend our perception of who is 'us' through forms of socialisation aimed at improving the individual's self-esteem and reducing his or her aggression.

However, the most important point in this debate is the very recognition that inter-group prejudice plays a very important role in our thinking. Indeed, Erikson warned us that to eradicate it altogether could endanger the more vulnerable among us, who would then forfeit the defence mechanism of projection and become essentially prejudiced against themselves (1950, pp.406–407). It is the ubiquitous nature of this differentiation between 'us' and 'them' and the fact that it also appears to occur among our closest relatives, the chimpanzees, that makes people inclined to attribute this phenomenon to our genes.

The implications of such a genetic causality are not difficult to predict: for example, the sociobiologist Wilson believes that we are innately programmed to see the 'other' as different which, he says, tends to make us fear strangers and to solve conflicts by aggression, rules he believes have conferred a biological advantage on those who conformed to them most (Wilson, 1978, p.119).

What has perhaps not been made clear in this debate is that, whatever our genetic predisposition may be in experiencing fear and aggression towards the 'other', we also know that such an attitude can be maintained, strengthened or weakened by powerful psychological mechanisms and processes whose roots lie in the very social system into which we are born It is becoming more and more apparent that socio-cultural factors such as male–female inequality and widespread child maltreatment can induce psychic manifestations which contribute to the genesis of violence by inducing rage and disturbances in the attachment system.

In order to get some idea of how cultural forces can also promote the dehumanisation of the other, we need to return to the rainforests of Zaire or to those of Borneo for a glimpse of a childhood that is not subject to our specific cultural pressures. Though life in the tropical forest is a physically demanding existence and at times frankly dangerous, the Punan hunter–gatherer, like the pygmy, does not envy the life of his agricultural neighbours, the Dayaks: among other things, he believes that they have to work much too hard! (personal communication). Punan life is one of environmental equilibrium with the forest: in small groups of up to 25, these people and their dogs gather, hunt and enjoy their family and community life. There is no hierarchy in this social organisation, no strongly demarcated status-linked male–female sex roles: indeed, though he is the hunter, the Punan father may be the only man in the world normally to assist his wife in childbirth. The Punan children are not subject to violent forms of upbringing nor do the adults go to war, unlike their Dayak neighbours whose warriors were practising headhunters until not so very long ago. Punans are peaceful people doomed to die with the forests they know so well: they do not have rigidly defined sexual roles or any other form of social stratification founded on the belief that certain individuals are more important than others; though they may criticise and make fun of the lives of their more 'advanced' Dayak neighbours, they do not display any racial or other forms of established social prejudice.

However, even for hunter–gatherers, both MaButi pygmies and Punans are exceptionally egalitarian. This is attributed by Leaky to the limited importance of meat in these societies living off the rich variety of food provided by the rainforest: he maintains that the greater the importance attached to meat in such hunter–gatherer communities, the greater the importance of the male hunter. As the man's status rises, the woman's status declines (Leaky, 1977, p.235). For instance, among the !Kung who eat more meat (30% of their diet), the men have a higher status than the women. As for the Eskimos who eat only meat which is obtained by the men, their women are treated as sex objects and have no control over their own fate. It appears that as hunter–gatherers moved north and hunting became more sophisticated and time consuming, so did the status of men. A survey by Richard Lee shows that out of 58 hunting–gathering groups from around the world, only 19% are primarily dependent on hunting for their food. The latter tend to live in the very cold regions of the globe, whereas gathering takes place mainly on the Equator (Reader, 1988, p.142).

Nomadic hunter–gatherers carry on with a way of life that has been the lot of humankind for about 3 million years. Five hundred years ago, when the world population was an estimated 350 million, only 1% of people still hunted and gathered for food. By 1987, 4.8 billion people lived on our planet but only 0.0001% followed the lifestyle that had nurtured us for 99% of our existence (Reader, 1988, p.143).

If we have often referred to the few surviving communities of hunter–gatherers, it is because much has been made of our hunting past by those men who, like Ardrey and Dart, believe man to be essentially violent and war-loving. Their work was discussed earlier (see Chapter 3). Little has been made of our 'gathering' past, no doubt because such research underlines the importance of women in pre-agricultural societies. Hunter–gatherers live in small groups of about 25 people. Although men tend to do the hunting and women the gathering, this is not always the case. Among the Agta in the Philippines, women not only have considerable authority, they hunt animals and fish in the rivers with men and barter with other tribes for goods and services (Estioko-Griffin and Griffin, 1981, pp.121–151). When the women go hunting, their children are looked after by the extended family.

There is, however, one aspect of human society that has never changed and which it shares with all mammals. The course of evolution has brought about an ever closer psychophysiological coadaptation of the mother and infant, a specialisation that tends to leave the father on the periphery of family life. We noted that in the MaButi as in the Punan societies, fathers do maintain a certain, albeit minor, role in bringing up their infants and become more involved as the child grows up; however, with the human migration northwards and the more time-consuming nature of hunting, men appear to have played less and less of a parental role in family life: such an outcome was believed by the Sutties to be very unsatisfactory for men, who, like women, can also have strong wishes to be parents (Suttie and Suttie, 1932). Though hardly any data exist describing the biological influences on male care, men do express strong wishes to be involved in parenting. Not only have they been through the same upbringing as females but, in some communities, the male has an important and positive contribution to make in the upbringing of his children, as we have seen with the MaButi pygmies and other hunter–gatherers (Lamb, 1987). We also know that specific attachment behaviours are demonstrated towards fathers (Lamb, 1977). Field suggests that mothers and fathers attend to different aspects of the stimulation and arousal modulation required by the infant (Field, 1985 p. 435).

The Sutties (1932) go as far as maintaining that this loss is at the root of the patriarchal system with its accompanying polarisation of sex roles as they exist today. When fathers have the time to care for their infants, the arrival of a new-born baby poses little threat to them. However, when sex roles become more differentiated, the human male is at risk of losing out on two counts: he cannot share in the pleasures of parenting and he also faces the consequences of being a man in a male-dominated culture.

Indeed, by virtue of his new sex role the human male has to aquire certain attributes his female counterpart does not need to possess and vice versa: this splitting of sex-linked attributes becomes increasingly important as sex roles become more sharply defined. As a result, the male's individual development becomes increasingly determined by the sex role his culture expects of him. This has very important consequences for the male infant, who needs to become masculine by denying his early feminine identification with mother. The psychological implications of this process are enormous, as will become evident. The final result is that father is left out of the mother–infant relationship which, by reminding him of the relationship he once had with his own mother, also stirs up the feelings of loss and jealousy he had to endure when he had to lose her during his childhood.

If we compare the development of boys with that of girls, the girl's attachment relationship induces her to accept a male substitute for mother whereas, for the male, heterosexual activity can actually enhance the mother–child attachment bond, so that mating would be a reinstatement of the situation. This is why the arrival of the baby can so easily produce jealousy in the father, so much so that the Sutties see this as the main threat to the nuclear family (1932, p.213).

Mythology is full of examples of violent paternal jealousy: one famous myth is that of Zeus who, by ingesting both mother and child, acquired the capacity for maternity: his daughter Athena sprang full grown from his head. In certain Teuto-Celtic cultures the jealousy of the father was reduced by requiring the mother to give less attention to her child and more to her mate. In other cultures, the father's potential fury and envy of mother is dealt with by the custom of 'couvade' where the man is treated by his mother as if he is also about to give birth. Roheim provides an even more extreme illustration of the masculine envy of motherhood when he describes the Australian aborigine custom of subincision, whereby the 'aralta' hole is made to bleed; the

Sutties see this custom as an obvious simulation of menstruation, particularly as the subincised penis is renamed after the female organs. The male is also believed to be able, in suitable circumstances, to produce children (Suttie and Suttie, 1932, p.217).

> The most direct, gratifying and natural expressions of paternal jealousy, however, are found in *patriarchal culture itself*. In this the male becomes *the* parent, the children are his and bear his name. His wife or wives, he buys or has bestowed on him by her father: his daughters he gives away or sells in the interests of the 'dynasty'.
>
> *(Suttie and Suttie, 1932, pp.217–218; Sutties' italics)*

For the Sutties then, the patriarchal family system provides a solution for the father and society: his jealous hostility regarding his children's relation to mother is 'bought off' and his services secured for the family. In buying his wife and children with food, a new equation arises whereby 'money is food; food is love'. On the social level this is translated as 'money is power: is esteem; esteem is love'. The authors believe that it is just such an equation that makes the patriarchal culture so passionately acquisitive and why the institution of property is both attacked and vigorously defended (1932, p.217).

The patriarchal culture is therefore both the product and the cause of affective tensions, and expresses itself in an intense religion whereby the powerful father image is made to take on all the power of the mother so that her image can be idealised and made 'gentle' and unthreatening.

Over a series of generations, patriarchy has perpetuated itself through the attachment system with all the repercussions such a parental system can have on the relations between men and women, parents and their children and social relationships in general. The psychological template of the patriarchal system is the caregiver–infant dyad within the context of the father–mother relationship. In honour of Freud, the Sutties refer to this culture as the Oedipus culture since, in their view, the psychoanalytic Oedipus complex is the expression of paternal jealousy of both mother and child, a jealousy which is denied by the father and projected on to the infant (1932, p.211). The initial jealousy does not come from the child and is not of a sexual nature as Freud would have us believe: it springs from the mother–infant relationship. If this primary attachment relationship has been unsatisfactory, the adult male will be more affected than the woman by virtue of the fact that paternity offers him less emotional reward; instead, the jealous child in him will refuse to be left out of the mother–infant relationship and will exhibit an aggressive intrusiveness which is then perpetuated in his children and down the generations. Such an outcome is the paradoxical result of the patriarchal system's inherent devaluation of women and motherhood (and mother worship). The more the father, backed by society, attacks his wife, depriving her of social interests and functions, the more she turns to her child.

Patriarchy has therefore had the paradoxical effect of increasing the Oedipus rivalry and hatred of father in both boys and girls. In such conditions the mother is unable or unwilling to help her child renounce his strong ties with her, with the result that the boy is not encouraged to be truly independent and he is left in a state of insecurity which he later seeks to remedy by finding a substitute mother, an 'ideal passive woman'. However, once married, the idealisation fails and the man ceases to trust his wife because of his earlier insecure attachment; he then becomes jealous of her involvement with their children. This pattern is repeated down the generations and is even intensified in cultural conditions where women are segregated from men, as happens in certain Islamic societies.

Though the Sutties tend to see the patriarchal system as a psychological and defensive solution to the mother–infant attachment relationship, it clearly cannot be divorced from the turbulent socio-political developments which began to take place in the Middle East during the third millenium before Christ. In response to the patriarchal warring tribes of the East, the mother goddess began to give way to father gods. In the first city states that followed the Agricultural Revolution, male-dominated social hierarchies became established with a widening gulf between producers and those who controlled the surpluses. War became increasingly important (Baring and Cashford, 1991, p.151). The invasion of this part of the world by both Aryans and Semites could be seen to have had a devastating and lasting effect on the civilisations that followed.

> A relationship with nature many thousands of years old was disrupted as people no longer felt safe in villages, and sought refuge first in towns and then in cities girdled by immense walls. A new social group – that of the warrior – came into being and the former close-knit group of farmers became little more than serfs.
>
> *(Baring and Cashford, 1991, p.157)*

The authors note that these changes were reflected in the new mythology as gods and goddesses became 'infected by the warrior ethos, ratifying the barbaric actions of kings whose territorial ambitions draw them ever more deeply into the compulsion to conquer and enslave other peoples' (1991, p.157).

Baring and Cashford attribute many of our current attitudes to these invaders: they are believed to have brought the view of nature as something 'other' to be conquered; similarly, death becomes the opposite of life, something final and remorseless rather than the old promise of rebirth.

As the Bronze Age progressed, a new terror took over, the terror of death by hand of man and by new diseases brought in by the conquering armies. Human violence was unleashed on a grand scale, destroying cities, bringing death, rape and slavery to countless people as well as great power to the conquerors.

These changes in attitude towards nature, life and the 'other' have become ours:

> 'Their legacy lives on in pervasive attitudes and structures of response to life that have not been questioned and still have a controlling influence on the psyche today ... No less a question than our vision of human nature is involved here. Are we to regard the values of these nomadic tribes as specific to their own experience of life or as a representative of the human race as a whole. If we see the ethos of conquest that they brought with them as specific to tribal consciousness only, then we do not need to generalise this vision of life and conclude that human nature itself is innately aggressive and war like.'

> *(Baring and Cashford, 1991, pp.157–158)*

As new empires were formed, an increasingly sedentary existence developed which brought with it the accumulation of property. Social organisation became centred round the control of production and the distribution of wealth in the community. The warrior class continued to play its crucial role in protecting those in power and in conquering. Religion took on an important role in the maintenance of male–female inequality: important men, like Odo de Cluny (AD 879–942), could be heard propounding profoundly misogynist views such as 'To embrace a woman is to embrace a sack of manure'. For Thomas Aquinas, women were simply 'defective and misbegotten'.

Men and women

The making of men and women

One of the main characteristics of the patriarchal system is therefore the inferior status of the woman. Through the parallel influence of cultural transmission through language and tradition, as well as through the psychobiological effects of the mother–infant transgenerational system we described earlier, the patriarchal system continues to provide the appropriate rearing conditions for the maintenance of this crucial and uneven male–female split, a psychological split that is prevalent the world over, even in the USA where some would have us believe that the battle between the sexes has been won by the women (Faludi, 1991).

Our particular interest in this sexual inequality focuses on how the upbringing and development of boys and girls in our culture may con-

tribute to the violence that now concerns us so much. In most primate
species, males are more aggressive than females and, when exposed to
maternal deprivation or abuse, males are more affected and become
extremely hostile (see Chapter 4). In humans there are also genetic differences between the two sexes which influence their behaviour, but
considerable interaction also takes place between biological determinants and cultural forces. This was illustrated when comparing male
sexual behaviour across different cultures (Sanday, 1981).

It is in the study of the development of the male and female self that
it begins to be possible to discover how gender identity is formed as a
result of these different interactional processes and how these might
predispose towards human violence. What is becoming apparent is that
one of the most important ways the self of a person is organised is
around his or her gender identity: our concept of ourselves as either
male or female not only structures our sense of self but is also one of
the major ways through which cultural expectations are channelled.

Women are said to have it easier during development because they
can directly identify with their mothers. Men, on the other hand, have
to forego their early identification with their mothers to become sexually potent. Stoller describes this process very lucidly: the first person
to be identified with is one's mother, a person whose psyche and body
are like the little girl's but so different from the boy's. The latter has to
ackowledge these differences and in time accept them. As he becomes
more masculine, he must separate himself in the outside world from
his mother's female body and in his inside world from his own already
formed primary identification with femaleness and feminity. This great
task is often not completed and, for Stoller, this is the greater promoter
of perversion, perversion being, as Stoller defines it, the 'eroticised
form of hatred', or the ultimate in separation, 'mother murder' (1975,
p.150).

> To break free of that first object, mother, and establish oneself requires that
> a barrier be set up to help keep one from succumbing to the urge to merge
> with her. This piece of character structure may be sustained by fantasies of
> harming mother: again a risky business.
>
> *(1975, p.121)*

Stoller goes on to make it clear that, in his view, the mother–infant
relationship involving boys is almost always doomed to failure:
whether the boy's experience is of a 'deprived symbiosis' or of 'good
enough mothering', his development is threatened. Indeed, Stoller
argues: 'Our culture, as do most others, defines masculinity – for better
or worse – by how completely one demonstrates that one is rid of the
need for symbiosis with mother' (1975, p.162). This involves the formation of a character structure that forces the inner mother down and

out of awareness (1975, p.150). What is implied is that to become masculine, a boy has to split off or repress his identification with his mother. To achieve this she must be seen to be bad, worthless or dangerous: she has to be dehumanised. Such a split enables him to hold onto an idealised view of mother and women which has no bearing on reality: both these attitudes are endorsed by society where the woman is often seen as either 'madonna' or 'whore'.

Masculinity is thus achieved by a culturally endorsed use of psychological defences such as splitting, dehumanisation and idealisation; these defences allow man to reject certain aspects of himself which are identified with his mother but they also lead on to a failure of empathy or an inhibited capacity to identifiy with others which interferes with full personal development and maturity (1975, p.134). The outcome of such a development is also the linking in men of sex and sadism. Freud wanted to see this link as inborn: 'The sexuality of most male human beings contains an element of aggressiveness – a desire to subjugate ... Thus sadism would correspond to an aggressive component of the sexual instinct' (Freud, 1905).

Stoller agrees with Suttie that male sexual perversions are linked to our current social system and in fact are important in preserving it. His view of masculine development helps to explain why homosexual men are hated and often violently attacked by 'conventional' heterosexual men: they present a threat to their masculinity, to a sexual identity that only appears to exist in relation to femininity, to all that is not masculine.

Stoller believed perversions only developed in men, but we now know that women also develop them but they tend to carry out their perverse acts against their own bodies or their babies, both of which they treat as part-objects (Welldon, 1988, p.72). With men, the act is carried out against an external part-object who usually represents the hated mother. The more the individual identifies the part-object of his perversion with the original object who forced him to develop these dynamics, the more dangerous the perversion.

In the case of the 'Yorkshire Ripper', women became the dehumanised objects of his hatred for his mother, a hatred he attempted to split off from his wife. Joan Smith, in her book *Mysogenies* (1989), points out that he wanted desperately to prove himself a man in his local culture, which meant being engaged in such activities as hard drinking, petty crime, fighting and casual sex, including going out with prostitutes. He proved himself such a failure, his father said of him: 'He was a right mother's boy from the word go' (Cameron and Frazer, 1987, p.137).

Peter Sutcliffe, as he was really called, was terrified of this father as were his siblings. The father would drink and beat up the family including his wife. He was also unfaithful to her. Peter was the most sensitive of the boys and could not identify with his father or any other man. He was eventually to find his manhood when he began stabbing, mutilating and destroying women's bodies (Smith, 1989, p.148). Unfortunately, his sense of relief was short lived and the compulsion to kill was therefore never satisfied.

A very important aspect of Joan Smith's account of the case involves trying to understand why the police took so long to identify Peter Sutcliffe as the murderer, since the incriminating evidence was available long before he was arrested. The author attributes this fatal delay to the fact that he shared so many of the policemen's own prejudices: to both him and the officers, the prostitutes he killed were not quite 'human': they were 'whores'. This made his apparent crusade against them understandable. He only became a really dangerous killer in their eyes when he mutilated and killed an 'innocent sixteen year old lass, a happy, respectable working class girl from a decent Leeds Family ...' (1989, p.139).

In fact, like another vicious killer Albert DeSalvo, the Yorkshire Ripper was seen as a hero in certain communities: he was sung about by the band Thin Lizzy in 'Killer on the loose'; football supporters in the north of England would sing 'There's only one Yorkshire Ripper' to the tune of Guantanamera and they also chanted 'Ripper 12, police nil'.

It seems that there are many men in the world who need to hate and violate women and for whom this is the only way of making them feel that they are real men. The male self in a patriarchal society tends to rely on the dehumanisation of the sexual 'other' to survive. Stoller vividly illustrates this when discussing pornography. For him there is no non-perverse pornography: all sexually exciting matter has hostility as a goal. However, since most pornography is aimed at the average heterosexual male, it is 'normal' in the statistical sense but not in the universal sense, because female nudity is not 'sexually fetishistic' in all societies.

The female sense of self is defined in relation to the needs of the male self: women will tend to identify with what men project onto them, both the dehumanised object role they are given and the idealised role and expectations they persistently attempt to meet.

The phenomenon of 'projective-identification' is therefore inherent to the psychic drama that takes place between men and women: each sex splits off the characteristics they perceive as belonging to the 'other'. As a result of this process of denial and splitting, these repressed parts of themselves are projected onto the 'other' of the opposite sex, who must then be controlled at all costs in an attempt to make good what has been lost. This process is particularly evident in the man who denigrates his femininity, projects it into 'his woman' and then needs to dominate her; it is also present in the masochistic role enactment of the woman who projects her fighting spirit and her potency onto her 'man'.

How is the split in male–female sexual identity made manifest? It is becoming clear that men are more likely to be abusers and females to be victims: in her study on the history of violence in 190 psychiatric outpatients, Herman found that 81% of the offenders were male whereas the majority of victims, 81%, were females. What really surprised her was to discover that 10% of the men had been sex offenders. The majority of the reported violence had taken place in the family (Herman, 1986).

Kaplan attributes this difference to how boys and girls are brought up (1988, pp.127–139). She describes the woman's model of development as 'the self in relation' model.

> It posits that, for women, the core self-structure is a relational self that evolves and matures through participating in and facilitating connection with others and through attending to the components of the relational matrix, especially affective communication.
>
> *(1988, p.128)*

As Kaplan explains, this is achieved through the identification with the mother, a nurturing adult, and by discovering that her sense of self, as a girl, is enhanced and developed by moving into relations with others. Interestingly, this does not mean that women do things for others but rather that they look for 'empowerment' through the process of affirming themselves and manifesting empathic understanding of others (1988, p.129). This is carried from the home into the labour force.

Like Stoller, Kaplan thinks that boys are subjected to pressures to refrain from identifying with their primary female caregiver and with the nurturing functions she represents. Instead, they are encouraged to identify with the image of the paternal presence. Such an identification is usually fragile because the real father is often absent and the nature of his work is also remote. As a result, bonding in a close caring relationship with the opposite sex is a threat to the self and is avoided by moving away from the relationship. Thematic Apperception Tests show that men are more threatened by intimacy and women by isolation.

Thus, throughout their development, boys go for independence, isolated achievement and the inhibition of affect in intimate relationships. The male self's main source of self-esteem lies within the world of 'work'. Marriage and family are of secondary importance. These conclusions appear to confirm what Shere Hite found in her report on *'Love, Passion and Emotional Violence'*: one of the most frequent complaints American women have about their male partners is that they do not or cannot communicate, so much so that 98% of the 45 000 women interviewed want to make basic changes in their relationships and improve the emotional relationships they have with men (1991, p.4).

The prevalence of male–female abuse

When one looks at the prevalence of abusers in the USA, 10–20% of men acknowledge they have been abusive (Finkelhor, 1979; Russell, 1984). Malamuth interviewed college men and discovered that 25% said they were prepared to use force to get sex and that 51% said they would attempt rape if they knew they could get away with it! (1981).

These findings tie up with those relating to yet another form of family violence, that of rape in the marriage, which reflects the same cultural trends and which is still legal in much of the USA and most other countries of the world. Diana Russell's study *Rape in Marriage* (1982) involved a survey of 930 women in San Francisco: 14% of the married women in the sample reported sexual assaults by their husbands; 12% had been forced to have intercourse and 2% had been forced to experience other types of forced sex. These findings were confirmed by Finkelhor and Yllo in Boston (1988). In the UK women are seven times more likely to be raped by their husbands than by a stranger: in half of these cases violence was used or threatened. This means that 1370 000 wives or ex-wives have been the victims of rape in the UK (Dyer, 1990). Three out of four reported rapes do not get a conviction in England.

Kaplan suggests that such high figures indicate that we are dealing with a real social problem which derives from the normative pattern of male development.

> The prevalence of violence in men seems to be anchored in men's internalisation of cultural prescriptions. In patriarchal society, men are given permission to expect gratification of individual needs and to use their dominant status to seek such gratification.
>
> *(1988, p.136)*

As she says, if men do feel that this is the case, then there are really no built-in constraints against men using force to get what they want. In fact, as we have seen before, our culture condones the use of force to resolve disputes. This ties up with the findings of Baron, Straus and Jaffee which showed a direct relationship between legitimate violence, violent attitudes and rape (1988). Similar findings were made cross-culturally: interpersonal violence is rarely found in rape-free societies (Sanday, 1981).

Murder is the end result of male–female inequality and the implicit dehumanisation it entails: every three days in Britain, a woman dies at the hands of her male partner. As Pamela Smith points out, the men who commit these crimes often appear 'as "model husbands" – quiet, solicitous, even retiring, men' (1989). The majority have no history of violence or aggression. Then, one day, 'under pressure', they kill. Their calm coping exteriors belied their vulnerability, the vulnerability of men who cannot reconcile themselves to the aggressive manifestations of their psychological splits, the very splits that allowed them to feel that they were men.

Kaplan states that for women, the developmental problem does not lie in why they become victims, because all women are vulnerable to becoming victims in our society. It is how women behave once they have been abused or traumatised that appears to be related to their upbringing. If their self-identity and self-esteem reside in their capacity to take care of relations, then they may feel more threatened by the loss of this attribute than by the physical or emotional harm they are risking. Such an attitude is reinforced by the strong tendency to blame women for their personal experiences of abuse, an attitude with which women easily identify.

Implications of the sexual conflict

Male and female problems are intrinsic to our culture and if they are to be changed, they require collective support that is then reflected in changes in the social structure. What is becoming clearer is that we live in a culture in which the more rigid masculine self is shored up at the expense of the female self. Masculinity, in most social groups, requires of boys that they devalue and deny the importance of their first and most important attachment relation. Even with a 'good enough' mother, all the qualities associated with mothering, her tenderness and her ability to nurture and to be emotionally responsive, must be repressed and, if possible, projected into the female 'other', leading to a depletion in the male self and to his permanent need for those very attributes he has had to deny himself. Having, so to speak, killed off the mother in himself, a rigidly masculine individual is permanently insecure in his sexual identity, infantilised by these inner splits and outer projections, bereft of the security of an attachment relation he has either never known or needed to 'cut off'. He is also deprived of the social support women develop towards one another. The result of this cultural denial of man's femininity is a deep dread of women whom men often envy and therefore also hate.

The man's comfort lies in the male group where male values are reinforced, usually at the expense of a socially inferior 'other'. When discussing this book with Bowlby, he reminded me that the Second World War, for many men like himself, had brought with it a sense of 'male camaraderie' he had deeply valued, an experience he felt that I, as a woman, would not be able to appreciate. My response was one of sadness that men should be dependent on violence for some of their closest experiences with other men.

Tiger makes it clear that the essential component of successful male bonding goes hand in hand with 'a ready proneness to aggress externally' (1969, p.190). The implications are that the more potentially aggressive people are, the greater their need for a 'them' and 'us' group experience both to prevent intragroup violence and to boost the self through the externalisation of personal violence onto outsiders.

The woman unconsciously takes on the dehumanising projections of her male partner and re-enacts them at her expense. She also learns to suppress any feelings of anger and destructiveness towards those who abuse her. Instead, when traumatised, she tends to turn her rage against herself in some form of self-destructive behaviour (van de Kolk 1988, p.175).

A pattern is emerging between male–female inequality and family violence. This can take the form of physical assaults between parents and marital rape, as well as physical and child sexual abuse. In her book on 'Father–Daughter Incest', Judith Lewis Herman states that child sexual abuse is the result of male–female inequality and the patriarchal family structure. Reflecting the views of many modern sociologists and psychoanalysts, she also believes that any long-term hope of changing the psychology of men and women rests on both sexes sharing the responsibility for the care of the children.

> Boys might be able to establish the same kind of secure gender identity that girls do, based on a primary identification with a nurturing father. Girls might be able to establish a sense of autonomy and self respect based upon identification with a mother who is not perceived as inferior...Children raised by parents of both sexes presumably would not reach adult life expecting nurturance, sacrifice and service only from women. The capacities for caretaking would be developed in both boys and girls, making it possible for grown men and women to share in the rearing of the next generation.
>
> *(1981, pp.212–213)*

As Herman says, the idea of involving men more in child rearing may sound simple but is extremely radical, so radical that it is dismissed by most people. No 'new' political system, not even the Socialist one, ever made a serious attempt at involving men in the work of child care. The reality is that men are totally absent from an increasing proportion of families. About 25% of American families are now single parent families, that is, mother-led households. In the UK, there were over 1 010 000 one-parent families in 1986, that is, about 14% of families with children.

In two-parent families, though the father contributes financially to the care of the children, he does not have any direct child-care responsibilities. One American study shows men spending 15 minutes of the day in direct interaction with their children and another study showed that they spent, on average, 37.7 seconds per day talking to their infants (Herman, 1981, p.213). An increasing amount of research into the effects of a father's absence from the home shows that, if 'paternal neglect' is a problem, then most children suffer from it. In fact, it is beginning to emerge that children form strong attachments with their fathers from which they benefit considerably and they also suffer from paternal rejection, indifference or hostility. It seems quite clear that fathers are very important in the development of their children. However, can men be persuaded to involve themselves with a task they have spent several thousand years devaluing and which requires a great deal of change in the organisation of production? As long as the idea of male–female equality over child care is seen as a 'feminist' issue, most men will dismiss it. However, if the links between male–female inequality, child care and social violence are made increasingly obvious, then more men and women may begin to see the value of questioning and changing the system they have so far supported.

Now that more and more women are entering into the paid labour force without any real reduction in child-care responsibility, they feel increasingly cheated of their rights and critical of their male partner's failure to share in the child care. The marital stresses that this state of affairs has produced are there for all to see in the rapid rise in divorce rates. In the UK, one in four marriages ends in divorce and the figures are predicted to rise to one in three very soon. This means that 150 000 British children per year have divorced parents. Since many of them continue to be looked after by their mothers who cannot go to work, the financial cost to the state is enormous. However, the long-term psychological and social cost of this breakdown of the family is even more devastating for the children. Research shows that children exposed to marital conflict do suffer: whereas childhood problems arising from divorce used to be attributed to the effects of separation, the evidence now shows that current interparental conflict is the main explanation for these difficulties (Emery, 1982). (This does not mean, however, that separation does not affect the child.) This marital turmoil affects boys more than girls and, though a good relationship with the mother can buffer the child, the negative effects of the marital turmoil still arise. As Robin Skynner states:

> Children absorb not just models of the behaviour of people in isolation, but also of their relationship to one another. In particular, the internalised model of the parents *as a couple,* rather than as separate individuals alone, will have a deep influence on the quality of the marriages of their children.

> *(1976, p.123; Skynner's italics)*

This marital turmoil can be a great source of fear in children: because fathers expect to be in charge at home, they can experience their wives, failings as direct attacks on their very selves; the wifebeater husband will then lash out with indescribable passion. He will do it because he feels his wife deserves it and because he believes he has a right to do it to her.

People working with wife batterers (such as Jim Wilson or Adam Jukes in the UK) believe that domestic violence comes from two things: the authority the man feels he should have over his wife and the services he expects from her. They believe that men who abuse women physically or emotionally (i.e. nearly all men in their view) suffer from an inability to see women as separate independent people. In our culture, women are defined as what men need to complete themselves: for this reason they need to control 'their women', often by inflicting pain.

With such internalised parental relationships and sex role models, it is not surprising that the male–female conflict is so acute. Essentially, what the dehumanisation of the 'other' is all about is creating the psychological template for men to be able to exploit, abuse and if necessary kill the 'other'.

By subjecting infants to deprivation or maltreatment and by condoning physical and emotional abuse in the upbringing of our children, society produces a human psyche which is primed to hate the 'other'. This 'other' will usually be defined by the group to which the individual belongs. All of us carry within us these split-off templates of abuse: though they may remain dormant for months or years, their reactivation is potentially a violent one, the manifestation of both a damaged attachment system and a narcissistically injured self.

The exploitation of children

As a result of this dehumanisation of the 'other', exploitation and violence have become intrinsic to the Western way of life and its underlying political and economic structures. One of its main manifestations is the exploitation, abuse and murder of millions of children. Though the children of the UK are no longer being made to work long hours in the appalling conditions of the mines, the mills and factories of the Industrial Revolution, their counterparts in the poor countries of the Third World are facing just such 'Victorian' working conditions. According to UNICEF, 200 million children between the ages of 5 and 15 work for miserable wages both to survive and to help their parents (Backmann, 1991). This means that in India alone, 128 million do not go to school because they work: half of them work in industry for pitiful wages and 5 million as slaves.

Despite widespread laws to protect children from being exploited in this way, only the wealthy countries consider the use of child labour as a social problem. It is essentially in the poor developing countries that children are being ruthlessly exploited: an estimated 100 million children roam the streets of the large cities in search of a living. In South

America, they are now the victims of the police or paid killers who shoot them down by the hundreds with impunity.

In Thailand, as in other countries of the Far East where tourism and prostitution are linked, thousands of children are sold or kidnapped to satisfy the sexual needs of adults. In the Philippines, some houses of prostitution specialise in providing 5 year old children for American or European paedophiles, and girls of less than 16 are available to the sailors of the American fleet.

Few Westerners believe that slavery still exists: yet, even in the countries of the Gulf, our recent allies, thousands of young Asian women and small children are made into slaves without any rights or freedom. Children are also being bought or sold all over the world. Even Britain was exporting her children over the last 350 years; they were to be used as slave labour or as future 'bearers of white man's burden' (Bean and Melville, 1990).

One of the central tenets underlying the use of child labour is the belief that children are the 'possessions' of adults. Their dehumanisation goes hand in hand with the current economic system; what is happening in the developing countries is what took place in our Western countries over the last few centuries. But, even today, there is still glaring evidence of the need to exploit and abuse children in the more developed countries of the West: in the USA, for instance, thousands of children are being offered in prostitution (Backmann, 1991). The West is also very much involved in the 'harvesting', of organs for transplantation, from children who are kidnapped or 'adopted' in the Third World (Pinero, 1992).

Racism

In South Africa, hundreds of children and adults have been killed by the police or the army and thousands detained without charge and often tortured. Malnutrition, infantile deaths and general morbity figures are higher for black South African children than their white counterparts. These differences stem from yet another dehumanisation process, that of apartheid which has as its central premise, the inferiority of the black person in relation to the white. Though racism was systematically developed by the West to justify the slave trade, it took root very easily because of patriarchal society's highly developed capacity to dehumanise the 'other' (Pope-Hennessy, 1967). Indeed, though born out of the male–female divide, the psychological template of dehumanisation and abuse is central to the establishment of all forms of racism and rigid social hierarchies. Racism is but another example of the 'legitimate dehumanisation' that Western culture encourages. 'Slavery', wrote Voltaire in the eighteenth century, 'is as ancient as war, and war as human nature.'

The famous African explorer, Captain Richard Burton, wrote the following when he reached the shores of Lake Tanganyika:

> The study of the Negro is the study of Man's rudimental mind. He would rather appear a degeneracy from the civilized man than a savage rising to the first step, were it not for his total incapacity for improvement. He seems to belong to one of those childish races which, never rising to Man's estate, fall like worn out links from the great chain of animated nature.

(Davidson, 1984, p.15)

'The raw native', affirms a Portuguese Colonial authority as late as 1950, 'has to be regarded as an adult with a child's mentality' (Davidson, 1984, p.206). The racist often attributes childish attributes to the inferior coloured 'other', an interesting phenomenon if we bear in mind how Western children are perceived as needing to be dominated and punished 'for their own good'. Similar attitudes were prevalent towards the black African slaves and in the (Western) colonies.

What racism implies psychologically, is that the 'black' person is legitimately dehumanised and can therefore be exploited both physically and psychologically. Racism therefore begins, as all acts of dehumanisation do, by a distortion of perception: the 'other' is literally perceived to be different, filthy, stupid, bad, childlike etc. This cognitive process originates, as was shown earlier, from the experience of abuse which the infant or child attempts to ward off by identifying with the aggressor. It can also be culturally transmitted through learning and modelling, but it is my belief that such learning only takes place where the psychic template of dehumanisation already exists: the seeds of abuse, racism and murder are sown in the emotional wounds of the abused and traumatised. They are then reinforced by the cultural beliefs of the time. It may be worth returning to Frodi's experiment to remind ourselves of how a parent's perception and response to a crying baby was determined by what the researchers said about the infant (who in fact was always the same baby on video): the parents of both sexes in Frodi's tests were all aversively aroused by the crying, but those who were told the baby was 'premature' or 'difficult' were even more negatively aroused. 'This experimental manipulation created a cognitive set that affected the parents' autonomic arousal as well as their subjective feelings' (Frodi, 1985, p.356). Abusive mothers subject to the same experiment showed an even greater aversive arousal response to crying babies and this also extended to the smiling baby. These last results show that these mothers had an acquired aversive cognitive set that had generalised to cover all child-related stimuli, smiles and cries.

The racist's perception of some people being 'black' and hence inferior, is also determined by his culturally imposed cognitive sets, superimposed upon the earlier experiences of dehumanisation. This was shown most clearly when Europeans discovered the huge and impressive walls of Great Zimbabwe. They could not contemplate the possibility that this structure arose from the 'Negro's rudimental mind'. To do so would have meant questioning the entire psychological infrastructure that underlay the economic foundations of colonialism. So, the walls were attributed to the Phoenicians, to King Solomon's mines, but never to the great African civilisation that built them around 1300 AD (Davidson, 1984, pp.66–67).

Such distortions in perception are what made it possible for 'industrious honest people' to work in the slave trade. A certain Captain John Newton is described by Pope-Hennessy in his book on slavery (1967, pp.264–272). This man was the captain of an eighteenth-century slave ship. He was a 'respectable' person whose love-letters to his wife were sensitive and affectionate. In one of them he describes how men on his ship come and go at his command: they could not eat without his permission or go to sleep if Newton should leave his ship, no matter how late the hour. These customs were justified by the fact that 'without them the common sailors would be unmanageable' (1967, p.269). This apparently 'sensitive' man had no difficulty working in a trade where slaves were exposed to countless torments: some of these were unmerciful whippings which were

> continued till the poor creatures have not had power to groan under their misery, and hardly a sign of life remained. I have seen them agonising for hours, I believe for days together, under the torture of the thumbscrews, a dreadful engine, which, if the screw be turned by an unrelenting hand, can give intolerable anguish.
>
> *(1967, p.271)*

After 9 years, Newton left the slave trade following an apoplectic attack. He became an ardent abolitionist who could think of no commerce 'so iniquitous, so cruel, so oppressive, so destructive, as the African Slave Trade' (1967, p.271).

Pope-Hennessy ponders as to how men in appearance so cultivated and religious as Newton could become slave traders? He concludes that

> He belonged to that vast and dangerous multitude of human beings who take the established order for granted, and who lack both the courage and the time to question every single general assumption – to think, in fact, for themselves.
>
> *(1967, p.272)*

The problem is that people are not encouraged to think for themselves: they are encouraged to be obedient, respectful of authority and to submit to the rule of force like Newton's sailors. Like so many men in authority, John Newton probably treated his sailors as he had been treated as a child; like so many respectable men of his and our time, his

potential for violence was split off from his love-life and 'civilised' existence to be re-enacted with his sailors and even more freely with his
slaves, on whom he could project all that felt incongruous with his
own self-image, his 'blackness', sensuality and foregone childishness,
all the vestiges of the earlier childhood trauma that was inflicted on
him in order to make a 'man' of him.

The power of racial violence was vividly illustrated in the Los
Angeles riots of May 1992. These followed a court case where four
police officers went on trial for beating up a man: the 'victim' was black
and the officers were 'white' as was most of the jury. The world was
able to witness on their televisions the video recording of what looked
like a man being beaten up by the police. What followed next stunned
many viewers: the police officers were acquitted. A television interview
of one of the female white jurors seemed to suggest that the verdict
was prejudiced against the victim: she had voted to acquit the police-
man because she was convinced that 'Rodney King was controlling the
whole show with his actions ...'. For her the use of force was therefore
justified.

There is no doubt that the origins of the beatings and the reasons
for the acquittals are much more complicated than the media made
out. However, to those who identified with the black man being
attacked by the police, the jurors' verdict could easily have appeared
like a racist justification for what appeared unjustifiable.

It is interesting to note that the defence used by the juror was the
same as that given by countless parents in authority who justify beating
their children to keep them under control. 'He thinks he is the boss –
all the time trying to run things – but I showed him who is in charge
here!' a father says of his 9-month-old boy whose skull he has split' (de
Mause, 1974, p.8). Lloyd de Mause believes that children are used by
adults as 'toilets' for their own projections, a process he also believes.
is behind the whole notion of 'original sin'.

Could it be that the 'blacks' in the USA, like the Jews in Germany
and Austria, fulfil the same function of carrying the projections of a
society riddled with pain and abuse? Faced with what appeared on television as a blatant denial of the pain and violence inflicted upon one of
'them', the younger 'blacks' and Hispanics, victims of the social system,
took to the streets in a display of wanton destruction and revenge. LA
went up in the flames of narcissistic rage, a rage that had its origins in
the denigration or traumatisation of the coloured people of America.
We may recall how young soldiers faced with the death of a member of
their group can experience this loss as an injury to the self, a self that is
completely identified with the group. The rage felt is so intense that
revenge is their only satisfaction, albeit short-lived. When in the throes
of such narcissistic rage, the enemy becomes the 'object' of revenge,
his annihilation becomes central to the restoration of the self. As Kohut

put it, the enemy is seen by the narcissistically vulnerable as 'a flaw in a narcissistically perceived reality'.

The jury's acquittal and the violent riots on the American streets were the consequences of both the dehumanisation of the 'other' which is at the centre of Western society, and the widespread legitimisation of violence.

Conclusion

The 'blacks' shore up the vulnerabilities of the 'whites', in much the same way as women shore up the sexual identity of men and as children act as the family 'toilets' for their parents' projections. The consequences of these massive psychological splits and projections required by a social order based on male–female inequality can only be poorly contained by the individual: he or she therefore seeks the support of an in-group where personal fears and needs can be legitimately projected onto 'others'. The more fragile the individual self, the greater the need for a group self: the price is the increasing dehumanisation of the 'other': misogyny, racism, nationalism and violence are all symptomatic of individual and social disintegration. Scapegoats become essential to the maintenance of law and order, as do police forces and armies. In ancient times, this increased use of legitimised violence by the state was usually sanctified by the gods or the church; nowadays, the Western states need men of science to promote, develop and legitimise the activities of their politicians. The role of these scientific 'high priests' will be the subject of the next chapter.

Chapter 14
The Traumatic Origins of Legitimate Violence

'Science without conscience is but death of the soul.'

Montaigne, 1533–1592

So far, this has been a study of human violence in the broadest sense of the term, in how it relates both to the disruption of the attachment system, and to the psychological manifestations of a traumatised self (see Chapters 4 and 7). Certain important connections have been made between different forms of upbringing and the incidence of violence in a particular society (see Chapter 12). It is through the study of the possible relationships between violence and the sociocultural context in which it occurs that a demonstrable link was actually shown to exist between the incidence of rape and the degree of legitimate violence in a particular community (Baron, Straus and Jaffee, 1988). The cultural implications of these findings are enormous for, as the authors stress, various forms of legitimate violence are woven into the fabric of American culture.

Straus, for instance, is of the opinion that the physical punishment of children is itself a sanctioned form of abuse because it is essential to the American socialisation process (1991). This is because it has the important effect of legitimising violence as it is itself a legally permissible attack on children, an attack which fits exactly the definition of violence given by Gelles: 'Violence is an act carried out with the intention, or the perceived intention, of physically injuring another person' (Gelles, 1978).

For Straus, physical punishment and legitimate violence, such as capital punishment, are similar. As he notes, corporal punishment is used by: 'Authority figures who tend to be loved or respected and since it is almost always used for a morally correct end and when other methods fail, physical punishment teaches that violence can and should be used under similar circumstances' (1991, p.134).

These observations highlight the possible links between child abuse and legitimate violence, making it necessary to explore how and why people carry out acts of legitimate violence. It is interesting that there is no research study which focuses on this process except in an indirect way: one such study is Stanley Milgram's famous American research on *Obedience to Authority* (1974). This study does not attempt to look at violence at all but at the process of obedience that is involved when a subject is instructed by an authority figure to give electric shocks to a 'learner/victim'. However, this research project could also be described as the 'study of legitimate violence in obedience to authority' since the subject is instructed by a figure in authority to carry out an act with the perceived intention of causing pain to another person. When looked at from this particular perspective, Milgram's findings appear to confirm much of what has already been suggested regarding the process of human violence, only in this case it has been sanctioned by people in authority.

The following analysis is based on the hypothesis that some of Milgram's subjects obeyed instructions and gave electric shocks to the 'learner' because of their own past history of abuse in childhood. In the absence of any direct research on the links between violence and childhood abuse in the general population, I think that this hypothesis is worth considering, particularly as it offers an explanation for Milgram's results which ties in with the evidence so far given on the traumatic origins of violence (see Chapter 11). However, it is important to remember that this analysis and its conclusions remain hypothetical and that a lot more research clearly needs to be done in this field.

One of the problems that researchers will face when carrying out such a study are the major difficulties involved in assessing whether subjects have or have not been traumatised in childhood, as such painful memories are usually split off and repressed by those who have suffered from psychological trauma (see Chapters 9 and 11).

Under Orders

In what appears to be a sophisticated modern laboratory, a 50-year-old man called Mr Prozi is seated in front of an instrument panel which consists of lever switches set in a line. Each switch has a labelled voltage designation, ranging from 15 to 150 volts. There is also a verbal designation for each group of four switches: the last four are marked 'Danger: severe shock'. This is a shock generator.

A stern-looking man dressed in a technician's grey coat appears to be giving Mr Prozi instructions. In another room, a middle-aged man is strapped down to an electric chair, out of sight but not out of earshot. Every time Mr Prozi presses a switch, he appears to give the man in the chair an electric shock.

At the beginning, Mr Prozi looks calm and composed but, as time goes on, he appears more and more anxious; he is under orders to move one level higher on the shock generator each time the learner in the electric chair gives a wrong answer. After administering a 180-volt shock, Mr Prozi swivels round in his chair to address the man in the technician's coat. He appears agitated. He does not want to kill the person next door who is hollering. The man in the grey coat reminds him that the experiment requires that he continue. Mr Prozi then says: 'I refuse to take responsibility. He's in there hollering!'... The experimenter eventually replies: 'I'm responsible for anything that happens to him. Continue please ...' Mr Prozi continues but the victim next door yells: 'Let me out of here, you have no right to keep me here. Let me out of here, let me out, my heart's is bothering me, let me out!' Mr Prozi shakes his head, pats the table nervously and complains. The man in the grey coat only reminds him that the experiment requires that he goes on.

Mr Prozi continues up to 270 volts. He then says he will not give the learner 450 volts. However, he continues administering the shocks until he hears the victim howl and refuse to answer any more. There follows a gloomy silence from the other room. The experimenter instructs him further: 'If the learner doesn't answer in a reasonable time, about four or five seconds, consider the answer wrong. And follow the same procedures you have been doing for wrong answers ...' Mr Prozi obeys and gives the victim shocks of up to 375 volts when he suddenly stands up and addresses the experimenter: 'I think something's happened to that fellow in there. I don't get no answer. He was hollering at less voltage. Can't you check in and see if he's all right, please?' The man in the technician's coat calmly replies: 'Not once we've started. Please continue, Teacher.'

Mr Prozi sits down and continues only to swivel round again and face the experimenter. He is concerned about 'the man in there'. The man in authority tells him to continue. 'You accept all responsibility?' asks Mr Prozi again. The experimenter replies: 'The responsibility is mine. Correct. Please go on.' The subject continues giving shocks until he reaches the maximum voltage of 450, labelled 'Danger, severe shock'. The experimenter tells him to continue using the 450 volt switch for each wrong answer. Mr Prozi asks anxiously: 'Don't the man's health mean anything?' The man in the technician's coat appears unmoved. Mr Prozi insists: 'What if he's dead in there?' (He gestures towards the room with the electric chair.) 'I mean, he told me he can't stand the shock, sir. *I don't mean to be rude,* but I think you should look in on him. All you have to do is look in the door. I don't get no answer, no noise. Something might have happened to the gentleman in there, sir' (my italics). He is simply told to continue. Mr Prozi dutifully administers two more 450-volt shocks and it is the experimenter who finally discontinues the experiment.

This experiment, which appears very much like an act of torture, is being carried out by Stanley Milgram's team in the elegant Interaction Laboratory of Yale University (1974, pp.73–77). It is important to realise that no electric shocks were really given to the learner who was role-played by an accountant, whilst the experimenter's role was played by a school teacher. However, like all the other subjects in this experiment, Mr Prozi was not acting: he really believed he was giving electric shocks to his victim just as he believed his victim was suffering.

All subjects came to the laboratory in response to an advertisement to participate in 'a study of memory'. They were received by the experimenter who gave them an introductory talk on the theories of learning. In his speech, he made the link between corporal punishment and learning:

> One theory is that people learn things correctly whenever they get *punished for making a mistake. A common application of this theory would be when parents spank a child* if he does something wrong ... We want to find out just what effect different people have on each other as teachers and learners, and what effect punishment will have on learning in this situation. Therefore I am going to ask one of you to be the teacher here tonight and the other one to be the learner.
>
> *(1974, p.18; my italics)*

Both the subject and the actor–learner draw a slip of paper and are allotted their respective roles. The learner is strapped into his electric chair in front of the subject. The volunteer subject is told that he will be paid for coming whether he decides to cooperate with the experiment or not.

Returning to the case of Mr Prozi, Milgram makes several points (1974, pp.76–77). The first is that, despite the learner's verbal protests, the subject continues to administer the shocks ordered by the experimenter: this suggests 'a dissociation between words and action'. It was clear that Mr Prozi did not want to administer these shocks; it was a painful act for him and only took place because of his relationship to the experimenter.

It is also important to note how crucial it was for Mr Prozi that the experimenter should accept responsibility for what happened. Only when he had been able to project on to the man in authority his own sense of responsibility and guilt about the learner's life, was he able to continue with the experiment. Finally, it is also remarkable to see that, after he had done this, his language became that of an obedient child, both courteous and respectful. As Milgram states:

> Despite the considerable tension of the situation, a tone of courtesy and deference is meticulously maintained. The subject's objections strike us as inordinately weak and inappropriate in view of the events in which he is immersed. He thinks he is killing someone and yet he uses the language of the tea table.
>
> *(1974, p.77)*

This last comment could be seen as an indication that the submission to authority, which is exemplified by the majority of the volunteers in this study, could possibly be related to their childhood experience of legitimate abuse at the hands of their parents or school teachers. This hypothesis is based on the fact that corporal punishment continues to be widely used in American families, that it is officially sanctioned school policy in many states (Gelles, 1978) and that 92% of young adults report having been physically punished as children (see Chapter 12). It is therefore very likely that many of Milgram's research subjects had been on the receiving end of such treatment themselves; some of them could even have been severely abused in this way, with all the implications this has in terms of their dissociated rage and their potential for seeing the 'other' as a 'part object' in the re-enactment of their abuse (see Chapters 10 and 11). Since it is also known that those who have experienced corporal punishment believe that they deserved it and that its use is justified in teaching (Graziano et al., 1991), many of Milgram's volunteers probably had similar views. It seems that because of children's need to preserve their love for their parents, most people will identify with their parents' reasons for punishing them: the result is a tendency to identify with the aggressor which, in this somewhat similar situation, would mean taking sides with the experimenter against the victim.

Milgram found that 26 out of 40 of his original male subjects obeyed the orders of the experimenter to the end, punishing their victim until they reached the most potent shock available on the generator.

One such subject was Mr Batta, a 37-year-old welder: he had his victim/learner sitting next to him in the room, a factor that normally greatly reduced the number of subjects able to give maximum shocks. However, it had no such effect on Mr Batta who paid little attention to his victim. In fact, when the latter refused to put his hand on the shock plate after the 150-volt level, Mr Batta ignored his victim's pleas for mercy and forced the man's hand down on the plate. 'What is extraordinary is his apparent total indifference to the learner: he hardly takes cognizance of him as a human being. Meanwhile, he relates to the experimenter in a submissive and courteous fashion' (Milgram, 1974, p.46).

As Mr Batta increases the power of his shocks and subdues the screaming learner, his face remains hard and impassive. He seems to derive satisfaction from a job well done. At the end of the experiment, when asked if he had felt tense or nervous he replied: 'The only time I got a little – I wouldn't say nervous – I got *disgusted*, was when he wouldn't cooperate,' (Milgram's italics) Clearly, for Mr Batta, the learner was not a human being in pain; he was simply a threat to the smooth running of the experiment. The learner appears to come over as so dehumanised in Mr Batta's eyes that one is left wondering what dehumanising experiences Mr Batta had himself been subjected to?

Mr Jan Rensaaler, who emigrated from the Netherlands after the Second World War, reacts very differently to the experiment. When the victim complains at the 150 volt level, he asks the experimenter what he should do. He then continues to obey until he reaches the level of 255 volts when he stops. The experimenter tells him to continue: he has no choice (Milgram, 1974, p.51). Mr Rensaaler answers:

> I do have a choice. (Incredulous and indignant.) Why don't I have a choice? I came here on my own free will. I thought I could help in research project. But if I have to hurt somebody to do that, or if I was in his place, too, I wouldn't stay there. I can't continue. I'm very sorry. I think I h've gone too far already, probably.

This subject refused to assign any responsibility to the learner or experimenter. Looking back at the experiment, he wishes he had stopped when the learner first complained but

> I turned around and looked at you. I guess it's a matter of ... authority, if you want to call it that: my being impressed by the thing, and going on although I didn't want to. Say, if you're serving in the army, and you have to do something you don't like to do, but your superior tells you to do it. That sort of thing, you know what I mean?
>
> *(Milgram, 1974, pp. 51–52)*

Mr Rensaleer clearly understood what was at stake. He was most surprised to hear that a group of psychiatrists predicted that most subjects would not go beyond the 150-volt shock when the victim asked to be freed and that only one in a thousand would administer the highest shock on the board (Milgram, 1974, p.31). Basing himself on his experience of Nazi-occupied Europe, Mr Rensaleer correctly predicted a higher level of compliance to orders.

These three subjects represent different levels of obedience and what can begin to be seen is that (1) high levels of obedience to authority figures are associated with (2) high levels of violence towards the 'learner', (3) a strong tendency to dehumanise the victim and (4) a relinquishing of personal responsibility which becomes manifest in an almost childlike attitude towards people in authority.

These three features are central to our hypothesis, which suggests that about a third of these subjects are unconsciously reliving split off childhood experiences of abuse carried out by parents and teachers, only in this setting, their alliance with the authority figure allows them to become the victimiser rather than the victim. It is most important to note that both men and women were found to participate in this act of obedience to authority.

In another series of ingenious experiments, Milgram showed that subjects only obeyed commands made by a person in authority (1974, p.104). He also showed how group phenomena can either hinder or

help those in authority. Referring to Asch's brilliant research on conformity (1951), he devised a test whereby the subject is asked to teach
with two other teachers he believes to be volunteers like himself (1974,
pp.114–118). One of these 'teachers' drops out of the test when the
learner starts to complain. After a higher shock level of 240 volts, the
second 'teacher' also refuses to carry on with the experiment. It does
not take long before the subject decides to defy the experimenter and
stop obeying. Under this type of group pressure, 36 subjects out of 40
defy the experimenter, whereas only 14 do so in the absence of group
pressure.

Group dynamics are usually used to increase submission rather than
to resist it. Having made the obvious point that the less the subject is
aware of the consequences of his acts, the easier it is for him to obey,
Milgram removed the subject from the act of giving shocks to the learner: he gave this task to another participant and the naive subject was
left to carry out subsidiary acts which contributed towards the final
administration of the shock to the victim. In this test, only 3 out of 40
subjects refused to carry on till the end of the experiment (1974,
pp.121–122). As Milgram points out, any destructive bureaucratic system can organise itself so that only the most callous and obedient are
directly involved in the violence, whilst those more likely to disobey
would feel doubly absolved from their responsibilities: not only has
their work been 'legitimised' by the authorities, but they do not commit brutal acts themselves. This technique was very much in evidence
in Nazi Germany, where faceless bureaucrats were involved at all levels
in the destruction of millions of human beings.

Lifton believes that the same techniques have been used in the USA,
in what he calls the 'nuclear bureaucracy' of the Cold War. In *The
Genocidal Mentality* (Lifton and Markusen,1990), one senior official in
the Defence Department gives a description of his group of employees
engaged in the work of 'nuclear targeting', that is in decisions involving
the potential destruction of millions of 'enemy' lives:

> I and my colleagues, with whom I shared a large office, drank coffee and ate
> lunch, never experienced guilt or self criticism. Our office behaviour was no
> different from that of men and women who might work for a bank or insur-
> ance company.
>
> *(1990, p.181)*

These men and women lived ordinary lives whilst, in their minds, they
thought about who were to be the possible victims of a nuclear attack.
This process requires the individual to be able to see the 'targeted'
others as 'dispensable': dehumanisation is inherent to the military
business. This is perhaps made easier if the 'enemy' is only a number
on a sheet of paper or a character in a computer war game.

What is striking in Milgram's study is the fact that, throughout his experiments, the levels of tension were found to be very high in many of his subjects. Milgram attributes this tension to the conflict that develops within the subjects as they are told to administer electric shocks to someone they can hear and, in some cases, even see and touch. He perceives these subjects as struggling to reconcile their belief that they should not harm others with their equally compelling tendency to obey those in authority.

Disturbed to find so many decent men and women committing acts of violence under orders, Milgram attempts to understand this phenomenon. Being unaware of the vast body of evidence that has since come to light concerning the prevalence of child abuse and its potential for violence (see Chapter 12), he suggests that humans are born with a potential for obedience which interacts with social pressures to produce the 'obedient man', a man who can function in a hierarchical social structure. Using a cybernetic model, he concludes that when individuals enter a system of hierarchical control, the mechanism that normally regulates their individual impulses, that is their 'conscience', is suppressed and is transfered to a 'higher-level component' to satisfy the organisational needs of the hierarchy on which humans appear to depend.

Milgram then looks for the 'switch' that enables this change to take place, so that the individual no longer sees himself as an autonomous individual but as an agent in the service of another of a higher status (1974, pp.131–134). Milgram had the courage to demonstrate how easy it is for any one of us to 'pull the trigger' under orders. He was, as previously noted, not concerned with the origins of violence when he set up his experiment, because obedience for him had nothing to do with unconscious feelings of rage and hatred, let alone with childhood abuse. He was not aware of the immense potential for violence which is locked up in those millions of individuals who have suffered the effects of childhood maltreatment. And yet, because of his subjects' terrifying tendency to obey orders, however inhumane, he concludes that: 'Most men, as civilians will not hurt, maim or kill others in the normal course of the day' (1974, p.128). But, he adds later:

> The kind of character produced in American democratic society, cannot be counted on to insulate its citizens from brutality and inhumane treatment at the direction of malevolent authority. A substantial proportion of people do what they are told to do, irrespective of the content of the act and without limitations of conscience, so long as they perceive that the command comes from a legitimate authority.
>
> *(1974, p.189)*

His epilogue remains depressingly correct and relevant to most cultures, however democratic they may appear.

It is only now that there is the evidence regarding the extent of childhood abuse and its implications that a new hypothesis can be formulated to explain Milgram's extraordinary results. As has been observed before (see Chapter 12), most adults who were beaten up by their parents feel that these early authority figures were 'right' and, in order to preserve this belief, they have to split off from consciousness any memory of pain and rage they may have experienced. This dissociation is maintained through cultural pressures which continue to endorse the use of corporal punishment (Gelles, 1978). As a result, this form of childhood trauma and its accompanying rage are repressed. It is only in a context where an equally powerful 'parental figure' is present to sanction such feelings of revenge, that these can be accessed and re-enacted in identification with the aggressor–parent. Such a phenomenon could explain the behaviour of subjects like Mr Batta. It is important to note that, as with cases of child abuse, the full memory of the trauma does not return in the re-enactment of the abuse: it remains split off in the unconscious, too painful to be acknowledged or felt.

Milgram did not see that central to his experiment is not only the issue of obeying an authority figure but also of exerting power over the 'other'. In giving his orders, the experimenter not only insists on the subject's obedience, but 'in the interests of science', he also sanctions the dehumanisation of the other subject, the learner. The latter must learn what is 'right' and 'wrong', however painful the process is. The subject is faced with a perversion of the process of teaching as well as with the legitimate and arbitrary dehumanisation of his 'pupil', an experience that may be reminiscent of what he went through at school. But here any identification with the learner stops, for, thanks to the experimenter, the subject no longer needs to feel victimised; he has the power given to him by the 'experimenter' to do to another what may have been done unto him, that is, to be the victimiser rather than the victim.

As O'Brien says in George Orwell's terrible novel *Nineteen Eighty-Four*:

> 'The real power... is power over men.' 'How does one man assert his power over another, Winston?'...'By making him suffer. Obedience is not enough. Unless he is suffering, how can you be sure that he is obeying your will and not his own? Power is in inflicting pain and humiliation. Power is in tearing human minds to pieces and putting them together again in new shapes of your own choosing.'
>
> *(1949, p.211)*

When Milgram formulated his theory to explain his subjects' violent behaviour, he was not aware of the links between child abuse and violence, nor of the evidence provided by hunter–gatherers which shows that, in small nomadic societies without hierarchies and authority figures, humans can function without a potential for obedience. Obedience is therefore not the 'fatal flaw' in human nature Milgram hypothesised, but it is the fatal flaw of the type of society we currently live in, with its psychological infrastructure of human inequality and child abuse (see Chapters 12 and 13).

If I have gone in such detail into Milgram's work, it is because it is of central importance in understanding two very important factors in the genesis of violence. The first is that it clearly illustrates how predisposed people are in Western societies to obey and act out their violence when they are in a context that sanctions this. The second is how clearly it demonstrates the power of the 'scientific experimenter' in getting subjects to obey.

There has been another experimental study which confirms many of Milgram's findings. Once again, the analysis offered here is based on my hypothesis that a certain proportion of the subjects involved had been traumatised through abuse in childhood. This is not, however, what Zimbardo set out to show (Sabini and Silver, 1982). He simulated a prison environment with students arbitrarily assigned to either prisoner or warder roles. This study was focused on what people can do when they are given legitimate power over another. In fact, the reactions of both groups of subjects were so extreme that the experiment had to be stopped after only 6 days, when it was meant to go on for 2 weeks. Unfortunately, the way it was planned and executed was so much like the real thing, that prisoners and guards alike probably felt that they were in prison. People have been critical of the degrading prison rules arranged by the experimenters and of the way the prisoners were arrested in their homes by real policemen, so that they never quite knew if the arrests were genuine or not. However, the fact that the experiment got so out of hand is indicative in itself of the violence that can be unleashed when the setting encourages people to express their destructive feelings.

Unlike the volunteers in Milgram's study, the students participating in Zimbardo's experiment were highly selected: they had to fill in a questionnaire and be interviewed by one of the experimenters. Only the most stable, most mature and least involved in anti-social behaviour were selected to participate in the study. It is important to note here that a history of childhood abuse would not necessarily have been elicited in those who were selected: as has been noted before, such painful experiences are usually split off from consciousness (see Chapters 10 and 11).

The original findings were as follows: the guards were characterised as falling into one of three groups. There were the tough but fair guards who kept within prison rules. Then there were several guards who were especially good, according to the prisoners: these felt genuinely sorry for prisoners, carried out favours for them and never punished them. And finally, about a third of the guards were extremely hostile and despotic: they invented new forms of degradation and humiliation and appeared to enjoy the power they had when they put on their guard's uniforms and wielded their sticks. What is striking is how differently the three groups of wardens behaved towards the prisoners. The 'good guys' appeared to have a secure sense of self with a capacity to empathise with their maltreated colleagues; they appeared to have no need to be abusive towards them. Linking these findings with the studies on attachment, it could be hypothesised that these individuals were the adult version of the securely attached infants, the group-B infants.

As for the hostile guards, they were clearly unable to empathise with their charges: in fact, they wanted to abuse them and humiliate them, and appeared to get satisfaction from the pain and distress they caused their prisoners. The latter did not appear to be human beings for these guards. Were they in fact 'part objects' in the re-enactment of their guards' own history of abuse? It could be postulated, that with the apparent blessing of the experimenters, the sadistic guards were able to revenge themselves for what they unconsciously felt had been done to them during their childhood and that these individuals were the grown-up version of the group-A insecure infants or the victims of later childhood abuse? (It is interesting to note that the proportion of abusing guards is only slightly higher than that of the group-A infants who comprised 21% of the babies tested in the Strange Situation (Ainsworth et al., 1978).)

These findings drawn from both Milgram's and Zimbardo's experiments suggest that, in conditions where abuse is made legitimate (whether experimental or real), certain people who have been maltreated could re-experience their abuse either as victims or as abusers depending on the power they are given. According to this hypothesis, the act of giving subjects legitimate power to abuse an 'other' may have stimulated some subjects to re-enact an earlier abusive power relation in identification with the aggressor. Unlike Milgram's experiment, however, the prisoners in Zimbardo's study became the real victims of their guards' abuse: for some of these victims, this may also have meant reliving past traumas which were unbearable to them.

These assumptions are based on the evidence that environmental changes and their associated cues may reactivate past traumatic memories (van der Kolk, 1989). In Delgado's work on aggression in primates, he makes it quite clear that the most essential thing in the development of aggression and violence is the personal reception and processing of environmental information through the various mechanisms of the brain which, when activated, can induce violent responses.

It is not that there is a natural aggressive instinct in man to kill man ... The basis for human hostility is mainly cultural or environmental, and as proved by history, aggressive tendencies may be decisively modified by education. One of the tasks for future scientists is the experimental study of these problems, recognising that environmental stimuli may radically affect the physical and chemical development of every organ, including the brain.

(Delgado, 1968)

Such views tie up with the evidence on the effects of psychological trauma (van der Kolk, 1987) and with the results of different forms of attachment throughout infancy (Field, 1985; Kraemer, 1985; Panksepp, Siviy and Normansell, 1985).

In what way, though, does the presence of an authority figure act as a 'switch' to bring about both obedience and abuse of the other? From the studies examined so far, it was the scientific status of the experimenter that appears to have made some of the subjects feel that what took place under his orders was 'legitimate'. This legitimacy could be considered as the equivalent of parental approval for the child: it would allow the insecure child in the adult finally to feel that he or she has the possibility of being approved, provided, of course, that the parent's wishes are carried out or that the experimenter is obeyed. The more insecure the adult, the more desperate the need to obey authority and so become part of the group of those in charge, the group of those who know how to be powerful by dehumanising the 'other', by inflicting pain and even killing the 'other'. After all, does the experience of legitimate corporal punishment in childhood not vindicate the view that 'might is right'? The experimenter, the subject and their common victim form an essential triangle in the perpetration of abuse. It could be postulated that the 'scientist' in Milgram's experiment gives the subject the opportunity legitimately to take revenge on his or her victim. This victim is not just a dehumanised 'other'; he or she can also act as the scapegoat for the subject's own dissociated feelings of helplessness, pain and rage.

As was noted earlier, the process taking place in Milgram's experiments is very like what takes place in the torture chambers across the world. In a similar act of dissociation to that of the subject, the torturer can attack all that he has had to dissociate himself from in order to feel strong and potent: in this way, he can belong to the group of those in authority as well as revenge himself for what pain and violence he may have endured in his past.

It is important to note that nearly all torturers are men and that the process of torture often involves sexual abuse and rape; this may not be so surprising if we can recall the degree of splitting and projective identification, as well as the perversion that is likely to be involved in the development of the male sexual identity of those who have been deprived of a good enough parental experience (see Chapter 13).

When an Argentinian torturer was asked if he abused the women, he replied:

> You could not help but get excited when you were handling a naked body, totally at your mercy. The movement became demanding, their semiconscious vulnerability a temptation, you had to do it.

(Graham-Youll, 1984, p.11)

For these men, their victims were objects without feelings. In this way the reality of what they were doing could be denied to themselves:

> I never tortured. Torture is inflicting pain for personal pleasure. I dealt punishment to my enemy, under orders from my superiors. And if you want to know, we all get to the stage when it becomes a game...I am working to break him as quickly as possible. You feel sorry to cause them pain, but you work quickly. You don't look at the face, even when you put the prods in the mouth; you keep their eyes covered. The secret is not to look at their eyes. The other secret is not to draw blood, you leave that for the sick bastards or the young brutes. You can watch the body arch and bounce under electricity, but never draw blood...
>
> *(Graham-Youll,1984, p.11)*

This torturer's need to keep his victims' eyes covered suggests that if both their eyes were to meet he might not be have been able to dehumanise his victim so successfully.

It is, however, in the act of war that obedience to authority becomes of paramount importance for those men and women who are under orders to kill. It is, of course, only one of the many factors involved in war. These have been outlined by the signatories of 'The Seville Statement on Violence' signed in 1986: 'Modern war involves institutional use of personal characteristics such as obedience, suggestibility, and idealism, social skills such as language, and rational considerations such as cost-calculation, planning, and information processing' (Groebel and Hinde, 1989, p.xv).

The aspect of war that concerns us here is the violence that is implicit in the obedience of so many. Looking back at what took place in Milgram's laboratory, under the orders of the experimenter, it is perhaps not surprising that thousands, if not millions of apparently sensible people do follow their leaders into war. To achieve this end, however, an 'enemy' has to be created and dehumanised and his destruction sanctioned by those in authority. The resulting psychological effect on the individual is very similar to what happened to Milgram's subjects: for those whose past is one of unexpressed rage and pain, the war can provide an outlet for feelings which until then are split off and repressed. These can be re-enacted on the battle field, sometimes to the bewilderment of the individual. I have met one such patient who, after a childhood of deprivation and abuse, went to fight with the army in Northern Ireland. He was horrified to find that he had an overwhelming wish to kill. He now suffers from PTSD and his rage is directed against his leaders who encouraged him to fight when they knew he was 'sick'.

However, though the analogy with Milgram's experiment helps to explain how and why so many civilised individuals can participate in the act of killing when ordered to do so, it fails to address the important group dynamics which are also involved in the state of war. When acting under orders and accessing their past dissociated feelings of rage, individuals can lose their prior sense of autonomy: as a result, their need to become part of the 'national' ingroup becomes of paramount importance. Held together by a common belief, such as the glory of the nation, the purification of the race or the defence of democracy, the group process binds members together and allows split off feelings of narcissistic rage to be vented and acted out against the 'enemy' in a way that would never have been possible during peace time. This is what we are seeing in the terrible acts of murder, rape and 'ethnic cleansing' that are being carried out in what was Yugoslavia.

The perversion of the professional caring relationship

The study of human violence cannot ignore what is perhaps one of its most disturbing manifestations, the participation of the 'caring professions' in acts of abuse against those who are in their care. Whilst other powerful individuals like judges, military leaders or police officers can all be involved in the perpetration of violence through the misuse of their power, it is the participation of those involved in the direct care of sick or disturbed individuals that will be the focus of the rest of this chapter. The reason for this is that the professional–patient relationship could be postulated to lend itself to the re-enactment of childhood abuse, as the relationship is very similar to the parent–child relationship: the doctor or therapist is entrusted with the care of his or her patient, whereas the latter is invited to regress to more dependent forms of behaviour because of the nature of the treatment. A surgical patient has to trust her doctor even when unconscious under the anaesthetic; a psychiatric patient needs to feel safe in the bewildering and painful confusion of a psychotic breakdown; a psychotherapy patient relinquishes old defences at the risk of feeling very vulnerable and helpless. If any of these human interactions were to trigger off the re-enactment of an earlier experience of abuse in the caring professional, the outcome could be devastating for the patient, because of the unequal power relations that exist between therapists and their patients (see Chapter 9). Doctors address this particular danger when they swear the Hippocratic Oath: 'In whatsoever houses I enter, I will enter to help the sick, and I will abstain from all intentional wrongdoing and harm.'

Unfortunately, patient maltreatment can occur quite unintentionally. There can either be an unconscious collusion with the patient's own traumatic re-enactment, as happens sometimes with sexually abused victims, or the therapist can unconsciously impose his or her own traumatic experience, re-enacted in this professional context from the point of view of the victimiser rather than the victim.

This possibility of abuse in treatment has already been commented upon with regard to psychoanalytic psychotherapists treating patients who have been traumatised. This is particularly common with sexually abused women whose tendency to sexualise their relationships with intimate others puts them at risk of being further abused by the very people who should be protecting them (Kluft, 1990; Fahy and Fisher, 1992).

In my view, this tendency on the part of therapists to re-enact their patient's abuse is due partly to a denial of the importance of psychological trauma and to the persistent belief in the overriding importance of the internal phantasy world of the patient (Chapter 9): what is not consciously recognised can so easily be unconsciously re-enacted, especially if, in addition, the psychotherapist is also unaware of his or her own personal history of abuse.

It is possible that many of those who choose to train in psychotherapy have themselves suffered from deprivation and/or abuse and that they tend to deal with their own needs by projecting them and attending to them in their patients. These potential 'compulsive carers' require a personal therapeutic experience which addresses the reality of their traumatic past if they are to avoid both denying and recreating their patient's own traumatic experience within the therapeutic setting. Research needs to be carried out to ascertain the prevalence of trauma and/or abuse among trainees in this field: such a study might help psychotherapeutic training institutions to become more aware of the importance of past traumatic experiences in the lives of their trainees (Hopper, 1991, pp.619–620).

Another way to minimise the damage that can occur between therapist and patient is to make it a professional requirement that all therapists have either some degree of supervision or a peer group with whom they can share their work, however skilled they may be. Unconscious defensive and potentially rejecting reactions to a patient's painful or violent feelings are always possible, however many years of psychoanalysis an individual has been through. The importance of peer group supervision was clearly shown in Rachel's psychotherapeutic treatment (see Chapter 9).

If the unconscious re-enactment of abuse is clearly a possibility in psychoanalytic psychotherapy, and even more so in other more directive forms of therapy, it can also occur within psychiatry or medicine in general. In this field, very little, if any, attention is given to the possibility of re-enactment of abuse on the part of patients or doctors and yet it happens, as was illustrated by Rachel's psychiatric history and by the experiences of other patients whose treatment failed to acknowledge the reality and psychological importance of their past traumatic experience (see Chapter 11).

Although most caring professionals carry out their difficult and demanding work with considerable skill and sensitivity, there are few who have not also witnessed or been party to glaring examples of neglect or of minor abuse towards patients. This is to be expected since neither doctors nor nurses are likely to be exempt from the type of formative experiences which incline people towards acts of abuse towards themselves or others: as with therapists, men and women often go into medicine or nursing to help heal themselves in the 'other'. Johnson points out that:

> The literature on motivations to study medicine suggests, that for some doctors, a component of their decision is a response to unconscious drives to compensate for childhood experiences of parental impotence or emotional neglect.
>
> *(1991, p.318)*

One study on university students supports this view by showing that those who decided to study medicine, particularly in the high patient contact specialities like psychiatry, tended to describe their childhood as being less stable, their parents as more overprotective and their home environment as more distant than the other students. The authors conclude: 'Some physicians may elect to assume direct care of patients to give others the care they did not receive in their own childhood' (Vaillant, Sobowale and McArthur, 1972).

This professionally endorsed process of 'projective identification' in a vulnerable self works as long as the patient acts his or her prescribed part and the doctor can feel sufficiently successful and potent. It does, however, imply that some doctors will tend to become emotionally dependent on their patients. Being needed has indeed been found to be one of doctors' greatest sources of satisfaction, probably to maintain what Kohut would describe as a 'grandiose' sense of self and, at a more basic level, to satisfy a need to be loved. However, such a dependency can also generate feelings of anger in these same physicians (Johnson, 1991). Also, to retain such feelings of grandiosity, doctors both need to and are encouraged in their training to repress feelings and attributes which might interfere with their idealised self-image: this means developing a certain degree of emotional detachment and denying any sense of personal vulnerability. These narcissistic personality traits can make doctors particularly vulnerable to stress which they often deal with by abusing alcohol (RCGP, 1986) or drugs (Lask, 1987) in an attempt to ward off feelings of depression and failure. Doctors also show abnormally high rates of suicide. 'Doctors will readily present with "medical" problems ... to a colleague for advice, but are much more reluctant to present illnesses which have implications of weakness or of being unable to cope' (Richards, 1989).

Doctors might also deal with these same feelings of personal distress and impotence in a different way if the opportunity presented itself, that is by being involved in a violent process whereby the 'patient' becomes the 'legitimate' victim of the doctor's dissociated rage and the recipient of all his projected feelings of pain and helplessness. Such conditions, similar to those seen in Milgram's experiments, exist in the torture chambers of at least 90 countries of the world: these operate under the aegis of the state and doctors unfortunately play an important role in a sizeable minority of these centres (Amnesty International, 1984; BMA, 1986, 1992). Of course, torture can and does take place without the participation of doctors, but the fact that physicians do become involved in the deliberate maltreatment of detainees is of great concern to both the medical profession and to the public, for it involves a perversion of the doctor–patient relationship in the interests of power.

Torture as defined by the World Medical Association as the:

> ...deliberate, systematic or wanton infliction of physical and mental suffering by one or more persons acting alone or on the orders of an authority, to force another person to yield information, to make a confession, or for any other reason.
>
> *(Declaration of Tokyo, 1975)*

Doctors become involved in the act of torture by examining people to see that they are fit to be tortured, participating in torture, and treating them after they have been tortured, in some cases so that they may be tortured again. As a result of their findings, the British Medical Association concluded that:

> It is unethical for a doctor to carry out an examination on a person before that person is interrogated under duress or tortured. Even though the doctor takes no part in the interrogation or torture, his examination of the patient prior to the interrogation could be interpreted as condoning it.
>
> *(BMA, 1981, p. 49)*

This endorses the World Medical Association's Declaration of Tokyo on the question of torture (1975; Amnesty International, 1985)

The case of Alfonso illustrates how a doctor can be involved in the act of torture. In 1975, this electrician was arrested by the Argentinian police for having pamphlets of the left-wing Peronist Youth Movement. He was tortured with the 'picana', an electrical cattle prod, on his sensitive parts under the supervision of doctors who monitored his pulse and heart to see that he did not die.

Hundreds of people were treated in this way by the Argentinian government as part of a state-controlled machinery to suppress dissent. The Argentinian Medical Association did not complain to the Junta because many physicians, other than those employed by the state, supported the aims of the regime and therefore turned a 'blind eye' to what was going on (Hodges, 1981, p.36). The focus of interest here lies in what happens to the doctor–patient relationship in the act of torture: how is an essentially caring relationship perverted into an act of deliberate abuse?

An Uruguyan student reports what he felt about his doctor:

I was asked about my family tree, chronic illnesses, present illnesses, and any delicate areas of my body or organism that might be the result of previous illnesses.

I was half conscious and thought that this medical control might reduce that torture. But hours later I was able to verify the functions of such controls when I heard the unmistakable voice of the doctor saying 'It's alright, you can continue'.

I felt anger at an individual who is formed by society to save lives dedicating himself to delimiting how to torture people better.

(Hodges, 1981, p.34)

The BMA's report, *Medicine Betrayed* gives similar examples (1992). The doctors themselves often believe, as the subjects in Milgram's experiments did, that they are carrying out their duty to the state and that they have no responsibility for what they do to victims. In this way, the doctor–patient relationship is perverted in the service of state control and abuse. The psychological mechanisms involved are probably the same as those which were hypothesised in the Milgram and Zimbardo experiments, only that, in most cases of state torture, fear of persecution must be an important additional factor in the recruitment of doctors. However, it is now clear that fear is certainly not the only factor: the opportunity to gain power through the legitimised torture of the 'other' is unconsciously appealing to those whose life has been marked by abuse and/or neglect; it presents the ex-victim with a chance to get his or her revenge, and this time with the blessing of authority.

Another aspect of medical treatment which is beginning to cause concern is related to the 'harvesting' of organs for transplant purposes. In some countries, surgeons are known to use the organs of executed prisoners for their transplant operations. For instance, the People's Republic of China is involved in the trade of kidneys from executed prisoners to hospitals in Hong Kong: no consent for organ removal is given by either the prisoner or the family. In Argentina, Peru and Colombia, thousands of poor street children are being kidnapped or killed and their organs removed to be sold to the rich hospitals of the West (Pinero, 1992). Though many other officials are involved in this business, it is unlikely that doctors are not personally involved, too, in the removal of these organs and it is a fact that surgeons carry out the transplant operations. And yet, hardly any doctors have spoken out against this lucrative and deadly business.

Again and again, we are faced with the disturbing fact that doctors can all too easily condone and participate in abusive practices against individuals. Robert Jay Lifton carried out an extensive study into the minds of the Nazi doctors whose diligent work in the field of racial hygiene made their leader's nightmarish vision become a reality (1986). When a Nazi doctor was asked how he reconciled the killings in Auschwitz with his Hippocratic Oath, he replied: 'Of course I am a doctor and I want to preserve life. And out of respect for human life, I would remove a gangrenous appendix from a diseased body. The Jew is a gangrenous appendix in the body of mankind' (Lifton, 1986, p.16).

Lifton believes that the Nazi ideology was taken up because it offered a cure for a severe historical trauma, the humiliating defeat of the First World War. He also shows how psychological mechanisms, such as dissociation and splitting, enable people to protect themselves from the harmful effects of their own actions upon others. He describes an extreme form of this phenomenon he calls 'doubling', which results in the formation of a functional second self which is related, though more or less autonomous, to the original self. Thus, the formation of an 'Auschwitz self' allowed the German doctor both to work in the murderous environment of the concentration camp and to attend to his wife and children when he returned home. One of Lifton's most important conclusions is to warn us that the murderous potential of the Nazi doctor can occur anywhere (1986, p.503).

Whilst the process of 'doubling' is a useful shorthand way of describing an extreme form of dissociation, usually seen in childhood victims of trauma, the Nazi doctor's murderous activities involved more than this psychological mechanism; they also depended on the individual's capacity to dehumanise the 'other' and thereby destroy in cold blood such 'gangrenous appendages'. As in all forms of human violence, two processes are at work: the cognitive process of dehumanisation reinforced by historical, cultural and ideological factors, as well as the psychophysiological processes linked to past damage of the attachment system, resulting in 'split off' and temporarily repressed feelings of intense narcissistic rage.

As Alice Miller makes quite clear in her work, the violence of Nazi Germany was partly born out of its harsh traditional rearing patterns aimed at producing extremely obedient individuals; such training often involved physical and emotional abuse (1983). Racism and nationalism could be seen as the natural manifestations of such a culture's effects on the self and the attachment system of its members, including its doctors.

It is interesting that in Serbia, it is a respected consultant psychiatrist who has become the theorist of Serbian ideology: mixing nationalism with mysticism and supposedly Freudian theories, Jovan Raskovic appears to have provided his people with a belief system that justifies their policy of 'ethnic cleansing'. He became the head of the Serb Democratic Party in 1990 and was also elected member of the Academy of Science, a move that gave his propaganda work 'scientific' respectability. Just before the armed attack against Croatia in January 1992, he proudly stated on television:

> I am responsible because I prepared this war, even though not military preparations. If I hadn't caused this emotional tension in the Serb people nothing would have happened. My party and I have set fire to Serb nationalism ... We led this people by giving it an identity.
>
> *(Badou, 1993)*

After his death in 1992, the rape and killing that his theories advocate continued to be practiced under the leadership of another psychiatrist, Radovan Karadzic.

The abuse of medical power for non-medical ends is not, as some people might believe, simply due to the doctor's hierarchical position. Like all violence, it is partly rooted in the rearing patterns of the community and it is also related to the specifically caring nature of the doctor–patient relationship. As was outlined earlier in this chapter, such a relationship makes it quite easy for past abuse or deprivation to be re-enacted, particularly if the context in which this takes place is one that legitimises such an abuse of power. Such a context can be created in two ways: either by providing doctors with a theoretical framework which facilitates the process of dehumanisation of their patients, or by the state sanctioning the medical maltreatment of certain individuals.

This latter phenomenon was particularly evident in what was the USSR, where psychiatry became an instrument of State control which was used against political dissidents (BMA, 1992). By being declared 'insane', these prisoners were deprived of their right to be tried or to appeal, which was the legal entitlement of Russian political prisoners in the 1980s. By becoming mental patients, they could be indefinitely incarcerated and, in some cases, attempts were made forcibly to change their personalities through drugs.

It is important to note that this particular form of psychiatric abuse took place mainly in the Serbsky Institute of Moscow and that other psychiatrists, such as those in what was Leningrad, did their best to counterbalance this system. It is also important to realise that an authoritarian approach to patient care was related to the culture of the Soviet Union: this is illustrated by a comment made by two staff members of the USSR Academy of Sciences to their American visitors: 'In the medical practice of the USSR in general, and not only in psychiatry, it is not the accepted custom to discuss with patients methods for treating them ...' (Report of the United States Delegation, 1989; see BMA, 1992, p.70).

In 1991, the World Psychiatric Association visited the USSR and reported no new cases of political use of psychiatry, and a more recent report on conditions in mental hospitals acknowledges important changes in the law which give new civil rights to psychiatric patients. However, psychiatric treatment continues to remain quite repressive and old fashioned, prescribing treatments such as insulin therapy for schizophrenics.

Psychiatric abuse was also carried out in Cuba, where some political dissidents were treated in the same way as the 'criminally insane'. Brown and Lago give eye witness accounts of what was seen on the ward (1991). Mr de Sosa, a businessman, reports: 'There were about eighty men in this ward, all violently disturbed. The smell of urine and excrement was sickening. There would be brawls among the patients every so often and shattered, bloody bodies had to be carted out ...' Another eye witness, a professor in history, describes what he saw:

> The doctors never crossed the shadows of the bars, and the orderlies only entered when they had to remove someone forcibly to be subjected to electroshock treatment ... The most repulsive acts took place there, including rapes and beatings of defenceless elderly persons.
>
> *(1991)*

Electroconvulsive treatment was given to groups of patients, often in the presence of other inmates, on a wet excreta-covered floor.

As the authors point out, the treatment given to the 27 political prisoners was a form of torture. However, what is not sufficiently stressed is that such a 'barbaric' practice continues to be carried out on ordinary patients. If such appalling treatments were not available for genuine patients, they could not be used for political prisoners. The condoning of abusive treatment for the mentally ill, for whatever reason, makes psychiatry an easy tool for the torture or abuse of those with a vested interest in controlling others.

The British Medical Association's working party (1992) concludes that psychiatry has a built-in capacity to abuse which, according to psychiatrists like Bloch and Reddaway, is 'greater than any other field of medicine' (1977).

The study of medical involvement in Nazi Germany provides a very useful example of how psychiatrists can become involved in the legitimate perpetration of violence. In his editorial entitled 'Psychiatry and the Holocaust', Paul Weindling summarises the events in Germany leading up to the so-called euthanasia programme of the 1930s which preceded the Holocaust (1992). As he states:

> It would be comforting to attribute euthanasia to the brutality of Nazi gutter politics and to the tenets of racial ideology, and so having nothing at all to do with the medical profession or with psychiatric science. This view ignores the facts that it was a group of Nazi doctors close to Hitler who helped to persuade him that 'lives no longer worth living' should be exterminated, and that he used war as a convenient camouflage for a secret euthanasia order. Further, many of the psychiatrists involved were not Nazi party members: their actions had, by contemporary standards, purely medical rationales with a long and complex history.
>
> *(1992, p.2)*

The way in which German doctors were involved in the murder of psychiatric patients and other disabled and disadvantaged groups does indeed provide a terrible example of abuse by the medical profession under the guise of scientific expertise. One of the factors that is considered to be important when attempting to explain how doctors could do such terrible things to their patients is related to the prevalent medical belief in inherited constitutional anomalies. These narrowly deterministic explanations of mental illness made a comprehensive and more social approach less popular. These attitudes were also associated with an increasingly biomedical approach to psychiatric training which tends to view patients as self-contained entities, divorced from their social environment (van der Kolk, 1987, p.xi). In keeping with views expressed earlier (Chapter 10), Michael Burleigh points out how 'the objectification of the patient, and the increasingly technological nature of modern medicine, resulted in a form of "moral amnesia" towards the patient's actual or potential suffering' (1991, p.322).

These so-called medical advances took place just after the terrible mass slaughter of the First World War which was followed by widespread starvation in Germany. Hitler's calls for mass sterilisation of mental patients in 1924 and for the killing of the mentally ill in 1929 were seen as a policy of national survival in a time of crisis.

It is interesting to note that in 1910, Winston Churchill also wanted more than 100 000 'morally degenerate' Britons to be forcibly sterilised and others to be incarcerated in labour camps to halt the decline of the British race. This was based on a prevalent view of the time that the lower classes were the breeding grounds for increasing numbers of feeble-minded and insane individuals (Ponting, 1992). Fortunately, Churchill's ideas were dismissed, but Hitler's policies were enacted when he came into power in 1933. The Nazis appropriated the current medical way of thinking which placed the health of the social whole and of future generations above that of individuals. The psychiatrists led the way in having 360 000 people sterilised for being feeble minded or schizophrenic (Weindling, 1992, p.2). The German psychiatrists also allowed the SS to dominate their Psychiatric Institute, hoping in this way to get more funds, and then helped them with the putting into place of the covert T4 medical killing procedures in 1939, when all patients judged incurable were to be 'terminated'. Nearly 200 000 psychiatric patients died under the euthanasia programme in special medical killing centres and 6000 children were killed in 'special children's departments'. The T4 programme was abandoned because of opposition to it, but it provided the basis for the extermination programme that was to involve 6 million Jews and 5 million Gypsies and other stigmatised groups such as homosexuals and communists.

Most important, however, is to recall that leading psychiatrists, like Carl Schneider ((Lifton, 1986, p.122), were at the centre of the medical killing operation and that they were also involved in the deliberate starvation of patients and in the use of lethal medication (Weindling, 1992).

Why are psychiatrists so often party to abuse? This is what Bloch and Reddaway asked themselves:

> Several factors suggest themselves: psychiatry's boundaries are exceedingly blurred and ill-defined; little agreement exists on the criteria for defining mental illness; the mentally ill are often used as scapegoats for society's fears; and the psychiatrist commonly faces dual loyalty, both to the patient he is treating and to the institutions to which he is responsible.
>
> *(1977)*

The last factor is an important one: psychiatrists in Britain and many other countries are trained to act for the state right from the beginning of their career. Their psychiatric patients, whose behaviour is seen to be a danger to themselves or to others, can be legitimately detained and deprived of many of their civil rights. The legitimacy of the procedure is endorsed by the doctor's diagnosis. For this to happen, human emotional and behavioural problems need to be translated into a medical diagnosis, so that the individual can then be seen as a 'patient' requiring 'treatment' in hospital. Many safeguards have been introduced to protect patients, but these people still feel dehumanised by the diagnoses and treatments they receive (Chapter 9).

There is also another aspect of psychiatry which facilitates the process of abuse. As was pointed out earlier, failure to acknowledge the reality and severe implications of childhood abuse by psychoanalysts may well make repetition of the abuse in treatment more likely. Similarly, psychiatry's need to remain wedded to biological medicine often makes its practitioners impervious to the social and traumatic causes of their patients' problems. This can lead to a re-enactment of the trauma in treatment, or to the denial of the importance of social factors in the aetiology of psychiatric symptoms (see Chapter 10). The dangers inherent in current psychiatric practice are illustrated in the next example.

Dr Donald E. Cameron was an American professor in psychiatry who carried out government-sponsored research into brainwashing. He was also president of the American Psychiatric Association and of the World Psychiatric Association. He carried out his work in Canada, in the Allan Memorial Institute, because American law forbids experiments on humans. Here, he developed his 'psychic driving technique'. Unsuspecting psychiatric patients were subjected to long periods of drug-induced sleep, in between which they were given 30–60 electro-convulsive treatments within a short period of time. When awake, these patients were forced to listen over and over again to their own accounts of some traumatic period in their lives. These tapes were played through headphones for up to 18 hours a day. As a result of this 'treatment', many of Dr Cameron's patients were irremediably dam-aged. What is perhaps most disturbing is that reputable psychiatrists were aware of the nature of Dr Cameron's work, and of who was behind it, but as Dr Sargant, a British psychiatrist, said: 'You don't raise that sort of thing with a colleague' (Thomas, 1989, p.193).

Some psychiatrists might think that what has been discussed here is not the sort of thing to be raised in public either, but I feel, both as a psychiatrist and as a psychoanalytic psychotherapist, that the potential for abuse in the doctor–patient or therapist–client relationship is too important to be ignored, particularly if there is now a way of under-standing how it can come about and how it can also be avoided.

Conclusion

The study of attachment relationships and the impact of abuse and neglect on this motivational system shows that any caring relationship, whether professional or not, is potentially vulnerable to become one of abuse. It should therefore come as no surprise to find that those men and women who choose to become therapists, nurses or doctors in order to help others are perhaps at some risk of abusing their patients. The latter may become dehumanised 'objects' on to whom a trauma-tised therapist or doctor projects his or her unmet needs, disowned pain and helplessness. This is more likely to happen in an authoritarian setting which sanctions abusive professional relationships and allows the doctor's hitherto dissociated rage to be acted out. It can also hap-pen in the therapist's consulting room, particularly when the latter's theoretical approach is one that invalidates the reality of a patient's

traumatic experience. In both cases, patients are at risk of being maltreated either emotionally or physically.

Rather than berate this professional vulnerability or collude with it
by attributing it simply to the misuse of power in some individuals, it is
more helpful to understand how such professional abuse can come
about. Most doctors and therapists do not go into medicine to misuse
their power for non-therapeutic ends: their aim is usually to heal and
help others, a task to which they normally devote themselves. If doctors and nurses end up tormenting their patients, something has taken
place which is reminiscent of what occurs between child-abusing parents and their offspring: the caring parental relationship is perverted
into one of power of the self over the 'other', a defence against the
pain and the sense of helplessness that some children or patients elicit
in their caregivers. An individual with a wounded attachment system
and the accompanying narcissistic injury to the self will always be at
risk of either being victimised or being the victimiser: the latter is more
likely to take place in the therapeutic role.

If the potential for abuse could be seriously acknowledged by therapists in general, their professional organisations could make sure that
preventive measures were in place to reduce the possibility of maltreatment occurring. Some ideas were put forward in relation to this problem in psychotherapy earlier on in this chapter. Doctors, however, may
find it particularly difficult to accept their vulnerability, especially as
one of the reasons they go into medicine is both to deny it and to look
after it in the 'other'. Peer group supervision and regular audit meet-
ings are ways in which doctors can be helped to look at their work and
attend to the areas of difficulty that arise between them and their
patients.

However, as with psychoanalysis, both in medicine and in psychiatry
the theoretical underpinnings of the current psychopathological models need to be revised to take into account the long-term consequences
of post-traumatic stress disorder, not only in the adult but especially in
the developing human being whose trauma becomes manifest in both
somatic and psychological symptoms. This means recognising the
importance of the attachment system, our need to relate to the 'other'
and hence the power of the 'caring professions' in the treatment of
their patients.

Finally, if professional abuse has the same roots as the violence
enacted in Zimbardo's and Milgram's experiments, it is likely that the
psychological origins of legitimate violence lie in our culture's form of
childhood upbringing and the social inequality of the sexes (Chapter
13): legitimate abuse in society requires and depends upon the way we
raise our children. For as long as the rewards of such a system out-
weighed the costs, particularly for the male sex, there were understandable reasons for continuing much as before. But our violence and

the destructive capacity of our weapons, particularly of our nuclear weapons, is now such a threat to our very existence that, as Einstein said: 'We shall require a substantially new way of thinking if mankind is to survive'.

Chapter 15
Love and Hate

'To the sick man, sweet water tastes bitter in the mouth.'

El-Ghazali

Love and hate are blood relations

The relation between love and hate is far from universally accepted; indeed for some people it is important that no such connection is ever made; instead, humanity must be seen to suffer because of its inherent sinfulness, a wickedness that makes sense of life's pain and guilt. Whether people believe in Augustine's doctrine of original sin or in Freud's 'death instinct', they prefer feeling to blame rather than feeling totally helpless: this 'moral defence' protects those who believe in it from feeling impotent in the face of death and loss (see Chapter 2). But not only does a belief in humanity's inherent wickedness give people some sense of power, albeit a somewhat perverse one, it also explains away humanity's need to be violent and cruel: by believing that people are sinful or bad, our need to hurt the 'other' can be ascribed to an instinctual need over which we have little control. Some male authors like Tiger, Storr and the sociobiologists go even further: their very manhood appears to depend on being able to be violent (see Chapter 3).

As a result of this preoccupation with humanity's destructiveness, a vast amount of research on human development has been ignored. It is perhaps paradoxical that, in attempting to explore the reasons for human abuse, cruelty and murder, what has become increasingly evident is the importance of attachment as a major motivational system in human behaviour (Kraemer, 1985, p.140). Whereas it was originally conceived as a theoretical construct used to make sense of certain forms of infant behaviour towards caregivers, the attachment system is now known to involve a psychophysiological substrate.

As a result of the work done on separation and loss in primates and humans, attachment is now understood as a form of psychobiological attunement or synchrony which occurs in multiple relationships across the life span (Reite and Capitanio, 1985, p.235). Biological regulators which appear to be involved in the primary mother–infant interaction may well constitute the early stages in the development of psychological regulators which take over as the child grows up (Sander, 1977, p.133; Hofer, 1984, p.187). If this 'interactive self-regulatory system' is damaged in some way through separation or rejection, a process that is inherent in the act of abuse, the response of the organism to further separation may well be altered. As Field puts it so clearly, attachment describes a relationship that develops between one or more organisms as their psychological and physiological systems become attuned to each other: this means that they provide for each other a source of stimulation and arousal modulation, much as their primary caregiver once used to do (Field, 1985, p. 450). As a result, the loss of a partner (or selfobject) implies both a behavioural and a physiological disorganisation which can become manifest in depressed behaviour and, in some cases, vulnerability to disease as a result of changes of the immune system. These findings make it quite clear that it is necessary to understand the overt and underlying physiological behaviours of attached individuals if disruptions in attachment are to be really understood (Chapters 4 and 5).

Looked at from the perspective of the attachment system, a whole range of apparently disparate forms of human behaviour can now be understood as different manifestations of the attachment and attunement system gone wrong, such as child abuse, spouse abuse, murder, suicide, depression and other forms of psychopathology. What these disorders confirm is our need for the 'other' made manifest in our attachment relationships: violence results from attachment gone wrong (Field, 1985, p. 450).

These findings confirm Bowlby's view that human infants are preprogrammed to develop in a socially cooperative way and that whether or not they do so depends very much on how they are treated (1988, p.9). Such an argument is strengthened by findings which show that the neural pathways for altruism and aggression may be reciprocally related, so that aggression reflects a deficit in endogenous opiates, whereas their secretion reduces aggressiveness by promoting social comfort and play.

Love and hate may also be reciprocally related: according to this view, affiliative behaviour and destructiveness appear as two different manifestations of the same underlying attachment system (Panksepp, Siviy and Normansell, 1985). This connection becomes particularly apparent in the studies on primate behaviour which show how the differential abuse of the infant's attachment system allows for a tightening or loosening of the primate community's social bonds (see Chapters 4 and 5).

Although human destructiveness can begin to be understood in terms of a disruption in the attachment system with its resulting physiological manifestations, what also becomes apparent is that violence is also linked to a disruption at the level of the self. Attachment and attunement occur at a psychological as well as at a physiological level right from the beginning of the mother–infant relationship (Stern, 1985, p.140). Indeed, through the attachment relation that links her to her various caregivers, the infant develops an internal world of mental representations which become as important as actual people themselves. Hofer goes as far as suggesting that these mental representations, which help us endure temporary separations, do so because they come to serve as biological regulators, much as the sensory motor interactions with mother function for the infant (1984, p.192).

The process of internalising significant relationships has been the subject of much research in the field of attachment theory and, as a result, infant behaviour has been classified in terms of the attachment relationships she develops with her caregivers (Ainsworth et al., 1978). What has become increasingly apparent is that this primary relationship has very important and long-term effects on how an individual relates to others throughout his or her life. Links have also been shown between an infant's attachment patterns, the development of internal 'working models' or 'object-relations' and the development of the self. As a result, it has become clear that, whilst deprivation and loss can affect the more physiological substrate of human attachment behaviour, at the same time internal object-relations also affect the way individuals perceive the environment: this leads to the recreation of familiar self-affirming patterns of experience in their attachment relationships. Such a tendency, if not disconfirmed by experience or therapy, can lead to repeated self-destructive relationships as well as to child and spouse abuse (see Chapter 6).

The development of 'object-relations theory' and Kohut's 'self-psychology' have provided useful models for understanding human attachment and the impact of abuse and other forms of trauma on the self: the narcissistic rage that ensues plays a crucial part in the traumatic origins of human violence (see Chapter 7). It reflects in no uncertain way the importance of the self which must be preserved at all costs: for a weak self the 'other' must become the 'object' of a self that needs to be in control; all reminders of inner weakness or of pain must be banished, even at the cost of the self or dehumanisation of the 'other'. When cultural and familial conditions allow, the self develops self-esteem and empathy, a capacity to relate to different others and to make of affective relationships a source of strength. In this way, the self, rooted as it is in the psychophysiology of the attachment system, can be both the container and the instigator of human destructive feelings (see Chapter 8).

The study of psychological trauma confirms many of these findings, being itself defined as the 'sudden cessation of human interaction' and therefore equivalent to the sudden disruption of the attachment system. Violence can now be seen as both the expression of human rage due to severe narcissistic injuries to the self, and the expression of a disrupted attachment system (see Chapter 10). One of its manifestations is the victim's compulsion to repeat the trauma, a finding which lies at the heart of the traumatic origins of violence (see Chapter 11). Another psychological manifestation is the 'splitting off' of painful memories which can re-emerge, even if only partly, when triggered off by the appropriate environmental stimuli (see Chapters 9, 10 and 11).

It is when studying the prevalence of psychological trauma and abuse that it becomes clear why there is a cultural need to deny the importance of human relationships, an attitude that contributes considerably to the present difficulty in understanding human violence.

Primate and anthropological studies show that the most effective way of transmitting socio-cultural values is through the infant–caregiver attachment system. In a culture where corporal punishment is the norm, such as in the USA, the potential for violence in the population is very high: this becomes manifest in high rates of child abuse, murder, rape and legitimate violence (see Chapter 12).

But perhaps even more important to this study is the realisation that it is essentially the dehumanisation of the 'other' that is at the root of all human violence: this process appears to be almost intrinsic to the development of male–female role differentiation that exists in patriarchal cultures. The result is that men become 'men' at the expense of the female 'other'. The psychological template for sexual abuse and racism is the inevitable result of such a cultural system (see Chapter 13).

With such child-rearing practices in place, it is scarcely surprising to discover that a considerable proportion of the population is capable of very destructive violence once it has been sanctioned by those in authority. This applies both to the ordinary citizen and to the caregiving professional, whose relationship with his patient is one that predisposes itself to the re-enactment of a child-abusing relationship (see Chapter 14).

The fact that Western culture as we know it depends on such degrees of abuse and dehumanisation means that people are understandably reluctant to acknowledge the importance of these rearing practices in terms of the individual's attachment needs. And yet, it is now clear that no study of human violence can be complete without acknowledging the existence of humanity's capacity to be socially cooperative and even, dare I say it, loving or altruistic.

One of the few scientific works to directly address this subject is *Social and Biological Origins of Altruism and Aggression* by Zahn-Waxler, Cummings and Ianotti (1984). They describe altruistic behaviour in much the same way as we have described attachment behaviour. Central to their work is the now-familiar hypothesis that altruism and human aggression are two different manifestations of the same phenomenon, reflecting both our need for the 'other' and what happens when this need cannot be met.

There is one example from the field of primate research which illustrates most vividly how one species of primates has evolved very specific ways of using its attachment system to mediate social bonding, in marked contrast to the common chimpanzee which has been found to display some of our more violent characteristics (see Chapter 5). Of the same genus *Pan* and sharing 99.3% of the common chimpanzee's genetic material, this ape is called the bonobo or pigmy chimp of Zaire. Physically, it has a more slender build and longer legs than its cousin but it is in its social behaviour that it differs most: as Frans de Waal points out, the discovery of this ape has had quite an impact on the way we look at ourselves and, in particular, the way we interpret our sex life (1989, p.174). Indeed, long before the 'hippy' generation of the 1960s was even thought of, their slogan 'make love not war' had become a social reality for the bonobos in the forests of Zaire.

The bonobo social structure is quite different from that of the common chimpanzee: there are no adult bands of males; instead, their strongest bonds are between adult females and across the sexes. The result is that, in this society, the females play a much more important part and it is sex rather than aggression which appears to play such a crucial cohesive role for this society. Indeed bonobo sexual life is full of surprises: like humans, the bonobos assume a wide variety of positions for copulation including the face to face position, which is helped by the bonobo female's sexual canal being ventrally directed as it is in women; the male's genitals are said to be among the largest in the primate world; copulations can be initiated by either sex and the females are sexually receptive most of the month.

As Frans de Waal states, the sex life of the bonobos, like our own, is largely divorced from reproduction. Sex occurs between members of the same sex and even between adults and infants, though in these encounters sexual behaviour does not involve intromission or ejaculation for the adult males. The author points out that such sexual behaviour between human male adults and infants could well be described as child sexual abuse but it is not so for de Waal between the bonobos because, though genital contact does occur, the nature of the relationship between the adult and the child is tender and pleasurable for both, with no evidence of coercion; for him abuse only occurs when the relationship is sought purely for the adult's gratification. Many would not agree with this argument, at least not as far as children are concerned. The adult female bonobos also engage in intensive sexual contacts among themselves, including mutual 'genito-genital-rubbing' activities which appear to give them a sexual climax. Masturbation is common (though never to a climax in the males), and the juveniles often indulge in erotic games including oral sex or 'tongue kissing'.

Frans de Waal believes that the bonobos do not have sex just for fun, but do so in order to preserve group harmony: the majority of mounts and matings occur in tense situations and during meal times. Sexual behaviour is part of the species' begging and food sharing behaviour; sex appears to attenuate the competitive tendencies that naturally emerge at these times (1989, p.213). Japanese researchers studying bonobos in the wild have come to the same conclusions: they found that peaceful aggregation is made possible 'by changing the character of sexual behaviour into affiliative behaviour in which all individuals can participate, and by decreasing the reproductive meaning' (de Waal, 1989, p.214).

Increased sexual contact after aggression is also a widespread phenomenon: it appears to be used to prevent further aggression. However, though bonobos do appear to be less belligerent in captivity than other primate species, it is not yet known if territorial violence occurs in the wild as it does with the common chimpanzee.

The bonobo provides a fascinating example of sexual conflict resolution and makes a nonsense of the commonly held view that male sexuality in primates is intrinsically aggressive or even violent as Lorenz, Wilson and Tiger would have us believe (see Chapter 3). De Waal suggests that this sexual form of conflict resolution is particularly important for the bonobo females as it creates a close balanced relationship between the sexes and among the females themselves (1989, p.227).

The bonobos' use of sexual behaviour to maintain social cohesion has many implications for human beings, all the more so since genetic differences between us and the bonobo are scarcely much greater than those found between the two chimpanzee species. There is only a 0.7% difference in genetic material between the common chimpanzee and the pygmy chimp to account for their differences, and only just over 1% between us and the chimpanzee. This raises the question of how such marked changes in social behaviour can result from such minor differences in genetic material.

For Robert Cairns, such a question makes little sense because, as he says, social behaviour patterns – as opposed to non-social ones – should be especially vulnerable to change both in a species' evolutionary history and in an individual's developmental history. 'To the extent that behavioural patterns serve as a leading edge of biological adaptation, they constitute that part of the organismic system that is the most flexible' (Cairns, 1984, p.82).

Cairns's own research on mice demonstrates how social behavioural processes are open to extreme and rapid change through the interplay between both genetic and developmental factors operating through the attachment system (Cairns, MacCombie and Hood, 1983); the latter lends itself readily to such modifications, as was seen when comparing the effects of minor changes in upbringing between bonnet and pigtail macaques (Chapter 12). In the bonobo chimpanzee, the sexualisation of the attachment bond appears to have allowed intense affiliative behaviours to override aggressive and violent behaviour within the group. De Waal believes, as Harlow (1974) does, that violence only occurs in primates when peacemaking efforts such as those described above fail.

Whilst our two chimpanzee cousins appear to have developed quite markedly different forms of social organisation through minor changes in the manifestation of their attachment systems, what about the 'third chimpanzee'? How does the human species alter its social behaviour to adapt to the multiplicity of its different habitats?

As a result of studies in both child development and primate behaviour, researchers have begun to realise that human intelligence developed as it did not so much to improve human hunting skills, as was once believed, but in order to improve our social interaction. Living in social groups appears to be the key adaptation that ensures survival under a variety of environmental conditions encountered by most primate species. The intricacies of these social interactions have been clearly illustrated in the common chimpanzees. As Jane Goodall points out, we have much in common with this species – the affectionate, longstanding and often supportive behaviour between family members, similar reactions to loss and deprivation, both of which derive from our common attachment behaviour, the long period of childhood dependency, the importance of learning, the use of tools, cooperation in hunting and sophisticated forms of non-verbal communication patterns and social manipulations (Goodall, 1990, pp. 173–175). Research in this field now shows that the chimpanzee's mind is uncannily like our own: chimpanzees have pre-mathematical skills and can be taught American Sign Language, the sign language used by the deaf in the USA. They can string words together in meaningful ways and even invent signs (Rumbaugh and Gill, 1977).

However, what does differentiate humans from chimpanzees is the ability to communicate through the use of a sophisticated spoken language: the resulting gap between the chimpanzee's social life and ours is enormous. This difference is due to the increasing use of symbolic language and to its effects, both on the human brain (with the resulting specialisation of the two hemispheres) and on our culturally derived way of life. Once human beings could talk to one another, they could share their experiences and plan for the future; they could teach their children and make sense of their external and internal world through increasingly complex conceptual representations. This creative interplay between human thought processes and environmental activities is what is referred to as 'culture': it is the product of a human mind in interaction with its environment. This means that culture is both out there and within ourselves, closely tied up with the formation of the self which could be described as our cultural representative. This same self is also the instrument through which we endeavour to achieve optimum social interactions, a self born through attachment and attunement with all the cultural pressures and vulnerabilities this implies (see Chapter 7)

As long as the infant's early experience is one of attunement with her caregivers, she will develop a positive attitude towards the self and the 'other', an attitude which makes human interaction a potentially gratifying experience. The sense of empathy that is born from such a development is essential for good and satisfying social interactions (Staub, 1984, p.142; Stern, 1985, p.127). If such a development cannot take place as a result of parental or other failures, the self becomes constricted by the defensive need to split off and project feelings and traits with which the individual feels unable to cope. Interpersonal gratification gives way to the dehumanisation of the self and the 'other' and the potential for violent behaviour (see Chapter 8).

As a result of the interplay between western cultural pressures and the human attachment system, violence has become so commonplace that it has come to be seen as an instinctual part of human nature and quite distinct from altruism; the latter is usually seen as another inherited predisposition. Sociobiology was in fact created in response to a need to reconcile altruistic behaviour with neo-Darwinian principles of evolution through natural selection (Porter and Laney, 1980). Having defined altruism as behaviour that benefits another organism to the detriment of the organism performing the behaviour, the sociobiologist is left wondering: 'How can altruism, which by definition reduces personal fitness, possibly evolve by natural selection?' (Wilson, 1975, p.1).

Darwin himself had no such difficulties, for in *The Descent of Man*, he acknowledges the existence of man's social instincts and moral qualities:

> The development of the moral qualities is a more interesting problem. The foundation lies in the social instincts, including under this term the family ties. These instincts are highly complex, and in the case of the lower animals give special tendencies towards certain definite actions; but the more important elements are love, and the distinct emotion of sympathy. Animals endowed with the social instincts take pleasure in one another's company, warn one another of danger, defend and aid one another in many ways. These instincts do not extend to all individuals of the species, but only to those of the same community. As they are highly beneficial to the species they have in all probability been acquired through natural selection...
>
> Man is impelled by the same general wish to add his fellows; but has few or no special instincts...The motive to give aid is likewise much modified in man: it no longer consists of a blind instinctive impulse, but is much influenced by the praise or blame of his fellows. The appreciation and the bestowal of praise and blame both rest on *sympathy: and this emotion, as we have seen, is one of the most important elements of the social instincts.*

(1899, pp.610–611; my italics)

In stressing the importance of 'sympathy', Darwin acknowledges the value of empathy in altruism; he also appears to have been aware of the close links between the social instincts and family ties, ties which could be now described as attachment relationships. Indeed, unlike the neo-Darwinians and their successors, the sociobiologists, Darwin does not hesitate to underline the importance of love and empathy in the origins of altruism; nor does he fail to appreciate that in man, unlike other animals, the development of empathy is very much influenced by his social environment, by how much praise and blame he has himself been subject to.

Empathy does indeed appear to be the most important element in the development of altruism and, as was shown earlier, its development goes hand in hand with the psychobiological capacity to tune into the 'other' and a high self-esteem, both of which are the outcome of a secure infant–caregiver attachment relationship (Chapter 6).

Since the sociobiologists have to deny the importance of attachment behaviour, altruism is understood in terms of what Wilson defines as 'kinship':

> If the genes causing the altruism are shared by two organisms because of common descent, and if the altruistic act by one organism increases the joint contribution of these genes to the next generation, the propensity to altruism will spread through the gene pool.
>
> *(1975, pp. 1–2)*

The same phenomenon is also described by a genetic mathematical model devised by W.D. Hamilton (1964) and labelled 'inclusive fitness'. Species following this model would evolve behaviour such that each individual organism appears to be trying to maximise its inclusive fitness, that is its own reproductive success and that of those with whom it interacts. However, in his review of the literature on 'Kin selection theory', Jeffrey Kurland (1980) points out that this is yet another term used to define the same phenomenon hitherto described as 'inclusive fitness' or 'the selfish gene'. He makes the point that: 'Kin selection forces us to confront a central problem of evolutionary biology: namely at what level natural selection most effectively operates in producing adaptive change: gene, individual or group' (1980, p.258).

Kurland makes the very important point that what sociobiology fails to do is to research the role of kin selection (such as has been observed in child abuse and neglect) in the evolution of human social behaviour: for instance, could the prevalence of child abuse in our culture be demonstrably linked to our social requirements for legitimate violence? Without such empirical studies, Kurland foresees that human sociobiology will remain 'the domain of shrill and sanctimonious politics' (1980, p.265).

It is my view that as long as sociobiology continues to ignore the manifestations of the cultural or group self rooted in the psychobiology of the individual's attachment relations, it can never really address the sociobiological origins of either violence or altruism. The sociobiologists' refusal to take into account the social and psychophysiological implications of the attachment system, despite the fact that it is in itself genetically derived, illustrates to what extent sociobiology is more the pseudoscientific manifestation of a particular view of human nature than a real attempt to understand the origins of human violence or altruism (Chapter 3).

One psychologist who has contributed considerably to the understanding of both violence and altruism is Ervin Staub (1989). For him, altruistic behaviour is intended to help others with the single purpose of improving their welfare. Prosocial behaviour, on the other hand, is about benefiting others but without excluding self gain. Staub believes that in altruism the primary instigator is our need for others and that violent aggression results from loss or a threatened sense of self. He is one of the few authors whose work in the field of violence encompasses most of the issues raised here: he acknowledges the importance of the infant–caregiver relationships in the development of empathy and its role in reducing violence (1984, pp.141–142); he also dwells on the crucial role of the self born into a cultural group matrix with the ever-present need to bolster itself at the expense of the 'other' (1985). As he says, a weak sense of self and a low self-esteem contribute greatly to human violence.

Staub also attaches a lot of importance to how children are brought up: referring to research in this field, he points out that prosocial behaviour is influenced by

1. A combination of parental warmth and nurturance.
2. Firm control by the parents so that children actually behave in accordance with important values and rules.
3. Teaching through 'induction', which means pointing out to children the consequences of their behaviour on other people.

> The more parents and socializers in other settings, such as schools, particularly in the early school years, use such a pattern, the more we can expect a prosocial orientation, empathic responsiveness, and behavioural tendencies for increased altruism and less aggression in children.

(1984, pp.150–151)

As Staub points out, the practices that contribute to a prosocial orientation and positive behaviour in children are similar to those that contribute to a positive self-esteem. It is striking how well Staub's conclusions match up with the literature reviewed so far and with the conclusions of recent research on the altruistic personality.

Samuel and Pearl Oliner carried out a study of the gentiles who took the risk of rescuing the Jews in Nazi Europe (1988). For these researchers, behaviour is defined as altruistic when it is directed towards helping another and involves some risk or sacrifice for the actor; it is accompanied by no external reward and is completely voluntary. The Oliners were to discover that the key to altruism lay in the values that their subjects had learnt from their parents.

Their study involved three groups: those who were known to have rescued Jews, the *rescuers;* those who did nothing either to help people or to resist the Nazis, the *bystanders;* and those who said they did help the Jews but who had no corroborating evidence, the *non-rescuers.*

Rescuers' parents were similar to non-rescuers' parents with respect to communicating positive perceptions of the Jews, but they differed in communicating significantly less negative stereotypes of Jews (3% compared to 10% of non-rescuers and 16% of bystanders) and in showing a greater tendency to assess Jews as individuals rather than as group members (1988, p.150).

Rescuers appear to have been motivated mainly by concerns with equity and care: they were concerned with equal standards for all and with fairness. More rescuers than non-rescuers had taken on their parents' caring values (44% versus 25%) – the need to be helpful, hospitable, concerned and loving. In fact, the most important characteristic of the rescuers was their need to apply ethical values on a universal basis. This sense of universalism was based on the fact that they tended to see others like themselves, whether rich or poor, Christian or Jew: in summary, they did not need to dehumanise the 'other' (1988, p.176).

The Oliners explored the roots of the rescuers' attachments and their findings appear to confirm the view that their altruism can be seen as the consequence of satisfactory family relationships. Rescuers appeared to have had closer attachments with their parents, and in particular with their mothers, compared to non-rescuers, and with their fathers compared to bystanders.

The rescuers were found to differ from the non-rescuers in their empathic response to the pain of others which made them feel responsible and committed to help. They had a strong sense of inner control compared to non-rescuers. Interestingly their sense of self-esteem was no greater than that of others. The Oliners wondered what kind of development these people had been through. Their conclusions are very much in keeping with our earlier findings: they believe that a critical influence in their development was the way their parents disciplined them (see Chapter 12). 'The extent to which discipline – from teaching to punishing – is a central focus of the parent–child interaction is probably vastly underrated as an influence in development' (1988, p.178).

The Oliners refer to a study which shows that by the age of two, children are often pressured by their parents to change their behaviours an average of once every 6 or 7 minutes! Usually, the child complies but why she does so and how it is brought about will have longlasting effects on the child's view of relationships. Punitive strategies arouse aggression which, as has been shown, is often split off from consciousness to be projected on to some socially condoned target. What is significant in this study is that fewer rescuers than non-rescuers reported having been physically punished (32% versus 40% in the non-rescuers); many had been brought up through inductive reasoning (21% versus 6% of the non-rescuers) (1988, p.309).

An important difference between the groups lay in how they perceived the discipline they received: rescuers perceived their punishment as in some way related to their behaviour and they also reported it as an infrequent response of their parents; the non-rescuers perceived their punishment as gratuitous, as a release of aggression on the parents' part which had little to do with their childhood behaviour.

It is mainly in their reliance on reasoning, explanation, persuasion and advice that the parents of rescuers differ most. This approach communicates a message of trust and respect in their children which in turn enables the latter to feel more trusting and reliable with others. As the Oliners emphasise, such an attitude is based on a 'presumption of error rather than a presumption of evil intent' (1988, p.182).

> In contrast, punishment implies the need to curb some intrinsic wildness or evil intent. Routine gratuitous punishment implies that powerful people have the right to exert their will arbitrarily. Children who experience such treatment are likely to accept that view of the rights of the powerful over the less powerful. They have little reason to trust others and many reasons to fear them. Having little influence over their parents' behaviour, they are more inclined to feel a sense of helplessness in influencing others generally...Human relationships are construed in power terms, superordination and subordination viewed as the inherent social condition of humankind. The best one can do in the face of power is to succumb; but one of the uses of power is to satisfy one's desires. In the context of such relationships, the only restraints on behaviour are external ones. 'Might makes right' becomes a fundamental law of human relationships.

> *(1988, p.183)*

The authors make it clear that societal norms support the parents' authoritarian position, affirming the rights to humiliate and hurt and at the same time condemning children who might retaliate. So, when adults voluntarily abdicate the use of this power and resort to reasoning instead, they are modelling the right behaviour towards the weak on behalf of the strong. Their children will therefore have at their disposal an internal model or script when dealing with the powerless and

abused. As a result of having internalised their parents' values, the rescuers saw themselves as more caring and responsible as well as more
honest and helpful than the non-rescuers.

In outlining the developmental course of rescuers versus nonres-
cuers, the Oliners describe those who are resistant to altruism as people whose lives have been characterised by 'constrictedness'. These
people experience the world as largely peripheral except insofar as it
may be instrumentally useful. Centred on themselves and on their personal needs, these people pay little attention to others, unlike the
'extensive' altruistic individuals who have strong attachments and a
sense of inclusive obligations. The 'constricted' individual has been
brought up on a diet of routine physical punishment, with family values centred on the self and social conventions. Relationships with
others are guarded and usually seen as commodity exchanges; stereo-
typing or the dehumanisation of outsiders is common.

These findings concur with those of Adorno and his colleagues
(1950). Their study of 'ethnocentric ideology', carried out after the
Second World War, was an attempt to find out what caused Europeans
in the 1930s to become so involved in the elimination of the Jews.
Their research went beyond racial prejudice in that it also addressed
the group dynamics involved in the process; these were described as a
sense of inner cohesion and of devotion to the ingroup, which made its
members believe themselves to be superior to the outgroup and ready
to defend the interests of the ingroup against the outgroup.

What Adorno and his colleagues found was that these tendencies
were most clearly represented in people described as 'conventional
and authoritarian'. These men and women resemble the 'constricted'
non-rescuers in the Oliners' study: they, too, shared the experience of
having been brought up by status-driven and harsh, punitive parents.

Summarising the attitudes of the prejudiced authoritarian subjects,
Adorno and his colleagues state that they showed little evidence of real
love for their parents. Though they needed to idealise them, strong
resentment and feelings of victimisation would sometimes break
through during their interviews which they would then deny. The
authors felt that these subjects' underlying anger had to be suppressed
because it was so strong and because it threatened the desire, still present in these adults, to be taken care of by their parents. Such a conflict
leads to submission to parental figures in authority but also to a deep
underlying rage which, though not admitted and usually 'split off', is
nonetheless active and often projected onto significant others or 'outgroups' (1950, p.357).

What also emerges is that these prejudiced subjects had many of the
features found in the insecurely attached individual of the 'avoidant'
type, who fears close contact with others, has difficulties with intimacy
and a propensity to become violently aggressive (see Chapter 6). By

repressing their painful memories and their feelings of anger against their parents, Adorno's prejudiced subjects had come to identify with power and to reject or abuse the weak, whom they easily perceived as suitable targets for their violent feelings.

Dehumanisation or 'ethnocentrism' is thus intrinsic to the 'authoritarian' or 'bystander' personality structure, which desperately needs to bolster itself at the expense of the 'other', be it a woman, a child or a 'foreigner'. In order to survive, 'them' and 'us' distinctions are of the essence in such personalities, with the associated psychological need to see others as stereotypes. The result is that though the outgroups are usually objectively weaker, they are perceived by those in the ingroup as threatening and power-seeking because of the feelings such prejudiced people project onto others they deem as 'different' (1950, p.148).

The ingroup is idealised and blindly submitted to: obedience and loyalty are required of the ingroup members, just as they were with their parents, only in this case, the group imbues its members with a sense of power and status they never had as children. To keep the ingroup pure and strong, the outgroups must be either liquidated, or kept entirely subordinated or segregated so as to minimise contact: these methods were all used in Nazi Germany against the Jews, the mentally ill, the Gipsies, the homosexuals, and later, in South Africa, by the ruling elite against the black population.

The unprejudiced subjects of Adorno's study, on the other hand, had very similar loving feelings towards their parents as did the 'rescuers' in the Oliners' study. They also felt more independent of their parents and had developed instead a greater love-oriented dependence on other people who, by becaming alternative selfobjects, provided them with important sources of gratification.

Though Adorno and his colleagues' work was carried out over 40 years ago and has been rightly criticised for some of its assumptions and failings, it still raises many issues of crucial importance. For one, the prejudiced character-structure is seen as the natural outcome of our present civilisation:

> The increasing disproportion of the various psychological 'agencies' within the total personality is undoubtedly being reinforced by such tendencies in our culture as the division of labour, the increased importance of monopolies and institutions, and the dominance of the idea of exchange and of success and competition
>
> *(1950, p.389)*

What is being referred to here is the marked tendency in such people towards an increased fragmentation of the self, brought about through splitting and projection, in a society where the intrinsic need for the 'human other' is being denied in favour of relationships where the 'other' is commercially exploited and thereby becomes increasingly 'objectified'.

A look at the prejudiced individual's sexual relationships is particularly revealing in terms of our previous analysis of sex roles (see Chapter 13). Prejudiced subjects tend to see sex as a means of obtaining status and they also need to rationalise any failures in this area. Unprejudiced men can openly admit to their sexual difficulties. Prejudiced men will display the characteristic ambivalent attitude towards women that we explored in perverse sexual relationships: women are divided into 'pure' or 'bad' women. There is little integration of sex with affection in these men: the underlying resentment against their mother is split off to be projected on to one type of woman, the 'whore', whereas the other, 'madonna'-like, woman is idealised in a desperate attempt to preserve some link with the original mother (see Chapter 13).

The unprejudiced men have more personalised sexual relationships and show more respect for women, whereas their prejudiced counterparts express underlying disrespect and resentment. It is interesting to note that, in keeping with our earlier findings, the unprejudiced individual also shows a great deal of conflict regarding his sexuality, reflecting the inherent problems that exist in a society where men and women tend to rely on mechanisms of projective identification to bolster up their sexual identity (see Chapter 13).

The same pattern of relationships that was seen in relation to parents and sexual partners was recreated in the field of interpersonal relationships and work: the prejudiced character chose friends who would help him become successful and work that was likely to give him success and power. (Adorno saw this association with power as a means of keeping projected hostile feelings at bay.)

The unprejudiced individuals formed affectionate relationships with people whom they liked and they also invested considerable personal aspirations into their work. They were generally on better terms with themselves, though they suffered from a great longing to be loved. The prejudiced men aimed at being energetic, decisive and aggressive in competition, but such strong assertions of independence betrayed underlying feelings of dependence, passivity and helplessness as well as self contempt at times: these unacceptable feelings were projected onto suitable others. The result was a 'constriction' of the personality similar to the Oliners' 'constricted' personality, with a conscious need to be conventional and a marked tendency to deny any childhood experiences which might threaten their adult self-image.

In their conclusion, Adorno and his colleagues pointed out that these two opposite personality types only emerged as a result of their statistical analysis and must therefore be considered as syndromes rather than real personalities. And yet, as they also admit, Sartre's description of an 'anti-Semite' is just like the ethnocentric subject of their study. Perhaps this is not surprising, for the ethnocentric individual with his 'constricted' personality structure could be seen as a caricature of what he could have been if as a child he had received sufficiently loving care. The sense of self of the ethnocentric personality is the outcome of multiple defensive splits and projections. To preserve his threatened attachment with his caregivers, the physically abused child of harsh punitive parents must deny his trauma, split off the resulting rage and conform, through a process of identification, with his parents and their values. His sense of vulnerability and anger are split off to be projected on to others, who become themselves the representatives or even the victims of his thwarted rage. The need for such people to be seen to be strong and hard makes it also necessary for them to disown the sensitive aspects of their personality. This defensive process is particularly marked in men: in fact, as was observed earlier, such a denial with its associated splitting and projection of all that is considered 'feminine' into women, is what turns male infants into socially acceptable men (see Chapter 13).

What is being demonstrated is how 'splitting', which is intrinsically a defence against trauma, has become the hard currency of social adaptation in societies where violence is legitimised and sex roles are more or less rigidly defined. Such cultures bring about a narrowing of consciousness and of the personality such that the self can only survive at the expense of the 'other'.

The best prescription for social violence may well be to create psychological conditions which can only be survived through the use of such defences as denial, splitting, projection and projective identification. In a society where these psychological processes have become established ways of bolstering the individual's self-esteem, the potential for violence becomes intimately linked to the social structure that has produced it: abuse, murder and the dehumanisation of the 'other' in all its various forms become a way of life, a way of being and perceiving reality and, in a sense, splitting becomes a way of thinking.

Such a form of thinking or 'not-thinking' has been enhanced by the creation of the nuclear bomb. Living in the shadow of the bomb requires people to both deny its dangers and split off their terror on a daily basis. Studies on young children in Europe since the 1960s show that they worry a lot about the possibility of a nuclear war and its catastrophic consequences; girls appear more affected than boys (Solantaus, 1991). However, as the children grow older they become less concerned; this is attributed by the researcher to the internalisation of the dominant culture in which there is very little concern about nuclear weapons. The 'worry' is safely 'split off' and life goes on as normal, but the fact is that in so doing people increase the fragmentation of their minds and become silent bystanders in a genocidal programme that is justified, rightly or wrongly, on the grounds of 'self-defence'.

Belief systems and the maintenance of the self

In the light of these conclusions, the current polarisation between those who believe that humans are innately violent and those who believe we are born to be socially cooperative is understandable, as both sides are intent on upholding the belief that is most precious to them and on which their self-esteem depends.

For men and women who have known deprivation, abuse and trauma, whose capacity to be at one with the 'other' has been damaged and whose perception of the 'other' is not 'inclusive', the concept of original sin disguised as the 'death instinct' is a relief. It protects people from the overwhelming fear of death and the unknown, from the need to acknowledge human vulnerability and the traumatic effects of pain. Above all, it favours the 'status quo' and an egocentric belief in the individual which is a way of denying our interdependence and protecting us from the pain of loss and of not knowing the deeper joys of being at one with the other.

The male authority figures who uphold the instinct theory of violence and who deny the importance of attachment theory tend to show some of the characteristics of Adorno's authoritarian personality, a need to dehumanise the 'other', usually women, and a belief in male sexuality as inherently aggressive if not violent (see Chapter 3). Their attitude to those who uphold the importance of attachment behaviour in human relationships is often one of such contempt that the observer is left wondering what the idea of social cooperation and interdependency evokes in these men that it seems so repugnant to them. Are they, like the ethnocentric individuals in Adorno's study, fighting to preserve a vulnerable self-esteem at the expense of the 'other'?

Fortunately, not all believers in humanity's innate capacity to be violent share the views mentioned above: many simply limit themselves to a view of humanity driven by destructive instincts. This allows some psychotherapists to forego exploring too deeply their own pain and rage in the treatment of their traumatised patients. As long as trauma can be seen as the external manifestation of an internal scenario, it is controllable and explicable. The belief in a 'death instinct' also protects psychotherapists from the need to think about the social implications of what their patients tell them.

In this way, the intellectual infrastructure of the current system is being upheld by all those who feel a sense of affinity with the theories and attitudes that mirror the system they live in. Paradoxically, the most psychologically damaged are the very people most likely to defend the self-same system that led to their experience of abuse or loss.

However, the evidence which has been reviewed from the field of child development, ethology, anthropology, psychology and psychiatry repeatedly shows that not only do humans need to be attuned to the 'other' in order to survive, but that the rupture of their essential attachments, be it through neglect, loss or trauma, is at root of the human propensity for violence.

Such a conclusion could be perceived by some as a defensive need to deny our own 'primitive' feelings of envy and destructiveness. What is interesting, however, is that researchers and psychoanalysts who believe in the primary importance of human attachments do not deny the existence of these destructive feelings; however, they postulate that envy and hate are secondary to the sense of intense vulnerability and despair which accompanies our all-too-frequent experiences of loss, deprivation and trauma in early life. As a result of this approach, humanity's real fear of death, whether psychic or physical, is no longer ignored. As for our propensity to be violent and cruel, these feelings are far from denied: on the contrary, the concepts of narcissistic rage and psychological trauma explain only too well why violence is an everyday occurrence.

It is essentially the belief that human destructiveness arises as a result of psychological trauma that makes this approach so different from that taken by those who perceive violence as innate, a small difference but with huge implications. Indeed, what Bowlby and those who share the same basic assumptions maintain is that the human infant is born with a real need to love and to be loved: this implies that not only can the human condition be improved, but that it needs to be improved.

Adorno and his colleagues were to come to the same conclusion nearly 50 years ago: children need to be genuinely cared for and treated as human beings. Such a proposition appeared so simple and yet they found it fraught with difficulties. The first centred round finding 'good enough' parents to care for deprived or abused children when so many adults need to project on to their children the unacceptable aspects of themselves. And as for the parents who did love their children, how could they be asked either to bring up children for a society that does not exist or to aim towards goals that are only shared by a minority? For Adorno and his team, the answer was clear:

> It seems obvious therefore that the modification of the potentially fascist structure cannot be achieved by psychological means alone. The task is comparable to that of eliminating neurosis, or delinquency, or nationalism from the world. These are the products of the total organisation of society and are to be changed only as that society is changed.
>
> *(1950, p.975)*

Attachment theory and what it implies appears to fly in the face of established Western thinking and to have little to do with the socio-economic system in which we live. However, the belief that humanity is essentially cooperative by nature is as old as the concept of original sin and represents a long held belief in our culture, a belief that now has plenty of evidence to support it.

The traumatic origins of violence

It is beginning to become apparent, through research in the field of primate and child development, that not only are humans attached to
others through the psychophysiological manifestations of their attachment system, but that their self-esteem is linked with our capacity to be
attuned to the 'other'. This capacity is developed in the infant–caregiver relationships of early life (see Chapter 4).

These discoveries and observations imply that, if humanity's attachment needs are to be taken seriously, we must acknowledge our need
for others and our inherent capacity to be tender and caring. The
implications of such findings are clearly momentous, because affiliative
needs also imply an inherent vulnerability to deprivation, to loss and to
death. Such dependence on others for our self-esteem and our stimulation and arousal modulation needs (Field, 1985) means that these
attachment bonds with significant others are of the utmost importance
and have to be maintained throughout life. We are, as Kohut believes,
in continuous need for such 'selfobjects' and are never fully
autonomous. These resulting 'selfobjects' are essential for our sense of
well-being, so much so that those who have suffered deficiencies in
their earliest relationships also suffer from inadequate internalised
object representations, for which they then compensate by highly
dependent, addictive or perverse relationships (see Chapter 8).

Once the intrinsic human need for the other has been established, it
is not difficult to see how human violence can be linked to this need
for the 'other'. A selfobject failure, in a vulnerable or insecure personality, is tantamount to an attack on the self, with all that this entails in
terms of destructive rage and its associated cognitive and physiological
manifestations, both of which are the result of a disruption of the self
and its constituent attachment bonds. Such an experience can be
brought about through deprivation, loss, rejection or trauma.

This view of human violence has little to do with the widespread
belief in our innate destructiveness, the modern equivalent of
Augustine's myth of original sin (Chapter 2). The latter is not only central to Western thinking, but it also mirrors the defensive attitude of
those men and women, referred to earlier, who have perhaps not
known the rewarding qualities of intimate relationships. Theirs is a
world where intimacy and dependency are dangerous and to be avoided through splitting, denial and projective identification. For men and
women who lack a sense of self-validation through the experience of
attunement with the 'other', human relationships only exist to provide
for the individual's instrumental needs and not because they have an
intrinsic value of their own: theirs is an individual-oriented experience
of the world, a world whose theoreticians believe humankind to be
innately destructive and power-seeking, where violence is the manifes-

tation of our 'evil' nature; for them, attachment theory makes little sense. For such people, like Anthony Storr, men only learn to cooperate and communicate because they would destroy themselves if they did not.

One of the most interesting implications of this particular belief about human nature is that, by minimising the importance of the 'other', it also protects its believers from the impact of loss, trauma and death. Instead, the belief in mankind's innate violence gives its followers a culturally approved 'moral defence' which makes sense of the 'badness' in this world and of the need to see the 'other' as less than human; it also legitimises violent methods of upbringing such are currently being advocated by the American child psychologist, James Dobson and other religious educators (Storm, 1993).

I agree with Greenberg and Mitchell that the difference between the drive model and the relational model in psychoanalysis reflects essentially two different and profoundly incompatible visions of life and of the fundamental nature of human experience, a polarisation of views that has been observed throughout this study of human behaviour (1983, p.406).

The drive model is based on the assumption that our primary need is to discharge our instincts; such a view is most eloquently expressed by the British philosopher Hobbes, who maintained that the search for individual gratification at all levels is what drives mankind. The result is that the state is there to make sure that the needs of one individual do not completely override the needs of another individual.

> Hereby it is manifest, that during the time men live without a common Power to keep them all in awe, they are in that condition which is called War; and such a War, as is of every man against every man.

> *(1651, p.185)*

These premises form the basis of American political institutions. The assumed price of a government institution is that the individual must inevitably curb some of his more antisocial drives which stem from 'natural' man's need for violent gratification. These views are also held by Lorenz, Tiger and many others who believe in the instinctual origins of human violence. Indeed Locke, another British philosopher, wrote on the same subject as follows: 'To avoid this State of War...is one great reason of men putting themselves into society and quitting the State of Nature' (1690, p.323). The belief in the innateness of human violence is therefore very much in keeping with our present political systems and it should come as no surprise to find that the same assumptions and beliefs permeate all the different manifestations of our cultural system, including the upbringing of our children. One possible result is that a belief system based on a particular assumption about human nature can well become a social reality. For instance, in a cultural context where it is assumed that human beings are innately violent, child physical abuse can be defined as both an essential and legitimate form of socialisation: as a result of such an upbringing, there will be more potentially violent men and women than in a culture where violence towards children is not seen as legitimate (see Chapter 13).

Since violence begins with the violation of children's affiliative needs, the denial of such needs becomes essential for the preservation of the 'status quo', be it at the level of the psyche or at the level of society. Certain professionals and experts in the field of human behaviour, such as the sociobiologists, play their part in keeping the myth of human violence alive and well and, in so doing, reflect just such a tendency to preserve things as they are.

But, if the human need for attachments and non-abusive parental care is still being repudiated in the field of child development and human behaviour, the importance of attachment relations can no longer be denied by researchers in the field of post-traumatic stress disorder: here psychological trauma and its violent manifestations are seen as the natural consequences of the victim's disrupted affiliative bonds (see Chapters 9, 10 and 11); here, violence can be seen as the reciprocal manifestation of a damaged attachment system: through trauma, love and hate have once again become blood relations.

What has become apparent is that, for violence to take place, there must be a cognitive process of dehumanisation of the 'other' backed up by the narcissistic rage of the traumatised self, in addition to the neurophysiological manifestations of a disrupted attachment system. This is what appears to take place when PTSD victims re-enact their violent experiences. To understand this phenomenon, researchers have explored the neurophysiological matrix of attachment behaviour and they have found that its disruption, through trauma, results in a violent form of behaviour arising from the disruption of the brain's neurophysiological structures involved in attachment and attunement behaviour patterns. The resultant manifestations of this process are essentially twofold: at the neurophysiological level, the damage is made evident by a disruption in the attunement process and by a marked physiological and cognitive disarray; at the psychological level of the self and its links with the 'other', there is a disruption in the sense of identity, a loss of empathy and of the capacity to maintain affiliative relations, in general resulting in a marked sense of isolation. The final outcome is a shattered self.

These findings in the field of psychological trauma make it only too clear that to deny the reciprocal relationship that exists between attachment behaviour and violent aggressive behaviour no longer makes sense if we really want to begin to understand the origins of human violence. Attachment theory has become a legitimate focus for debate and research into human behaviour. No one truly interested in both understanding human violence and in reducing its prevalence can now afford to ignore these studies and their conclusions. Violence is not an innate biological instinct: it is the manifestation of both our disrupted attachment bonds and our shattered self.

As Alice Miller points out, it is only too easy to paint an apocalyptic picture of this century with its wars and destruction, an apparently endless catalogue of pain and terror. However, what really needs to be made known is that people are now acquiring scientific knowledge about themselves as a species that is utterly new in human history. The remedy against violence lies within us: humans are all potentially capable of making loving relationships; indeed it is in their nature to do so. Every infant born into this world has within its genes the power to make the other intensely special and lovable. However, for this power to be allowed to unfold and develop, it is necessary to to change the way people think about themselves and the world they live in.

A revision of cultural and scientific assumptions seems long overdue. As Irwing Thompson points out, two different biologies are beginning to define themselves, reflecting two different politics because they are essentially two different world views: 'one provides the scientific apologetics for the crisis management of the disintegrating modern world system; the other provides the scientific foundation for the politics of a new planetary culture' (1987, p.26).

One of the most recent and important changes in the world of science is the realisation that reality is a construct of our minds. This has been made very clear in our attempt to understand the origins of human violence. Those men and women who have known much pain and fear have to see the world in a way that makes sense of their suffering and of their life experience: theirs is a belief in man's innate destructiveness. Those who feel more secure in their capacity to love and be loved have another view of the world and of humanity, a view that recognises the importance of human relations and the need to value the 'other'. Most of us struggle in the confusion created by these two opposing world views of life and human nature: our mistake has been not to realise that such differing views of human nature reflect deeply held convictions that are essential to the preservation of the individual's sense of self. Our current beliefs, like predisposition to violence, are the last chapters of a long life-story: they need to be treated with respect and humility.

It is my hope that at the end of this book, a few of us may feel empowered to achieve some of the changes required to make the lives of our children safer and less painful wherever we may live. For others, it may simply be enough to be able to tolerate the fact that different ways of thinking about human nature are in themselves a reflection of an individual's personal and cultural past, a way of making sense of the world as each one of us has known it. This acknowledgement is in itself an act of scientific humility which will help us achieve a little progress on the long road to peace.

Bibliography

ADAM, K.S. (1982). Loss, suicide and attachment. In: C.M. Parkes and J. Stevenson-Hinde (Eds), *The Place of Attachment in Human Behaviour*. London, New York: Tavistock.

ADORNO, T.W., FRENKEL-BRUNSWICK, E., LEVINSON, D.J. and SANDFORD, R.N. (1950). *The Authoritarian Personality*. New York, Evanston, London: Harper and Row .

AINSWORTH, M.D.S., BLEHAR, M.C., WATERS, E. and WALL, S. (1978). *Patterns of Attachment: a Psychological Study of the Strange Situation*. Hillsdale, NJ: Lawrence Erlbaum Associates.

ALEXANDER, R.D. (1974). The evolution of social behaviour. *Annual Review of Ecological Systems* 5, 325–383.

AMERICAN PSYCHIATRIC ASSOCIATION (1980). *Diagnostic and Statistical Manual of Mental Disorders*, 3rd edn. Washington DC: APA.

AMNESTY INTERNATIONAL (1984). *Torture in the Eighties*. London: Amnesty International Publications.

AMNESTY INTERNATIONAL (1985). The Declaration of Tokyo. *Ethical Codes and Declarations Relevant to the Health Professions,* 2nd edn, pp. 9–10. London: Amnesty International Publications.

AMNESTY INTERNATIONAL (1989). *When the State Kills ... The Death Penalty Versus Human Rights*. London: Amnesty International Publications.

ANDERSON, C. O. and MASON, W. A. (1978). Competitive social strategies in groups of deprived and experienced rhesus monkeys (*Macaca mulatta*). *Journal of Comparative and Physiological Psychology* 87, 681–690.

ARCHER, D. and GARTNER, R. (1984). *Violence and Crime in Cross-National Perspective*. Newhaven: Yale University Press.

ARIES, P. (1962). *Centuries of Childhood*. Harmondsworth: Penguin Books.

ASCH, J.E. (1951). Effects of group pressure upon the modification and distortion of judgement. In: H. Guetzkow (Ed.), *Groups, Leadership and Men*. Pittsburgh: Carnegie Press.

ATTENBOROUGH, D. (1987). *The First Eden. The Mediterranean World and Man*. London: William Collins

AUGUSTINE (1961). *Confessions*. London: Penguin Books.

BACKMANN, R. (1991). The slave children. *Nouvel Observateur*, 25 April, pp. 4–15.

BADOU, G. (1993). The brains of purification. From *l'Express*, Paris 11 February. Translated in *Medical Group Newsletter* 5, 1.

BAILEY, K. (1987). Human paleopsychology. In: G. Newman (Ed.), *Origins of Human Aggression*, pp. 50–63. New York: Human Science Press (Plenum)

BANDURA, A. and WALTERS, R. (1959). *Adolescent Aggression*. New York: Ronald Press.

BARING, A. and CASHFORD, J. (1991). *The Myth of the Goddess*. London: BCA.

BARON, L. and STRAUS, M.A. (1987). Four theories of rape: a macrosociological analysis. *Social Problems* 34, 468–488.

BARON, L. and STRAUS, M.A. (1988). Cultural and economic sources of homicide in the United States. *The Sociological Quarterly* 29, 371–390.

BARON, L., STRAUS, M.A. and JAFFEE, D. (1988). Legitimate violence, violent attitudes, and rape: a test of the Cultural Spillover Theory. In: R.A. Prentky and V.L. Quinsey (Eds), *Human Sexual Aggression: Current Perspectives*, pp. 79–110. New York: New York Academy of Sciences.

BATESON, P. (1989). Is aggression instinctive? In: J. Groebel and R.A. Hinde (Eds) *Aggression and War*, pp.35–47. Cambridge: Cambridge University Press.

BEAN, P. and MELVILLE, J. (1990). *Lost Children of the Empire*. London: Unwin Hyman.

BECKER, E. (1973). *The Denial of Death*. New York: Free Press.

BELSKY, J. (1988). Infant day care and socioemotional development: The United States. *Journal of Child Psychology and Psychiatry* 29, 397–406.

BERKE, J.H. (1989). *The Tyranny of malice*. London: Simon and Schuster.

BERTALANFFY, L. von (1967). *Robots, Men and Minds: Psychology in the Modern World*. New York: George Braziller.

BETTELHEIM, B. (1943). Individual and mass behaviour in extreme situations *Journal of Abnormal Psychology* 38, 417–452.

BLANCHARD, M. and MAIN, M. (1979). Avoidance of the attachment figure and social-emotional adjustment in day-care infants. *Developmental Psychology* 15, 445–446.

BLOCH, S. and REDDAWAY, P. (1977). *Russia's Political Hospitals*. London: Gollancz.

BOWER, G.H. (1981). Mood and memory. *American Psychologist* 36, 129–148.

BOWLBY, J. (1958). The nature of the child's tie to his mother. *International Journal of Psychoanalysis* 39, 350–373.

BOWLBY, J. (1969). *Attachment*, Vol. 1, *Attachment and Loss*, 2nd edn. London: Hogarth Press; 1982; Harmondsworth: Penguin, 1971.

BOWLBY, J. (1973). *Separation: Anxiety and Anger*, Vol. 2 *Attachment and Loss*. London: Hogarth Press; Harmondsworth: Penguin, 1975.

BOWLBY, J. (1980). *Loss, Sadness and Depression*, Vol. 3, *Attachment and Loss*. London: Hogarth Press; Harmondsworth: Penguin, 1981.

BOWLBY, J. (1984). Violence in the family as a disorder of the attachment and caregiving systems. *The American Journal of Psychoanalysis* 44, 9–27

BOWLBY, J. (1988). *A Secure Base: Clinical Applications of Attachment Theory*. London: Routledge.

BRACKEN, P.J., GILLER, J.E. and KABAGANDA, S. (1992). Helping victims of violence in Uganda. *Medicine and War* 8, 155–163.

BRAUN, B.G. (1990). Dissociative disorders as sequelae to incest. In: R.P. Khuft (Ed.), *Incest Related Syndromes of Adult Psychopathology*, pp. 227–245. Washington, London: American Psychiatric Press.

BREIER, A.B., KELSOE, J.R. KIRWIN, P.D., BELLER, S., WOLKOWITZ, O.M. and PICKAR, D. (1988). Early parental loss and development of adult psychopathology. *Archives of General Psychiatry* 45, 987–993.

BREUER, J. and FREUD, S. (1893). On the psychical mechanism of hysterical phenomena: preliminary communication. In: *Studies on Hysteria* (1893–1895), pp. 1–251, Standard Edition 2. London: Hogarth Press.

BREUER, J. and FREUD, S. (1893–1895). *Studies on Hysteria*, standard edition 2. London: Hogarth Press.

BRITISH MEDICAL ASSOCIATION (1981). *Handbook of Medical Ethics*. London: BMA.

BRITISH MEDICAL ASSOCIATION (1986). *The Torture Report*. London: BMA.

BRITISH MEDICAL ASSOCIATION (1992). *Medicine Betrayed*. London: BMA.

BROWN, G. and ANDERSON, B. (1991). Psychiatric morbidity in adult inpatients with childhood histories of sexual and physical abuse. *American Journal of Psychiatry* 148, 55–61.

BROWN, G. W. and HARRIS, T. (1978). *Social Origins of Depression: a Study of Psychiatric Disorder in Women*. London: Tavistock Publications.

BROWN, C. and LAGO, A.M. (1991). *The Politics of Psychiatry in Revolutionary Cuba*. New Brunswick, London: Transaction Publishers.

BROWNE, A. and FINKELHOR, D. (1986). Impact of child sexual abuse: a review of the research. *Psychological Bulletin* 99, 66–77.

BURGESS, A. and HOLMSTROM, L. (1979). Adaptive strategies and recovery from rape. *American Journal of Psychiatry* 136, 1278–1282.

BURLEIGH, M. (1991). Surveys of developments in the social history of medicine: lll. Euthanasia in the Third Reich: some recent literature. *The Society for the Social History of Medicine*, 317–328.

BYERS, B. (1976). Biological rhythms as information channels in interpersonal communication behaviour. In: P.P.G. Bateson and H. Klopfer (Eds), *Perspectives in Ethology*. New York: Plenum.

CAIRNS, R.B. (1984). An evolutionary and developmental perspective on aggressive patterns. In: C. Zahn-Waxler, E. M. Cummings and R. Ianotti (Eds), *Social and Biological Origins of Altruism and Aggression*, pp. 58–87. Cambridge: Cambridge University Press.

CAIRNS, R., MacCOMBIE, D.J. and HOOD, K.E. (1983). A developmental-genetic analysis of aggressive behaviour in mice: l. Behavioural outcomes. *Journal of Comparative Psychology* 97, 69–89.

CAMERON, D. and FRAZER, E. (1987). *The Lust to Kill. A Feminist Investigation of Sexual Murder*. Cambridge: Polity Press.

CAPITANIO, J.P. (1986). Behavioural pathology. In: G. Mitchell (Ed.), *Comparative Primate Biology*, Vol 2A, *Behaviour, Conservation and Ecology*, pp. 411–454. New York: Liss.

CAPITANIO, J.P., WEISSBERG, M. and REITE, M. (1985). Biology of maternal behaviour: recent findings and implications. In: M. Reite and T. Field (Eds), *The Psychobiology of Attachment and Separation*, pp. 51–92. London: Academic Press.

CARLSON, E.T. (1986). The history of dissociation until 1880. In: J.M Quen (Ed.), *Split Minds, Split Brains*, pp.7–30. New York, London: New York University Press.

CARMEN, H., RIEKER, P.P. and MILLS, T. (1984). Victims of violence and psychiatric illness. *American Journal of Psychiatry* 141, 378–383.

COE, C. L., WIENER, S. G., ROSENBERG, L. T. and LEVINE, S. (1985). Endocrine and immune responses to separation and maternal loss in nonhuman primates. In: M. Reite and T. Field (Eds), *The Psychobiology of Attachment and Separation*, pp.163–199. London: Academic Press.

COLLINS, J.J. and BAILEY, S. (1990). Traumatic stress disorder and violent behaviour. *Journal of Traumatic Stress* 3, 203–220.

CROCKENBERG, S. (1981). Infant irritability, mother responsiveness, and social support influences on the security of infant–mother attachment. *Child Development* 52, 857–865.

CROWELL, J. and FELDMAN, S. (1988). Mothers' internal models of relationships and children's behavioural and developmental status: a study of mother–child interaction. *Child Development* 59, 1273–1285.

CYDILO, L. (1993). The rebels who were silenced by the syringe. *Financial Times Weekend*, 24/25 April.

DART, R. (1954). The predatory transition from ape to man. *International Anthropological and Linguistic Review* 1, 207–208.

DARWIN, C. (1871). *The Descent of Man*, 2nd edn. London: John Murray.

DAVIDSON, B. (1984). *The Story of Africa*. London: Mitchell Beazley.

DAWKINS, R. (1976). *The Selfish Gene*. Oxford: Oxford University Press.

DE WAAL, F. (1989). *Peacemaking among Primates*. London: Penguin Books.

deMAUSE, L. (Ed.) (1974). *The History of Childhood: The Untold Story of Child Abuse*. London: Bellew Publishing.

DEAN, A., MALIK, M., RICHARDS, W. and STRINGER S. (1986). Effects of parental maltreatment on children's conceptions of interpersonal relationships. *Developmental Psychology* 22, 617–626.

DELGADO, J. M. R. (1968). Recent advances in neurophysiology. In: *The Present Status of Psychotropic Drugs* Excerpta Medica International Congress Series 180, pp. 36–48. New York.

DELGADO, J. M. R. (1971).The neurological basis of violence. In: *Understanding Aggression, International Social Sciences Journal* 23, pp.27–35.

DELL, P.F. (1980). The Hopi family therapist and the Aristotelian parents. *Journal of Marital and Family Therapy* 6 123–130.

DOBSON, J. (1993). *The New Dare to Discipline*. London: Kingsway.

DURBIN, E.F.M. and BOWLBY J. (1939). *Personal aggressiveness and war*. Originally published in symposium on 'War and Democracy' (1938). Present version published separately in 1939. London: Routledge & Kegan Paul.

DYER, C. (1990). Conjugal wrongs. *Guardian*, 28 November.

EAGLE, M. N. (1984). *Recent Developments in Psychoanalysis: A Critical Evaluation*. New York: McGraw-Hill.

EGELAND, B., JACOBVITZ, D. and PAPATOLA, K. (1987). Intergenerational continuity of parental abuse. In: Gelles R.J. and Lancaster, J.B. (Eds), *Child Abuse and Neglect*, pp. 225–276. New York: Aldine de Gruyter.

EGELAND, B. and SROUFE, L.A. (1981). Attachment and early maltreatment. *Child Development*, 52, 44–52.

ELLIS, D. (1992). *Time*. The deadliest year yet. January, p.25.

'ELRO' (1978). *I Did Survive*. London, New York: Regency Press.

EMERY, R.E. (1982). Interparental conflict and the children of discord and divorce. *Psychological Bulletin* 92, 310–330.

ERIKSON, E.H. (1946). Ego development and historical change. In: A. Freud, H. Hartmann and E. Kris (Eds), *Psychoanalytic Study of the Child*, Vol. 2, pp. 359–396. New York: International Universities Press.

ERIKSON, E.H. (1950). *Childhood and Society*, 2nd edn. London: Hogarth Press, 1965; Harmondsworth: Penguin.

ESTIOKO-GRIFFIN, A. and GRIFFIN, B. (1981). Woman the hunter: the Agta. In: F. Dahlberg (Ed.), *Woman the Gatherer*, pp. 121–151. New Haven, London: Yale University Press.

EVANS, G. R. (1982). *Augustine on Evil*. Cambridge: Cambridge University Press.

EVANS, H. (1966). Biology: the new salvation of man. *Harper's Magazine*, September, pp. 107–108.

FAHY, T. and FISHER, N. (1992). Sexual contact between doctors and patients. *British Medical Journal* 304, 1519–1520.

FAIRBAIRN, R. (1952). *Psychoanalytic Studies of the Personality*. London: Routledge & Kegan Paul.

FALUDI, S. (1991). *Backlash: The Undeclared War against Women*. London: Chatto and Windus.

FARQUHAR, C.M., ROGERS, V., FRANKS, S., PEARCE, S., WADSWORTH, J. and BEARD, R.W. (1989). A randomised controlled trial of medroxyprogesterone acetate and psychotherapy for the treatment of pelvic congestion. *British Journal of Obstetrics and Gynaecology* 96, 1153–1162.

FERENCZI, S. (1949). Confusion of tongues between the adult and the child. The language of tenderness and the language of passion. *International Journal of Psychoanalysis* 30, 225–230. (First published, 1932, in German.)

FIELD, T. (1983). Child abuse in monkeys and humans: a comparative perspective. In: M. Reite and N.G. Caine (Eds), *Child Abuse: The Nonhuman Primate Data*, pp. 151–174. New York: Alan R. Liss.

FIELD, T. (1985). Attachment as psychobiological attunement: being on the same wavelength. In: M. Reite and T. Field (Eds), *The Psychobiology of Attachment and Separation*, pp. 415–454. London: Academic Press.

FIELD, T. and REITE, M. (1984). Children's responses to separation from mother during the birth of another child. *Child Development* 55, 1308–1316.

FIGLEY, C. (Ed.) (1985). *Trauma and Its Wake: The Study and Treatment of Post-traumatic Stress Disorder*. New York: Brunner Mazel.

FIGLEY, C.R. (1992). Post-traumatic stress disorder. Part ll. Relationship with various traumatic events. *Violence Update*, May, pp. 1 and 8–10.

FINKELHOR, D. (1979). *Sexually Victimised Children*. New York: Free Press.

FINKELHOR, D. (1984). *Child Sexual Abuse: New Theories and Research*. New York: Free Press.

FINKELHOR, D. and YLLO, K. (1988). Rape in marriage. In: M.B. Straus (Ed.), *Abuse and Victimisation Across the Life Span*, pp. 140–152. Baltimore, London: The Johns Hopkins University Press.

FOX, R. (1974). Narcissistic rage and the problem of combat aggression. *Archives of General Psychiatry* 31, 807–811.

FREUD, A. (1936). *The Ego and the Mechanisms of Defence*. London: Hogarth Press.

FREUD, A. and DANN, S. (1951). An experiment in group upbringing. In: Rackbill and Thompson (Eds) *Behaviour in Infancy and Early Childhood*, New York: Free Press, 1967.

FREUD, S. (1894). The neuro-psychoses of defence. In: *The Complete Psychological Works of Sigmund Freud*, Vol. 3, pp. 43–61.

FREUD, S. (1896a). The aetiology of hysteria. In: *The Complete Psychological Works of Sigmund Freud*, Vol. 3, pp. 187–221. London: Hogarth Press

FREUD, S. (1896b). Further remarks on the neuropsychoses of defence. In: *The Complete Psychological Works of Sigmund Freud*, Vol. 3, 159–185. London: Hogarth Press.

FREUD, S. (1900). The interpretation of dreams. In: *The Complete Psychological Works of Sigmund Freud*, Vols 4 and 5. London: Hogarth Press

FREUD, S. (1905). Three essays on the theory of sexuality. In: *The Complete Psychological Works of Sigmund Freud*, Vol. 7 pp.125–245. London: Hogarth Press

FREUD, S. (1917). Mourning and melancholia. In: *The Complete Psychological Works of Sigmund Freud*, Vol. 14 pp.237–258. London: Hogarth Press.

FREUD, S. (1920). Beyond the pleasure principle. In: *The Complete Psychological Works of Sigmund Freud*, Vol. 18, pp. 3–64. London: Hogarth Press.

FREUD, S. (1924). The economic problem of masochism. In: *The Complete Psychological Works of Sigmund Freud*, Vol. 19, pp. 155–170. London: Hogarth Press.

FREUD, S. (1930). Civilisation and its discontents. In: *The Complete Psychological Works of Sigmund Freud*, Vol. 21, pp. 59–145 London: Hogarth Press; or New York: W.W. Norton.

FREUD, S. (1933) The dissection of the psychical personality. Lecture 31. New Introductory Lectures on psycho-analysis. In: *The Complete Psychological Works of Sigmund Freud*, Vol. 22, 1–182. London: Hogarth Press.

FREUD, S. (1940) The theory of the instincts, pp.148–151. In: *An Outline of Psychoanalysis, The Complete Psychological Works of Sigmund Freud*, Vol. 23, 139–207. London: Hogarth Press.

FREUD, S. (1950). *The Origins of Psychoanalysis: Letters to Wilhelm Fliess, Drafts and Notes: 1887–1902*. New York: Basic Books.

FRODI, A. (1985). Variations in parental and nonparental response to early infant communication. In: M. Reite and T. Field (Eds), *The Psychobiology of Attachment and Separation*, pp. 351–367. London: Academic Press.

FROMM, E. (1970). *The Crisis of Psychoanalysis*. Harmondsworth: Penguin Books, 1973.

FROMM, E. (1974). *The Anatomy of Human Destructiveness*, pp. 24–26. Harmondsworth, Penguin Books, 1987.

FUSSEL, P. (1989). The brutal cut-off. *The Guardian*, 1 September.

GAENSBAUER, T.J. and HARMON, R.J. (1982). Attachment behaviour in abused/ neglected infants: implications for the concept of attachment. In: R.N. Emde and R.J. Harmon (Eds), *The Development of Attachment and Affiliative Systems*, pp. 263–280. New York: Plenum.

GAL, R. and MANGELSDORFF, D. (1991). *Handbook of Military Psychology*. Chichester: John Wiley.

GAZZANIGA, M.S. (1983). Right hemisphere language following brain bisection. *American Psychologist*, May, 525–537.

GAZZANIGA, M.S, and Le DOUX, J.E. (1978). *The Split Brain and the Integrated Mind*. New York: Plenum Press.

GELLES, R.J. (1978). Violence toward children in the United States. *American Journal of Orthopsychiatry* 48, 580–592.

GELLES, R.J. and LANCASTER J.B. (1987). *Child Abuse and Neglect: Biosocial Dimensions*. New York: Aldine de Gruyter.

GEORGE, C. and MAIN, M. (1979). Social interactions of young abused children: approach, avoidance and aggression. *Child Development* 50 306–318.

GIMBUTAS, M. (1992). *The Civilisation of the Goddess: The World of old Europe*, J. Marler (Ed.). San Francisco: Harper Collins.

GLASSER, M. (1979). Some aspects of the role of aggression in the perversions. In: I. Rosen (Ed.), *Sexual Deviation*, pp.278–305. Oxford: Oxford University Press.

GLENNY, M. (1992). *The Fall of Yugoslavia*. London: Penguin Books.

GLOVER, E. (1960). *The Roots of Crime*. London: Imago. Reprinted by International Universities Press, New York, 1970.

GOLDSTEIN, J.H. (1989). Beliefs about human aggression. In: J. Groebel and R.A. Hinde (Eds), *Aggression and War*. Cambridge: Cambridge University Press.

GOLEC, J. (1980). *Aftermath of disaster: the Teton dam break*, PhD dissertation. Columbus, OH: Disaster Research Centre, Ohio State University.

GOODALL, J. (1988). *In the Shadow of Man*, 2nd edn. London: Weidenfeld and Nicolson.

GOODALL, J. (1990). *Through a Window: 30 Years with the Chimpanzees of Gombe*. London: Weidenfeld and Nicolson.

GORST-UNSWORTH, C. (1992). Adaptation after torture: some thoughts on the long term effects of surviving a repressive regime. *Medicine and War* **8**, 164–168.

GRAHAM-YOULL, A. (1984). The mind of the torturer. *Observer*, 15 January, 11.

GRAZIANO, A.M., KUNCE, L., LINDQUIST, C.M. and MUNJAL, K. (1991). Physical punishment in childhood and current attitudes: a comparison of College students in the U.S. and India. *Violence Update*, May, 4–5.

GREEN, B.L., WILSON, J.P. and LINDY, J.D. (1985). Conceptualising PTSD: a psychosocial framework. In: C. Figley (Ed.), *Trauma and Its Wake*, pp. 53–69. New York: Brunner/Mazel.

GREENBERG J.R. and MITCHELL S.A. (1983). *Object Relations Theory in Psychoanalysis.* Cambridge, MA, London: Harvard University Press.

GROEBEL, J. and HINDE, R.A. (1989). *Aggression and War.* Cambridge: Cambridge University Press.

GROSSMAN, K., GROSSMAN, K.E., SPANGLER, G., SUESS, G. and UNZNER, L. (1985). Maternal sensitivity and newborn's orientation responses as related to quality of attachment in northern Germany. In: I. Bretherton and E. Waters (Eds), *Growing Points of Attachment Theory and Research.* Monographs of the Society for Research in Child Development Vol. 50 (1–2, serial no. 209), pp. 233–256.

GUIDANO, V. F. (1987). *Complexity of The Self: A Developmental Approach to Psychopathology and Therapy.* New York, London: Guilford Press.

GUNN, J. (1973). *Violence in Human Society.* Newton Abbot: David and Charles.

GUNTRIP, H. (1969). *Schizoid Phenomena, Object Relations and The Self.* London: Hogarth Press.

GUZE, S. (1989). Biological psychiatry: is there any other kind? *Psychological Medicine* **19**, 315–323.

HALEY, S.A. (1974). When the patient reports atrocities. *Archives of General Psychiatry* **30**, 191–196.

HAMILTON, J.W. (1976). Some comments about Freud's conceptualisation of the death instinct. *International Review of Psychoanalysis* **3**, 151–164.

HAMILTON, W.D. (1964). The genetical evolution of social behaviour. 1. *Journal of Theoretical Biology* **7**, 1–16.

HARLOW, H.F. (1974). *Learning to Love*, 2nd edn. New York, London: Jason Aronson.

HARLOW, H. F. and MEARS, C. (1979). *Primate Perspectives.* New York, London: John Wiley and Sons.

HARRIS, M. (1977). *Cannibals and Kings: The Origins of Culture.* New York: Random House.

HENDIN, H. (1991). Psychodynamics of suicide, with particular reference to the young. *American Journal of Psychiatry* **148**, 1150–1158.

HERMAN, J.L. with Lisa Hirschman (1981). *Father–Daughter Incest.* Cambridge, MA, London: Harvard University Press.

HERMAN, J. (1986). Histories of violence in an outpatient population: an exploratory study. *American Journal of Orthopsychiatry* **56**, 137–141.

HERMAN, J.L., PERRY, J.C. and van der KOLK, B. (1989). Childhood trauma in borderline personality disorder. *American Journal of Psychiatry* **146**, 490–495.

HINDE, R.A. (1974). *Biological Bases of Human Social Behaviour.* New York: McGraw-Hill

HINDE, R. A. (1976). On describing relationships. *Journal of Child Psychology and Psychiatry* **17**, 1–19.

HITE, S. (1991). *The Hite Report on Love, Passion and Emotional Violence*, 2nd edn. London: Optima.

HOBBES, T. (1651). *Leviathan.* London: Penguin Books.

HODGES, C. (1981).This meeting unequivocally condemns the usage of medical personnel in enforcement of inhuman laws and degrading measures. *British Medical Association, News Review*, September, 32–40.

HOFER, M. A. (1984). Relationships as regulators: a psychobiologic perspective on bereavement. *Psychosomatic Medicine* 46, 183–197.

HOPPE, K. (1971). The aftermath of the Nazi persecution reflected in recent psychiatric literature. In: H. Krystal and W.G. Niederland (Eds), *Psychic Traumatisation: After Effects in Individuals and Communities*, pp. 169–204. Boston: Little, Brown & Co.

HOPPER, E. (1991). Encapsulation as a defence against the fear of annihilation. *International Journal of Psychoanalysis* 72, 607.

JANOFF-BULMAN, R. (1985). The aftermath of victimisation: rebuilding shattered assumptions. In: C. Figley (Ed), *Trauma and Its Wake*, pp. 15–35. New York: Brunner/Mazel.

JENSEN, G.D., BOBBITT, R.A. and GORDON, G.N. (1968). Effects of environment on the relationship between mother and infant pigtail monkeys. *Journal of Comparative Physiology and Psychology* 66, 259–263.

JOHNSON, W.D.K. (1991). Predisposition to emotional distress and psychiatric illness among doctors: the role of unconscious and experiential factors. *British Journal of Medical Psychology* 64, 317–329.

KAGAN, J. (1984). *The Nature of the Child*. New York: Basic Books.

KAPLAN, A.G. (1988). How normal is normal development? Some connections between adult development and the roots of abuse and victimisation. In: M.B. Straus (Ed.), *Abuse and Victimisation across the Life Span*, pp. 127–139. Baltimore, London: The Johns Hopkins University Press.

KARDINER, A. (1941). *The Traumatic Neuroses of War*. New York: P. Hoeber.

KAREN, R. (1990). Becoming attached. *The Atlantic Monthly*, February, pp. 35–70.

KAUFMAN, I.C. and ROSENBLUM, L.A. (1967). The reaction to separation in infant monkeys: anaclitic depression and conservation withdrawal. *Psychosomatic Medicine* 29, 648–675.

KERNBERG, O. (1976). *Object Relations Theory and Clinical Psychoanalysis*. New York: Jason Aronson.

KLEIN, H. (1971). Families of Holocaust survivors in the kibbutz: psychological studies. In: H. Krystal and W.G. Niederland (Eds), *Psychic Traumatisation: After Effects in Individuals and Communities*, pp. 67–92. Boston: Little, Brown & Co.

KLEIN, M. (1930). The importance of symbol-formation in the development of the ego. In: *Contributions to Psychoanalysis, 1921–1945*. New York: McGraw-Hill, 1964.

KLEIN, M. and RIVIERE, J. (1937). *Love, Hate and Reparation*. London: Hogarth Press.

KLUFT, R.P. (Ed.) (1990). Incest and subsequent revictimisation: the case of the therapist-patient sexual exploitation, with a description of the Sitting Duck Syndrome. In: *Incest-related Syndromes of Adult Psychopathology*, pp. 263–287. Washington DC, London: American Psychiatric Press.

KOHUT, H. (1977). *The Restoration of The Self*. Madison, CT: International Universities Press.

KOHUT, H. (1979). The two analyses of Mr Z. *International Journal of Psychoanalysis* 60, 3–27.

KOHUT, H. (1980). Summarising reflections. In: A. Goldberg (Ed.), *Advances in Self Psychology*. New York: International Universities Press.

KOHUT, H. (1985). *Self Psychology and the Humanities: Reflections on a New Psychoanalytic Approach* (co-editor: C.B. Strozier). New York, London: W.W. Norton.

KONNER, M. (1991). *Childhood*. London: Little, Brown & Co.

KORBIN, J.E. (Ed.) (1981). Introduction. In: *Child Abuse and Neglect: Cross Cultural Perspectives*, pp. 1–9. Berkeley CA: University of California Press.

KRAEMER, G. W. (1985). Effects of differences in early social experience on primate neurobiological–behavioural development. In: M.Reite and T. Field (Eds), *The Psychobiology of Attachment and Separation*, pp. 135–161. London: Academic Press.

KRYSTAL, H. (Ed.) (1968). *Massive Psychic Trauma*. New York: International Universities Press.

KRYSTAL, H. (1988). *Integration and Self-healing: Affect, Trauma, Alexithymia*. Hillsdale, NJ: Analytic Press.

KUHN, T. (1970). *The Structure of Scientific Revolutions*, 2nd edn. Chicago: University of Chicago Press.

KURLAND, J.A. (1980). Kin selection theory: a review and selective bibliography. *Ethology and Sociobiology* 1, 255–274.

LAMB, M. (1977). The development of mother–infant and father–infant attachments in the second year of life. *Developmental Psychology* 13, 637–648.

LAMB, M.E. (Ed.) (1987). *The Father's Role: Cross Cultural Perspectives*. Hillsdale, NJ: Lawrence Erlbaum Associates.

LASK, B.(1987). Forget the stiff upper lip. *British Medical Journal* 295, 1584 (editorial).

LAUFER, R.S., FREY-WOUTERS, E. and GALLOPS, M.S. (1985). Traumatic stressors in the Vietnam War and post traumatic stress disorder. In: C. Figley (Ed.), *Trauma and Its Wake: The Study and Treatment of Post-traumatic Stress Disorder*. New York: Brunner Mazel. .

LEAKY, R.E. and LEWIN, R (1977). *Origins*. London: Macdonald's and Jane's.

LEVI, P. (1960). *If This is a Man*. London: Sphere Books.

LEVIN, B. (1989). Blind in the mind. *The Times*, 15 May.

LEVINE, J.D., GORDON, N. C. and FIELDS, H, L. (1978). The mechanism of placebo analgesia. *The Lancet* ii, 654–657.

LEVINE, S. and LEVINE, R. (1981). Child abuse and neglect in sub-Saharan Africa. In: J.E. Korbin (Ed.), *Child Abuse and Neglect: Cross Cultural Perspectives*. Berkeley, CA: University of California Press.

LEWIN, K. (1948). *Resolving Social Conflicts*. New York: Harper. (First published in 1936.)

LEWIS, D.O. MALLOUH, C. and WEBB, V. (1989). Child abuse, delinquency and criminality. In: D. Cicchetti and V. Carlson (Eds), *Child Maltreatment: Theory and Research on the Causes and Consequences of Child Abuse and Neglect*, pp. 707–721. Cambridge: Cambridge University Press.

LEWIS, D.O., MOY, E., JACKSON, L.D., AARONSON, R., RESTIFO, N., SERRA, S. and SIMOS, A. (1985). Biopsychosocial characteristics of children who later murder: a prospective study. *American Journal of Psychiatry* 142, 1161–1167.

LEWIS, M., FEIRING, C., McGUFFOG, C. and JASKIR, J. (1984). Predicting psychopathology in six-year-olds from early social relations. *Child Development* 55, 123–136.

LI-REPAC, D. (1982). *The impact of acculturation on the child-rearing attitudes and practices of Chinese–American families*. Unpublished doctoral dissertation. Berkeley: University of California. (Cited in Sroufe, 1985.)

LIFTON, R.J. (1986). *The Nazi Doctors: A Study in the Psychology of Evil*. London: Papermac [date not Papermac].

LIFTON, R.J. and MARKUSEN, E. (1990). *The Genocidal Mentality: Nazi Holocaust and Nuclear Threat*. London: Macmillan.

LIFTON, R.J. and OLSON, E. (1976). The human meaning of total disaster. The Buffalo Creek Experience. *Psychiatry* **39**, 1–18.

LINDEMANN, E. (1944). Symptomatology and management of acute grief. *American Journal of Psychiatry* **101**, 141–149.

LOCKE, J. (1690). *Two Treatises of Government*. New York: Mentor, 1947.

LORENZ, K. (1966). *On Aggression*. London: Methuen.

LUCHTERHAND, E.G. (1971). Sociological approaches to massive stress in natural and man-made disasters. *International Psychiatry Clinic* **8**, 29–53.

McFARLANE, A.C. (1990). Vulnerability to PTSD. In: M.E.Wolf and A.d. Mosnaim (Eds), *PTSD: Aetiology, Phenomenology and Treatment*, p. 16. Washington DC, London: American Psychiatric Press.

McKINNEY, W.T. (1985). Separation and depression: biological markers. In: M. Reite and T. Field (Eds), *The Psychobiology of Attachment and Separation*, pp. 201–222. London: Academic Press.

MacLEAN, P.D. (1987). On the evolution of the three mentalities of the brain. In: G. Newman (Ed.), *Origins of Human Aggression*, pp. 29–41. New York: Human Science Press.

MacLEAN, P.D. (1985). Brain evolution relating to family, play, and the separation call. *Archives of General Psychiatry* **42**, 405–417.

McNEILL, W.H. (1976). *Plagues and Peoples*. London: Penguin Books.

MAHLER, M., PINE, F. and BERGMAN, A. (1975). *The Psychological Birth of the Human Infant*. New York: Basic Books.

MAIN, M. (1977). Analysis of a peculiar form of reunion behaviour seen in some day-care children: its history and sequelae in children who are home reared. In: R. Webb (Ed.) *Social development in Childhood: Day Care Programs and Research*, pp. 33–78. Baltimore, MD: The Johns Hopkins University Press.

MAIN, M. (1981). Avoidance in the service of attachment: a working paper. In: K. Immelman, G. Barlow, M. Main and L. Petrinovitch (Eds), *Behavioural Development: The Bielefeld Interdisciplinary Project*. New York: Cambridge University Press.

MAIN, M. and CASSIDY, J. (1988). Categories of response to reunion with the parent at age six: Predictable from infant attachment classification and stable over a one month period. *Developmental Psychology* **24**, 415–426.

MAIN, M. and GEORGE, C. (1985). Responses of abused and disadvantaged toddlers to distress in agemates: a study in the day care setting. *Developmental Psychology* **21**, 407–412.

MAIN, M. and SOLOMON, J. (1989). Procedures for identifying infants as disorganised/disoriented during the Ainsworth Strange Situation. In: M. Greenberg, D. Cichetti and E. M. Cummings (Eds), *Attachment During the Preschool Years*. Chicago: University of Chicago Press.

MAIN, M. and WESTON, D. (1981). The quality of the toddler's relationship to mother and father. *Child Development* **52**, 932–940.

MAIN, M., KAPLAN, N. and CASSIDY, J. (1985). Security in infancy, childhood, and adult-hood: a move to the level of representation. In: I. Bretherton and E. Waters (Eds), *Growing Points of Attachment Theory and Research*, Monographs of the Society for Research in Child Development, Vol. 50, pp. 66–104.

MAIN, M., TOMASINI, L. and TOLAN, W. (1979). Differences among mothers of infants judged to differ in security. *Developmental Psychology* **15**, 427–473.

MALAMUTH, N.M. (1981). Rape proclivity among men. *Journal of Social Issues* **37**, 4.

MASON, J. (1959). Psychological influences on the pituitary- adrenal cortical system. *Recent Progress in Hormone Research* **15**, 345–389.

MASON, W. A. (1971). Motivational factors in psychosocial development. In: W. J. Arnold and M. M. Page (Eds), *Nebraska Symposium on Motivation*, pp. 35–67. Lincoln: University of Nebraska Press.

MASSON, J.M. (1984). *The Assault on Truth: Freud's Suppression of the Seduction Theory*. Harmondsworth: Penguin Books.

MATAS, L., AREND, R.A. and SROUFE, A. (1978). Continuity of adaptation in the second year: the relationship between quality of attachment and later competence. *Child Development* 49, 547–556.

MATURANA, H. (1987). Everything is said by an observer. In: W.I. Thompson (Ed.), *Gaia, a Way of Knowing*, pp. 65–82. New York: Lindisfarne Press.

MEAD, G.H. (1934). *Mind, Self and Society from the Standpoint of a Social Behaviourist*. Chicago, London: University of Chicago Press.

MEADOW, R. (1989). Epidemiology of child abuse. *British Medical Journal* 298, 727–730.

MENZIES, I.E.P. (1970). *The Functioning of Social Systems as a Defence against Anxiety*. London: The Tavistock Institute of Human Relations.

MERSKY, H. (1992). The manufacture of personalities. The production of multiple personality disorder. *British Journal of Psychiatry* 160, 327–340.

MILGRAM, S. (1974). *Obedience to Authority: An Experimental View*. London: Harper and Row.

MILLER, A. (1983). *For Your Own Good: Hidden Cruelty in Child Rearing and the Roots of Violence*. London: Virago.

MIRSKY, J. (1992). China's baby girls 'killed by the million'. *Observer*, 26 January, p13.

MIYAKE, K., CHEN, S.J. and CAMPOS, J.J. (1985). Infant temperament, mother's mode of interaction and attachment in Japan: an interim report. In: I. Bretherton and E. Waters (Eds), *Growing Points of Attachment Theory and Research*, Monographs of the Society for Research in Child Development Vol. 50 (1–2, serial no. 209), 276–297.

MONTAGU, A. (1976). *The Nature of Human Aggression*. Oxford: Oxford University Press.

MOOREHEAD, C. (1989). *Betrayal: Child Exploitation in Today's World*. London: Barrie and Jenkins.

NASMYTH, P. (1991). The invisible army of the traumatised. *The Guardian*, 13 September.

NEUMAN, G. (Ed.) (1987). *Origins of Human Aggression*. New York: Human Science Press.

NEW INTERNATIONALIST (1989). **192**, pp. 8–9.

NEWCOMBE, N. and LERNER, J.C. (1982). Britain between the two Wars: the historical context of Bowlby's theory of attachment. *Psychiatry* 45, 1–12.

OGDEN, T.H. (1979). On projective identification. *International Journal of Psycho-Analysis* 60, 357–373.

OLINER, S.P. and OLINER, P.M. (1988). *The Altruistic Personality*. New York: The Free Press.

ORWELL, G. (1949). *Nineteen Eighty-Four*. London, Harmondsworth: Penguin Books.

OZ, A. (1989). *The Slopes of Lebanon*. London: Vintage.

PAGELS, E. (1988). *Adam, Eve and the Serpent*. London: Weidenfeld and Nicolson.

PAM, A. (1990). A critique of the scientific status of biological psychiatry. *Acta Psychiatrica Scandinavia Supplementum* 82 (S362), 1–35.

PANKSEPP, J. (1984). The psychobiology of prosocial behaviours: separation distress, play and altruism. In: C. Zahn-Waxler, E. M. Cummings and R. Ianotti (Eds),

Social and Biological Origins of Altruism and Aggression, pp. 16–57. Cambridge: Cambridge University Press.

PANKSEPP, J., SIVIY, S. M. and NORMANSELL, L. A. (1985). Brain opioids and social emotions. In: M. Reite and T. Field (Eds), *The Psychobiology of Attachment and Separation*, pp. 3–49. London: Academic Press.

PERRY, B. D. (1991). Neurobiological sequelae of childhood trauma. Post traumatic stress disorders in children. In: M. Murberg (Ed.), *Catbecholamines in Post-Traumatic-Stress Disorder: Emerging Concepts*, pp. 100–128. Washington DC: American Psychiatric Press.

PIAGET, J. (1929). *The Child's Conception of the World*. London: Paladin.

PINERO, M. (1992). The kidnapping of children and the sale of organs. *Le Monde Diplomatique*, August, pp. 16–17.

PITMAN, R.K., VAN DER KOLK, B.A., SCOTT, P.O. and GREENBERG, M.S. (1990). Naloxone-reversible analgesic response to combat- related stimuli in post traumatic stress disorder. *Archives of General Psychiatry* 47, 541–544.

PLIMPTON, E. and ROSENBLUM, L. (1983). The ecological context of infant maltreatment in primates. In: M. Reite and N.G. Caine (Eds), *Child Abuse: the Nonhuman Primate Data*, pp. 103–117. New York: Alan Liss.

POFFENBERGER, T. (1981). Childbearing and social structure in rural India: toward a cross-cultural definition of child abuse and neglect. In: J.E. Korbin (Ed.), *Child Abuse and Neglect: Cross Cultural Perspectives*. Berkeley CA: University of California Press.

PONTING, C. (1992). Churchill's plan for race purity. *Guardian*, 20/21 June.

POPE-HENNESSY, J. (1967). *Sins of the Fathers. A Study of the Atlantic Slave Traders 1441–1807*. London: Cassell.

PORTER, R.H. and LANEY, M.D. (1980). Attachment theory and the concept of inclusive fitness. *Merrill–Palmer Quarterly* 26, 35–51.

PRITCHARD, C. (1992). Is there a link between suicide in young men and unemployment? *British Journal of Psychiatry* 160, 750–756.

PUTNAM, F.W. (1986). The scientific investigation of multiple personality disorder. In: J.M. Quen (Ed.), *Split Minds, Split Brains*, pp. 109–126. New York: New York University Press.

PUTNAM, F.W. (1990). Disturbances of the self in victims of childhood sexual abuse, In: R.P. Kluft (Ed.), *Incest-Related Syndromes of Adult Psychopathology*, pp. 113–131. Washington DC, London: American Psychiatric Association.

QUARANTELLI, E.L.. (1985). As assessment of conflicting views on mental health: the consequences of traumatic events. In: C. Figley, (Ed.), *Trauma and its Wake*, pp. 182–220. New York: Brunner/Mazel.

RANK, O. (1945). *Will Therapy and Truth and Reality*. New York: Knopf, 1936; one volume edition, 1945.

READER, J. (1988). *Man on Earth*. London: Penguin Books.

REDER, P. (1989). Freud's family. *British Journal of Psychiatry*, 154, 93–98. .

REITE, M. and CAPITANIO, J. P. (1985). On the nature of social separation and attachment. In: M. Reite and T. Field (Eds), *The Psychobiology of Attachment and Separation*, pp. 223–255. London: Academic Press.

RICHARDS, C. (1989). *The Health of Doctors*. London: King's Fund Publishing Office.

RICKS, M.H. (1985). The social transmission of parental behaviour: attachment across generations. In: I. Bretherton and E. Waters (Eds), *Growing Points in Attachment Theory and Research*. Monographs of the Society for Research in Child Development, Vol. 50 (1–2, serial no. 209), 211–227.

RICTHIE, J. and RICTHIE, J. (1981). Child rearing and child abuse. The polynesian context. In: J.E. Korbin (Ed.), Child abuse and neglect: cross cultural perspectives, pp. 186–204. Berkeley CA: University of California Press

ROBERTSON, J. and BOWLBY, J. (1952). Responses of young children to separation from their mothers. *Courrier du Centre Internationale de l'Enfance* 2, 131–142.

ROBERTSON, J. AND ROBERTSON, J. (1971). Young children in brief separations. *Psychoanalytic Study of the Child*, 26, 264–315.

ROGERS, J.A. (1983). Child abuse in humans: a clinician's view. In: M. Reite and N.G. Caine (Eds), *Child Abuse: the Nonhuman Primate Data*, pp. 1–17. New York: Alan R. Liss.

ROSEN, J., REYNOLDS, C.F., YEAGER, A.L., HOUCK, P.R. and HURWITZ, L.F. (1991). Sleep disturbances in the survivors of the Nazi Holocaust. *American Journal of Psychiatry* 148, 62–66.

ROSENBLUM, L. and SUNDERLAND, G. (1982). Feeding ecology and mother–infant relations. In: L. W. Hoffman, R. Gandelmann and H. R. Schiffman (Eds), *Biological Basis of Parental Behaviour*, pp. 75–110. Hillsdale, NJ: Lawrence Erlbaum Associates.

ROSENFELD, A.A. (1979). Incidence of incest among 18 female psychiatric patients. *American Journal of Psychiatry* 136, 791–795.

ROWELL, T. (1972). *Social Behaviour of Monkeys*. Harmondsworth: Penguin.

ROYAL COLLEGE OF GENERAL PRACTITIONERS (1986). *Alcohol: A Balanced View*. London: RCGP.

RUMBAUGH, D. M. and GILL, T. V. (1977). Language and language type communication: studies with a chimpanzee. In: M. Lewis and L. A. Rosenblum (Eds), *Interaction, Conversation and the Development of Language*, pp. 115–131. London: Wiley and Sons.

RUPPENTHAL, G.C., ARLING, G.L., HARLOW, H.F., SACKETT, G.P. and SUOMI, S.J. (1976). A ten-year perspective of motherless mother monkey behaviour. *Journal of Abnormal Psychology* 85, 341–349.

RUSSELL, D. (1982). *Rape in Marriage*. New York: Macmillan.

RUSSELL, D. (1984). *Rape, Incest and Sexual Exploitation.* Los Angeles: Sage.

RUTTER, M. (1981). *Maternal Deprivation Reassessed*, 2nd edn. London: Penguin Books.

RYCROFT, C. (1968). *A Critical Dictionary of Psychoanalysis*. Harmondsworth, Middlesex: Penguin Books.

SABINI, J. and SILVER, M. (1982). *Moralities of Everyday Life*. Oxford: Oxford University Press.

SACKETT, G. P. (1972). Isolation rearing in monkeys: diffuse and specific effects on later behaviour. In: *Colloques Internationaux du C.N.R.S.* 198, *Models Animaux du Comportement Humain*, pp. 61–110. Editions du Centre National de La Recherche Scientifique, 15 Quai Anatole-France-Paris Vlle.

SAGI, A., LAMB, M.E., LEWKOWITZ,K.S., SHOHAM, R., DVIR, R. and ESTES, D. (1991). Security of mother, father and metapelet attachment among kibbutz-reared Israeli children. In: I. Bretherton and E. Waters (Eds), *Growing Points of Attachment Theory and Research*. Monographs of the Society for Research in Child Development 50 (1–2, serial no. 209), 257–275.

SANDAY, P.R. (1981). The socio-cultural context of rape: a cross -cultural study. *Journal of Social Issues* 37, 5–27.

SANDER, L. W. (1977). The regulation of exchange in the infant- caretaker system and some aspects of the context–content relationship. In: M. Lewis and L.A. Rosenblum (Eds), *Interaction, Conversation and the Development of*

Language, pp. 133–156. New York: Wiley.

SCHAPIRO, S.J. and MITCHELL, G. (1983). Infant directed abuse in a seminatural environment: precipitating factors. In: M. Reite and N.G. Caine (Eds), *Child Abuse: The Nonhuman Primate Data*, pp.29–48. New York: Alan R. Liss.

SCHETZKY, D. H. (1990). A review of the literature on the long- term effects of childhood sexual abuse. In: R.P. Kluft (Ed.), *Incest Related Syndromes of Adult Psychopathology*, pp. 35–54. Washington DC, London: American Psychiatric Press.

SCHLENGER, W.E., KULKA. R.A., FAIRBANK, J.A. HOUGH, R.L., JORDAN, B.K., MARMAR, C.R. and WEISS, D.S. (1992). The prevalence of PTSD in the Vietnam generation: a multimethod multisource assessment of psychiatric disorder. *Journal of Traumatic Stress* 5, 333–364.

SCHNEIDER-ROSEN, K. and CICCHETTI, D. (1984). The relationship between affect and cognition in maltreated infants: Quality of attachment and the development of visual self-recognition. *Child Development* 55, 648–658.

SCHUR, M. (1972). *Freud, Living and Dying*. New York: International Universities Press.

SCRIGNAR, C.B. (1988). *Post Traumatic Stress Disorder: Diagnosis, Treatment and Legal Issues*, 2nd edn (1st edn, 1984). New Orleans: Bruno Press.

SCURFIELD, R. (1985). Post trauma stress assessment and treatment: overview and formulations. In: C. Figley (Ed.), *Trauma and Its Wake*, pp. 219–256. New York: Brunner/Mazel.

SEGAL, H. (1989). Introduction. In: J. Steiner (Ed.), *The Oedipus Complex: Clinical Implications*, pp. 1–10. London: Karnac books.

SHAFII, M., CARRIGAN, S. WHITTINGHILL, J.R. and DERRICK, A. (1985). Psychological autopsy of completed suicide in children and adolescents. *American Journal of Psychiatry* 142, 1061–1064.

SHOSTAK, M. (1990). *Nisa, the Life and Words of a !Kung Woman*. London: Earthscan Publications.

SHWED, J.A. and STRAUS, M.A. (1979). The military environment and child abuse. Mimeographed manuscript. Durham, NH: Family Research Laboratory, University of New Hampshire.

SIMONDS, P. (1965). The bonnet macaque in south India. In: I.Devore (Ed), *Primate Behaviour: Field Studies of Monkeys and Apes*, pp. 175–195. New York: Holt, Rinehart and Wilson.

SIVARD, R.L. (1988). *World Military and Social Expenditures, 1978–1988*. Washington DC: World Priorities.

SKYNNER, A.C.R. (1976). *One Flesh: Separate Persons. Principles of Family and Marital Psychotherapy*. London: Constable.

SMITH, J. (1989). *Mysogenies*. London, Boston: Faber and Faber.

SMITH, P. (1989). Perfect murderers. *New Statesman*, 7 July.

SOLANTAUS, T. (1991). Young people and the threat of nuclear war. *Medicine and War* 7, supplement 1, January–March.

SOLOMON, Z., KOTLER, M., and MIKULENCER, M. (1988). Combat related post traumatic stress disorder among second generation Holocaust survivors: preliminary findings. *American Journal of Psychiatry* 145, 865–868.

SPIEGEL, D, (1990). Trauma, dissociation and Hypnosis. In: R.P. Kluft (Ed.), *Incest Related Syndromes of Adult Psychopathology*, pp. 247–261. Washington and London: American Psychiatric Press.

SPIER, L., HALLOWELL, A.I. and NEUMAN, S.S. (1941). Language, culture and personality. In: *Essays in the Memory of Edward Sapir*, p. 57. Menasha, WI: Sapir Memorial Fund.

SPITZ, R. A. (1945). Hospitalism: an enquiry into the genesis of psychiatric conditions in early childhood. *Psychoanalytic Study of the Child* 1, 53–74.

SPITZ R.A. (1946). Anaclitic depression. *Psychoanalytic Study of the Child* 2, 313–342.

SROUFE, L.A. (1985). Attachment classification from the perspective of infant–caregiver relationships and infant temperament. *Child Development* 56, 1–14.

SROUFE, L.A. (1989). Relationships, self and individual adaptation. In: A. Samerof and R. Emde (Eds), *Relationship Disturbances in Childhood*, pp. 70–94. New York: Basic Books.

SROUFE, L.A. and WATERS, E. (1977a). Attachment as an organisational construct. *Child Development* 48, 1184–1199.

SROUFE, L.A. and WATERS, E. (1977b). Heart rate as a convergent measure in clinical and developmental research. *Merrill–Palmer Quarterly* 23, 3–27.

STAUB, E. (1984). A conception of the determinants and development of altruism and aggression: motives, the self and the environment. In: C. Zahn-Waxler, E. M. Cummings and R. Ianotti (Eds), *Social and Biological Origins of Altruism and Aggression*, pp. 135–163. Cambridge: Cambridge University Press.

STAUB, E. (1985). The psychology of perpetrators and bystanders. *Political Psychology* 6, 61–85.

STAUB, E. (1989). *The Roots of Evil. The Origins of Genocide and Other Group Violence*. Cambridge: Cambridge University Press.

STERN, D. (1985). The interpersonal world of the infant: a view from psychoanalysis and developmental psychology. New York: Basic Books.

STEVENSON, L. (1974). *Seven Theories of Human Nature*. New York, Oxford: Oxford University Press.

STOLLER, R. J. (1975). *Perversion: The Erotic Form of Hatred*. London: Karnac.

STORM, R. (1993). Would God use the rod? *Guardian*, 11 May, p.14

STORR, A. (1968). *Human Aggression*. Harmondsworth, Penguin Books.

STRAUS, M.B. (1991). Discipline and deviance: physical punishment of children and violence and other crime in adulthood. *Social Problems* 38, 133–154.

STRAUS, M.B. (Ed) (1988). *Abuse and Victimisation Across the Life Span*, pp. 107–123. Baltimore, London: The Johns Hopkins University Press.

STROEBE, W. and STROEBE, M.S. (1987). *Bereavement and Health*. Cambridge: Cambridge University Press.

SULLIVAN, H.S. (1950). Tensions interpersonal and international: a psychiatrist's view. In: *The Fusion of Psychiatry and Social Science*. New York: W.W. Norton, 1964.

SULLIVAN, H.S. (1953). *The interpersonal theory of psychiatry*. New York, London: W.W. Norton.

SULLIVAN, H.S. (1956). *Clinical studies in psychiatry*. New York, London: W.W. Norton.

SULLIVAN, H.S. (1964). *The Fusion of Psychiatry and Social Science*. New York: W.W. Norton.

SUOMI, S.J. and RIPP, C. (1983). A history of motherless mother monkey mothering at the University of Wisconsin Primate Laboratory. In: M. Reite and N.G. Caine (Eds), *Child Abuse: the Nonhuman Primate Data*, pp. 49–77. New York: Alan R. Liss.

SUOMI, S.J., HARLOW, H.F. and NOVAK, M.A. (1974). Reversal of social deficits produced by isolation rearing in monkeys. *Journal of Human Evolution* 3, 527–534.

SUTTIE, I. D. (1935). *The Origins of Love and Hate*. Harmondsworth: Penguin Books.

SUTTIE, I.D. and SUTTIE, J.I. (1932). The mother agent or object. Part I and II. *British Journal of Medical Psychology* 12, 91–107, 199–233.

TARNAPOWLSKY, A. and BERELOWITZ, M. (1987). Borderline personality disorder: a review of recent research. *British Journal of Psychiatry* **151**, 724–734.

TAYLOR, G.J. (1987). *Psychosomatic Medicine and Contemporary Psychoanalysis.* Madison, CT: International Universities Press.

TERR, L. (1983). Chowchilla revisited, The effects of psychic trauma four years after a school-bus kidnapping. *American Journal of Psychiatry* **140**, 1543–1550.

TERR, L. (1991). Childhood traumas: an outline and overview. *American Journal of Psychiatry* **148**, 10–20.

THOMAS, G. (1989). *Journey into Madness. The True Story of Secret CIA Mind Control and Medical Abuse.* London: Bantam Books.

THOMPSON, W. I. (Ed.) (1987). *Gaia, A Way of Knowing.* New York: Lindisfarne Press.

TIGER, L. (1984). *Men in Groups*, 2nd edn. New York, London: Marion Boyars. (Originally published 1969.)

TITCHENER, J.L. and KAPP, F.T. (1976). Family and character change at Buffalo Creek. *American Journal of Psychiatry* **133**, 295–299.

TRIVERS, R.L. (1974). Parent–offspring conflict. *American Zoologist* **14**, 249–264.

TRONICK, E.Z., WINN, S. and MORELLI, G.A. (1985). Multiple caretaking in the context of human evolution: why don't the Efe know the Western prescription for child care? in: M. Reite and T. Field (Eds), *The Psychobiology of Attachment and Separation*, pp. 293–322. London: Academic Press.

TROY, M. and SROUFE, L.A. (1987). Victimisation among preschoolers: role of attachment relationship history. *Journal of American Academy of Child and Adolescent Psychiatry* **26**, 166–172.

TURNBULL, C. (1961). *The Forest People.* London: Pan Books/Picador.

TURNBULL, C. (1973). *The Mountain People.* London: Pan Books/Picador.

VAILLANT, G.E. SOBOWALE, N.C. and McARTHUR. C. (1972). Some psychological vulnerabilities in physicians. *New England Journal of Medicine* **287**, 372–375.

VAN DER KOLK, B.A. (1985). Adolescent vulnerability to Post traumatic stress disorder. *Psychiatry* **48**, 365–370.

VAN DER KOLK, B.A. (Ed.) (1987). *Psychological Trauma.* Washington: American Psychiatric Press.

VAN DER KOLK, B.A. (1988). Trauma in men: effects on family life. In: M.B. Straus (Ed.), *Abuse and Victimisation across the Life Span*, pp. 171–187. Baltimore, London: The Johns Hopkins University Press.

VAN DER KOLK, B.A. (1989). The compulsion to repeat the trauma.: re-enactment, revictimisation and masochism. *Psychiatric Clinics of North America* **12**, 389–411.

VAN DER KOLK, B.A. and VAN DER HART, O. (1989). Pierre Janet and the breakdown of adaptation in psychological trauma. *American Journal of Psychiatry* **146**, 1530–1540.

VAUGHN, B., EGELAND, B., WATERS, E. and SROUFE, L.A. (1979). Individual differences in infant-mother attachment at 12 and 18 months: stability and change in families under stress. *Child Development* **50**, 971–975.

VERNIER, D. (1988). The wound of (female) circumcision. *Le Monde Diplomatique*, October. (In French.)

WALL, F. DE (1989). *Peacemaking Among Primates.* London: Penguin Books.

WEINDLING, P. (1992). Psychiatry and the Holocaust. Editorial. *Psychological Medicine* **22**, 1–3.

WEISSBERG, M.P. (1983). *Dangerous Secrets: Maladaptive Response to Stress.* New York, London: W.W. Norton.

WEINGARTNER, H. MILLER, H. and MURPHY, D.L. (1977). Mood-state dependent retrieval of verbal associations. *Journal of Abnormal Psychology* **86**, 276–284.

WELLDON, E.V. (1988). *Mother, Madonna and Whore*. London: Free Association Books.

WILSON, E. O. (1975). *Sociobiology*. Cambridge, MA: Harvard University Press.

WILSON, E. O. (1978). *On Human Nature*. Cambridge, MA, London: Harvard University Press.

WILSON J.P., SMITH, W.K. and JOHNSON, S.K. (1985). A comparative analysis of PTSD among various survivor groups. In: C. Figley (Ed.), *Trauma and Its Wake*, pp. 142–172. New York: Brunner/Mazel.

WINNICOTT, D.W. (1950). Aggression in relation to emotional development. In: *Through Paediatrics to Psychoanalysis*. New York, International Universities Press, 1958.

WINNICOTT, D.W. (1958). The sense of guilt. In: *The Maturational Process and the Facilitating Environment*. New York, International Universities Press, 1965.

WINNICOTT, D.W. (1959). Classification: is there a psycho- analytic contribution to psychiatric classification. In: *The maturational process and the facilitating environment*. New York, International Universities Press, 1965.

WINNICOTT, D.W. (1960). Ego distortion in terms of true and false self. In: *The Maturational Process and the Facilitating Environment*. London: Hogarth Press, 1965

WOLF, E.S. (1988). *Treating the Self: Elements of Clinical Self Psychology*. New York, London: Guilford Press.

WOLKENSTEIN, D. and KRAMER, S.N. (1984). *Inanna*. London: Rider.

WORLD DEVELOPMENT REPORT (1991). Oxford: Oxford University Press.

WU, D. (1981). Child abuse in Taiwan. In: J.E. Korbin (Ed.), *Child Abuse and Neglect: Cross Cultural Perspectives*. Berkeley, CA: University of California Press.

ZAHN-WAXLER, C., CUMMINGS, E.M. and IANOTTI, R. (Eds) (1984). Introduction; altruism and aggression: problems and progress in research. In: *Social and Biological Origins of Altruism and Aggression*, pp. 1–45. Cambridge: Cambridge University Press.

ZANARINI, M.C., GUNDERSON, J.G., MARINO, M.F., SCHWARTZ, E.O. and FRANKENBURG, F.R. (1989) Childhood experiences of borderline patients. *Comprehensive Psychiatry* **30**, 18–25.

ZULUETA, F. DE (1984). The implications of bilingualism in the study and treatment of psychiatric disorders: a review. *Psychological Medicine* **14**, 541–557.

ZULUETA, F. DE (1987). 1893: J. Breuer and S. Freud. On the psychical mechanism of hysterical phenomena: Preliminary communication. In: C. Thompson (Ed.), *The Origins of Modern Psychiatry*, pp. 87–104. Chichester, New York: John Wiley and Sons.

ZULUETA, F. DE (1990). Bilingualism and family therapy. *Journal of Family Therapy* **12**, 255–265.

ZWI, A. (1991). Militarism, militarization, health and the third world. *Medicine and War* **7**, 262–268.

ZWI, A. and UGALDE, A. (1989). Towards the epidemiology of political violence in the Third World. *Social Science and Medicine* **7**, 633–642.

Index